Dynamite Er

The BOYS™
HIGHLAND LADDIE

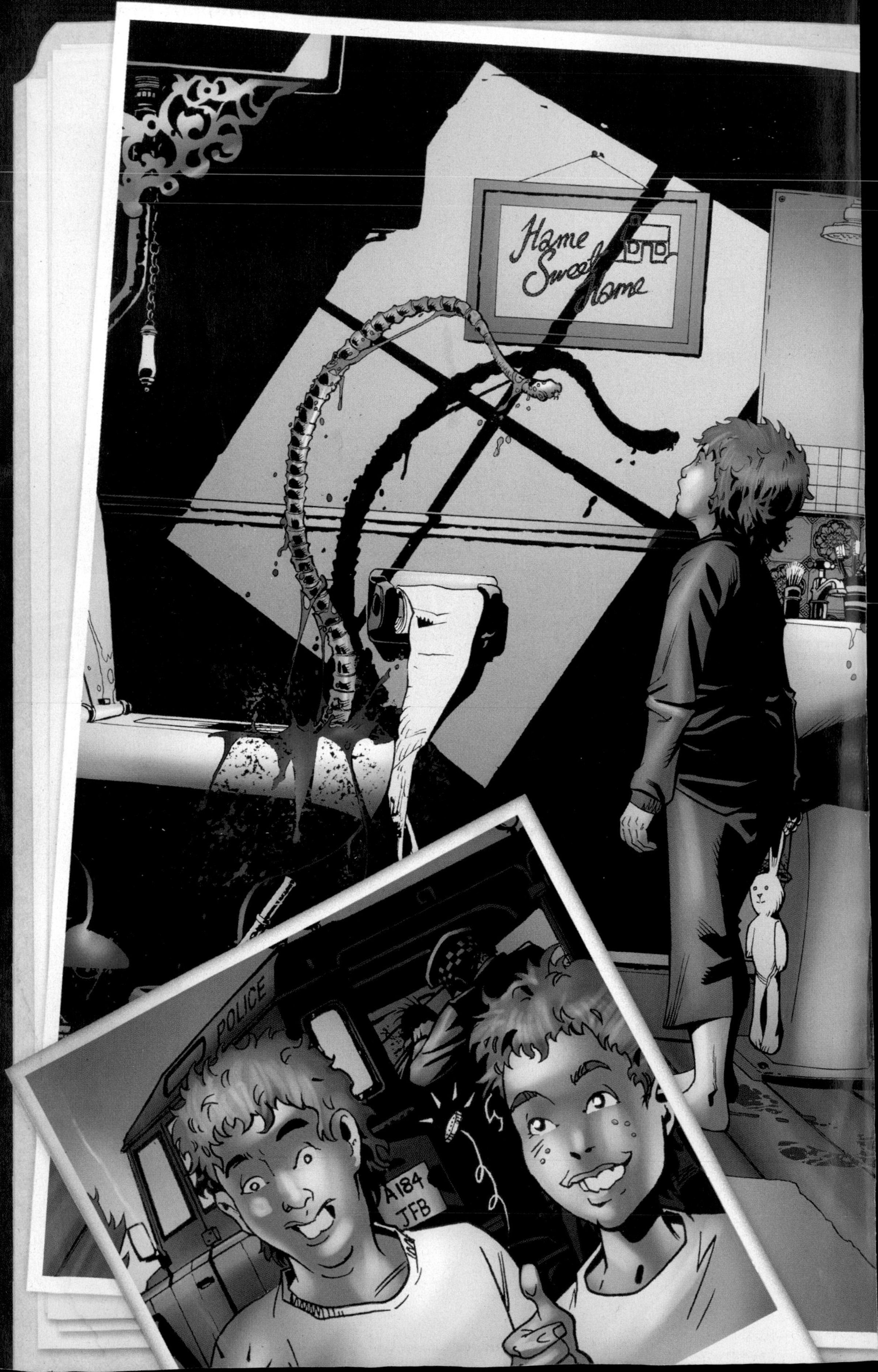

Home Sweet Home
POLICE
A184 JFB

volume eight: HIGHLAND LADDIE

Written by:
GARTH ENNIS

Lettered by:
SIMON BOWLAND

Illustrated by:
JOHN McCREA w/
KEITH BURNS

Coloured by:
TONY AVIÑA

Inks by:
KEITH BURNS w/
JOHN McCREA

Covers by:
DARICK
ROBERTSON
& TONY AVIÑA

The Boys created by:
GARTH ENNIS & DARICK ROBERTSON

Collects issues one to six of the Highland Laddie mini-series, originally published by Dynamite Entertainment.

Trade Design By: JASON ULLMEYER

THE BOYS: HIGHLAND LADDIE (VOL. 8)
ISBN: 9780857681454

Published by Titan Books, a division of Titan Publishing Group Ltd., 144 Southwark St., London, SE1 0UP. Contains material originally published in The Boys™: Highland Laddie #1-6. Copyright © Spitfire Productions Ltd. 2011 and Darick Robertson. All Rights Reserved. Dynamite, Dynamite Entertainment & The Dynamite Entertainment colophon ® 2011 DFI. All Rights Reserved. No part of this publication may be reproduced, stored in a retrieval system, or transmitted, in any form or by any means, without the prior written permission of the publisher. Names, characters, places and incidents featured in this publication are either the product of the author's imagination or used fictitiously. Any resemblance to actual persons, living or dead (except for satirical purposes), is entirely coincidental. A CIP catalogue record for this title is available from the British Library.

Printed in Canada.

First edition: April 2011

2 4 6 8 10 9 7 5 3 1

one

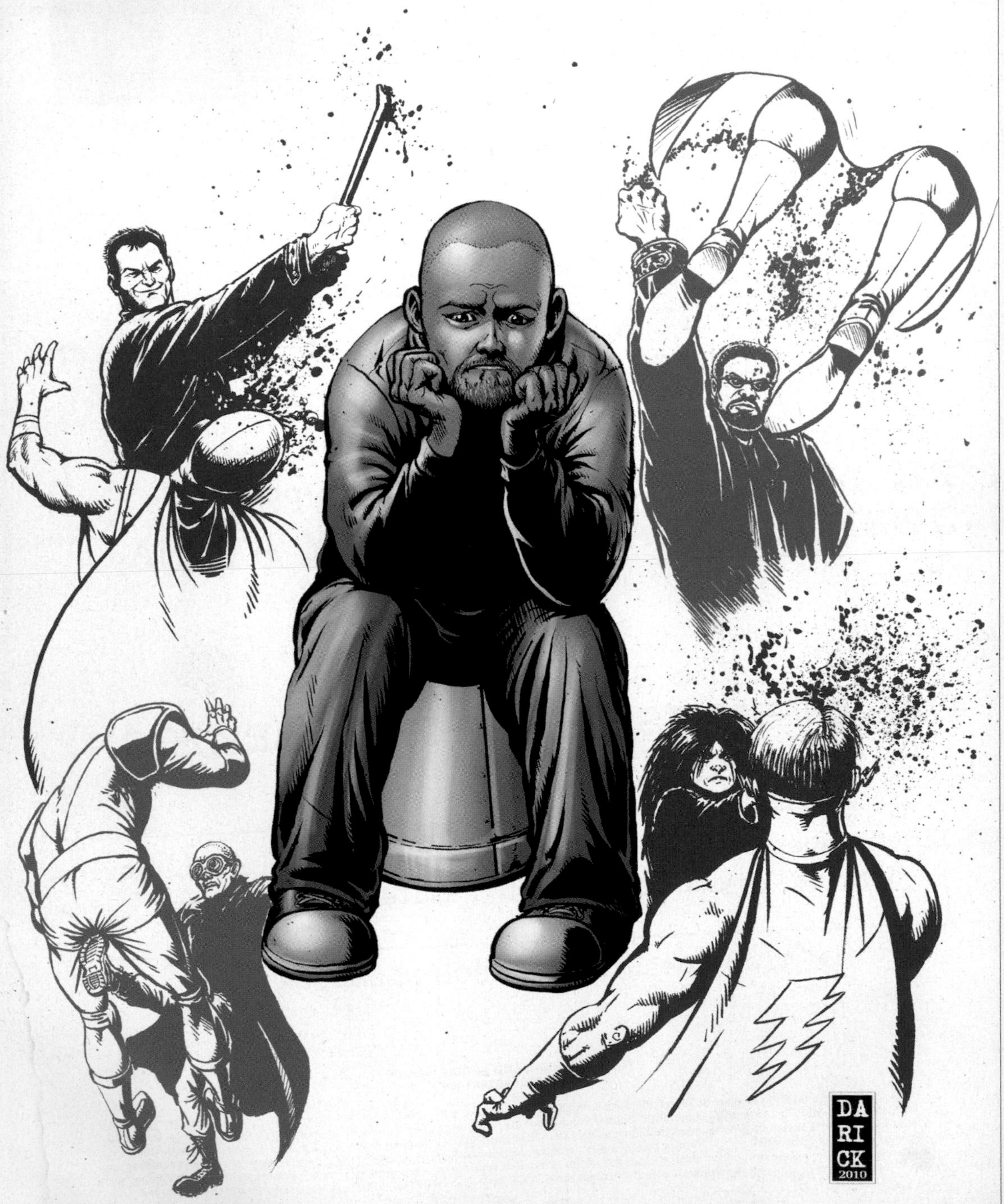
DA
RI
CK
2010

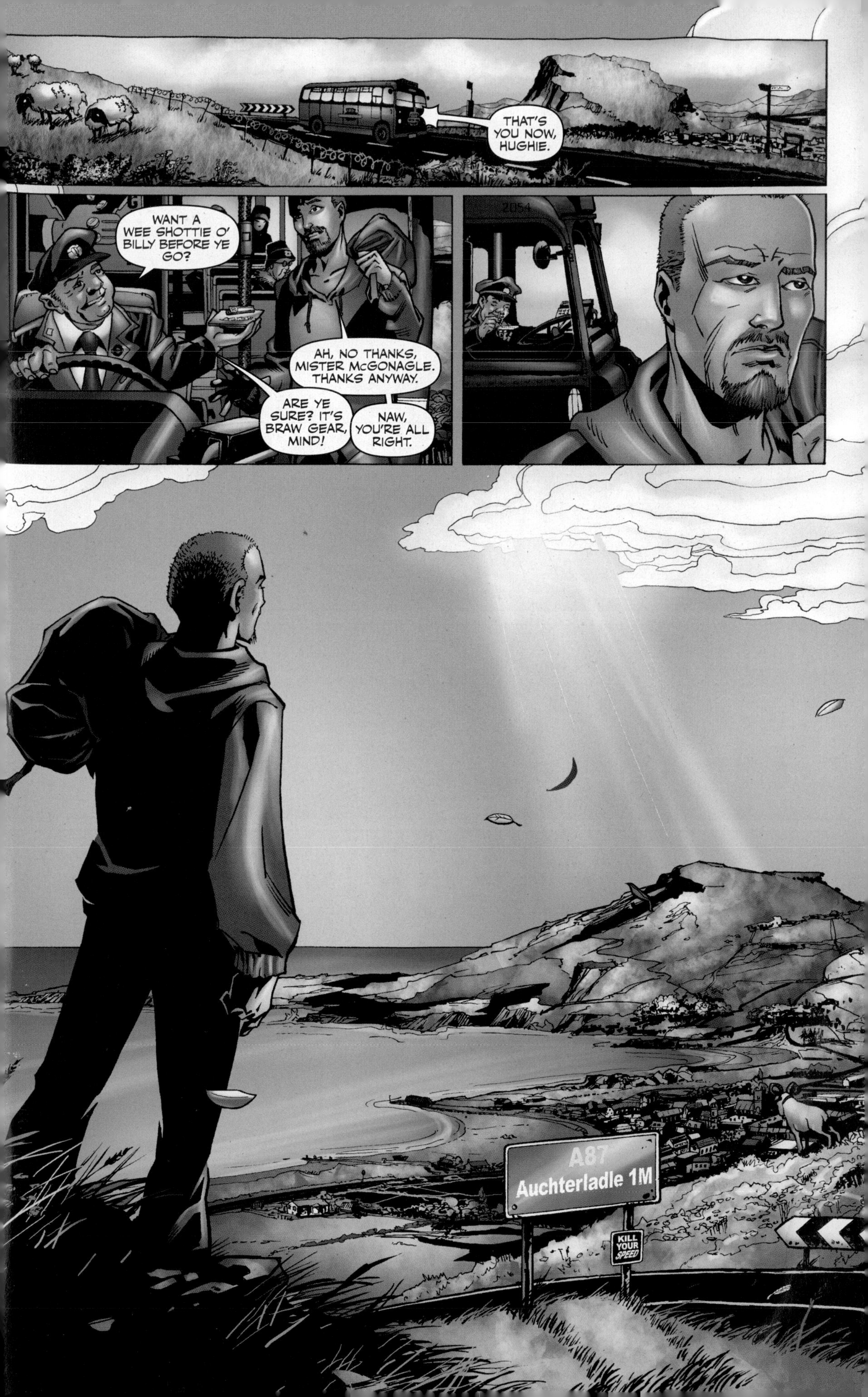
THAT'S YOU NOW, HUGHIE.
WANT A WEE SHOTTIE O' BILLY BEFORE YE GO?
AH, NO THANKS, MISTER McGONAGLE. THANKS ANYWAY.
ARE YE SURE? IT'S BRAW GEAR, MIND!
NAW, YOU'RE ALL RIGHT.
2054
A87
Auchterladle 1M
KILL YOUR SPEED

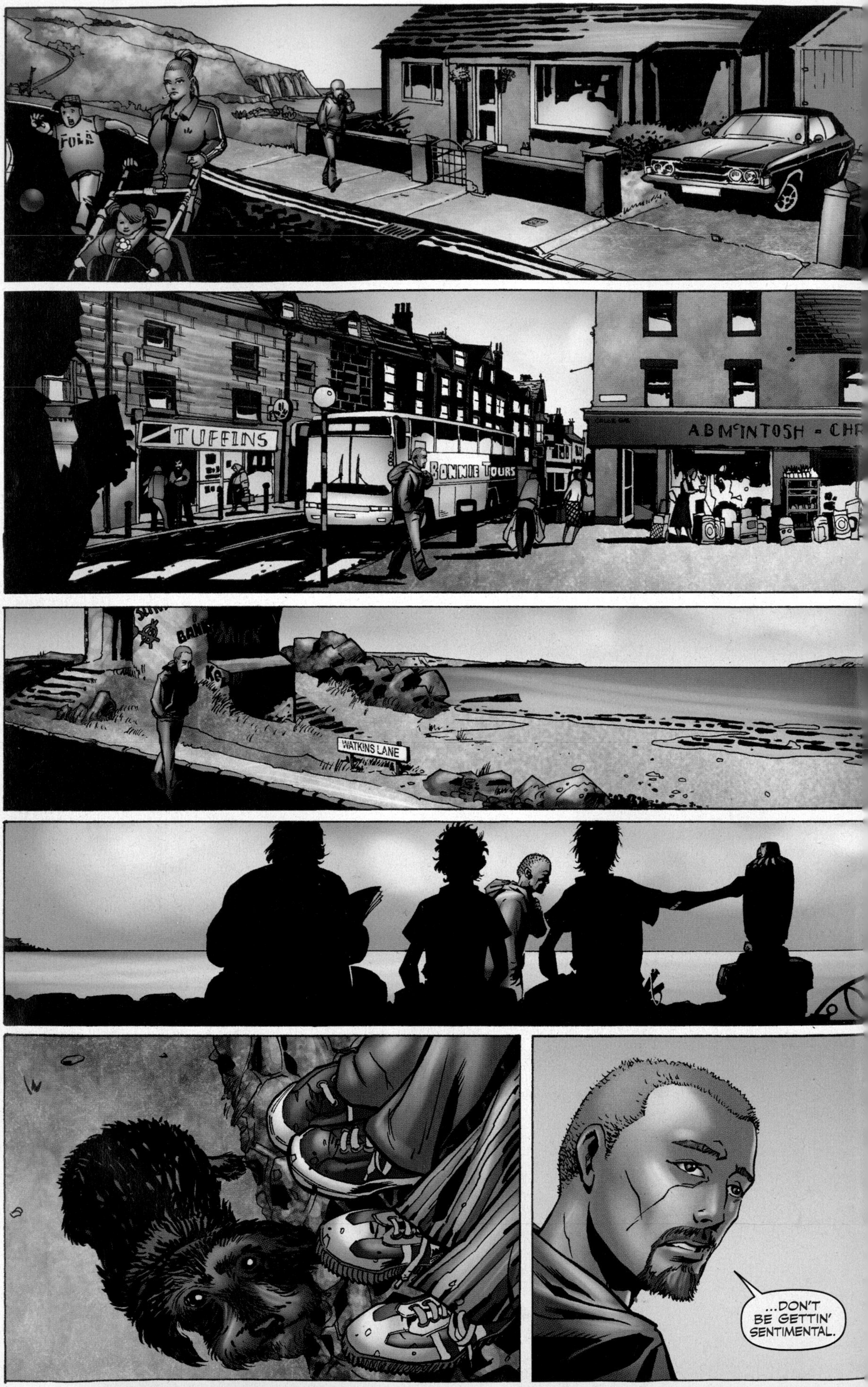
FOLK
TUFFINS
BONNIE TOURS
A B McINTOSH - CHR
WATKINS LANE
...DON'T BE GETTIN' SENTIMENTAL.

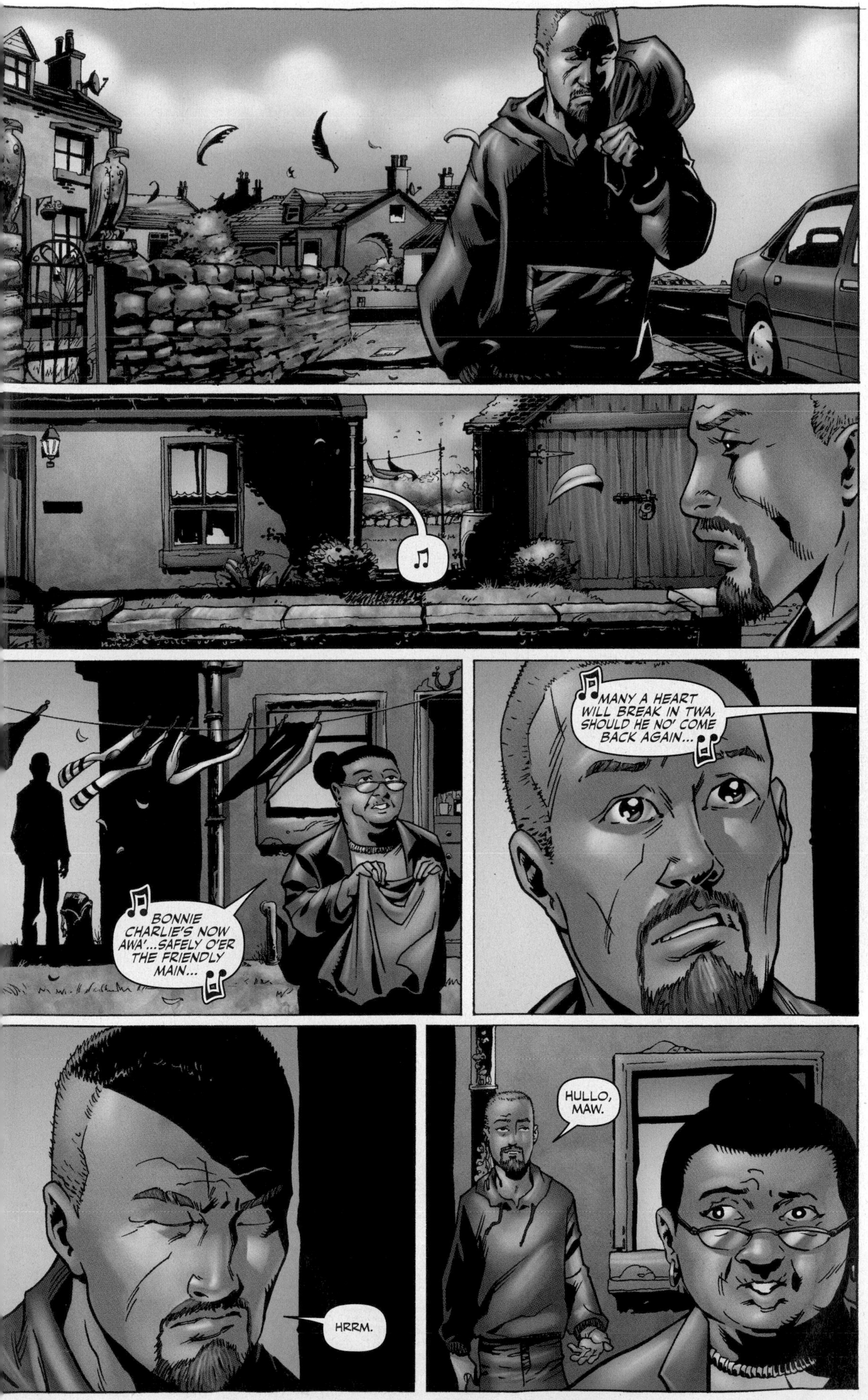
♫
BONNIE CHARLIE'S NOW AWA'...SAFELY O'ER THE FRIENDLY MAIN...
MANY A HEART WILL BREAK IN TWA, SHOULD HE NO' COME BACK AGAIN...
HRRM.
HULLO, MAW.

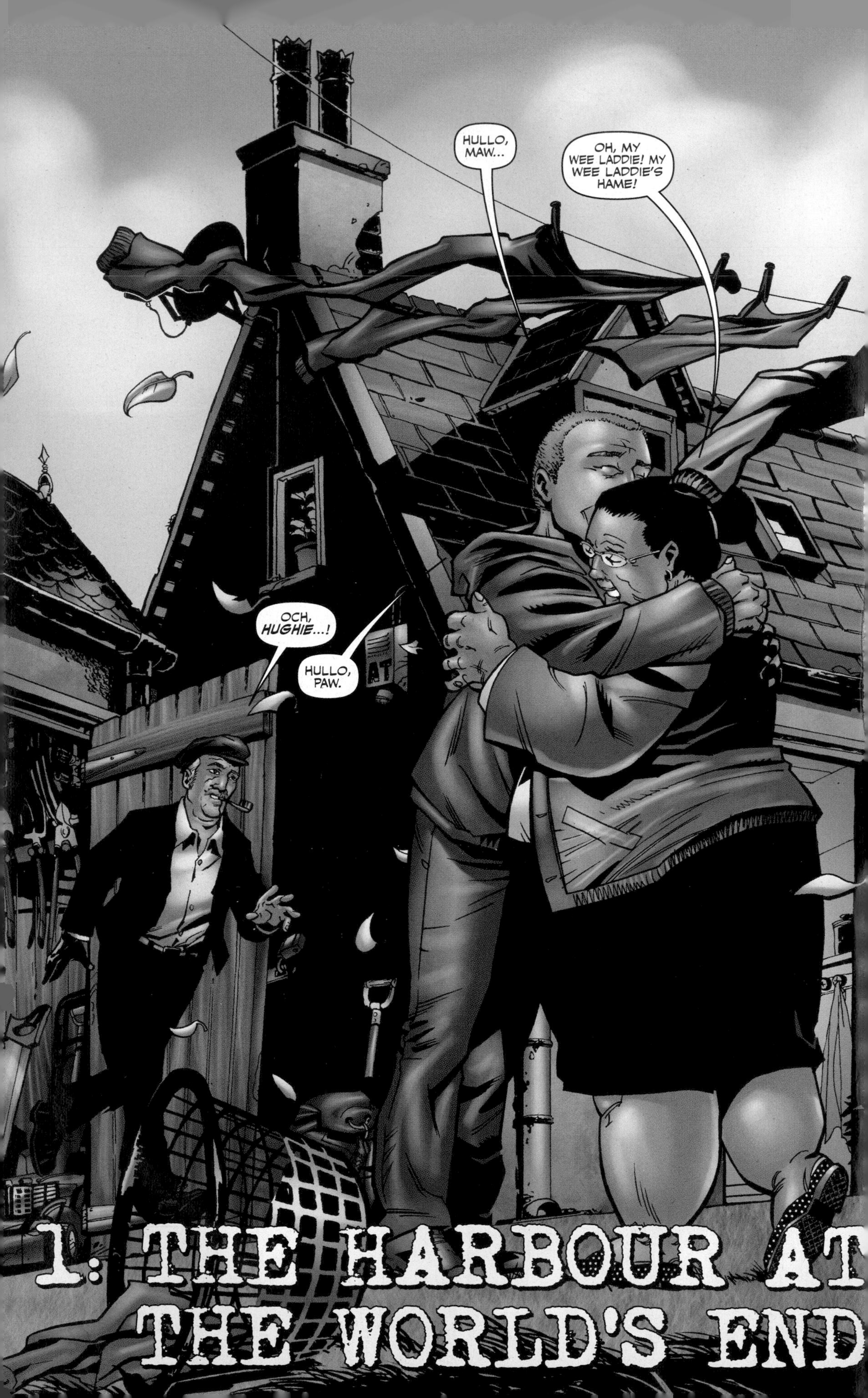
HULLO, MAW...
OH, MY WEE LADDIE! MY WEE LADDIE'S HAME!
OCH, HUGHIE...!
HULLO, PAW.
1: THE HARBOUR AT THE WORLD'S END

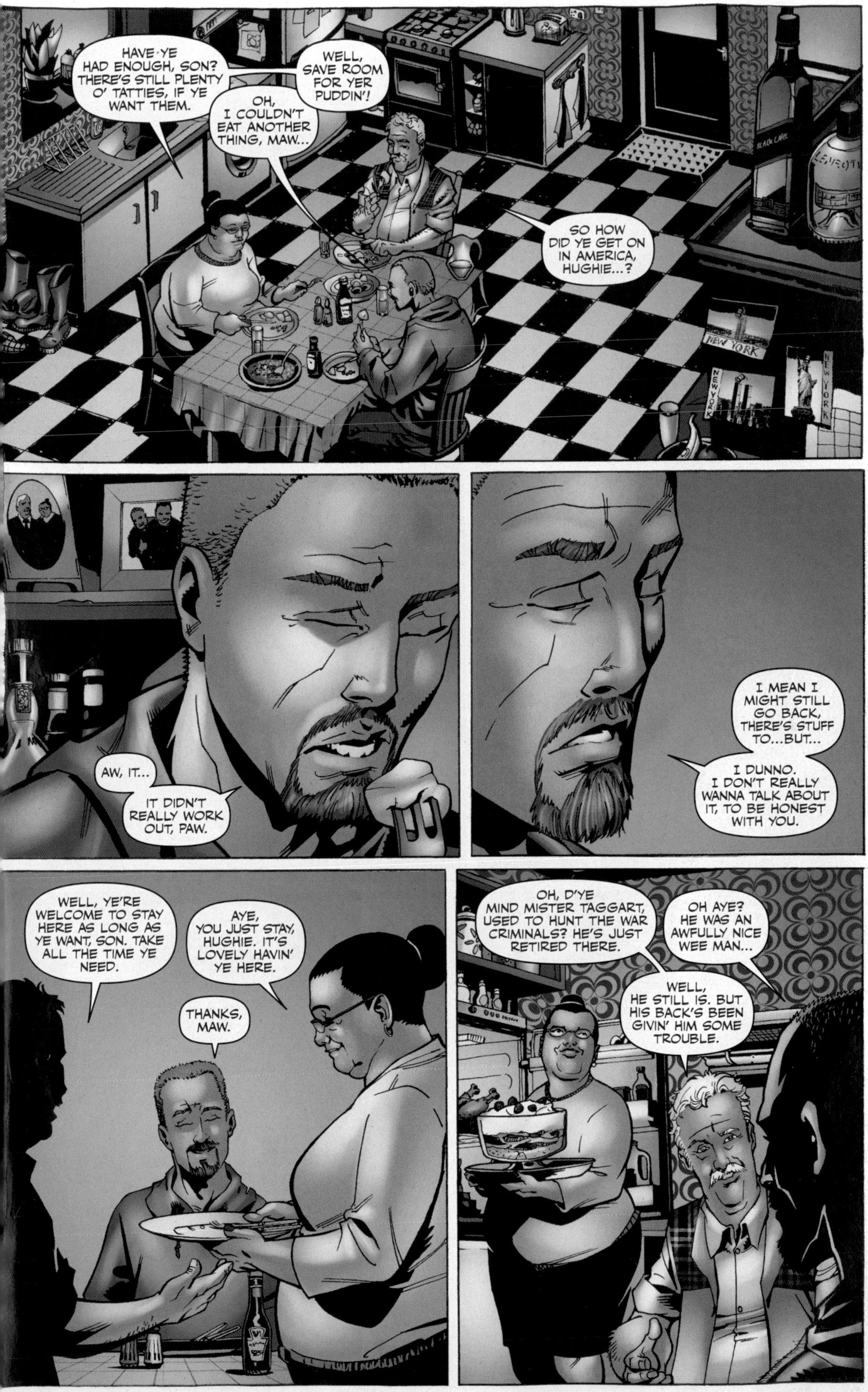
HAVE YE HAD ENOUGH, SON? THERE'S STILL PLENTY O' TATTIES, IF YE WANT THEM.
WELL, SAVE ROOM FOR YER PUDDIN'!
OH, I COULDN'T EAT ANOTHER THING, MAW...
SO HOW DID YE GET ON IN AMERICA, HUGHIE...?
NEW YORK
AW, IT...
IT DIDN'T REALLY WORK OUT, PAW.
I MEAN I MIGHT STILL GO BACK, THERE'S STUFF TO...BUT...
I DUNNO. I DON'T REALLY WANNA TALK ABOUT IT, TO BE HONEST WITH YOU.
WELL, YE'RE WELCOME TO STAY HERE AS LONG AS YE WANT, SON. TAKE ALL THE TIME YE NEED.
AYE, YOU JUST STAY, HUGHIE. IT'S LOVELY HAVIN' YE HERE.
THANKS, MAW.
OH, D'YE MIND MISTER TAGGART, USED TO HUNT THE WAR CRIMINALS? HE'S JUST RETIRED THERE.
OH AYE? HE WAS AN AWFULLY NICE WEE MAN...
WELL, HE STILL IS. BUT HIS BACK'S BEEN GIVIN' HIM SOME TROUBLE.

YE'LL BE WANTIN' TO SEE YER WEE FRIENDS, I DARESAY. BOBBY AND...DOT, IS IT?

DET, MAW. AYE, I GAVE HIM A CALL ON THE WAY HERE, I'M SEEIN' THEM BOTH LATER ON FOR A DRINK.

WHY IS IT YE CALL HIM *DET*, NOW?

SHORT FOR DETERGENT. WE USED TO SAY HE NEVER USES ANY.

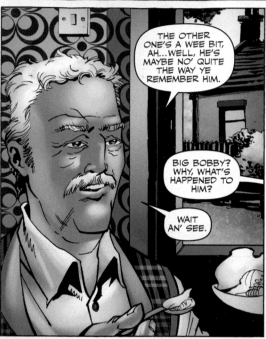

THE OTHER ONE'S A WEE BIT, AH...WELL, HE'S MAYBE NO' QUITE THE WAY YE REMEMBER HIM.

BIG BOBBY? WHY, WHAT'S HAPPENED TO HIM?

WAIT AN' SEE.

WELL THAT WAS A BRAW TRIFLE, DAPHNE. HUGHIE, WILL YE HAVE A WEE DRAM WI' ME?

AYE, WHY NO'. THAT'D BE SMASHIN'.

ECK, DON'T YOU BE LIGHTIN' THAT AULD PIPE IN HERE, NOW...

OCH, NOW HOW LONG IS IT SINCE I DID THAT? I KNOW BETTER THAN TO CHANCE MY ARM WI' YOU, HEN!

OH, GO ON WI' YE...!

WE'LL AWA' OUTSIDE, HUGHIE. A GOOD MAN KENS HIS LIMITATIONS, IS THAT NO' WHAT INSPECTOR CALLAHAN SAYS?

AYE.

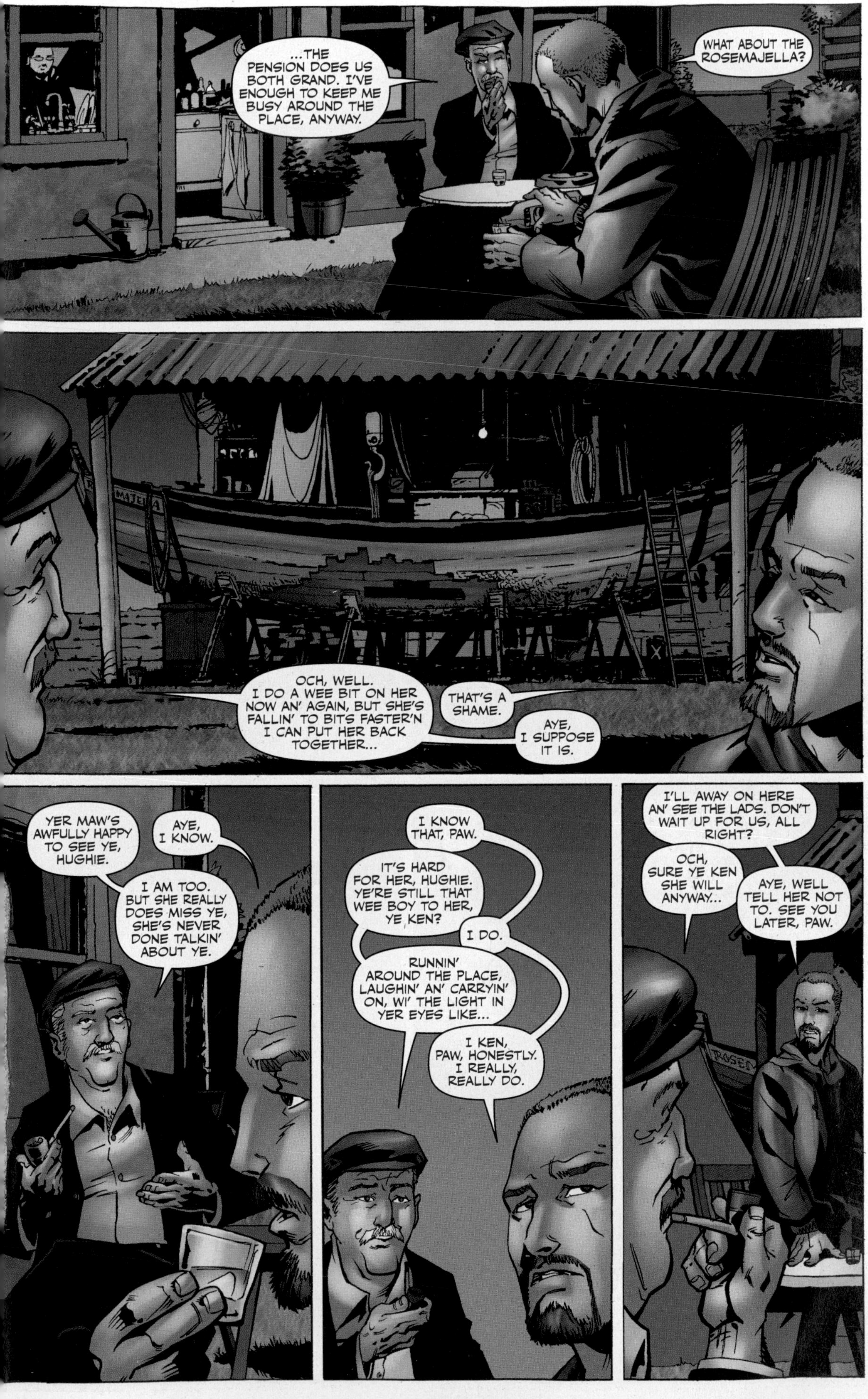
...THE PENSION DOES US BOTH GRAND. I'VE ENOUGH TO KEEP ME BUSY AROUND THE PLACE, ANYWAY.
WHAT ABOUT THE ROSEMAJELLA?
OCH, WELL. I DO A WEE BIT ON HER NOW AN' AGAIN, BUT SHE'S FALLIN' TO BITS FASTER'N I CAN PUT HER BACK TOGETHER...
THAT'S A SHAME.
AYE, I SUPPOSE IT IS.
YER MAW'S AWFULLY HAPPY TO SEE YE, HUGHIE.
AYE, I KNOW.
I AM TOO. BUT SHE REALLY DOES MISS YE, SHE'S NEVER DONE TALKIN' ABOUT YE.
I KNOW THAT, PAW.
IT'S HARD FOR HER, HUGHIE. YE'RE STILL THAT WEE BOY TO HER, YE KEN?
I DO.
RUNNIN' AROUND THE PLACE, LAUGHIN' AN' CARRYIN' ON, WI' THE LIGHT IN YER EYES LIKE...
I KEN, PAW, HONESTLY. I REALLY, REALLY DO.
I'LL AWAY ON HERE AN' SEE THE LADS. DON'T WAIT UP FOR US, ALL RIGHT?
OCH, SURE YE KEN SHE WILL ANYWAY...
AYE, WELL TELL HER NOT TO. SEE YOU LATER, PAW.

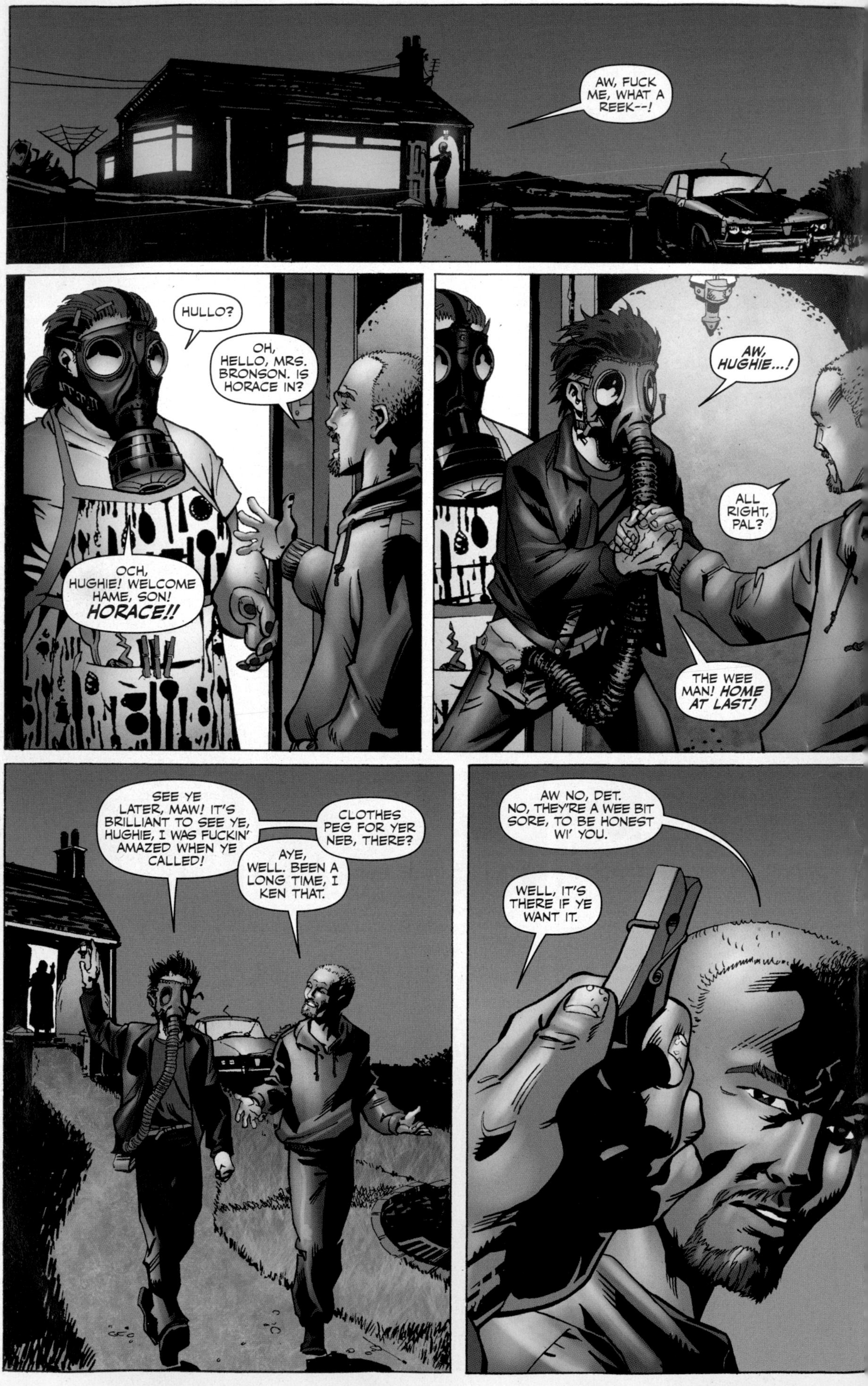
AW, FUCK ME, WHAT A REEK--!
HULLO?
OH, HELLO, MRS. BRONSON. IS HORACE IN?
OCH, HUGHIE! WELCOME HAME, SON! HORACE!!
AW, HUGHIE...!
ALL RIGHT, PAL?
THE WEE MAN! HOME AT LAST!
SEE YE LATER, MAW! IT'S BRILLIANT TO SEE YE, HUGHIE, I WAS FUCKIN' AMAZED WHEN YE CALLED!
AYE, WELL. BEEN A LONG TIME, I KEN THAT.
CLOTHES PEG FOR YER NEB, THERE?
AW NO, DET. NO, THEY'RE A WEE BIT SORE, TO BE HONEST WI' YOU.
WELL, IT'S THERE IF YE WANT IT.

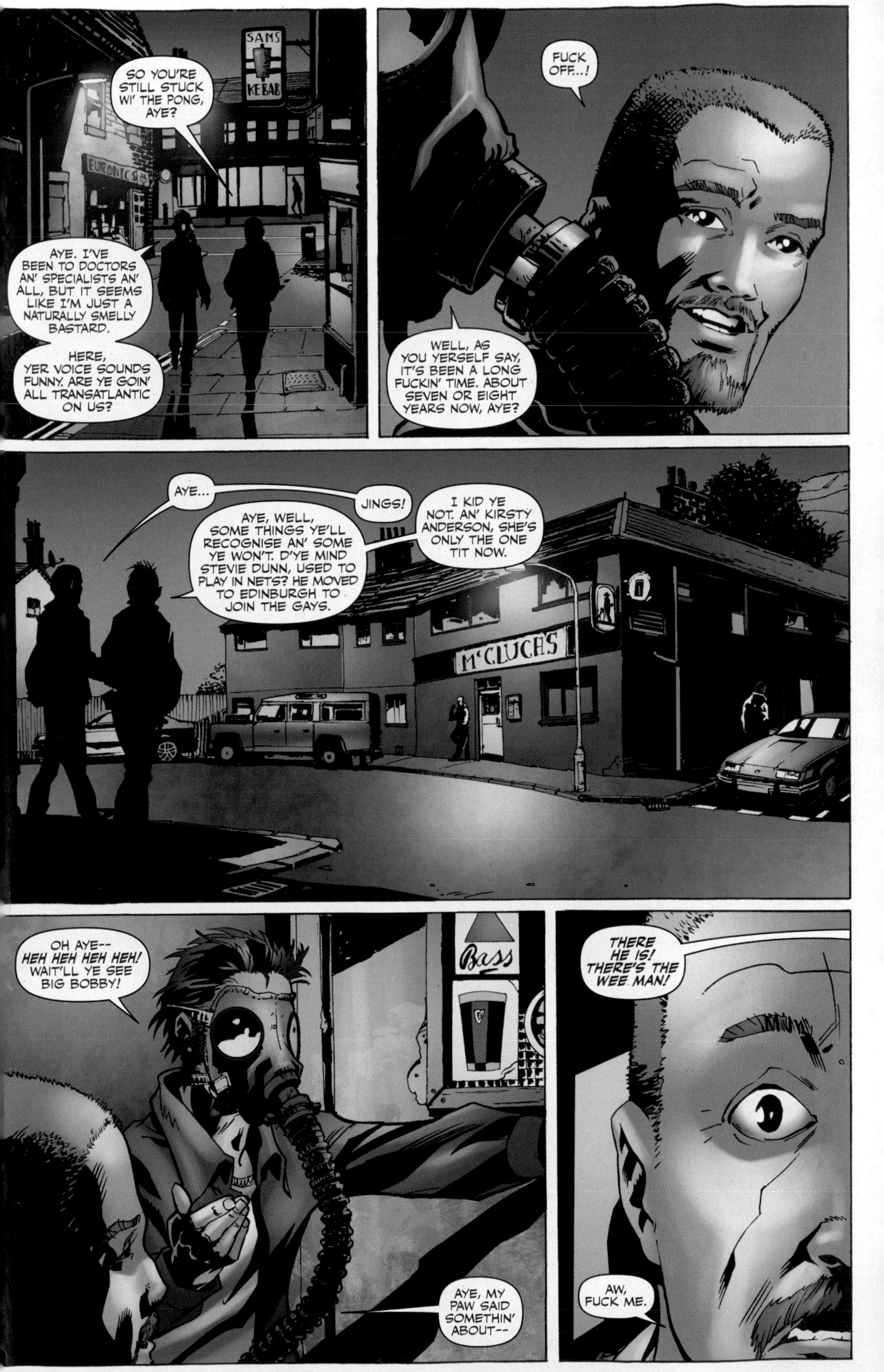
SAMS
KEBAB
SO YOU'RE STILL STUCK WI' THE PONG, AYE?
EURONICS
AYE. I'VE BEEN TO DOCTORS AN' SPECIALISTS AN' ALL, BUT IT SEEMS LIKE I'M JUST A NATURALLY SMELLY BASTARD.
HERE, YER VOICE SOUNDS FUNNY. ARE YE GOIN' ALL TRANSATLANTIC ON US?
FUCK OFF...!
WELL, AS YOU YERSELF SAY, IT'S BEEN A LONG FUCKIN' TIME. ABOUT SEVEN OR EIGHT YEARS NOW, AYE?
AYE...
AYE, WELL, SOME THINGS YE'LL RECOGNISE AN' SOME YE WON'T. D'YE MIND STEVIE DUNN, USED TO PLAY IN NETS? HE MOVED TO EDINBURGH TO JOIN THE GAYS.
JINGS!
I KID YE NOT. AN' KIRSTY ANDERSON, SHE'S ONLY THE ONE TIT NOW.
McCLUCAS
OH AYE-- *HEH HEH HEH HEH!* WAIT'LL YE SEE BIG BOBBY!
Bass
AYE, MY PAW SAID SOMETHIN' ABOUT--
THERE HE IS! THERE'S THE WEE MAN!
AW, FUCK ME.

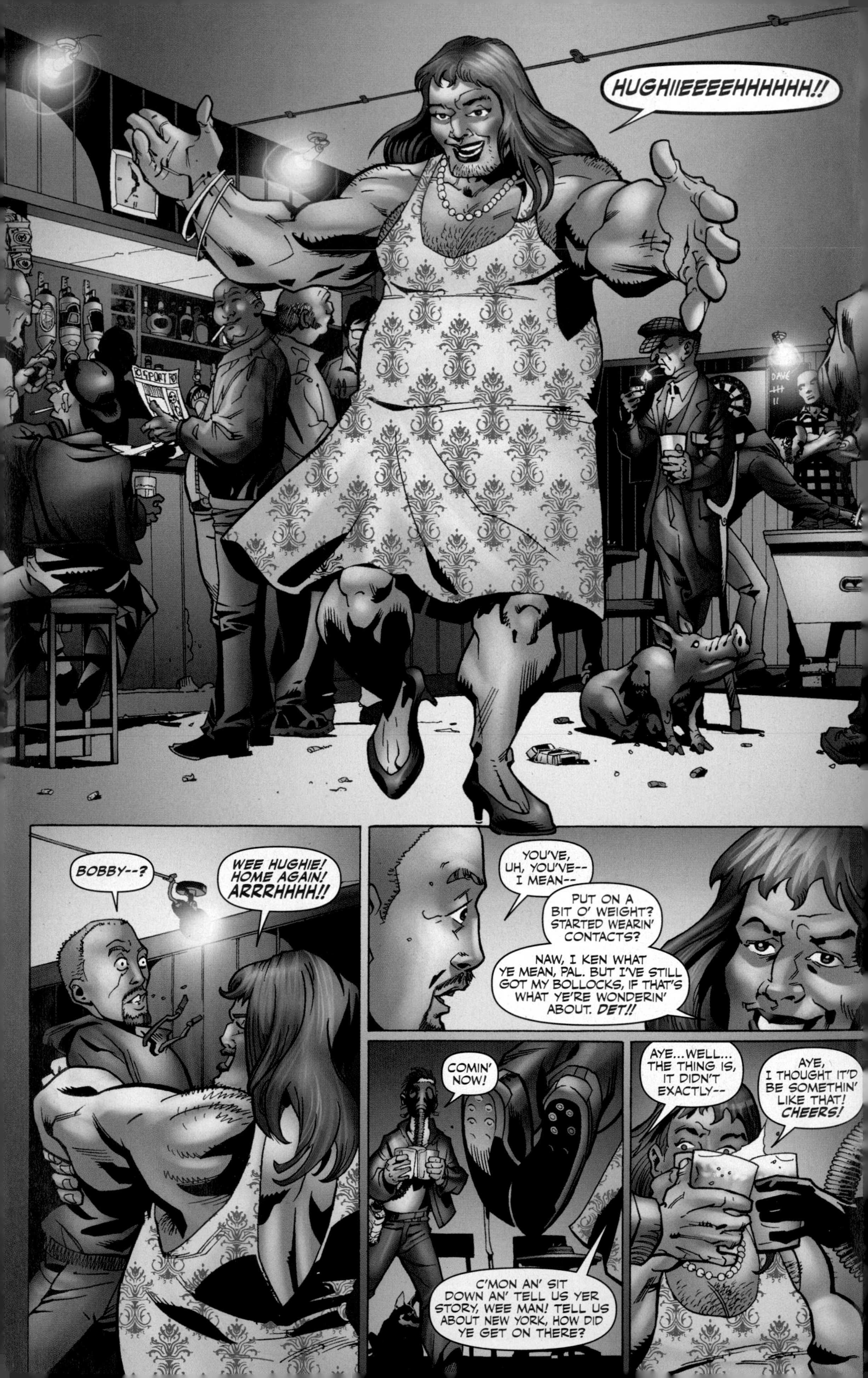
HUGHIIEEEEHHHHHH!!
DAVE
BOBBY--?
WEE HUGHIE! HOME AGAIN! ARRRHHHH!!
YOU'VE, UH, YOU'VE-- I MEAN--
PUT ON A BIT O' WEIGHT? STARTED WEARIN' CONTACTS?
NAW, I KEN WHAT YE MEAN, PAL. BUT I'VE STILL GOT MY BOLLOCKS, IF THAT'S WHAT YE'RE WONDERIN' ABOUT. DET!!
COMIN' NOW!
C'MON AN' SIT DOWN AN' TELL US YER STORY, WEE MAN! TELL US ABOUT NEW YORK, HOW DID YE GET ON THERE?
AYE...WELL... THE THING IS, IT DIDN'T EXACTLY--
AYE, I THOUGHT IT'D BE SOMETHIN' LIKE THAT! CHEERS!

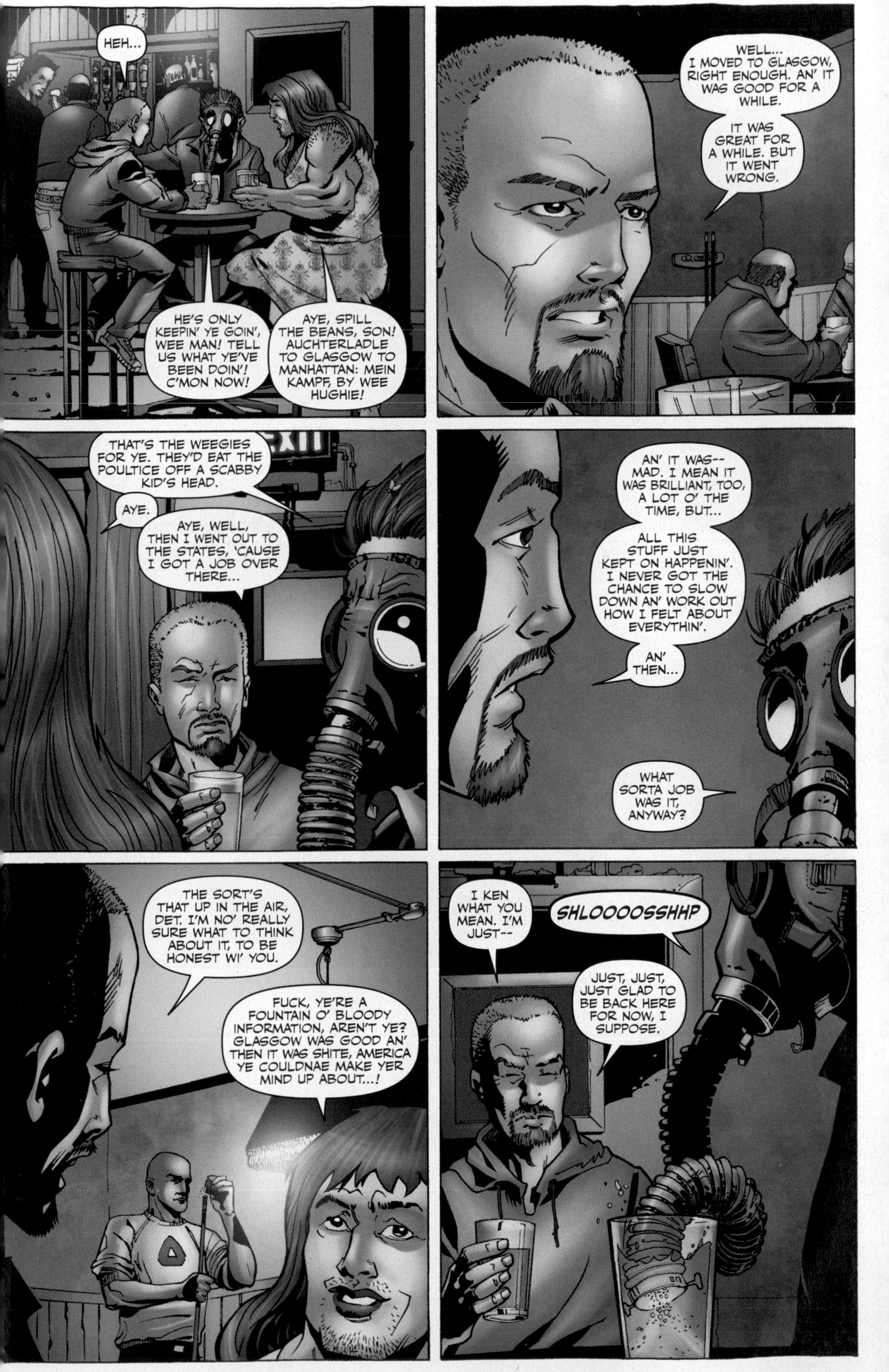
HEH...
HE'S ONLY KEEPIN' YE GOIN', WEE MAN! TELL US WHAT YE'VE BEEN DOIN'! C'MON NOW!
AYE, SPILL THE BEANS, SON! AUCHTERLADLE TO GLASGOW TO MANHATTAN: MEIN KAMPF, BY WEE HUGHIE!
WELL... I MOVED TO GLASGOW, RIGHT ENOUGH. AN' IT WAS GOOD FOR A WHILE.
IT WAS GREAT FOR A WHILE. BUT IT WENT WRONG.
THAT'S THE WEEGIES FOR YE. THEY'D EAT THE POULTICE OFF A SCABBY KID'S HEAD.
AYE.
AYE, WELL, THEN I WENT OUT TO THE STATES, 'CAUSE I GOT A JOB OVER THERE...
AN' IT WAS-- MAD. I MEAN IT WAS BRILLIANT, TOO, A LOT O' THE TIME, BUT...
ALL THIS STUFF JUST KEPT ON HAPPENIN'. I NEVER GOT THE CHANCE TO SLOW DOWN AN' WORK OUT HOW I FELT ABOUT EVERYTHIN'.
AN' THEN...
WHAT SORTA JOB WAS IT, ANYWAY?
THE SORT'S THAT UP IN THE AIR, DET. I'M NO' REALLY SURE WHAT TO THINK ABOUT IT, TO BE HONEST WI' YOU.
FUCK, YE'RE A FOUNTAIN O' BLOODY INFORMATION, AREN'T YE? GLASGOW WAS GOOD AN' THEN IT WAS SHITE, AMERICA YE COULDNAE MAKE YER MIND UP ABOUT...!
I KEN WHAT YOU MEAN. I'M JUST--
SHLOOOOSSHHP
JUST, JUST, JUST GLAD TO BE BACK HERE FOR NOW, I SUPPOSE.

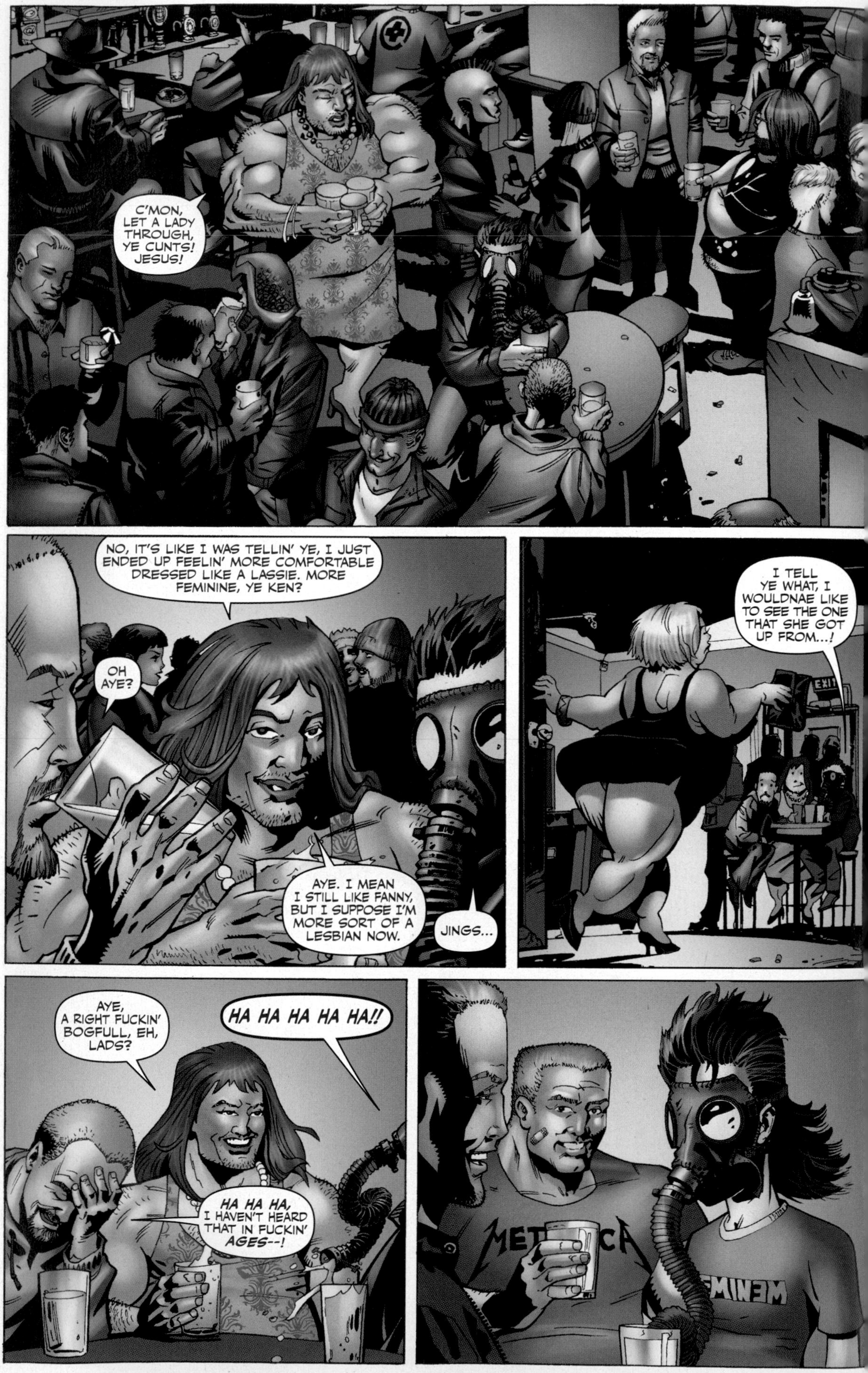
C'MON, LET A LADY THROUGH, YE CUNTS! JESUS!
NO, IT'S LIKE I WAS TELLIN' YE, I JUST ENDED UP FEELIN' MORE COMFORTABLE DRESSED LIKE A LASSIE. MORE FEMININE, YE KEN?
OH AYE?
AYE. I MEAN I STILL LIKE FANNY, BUT I SUPPOSE I'M MORE SORT OF A LESBIAN NOW.
JINGS...
I TELL YE WHAT, I WOULDNAE LIKE TO SEE THE ONE THAT SHE GOT UP FROM...!
EXIT
AYE, A RIGHT FUCKIN' BOGFULL, EH, LADS?
HA HA HA HA HA!!
HA HA HA, I HAVEN'T HEARD THAT IN FUCKIN' AGES--!
EMINEM

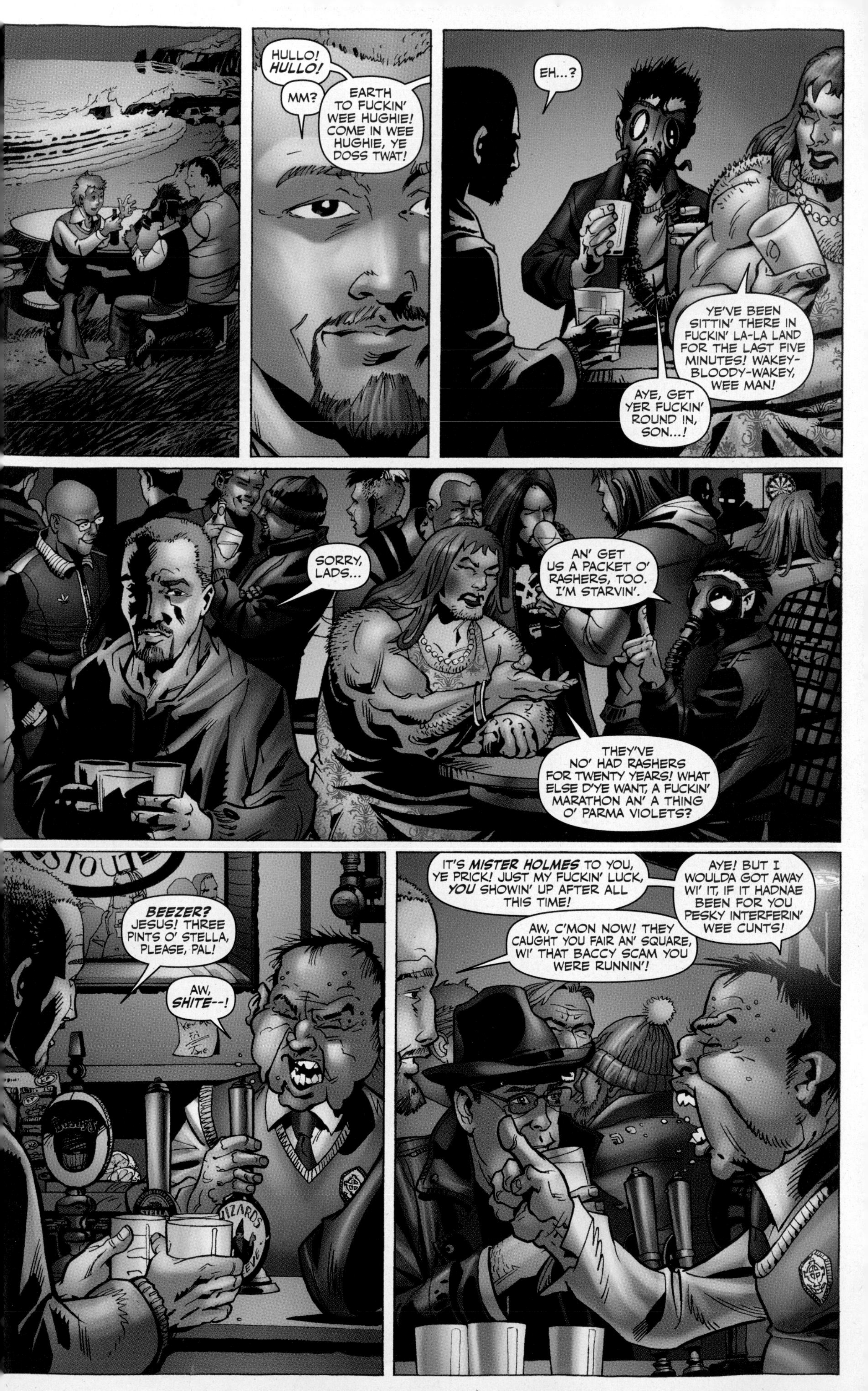
HULLO! *HULLO!*
MM?
EARTH TO FUCKIN' WEE HUGHIE! COME IN WEE HUGHIE, YE DOSS TWAT!
EH...?
YE'VE BEEN SITTIN' THERE IN FUCKIN' LA-LA LAND FOR THE LAST FIVE MINUTES! WAKEY-BLOODY-WAKEY, WEE MAN!
AYE, GET YER FUCKIN' ROUND IN, SON...!
SORRY, LADS...
AN' GET US A PACKET O' RASHERS, TOO. I'M STARVIN'.
THEY'VE NO' HAD RASHERS FOR TWENTY YEARS! WHAT ELSE D'YE WANT, A FUCKIN' MARATHON AN' A THING O' PARMA VIOLETS?
BEEZER? JESUS! THREE PINTS O' STELLA, PLEASE, PAL!
AW, *SHITE*--!
IT'S *MISTER HOLMES* TO YOU, YE PRICK! JUST MY FUCKIN' LUCK, *YOU* SHOWIN' UP AFTER ALL THIS TIME!
AW, C'MON NOW! THEY CAUGHT YOU FAIR AN' SQUARE, WI' THAT BACCY SCAM YOU WERE RUNNIN'!
AYE! BUT I WOULDA GOT AWAY WI' IT, IF IT HADNAE BEEN FOR YOU PESKY INTERFERIN' WEE CUNTS!

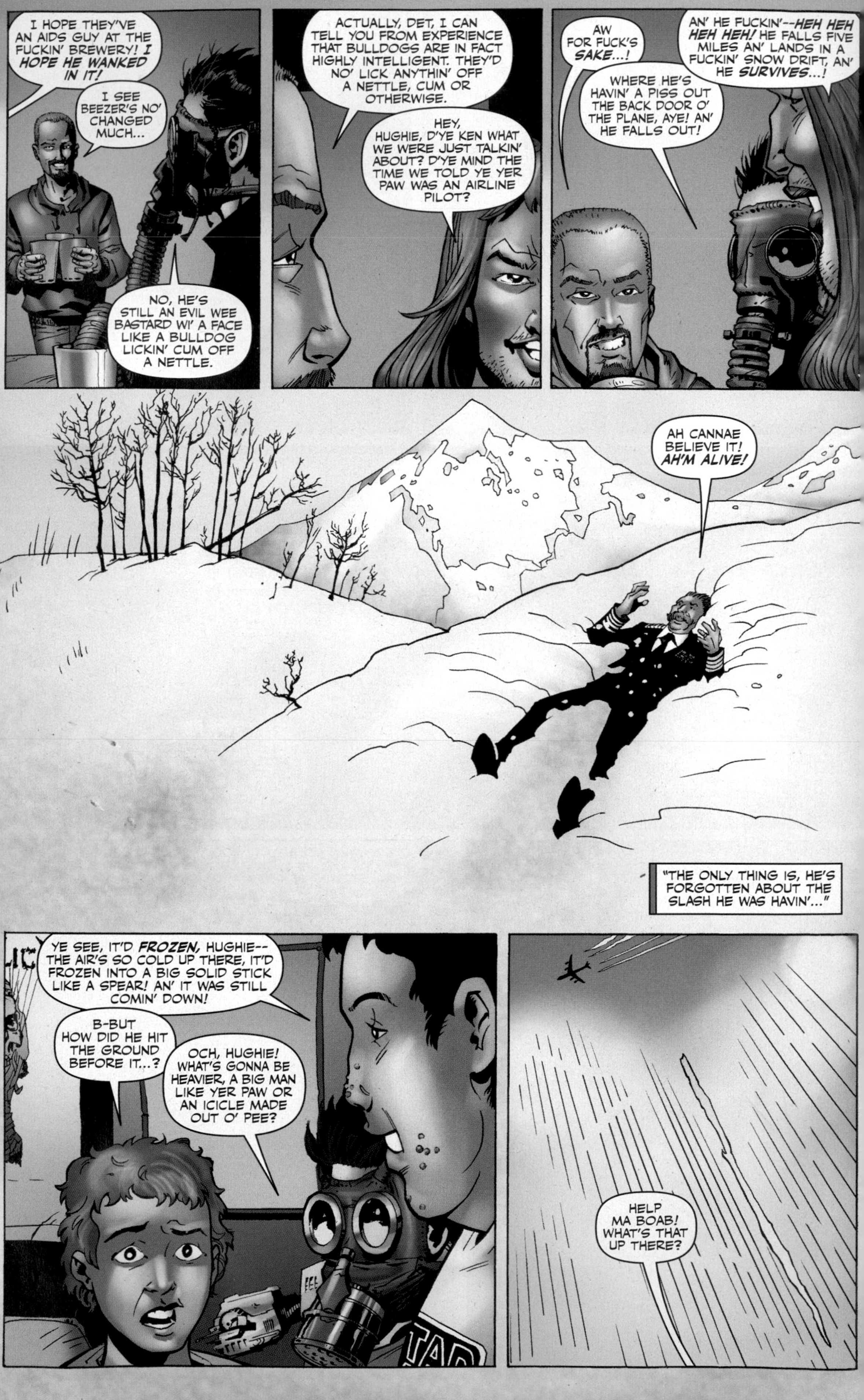
I HOPE THEY'VE AN AIDS GUY AT THE FUCKIN' BREWERY! I HOPE HE WANKED IN IT!
I SEE BEEZER'S NO' CHANGED MUCH...
NO, HE'S STILL AN EVIL WEE BASTARD WI' A FACE LIKE A BULLDOG LICKIN' CUM OFF A NETTLE.
ACTUALLY, DET, I CAN TELL YOU FROM EXPERIENCE THAT BULLDOGS ARE IN FACT HIGHLY INTELLIGENT. THEY'D NO' LICK ANYTHIN' OFF A NETTLE, CUM OR OTHERWISE.
HEY, HUGHIE, D'YE KEN WHAT WE WERE JUST TALKIN' ABOUT? D'YE MIND THE TIME WE TOLD YE YER PAW WAS AN AIRLINE PILOT?
AW FOR FUCK'S SAKE...!
AN' HE FUCKIN'--HEH HEH HEH HEH! HE FALLS FIVE MILES AN' LANDS IN A FUCKIN' SNOW DRIFT, AN' HE SURVIVES...!
WHERE HE'S HAVIN' A PISS OUT THE BACK DOOR O' THE PLANE, AYE! AN' HE FALLS OUT!
AH CANNAE BELIEVE IT! AH'M ALIVE!
"THE ONLY THING IS, HE'S FORGOTTEN ABOUT THE SLASH HE WAS HAVIN'..."
YE SEE, IT'D FROZEN, HUGHIE-- THE AIR'S SO COLD UP THERE, IT'D FROZEN INTO A BIG SOLID STICK LIKE A SPEAR! AN' IT WAS STILL COMIN' DOWN!
B-BUT HOW DID HE HIT THE GROUND BEFORE IT...?
OCH, HUGHIE! WHAT'S GONNA BE HEAVIER, A BIG MAN LIKE YER PAW OR AN ICICLE MADE OUT O' PEE?
HELP MA BOAB! WHAT'S THAT UP THERE?

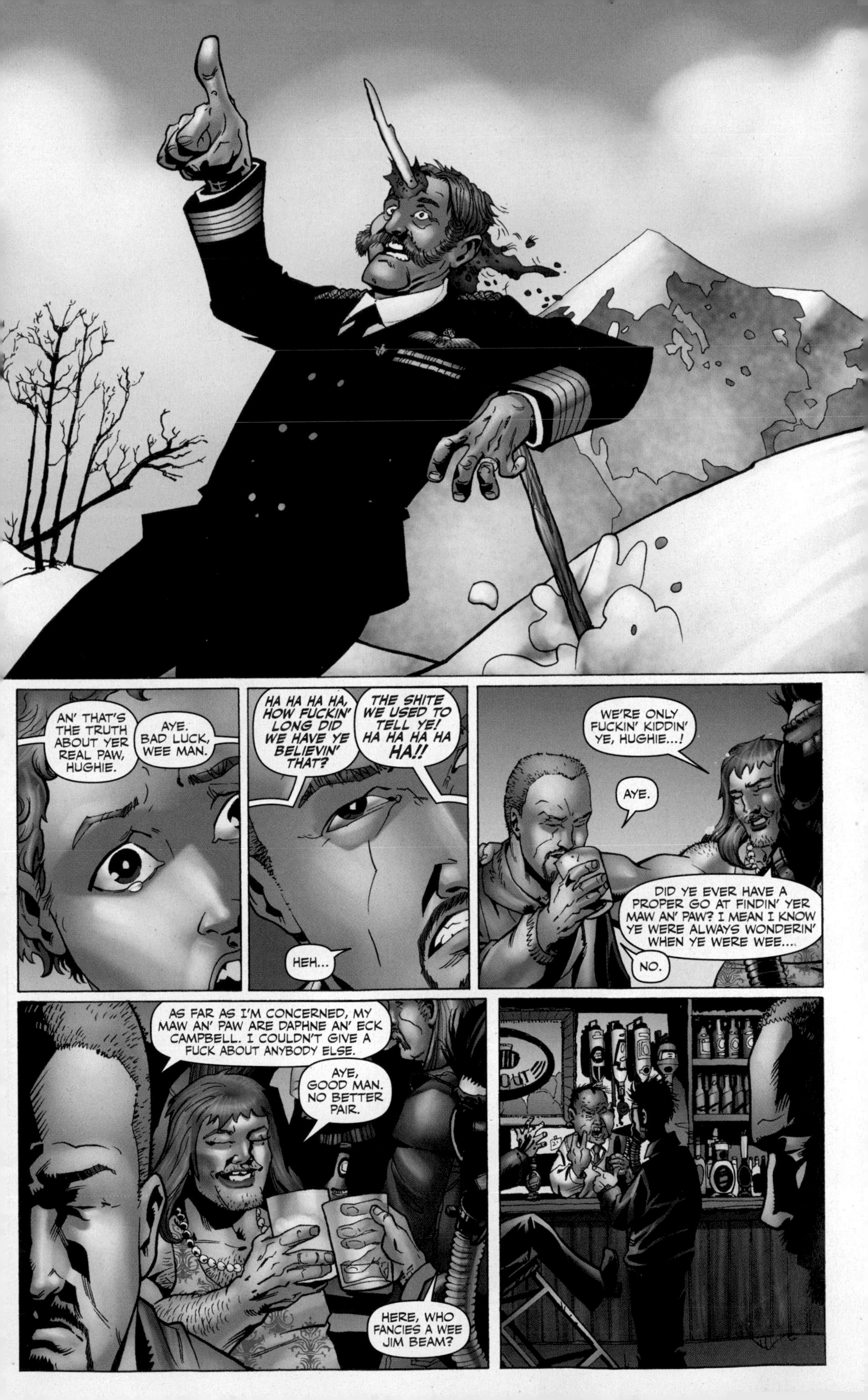
AN' THAT'S THE TRUTH ABOUT YER REAL PAW, HUGHIE.
AYE. BAD LUCK, WEE MAN.
HA HA HA HA, HOW FUCKIN' LONG DID WE HAVE YE BELIEVIN' THAT?
THE SHITE WE USED TO TELL YE! HA HA HA HA HA!!
HEH...
WE'RE ONLY FUCKIN' KIDDIN' YE, HUGHIE...!
AYE.
DID YE EVER HAVE A PROPER GO AT FINDIN' YER MAW AN' PAW? I MEAN I KNOW YE WERE ALWAYS WONDERIN' WHEN YE WERE WEE....
NO.
AS FAR AS I'M CONCERNED, MY MAW AN' PAW ARE DAPHNE AN' ECK CAMPBELL. I COULDN'T GIVE A FUCK ABOUT ANYBODY ELSE.
AYE, GOOD MAN. NO BETTER PAIR.
HERE, WHO FANCIES A WEE JIM BEAM?

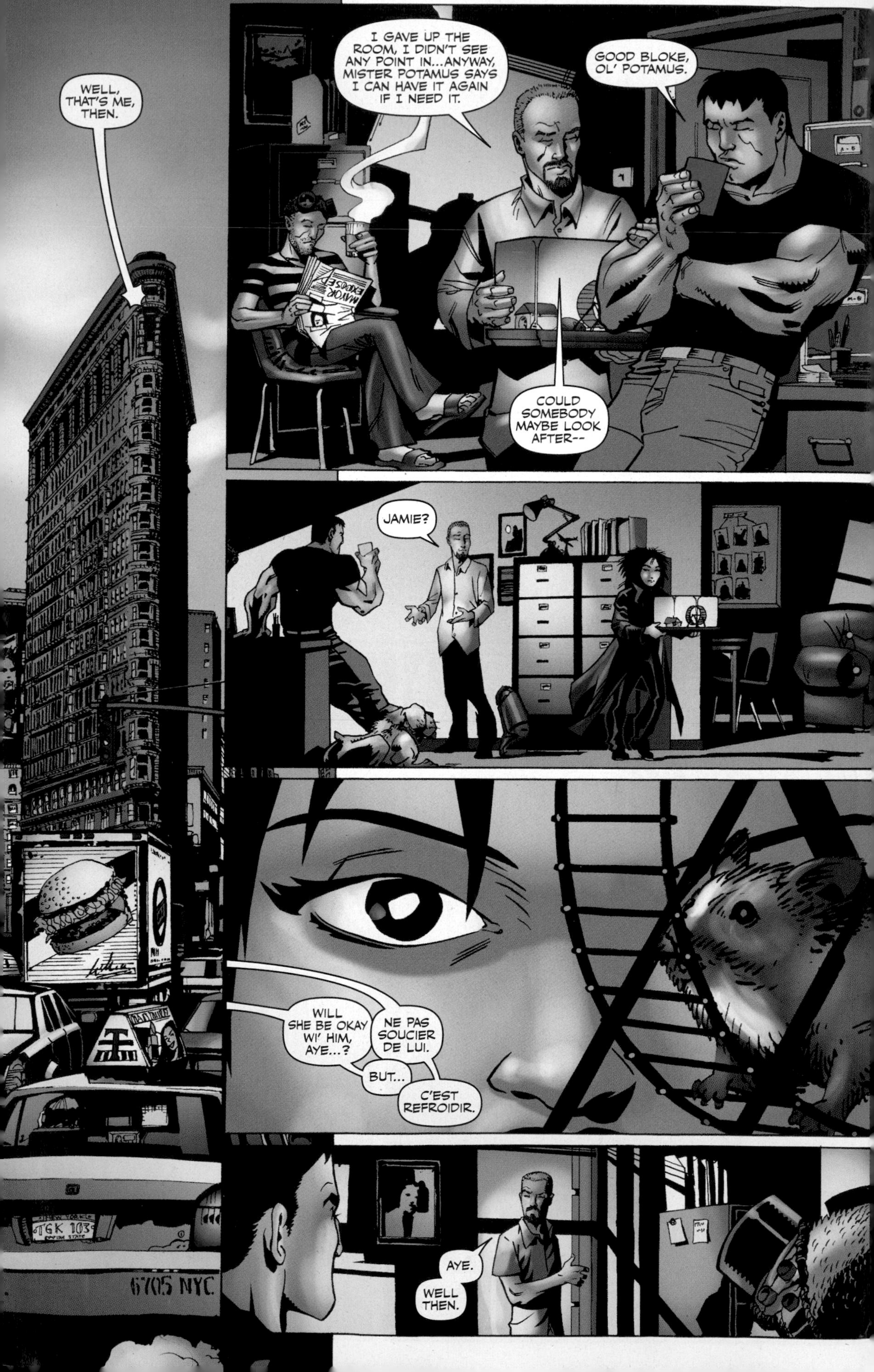
WELL, THAT'S ME, THEN.
I GAVE UP THE ROOM, I DIDN'T SEE ANY POINT IN...ANYWAY, MISTER POTAMUS SAYS I CAN HAVE IT AGAIN IF I NEED IT.
GOOD BLOKE, OL' POTAMUS.
COULD SOMEBODY MAYBE LOOK AFTER--
JAMIE?
WILL SHE BE OKAY WI' HIM, AYE...?
NE PAS SOUCIER DE LUI.
BUT...
C'EST REFROIDIR.
AYE.
WELL THEN.
6705 NYC

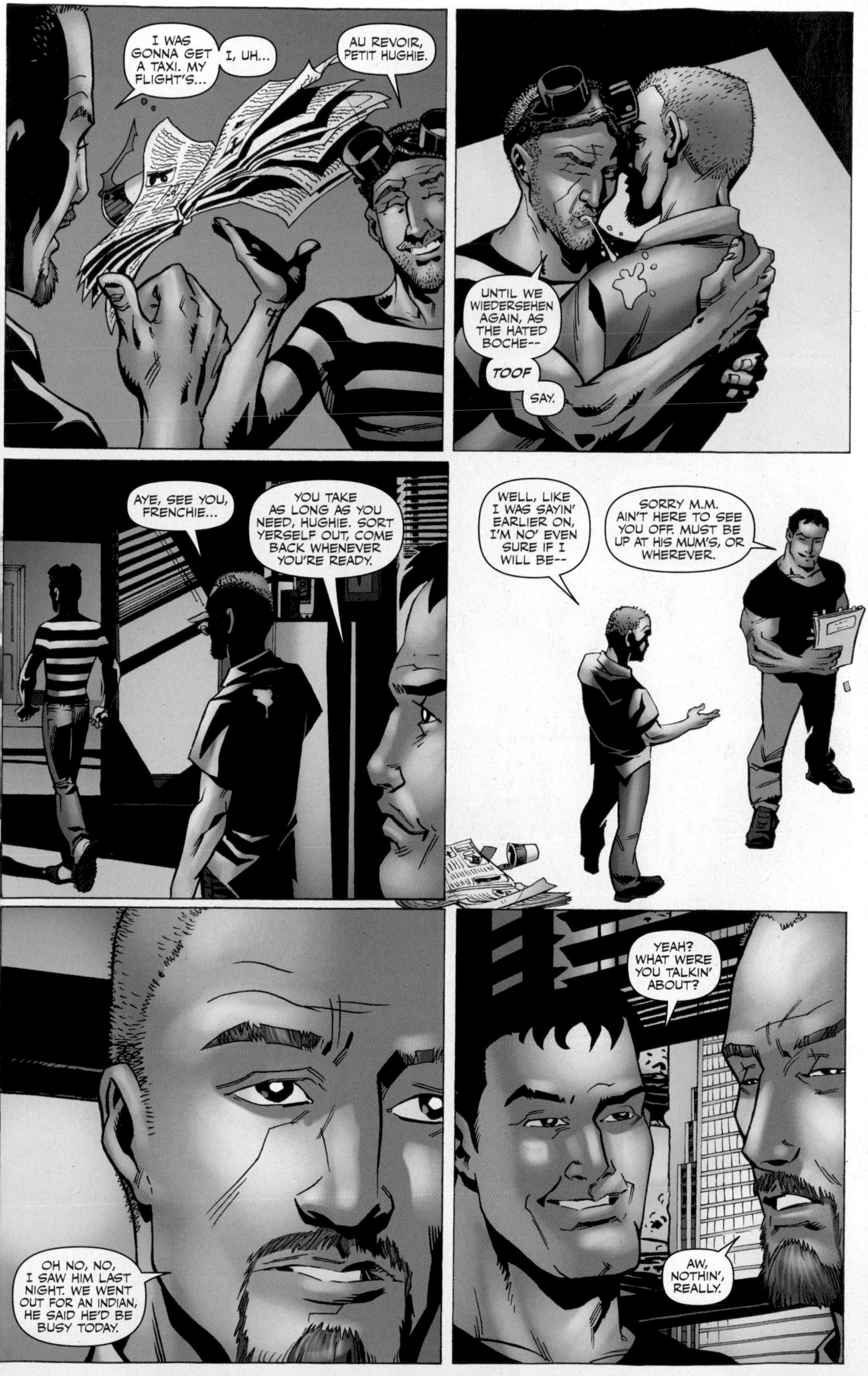

I WAS GONNA GET A TAXI. MY FLIGHT'S...
I, UH...
AU REVOIR, PETIT HUGHIE.
UNTIL WE WIEDERSEHEN AGAIN, AS THE HATED BOCHE--
TOOF
SAY.
AYE, SEE YOU, FRENCHIE...
YOU TAKE AS LONG AS YOU NEED, HUGHIE. SORT YERSELF OUT, COME BACK WHENEVER YOU'RE READY.
WELL, LIKE I WAS SAYIN' EARLIER ON, I'M NO' EVEN SURE IF I WILL BE--
SORRY M.M. AIN'T HERE TO SEE YOU OFF. MUST BE UP AT HIS MUM'S, OR WHEREVER.
OH NO, NO, I SAW HIM LAST NIGHT. WE WENT OUT FOR AN INDIAN, HE SAID HE'D BE BUSY TODAY.
YEAH? WHAT WERE YOU TALKIN' ABOUT?
AW, NOTHIN', REALLY.

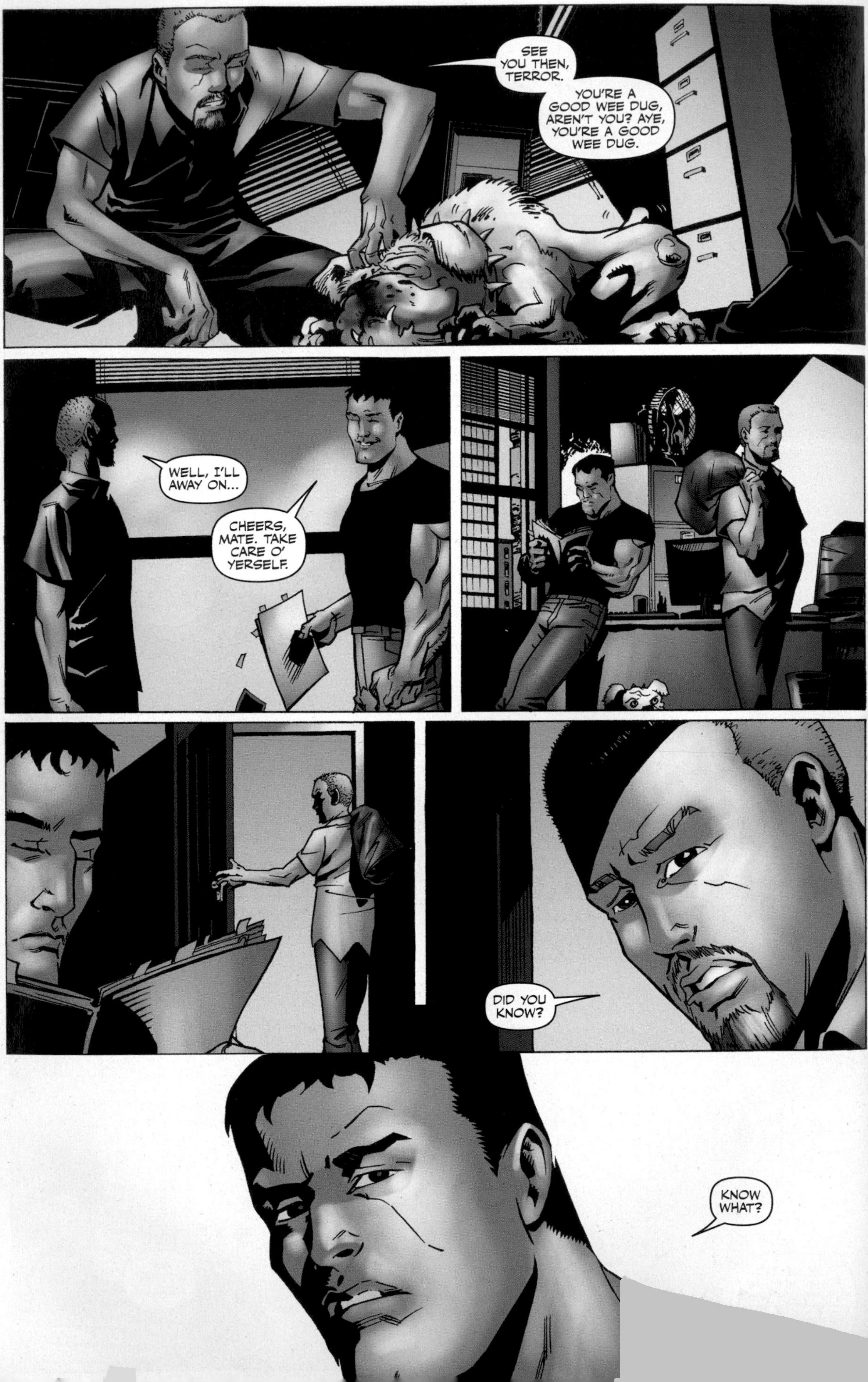
SEE YOU THEN, TERROR.
YOU'RE A GOOD WEE DUG, AREN'T YOU? AYE, YOU'RE A GOOD WEE DUG.
WELL, I'LL AWAY ON...
CHEERS, MATE. TAKE CARE O' YERSELF.
DID YOU KNOW?
KNOW WHAT?

PWORRNK

AYE, GET IT ALL OUT, SON. IT'S DOIN' YE NO GOOD.

ARE YE HEADIN' ON, ARE YE?

AYE, I THOUGHT I'D TAKE A WEE WALK DOWN THE SHORE. I'M NO' THAT TIRED YET.

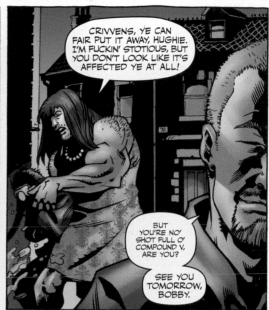

CRIVVENS, YE CAN FAIR PUT IT AWAY, HUGHIE. I'M FUCKIN' STOTIOUS, BUT YOU DON'T LOOK LIKE IT'S AFFECTED YE AT ALL!

BUT YOU'RE NO' SHOT FULL O' COMPOUND V, ARE YOU?

SEE YOU TOMORROW, BOBBY.

'EVENING.

HULLO THERE. ARE YOU PAINTIN' A PICTURE, AYE?

THAT I AM.

AW, THAT'S VERY GOOD...!

TRYING TO CAPTURE THE SIMMER DIM.

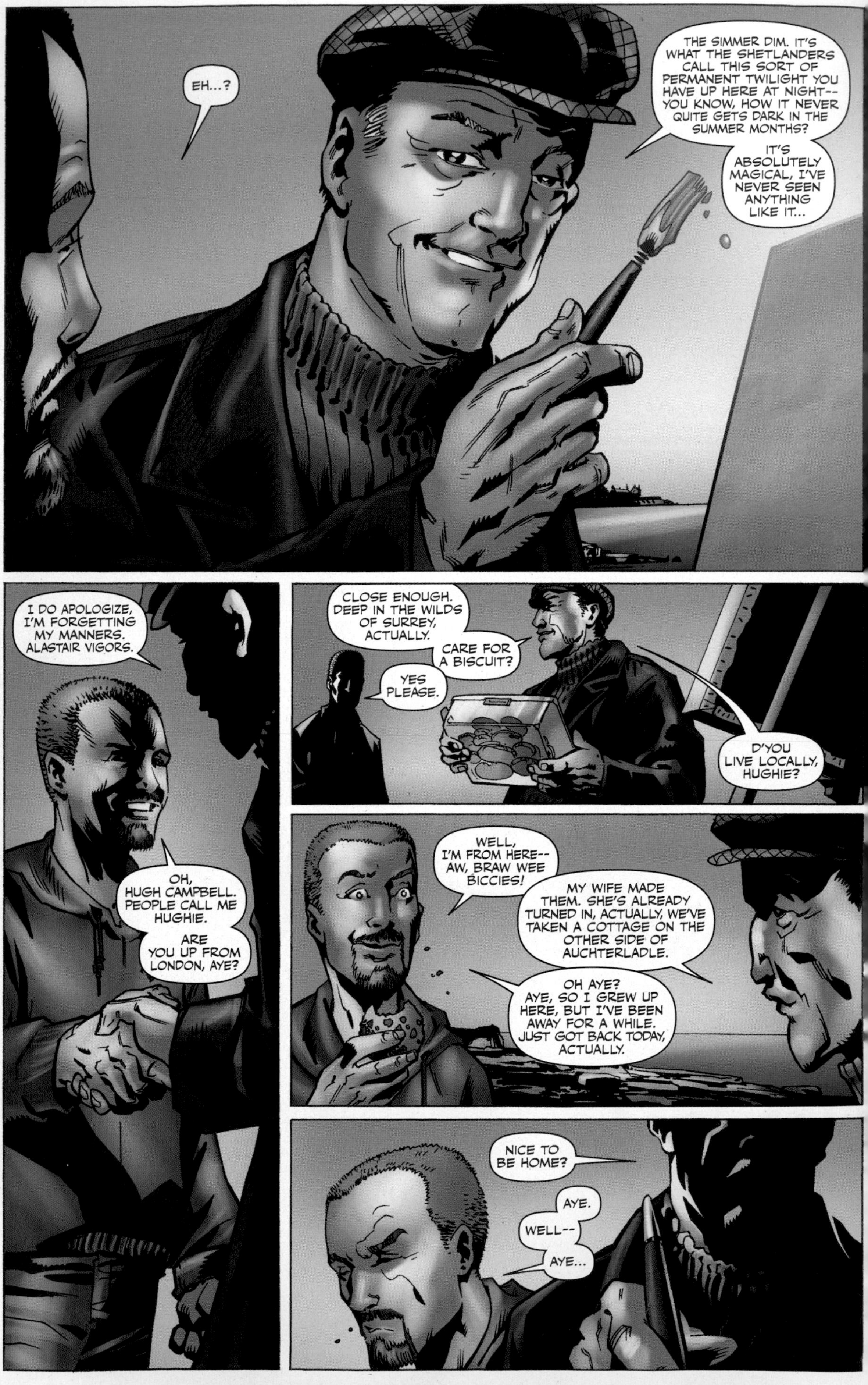
EH...?
THE SIMMER DIM. IT'S WHAT THE SHETLANDERS CALL THIS SORT OF PERMANENT TWILIGHT YOU HAVE UP HERE AT NIGHT-- YOU KNOW, HOW IT NEVER QUITE GETS DARK IN THE SUMMER MONTHS?
IT'S ABSOLUTELY MAGICAL, I'VE NEVER SEEN ANYTHING LIKE IT...
I DO APOLOGIZE, I'M FORGETTING MY MANNERS. ALASTAIR VIGORS.
OH, HUGH CAMPBELL. PEOPLE CALL ME HUGHIE.
ARE YOU UP FROM LONDON, AYE?
CLOSE ENOUGH. DEEP IN THE WILDS OF SURREY, ACTUALLY.
CARE FOR A BISCUIT?
YES PLEASE.
D'YOU LIVE LOCALLY, HUGHIE?
WELL, I'M FROM HERE-- AW, BRAW WEE BICCIES!
MY WIFE MADE THEM. SHE'S ALREADY TURNED IN, ACTUALLY, WE'VE TAKEN A COTTAGE ON THE OTHER SIDE OF AUCHTERLADLE.
OH AYE? AYE, SO I GREW UP HERE, BUT I'VE BEEN AWAY FOR A WHILE. JUST GOT BACK TODAY, ACTUALLY.
NICE TO BE HOME?
AYE.
WELL--
AYE...

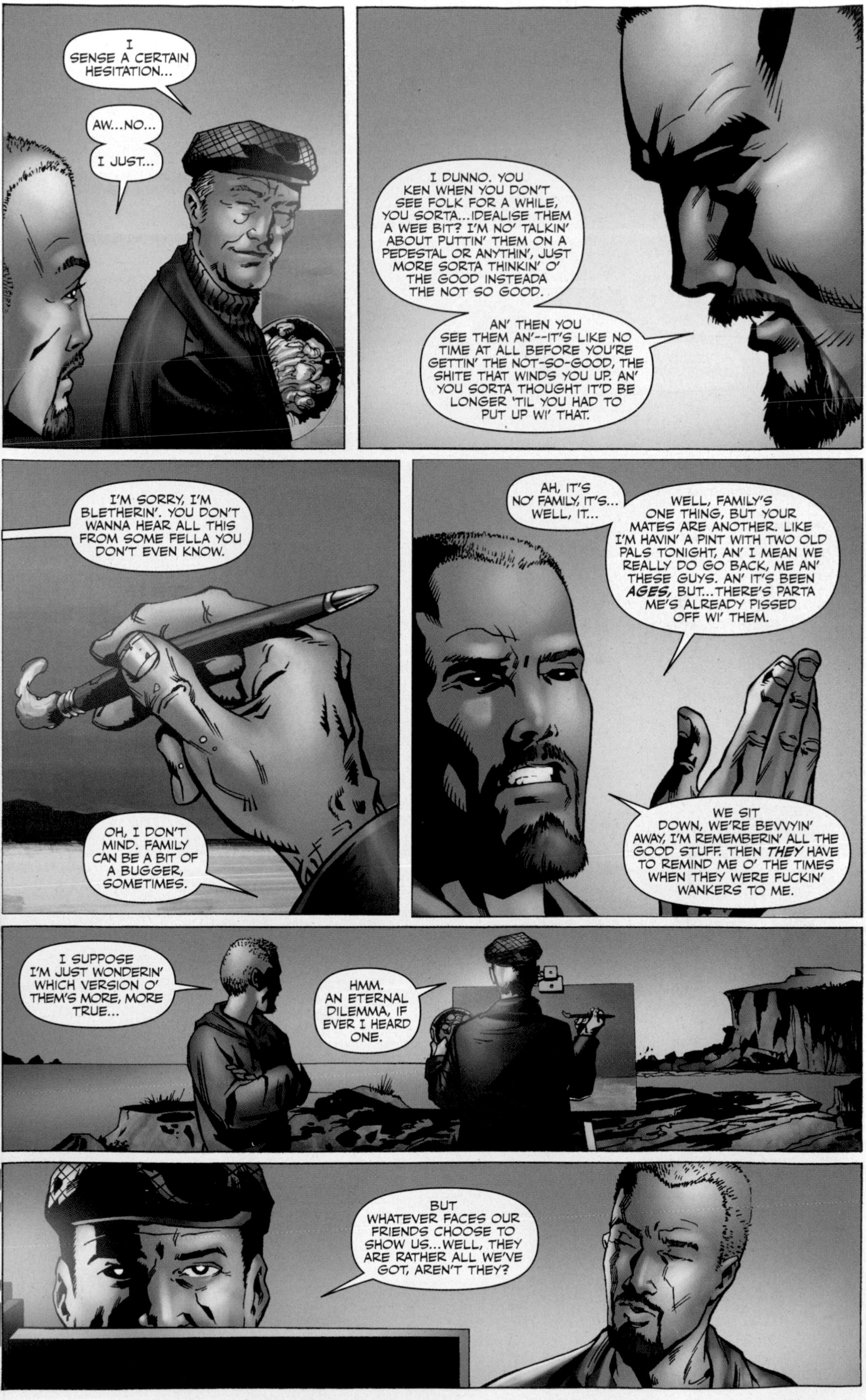
I SENSE A CERTAIN HESITATION...
AW...NO...
I JUST...
I DUNNO. YOU KEN WHEN YOU DON'T SEE FOLK FOR A WHILE, YOU SORTA...IDEALISE THEM A WEE BIT? I'M NO' TALKIN' ABOUT PUTTIN' THEM ON A PEDESTAL OR ANYTHIN', JUST MORE SORTA THINKIN' O' THE GOOD INSTEADA THE NOT SO GOOD.
AN' THEN YOU SEE THEM AN'--IT'S LIKE NO TIME AT ALL BEFORE YOU'RE GETTIN' THE NOT-SO-GOOD, THE SHITE THAT WINDS YOU UP. AN' YOU SORTA THOUGHT IT'D BE LONGER 'TIL YOU HAD TO PUT UP WI' THAT.
I'M SORRY, I'M BLETHERIN'. YOU DON'T WANNA HEAR ALL THIS FROM SOME FELLA YOU DON'T EVEN KNOW.
OH, I DON'T MIND. FAMILY CAN BE A BIT OF A BUGGER, SOMETIMES.
AH, IT'S NO' FAMILY, IT'S... WELL, IT...
WELL, FAMILY'S ONE THING, BUT YOUR MATES ARE ANOTHER. LIKE I'M HAVIN' A PINT WITH TWO OLD PALS TONIGHT, AN' I MEAN WE REALLY DO GO BACK, ME AN' THESE GUYS. AN' IT'S BEEN *AGES*, BUT...THERE'S PARTA ME'S ALREADY PISSED OFF WI' THEM.
WE SIT DOWN, WE'RE BEVVYIN' AWAY, I'M REMEMBERIN' ALL THE GOOD STUFF. THEN *THEY* HAVE TO REMIND ME O' THE TIMES WHEN THEY WERE FUCKIN' WANKERS TO ME.
I SUPPOSE I'M JUST WONDERIN' WHICH VERSION O' THEM'S MORE, MORE TRUE...
HMM. AN ETERNAL DILEMMA, IF EVER I HEARD ONE.
BUT WHATEVER FACES OUR FRIENDS CHOOSE TO SHOW US...WELL, THEY ARE RATHER ALL WE'VE GOT, AREN'T THEY?

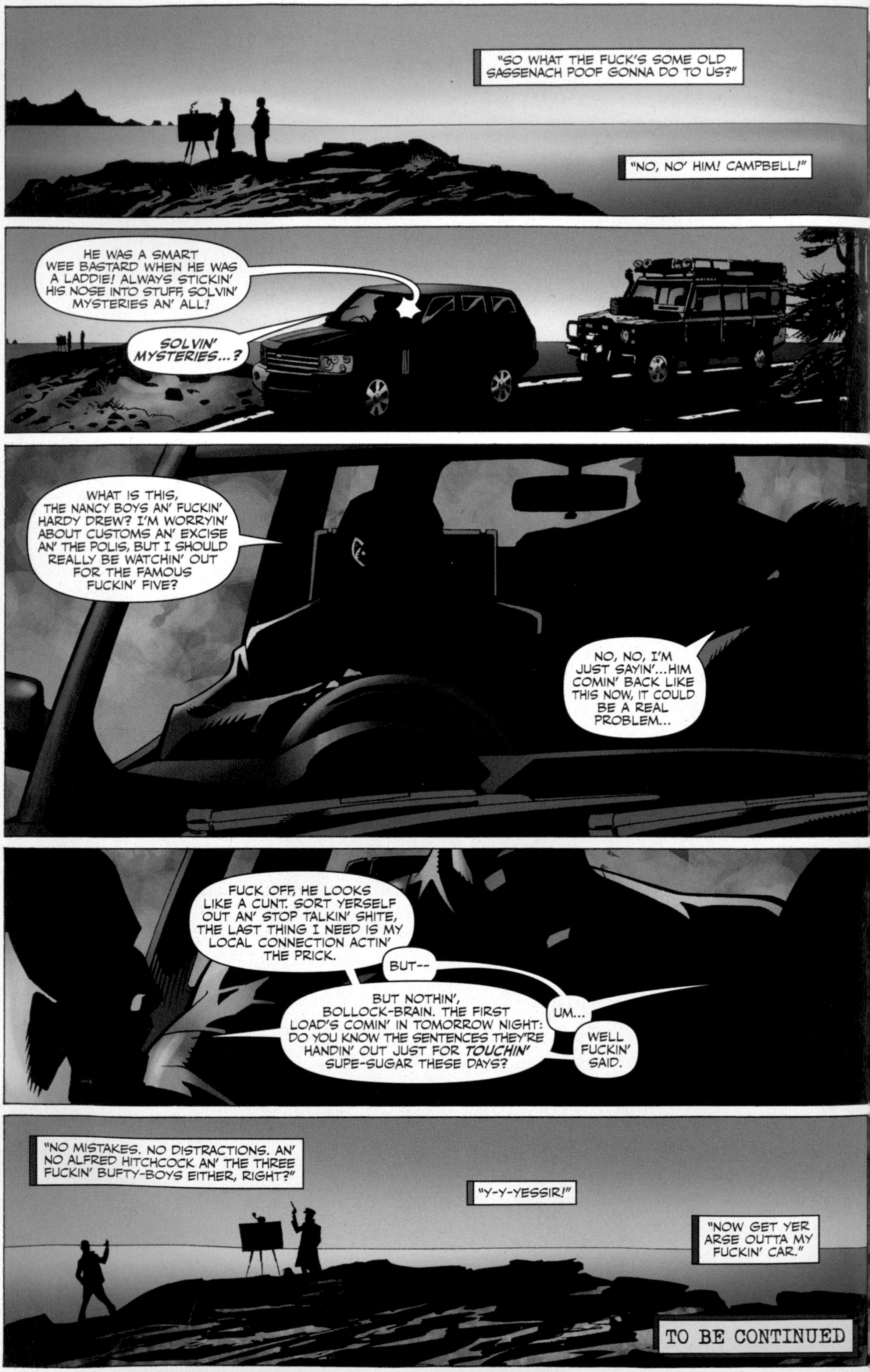
"SO WHAT THE FUCK'S SOME OLD SASSENACH POOF GONNA DO TO US?"
"NO, NO' HIM! CAMPBELL!"
HE WAS A SMART WEE BASTARD WHEN HE WAS A LADDIE! ALWAYS STICKIN' HIS NOSE INTO STUFF, SOLVIN' MYSTERIES AN' ALL!
SOLVIN' MYSTERIES...?
WHAT IS THIS, THE NANCY BOYS AN' FUCKIN' HARDY DREW? I'M WORRYIN' ABOUT CUSTOMS AN' EXCISE AN' THE POLIS, BUT I SHOULD REALLY BE WATCHIN' OUT FOR THE FAMOUS FUCKIN' FIVE?
NO, NO, I'M JUST SAYIN'...HIM COMIN' BACK LIKE THIS NOW, IT COULD BE A REAL PROBLEM...
FUCK OFF, HE LOOKS LIKE A CUNT. SORT YERSELF OUT AN' STOP TALKIN' SHITE, THE LAST THING I NEED IS MY LOCAL CONNECTION ACTIN' THE PRICK.
BUT--
BUT NOTHIN', BOLLOCK-BRAIN. THE FIRST LOAD'S COMIN' IN TOMORROW NIGHT: DO YOU KNOW THE SENTENCES THEY'RE HANDIN' OUT JUST FOR TOUCHIN' SUPE-SUGAR THESE DAYS?
UM...
WELL FUCKIN' SAID.
"NO MISTAKES. NO DISTRACTIONS. AN' NO ALFRED HITCHCOCK AN' THE THREE FUCKIN' BUFTY-BOYS EITHER, RIGHT?"
"Y-Y-YESSIR!"
"NOW GET YER ARSE OUTTA MY FUCKIN' CAR."
TO BE CONTINUED

two

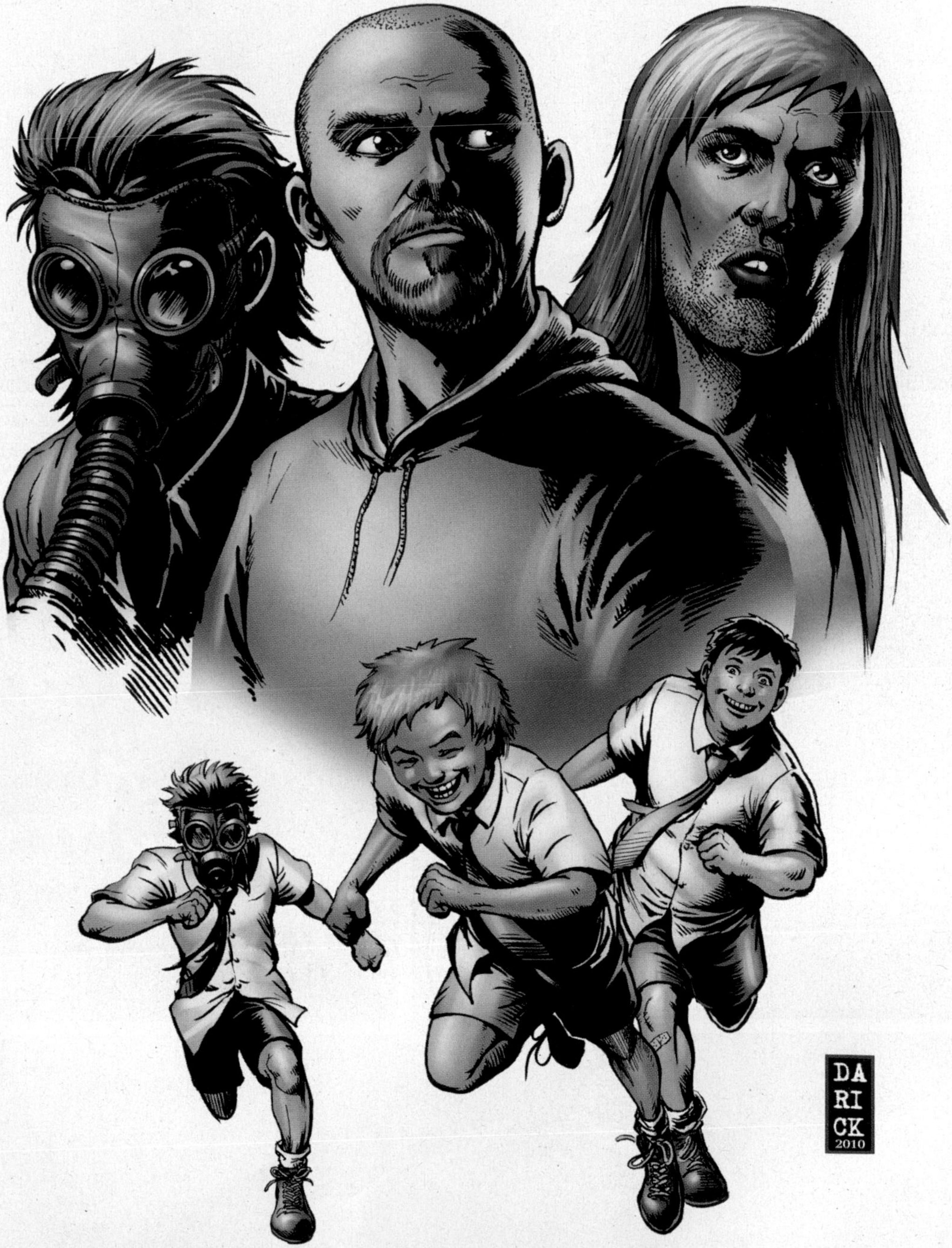
DA
RI
CK
2010

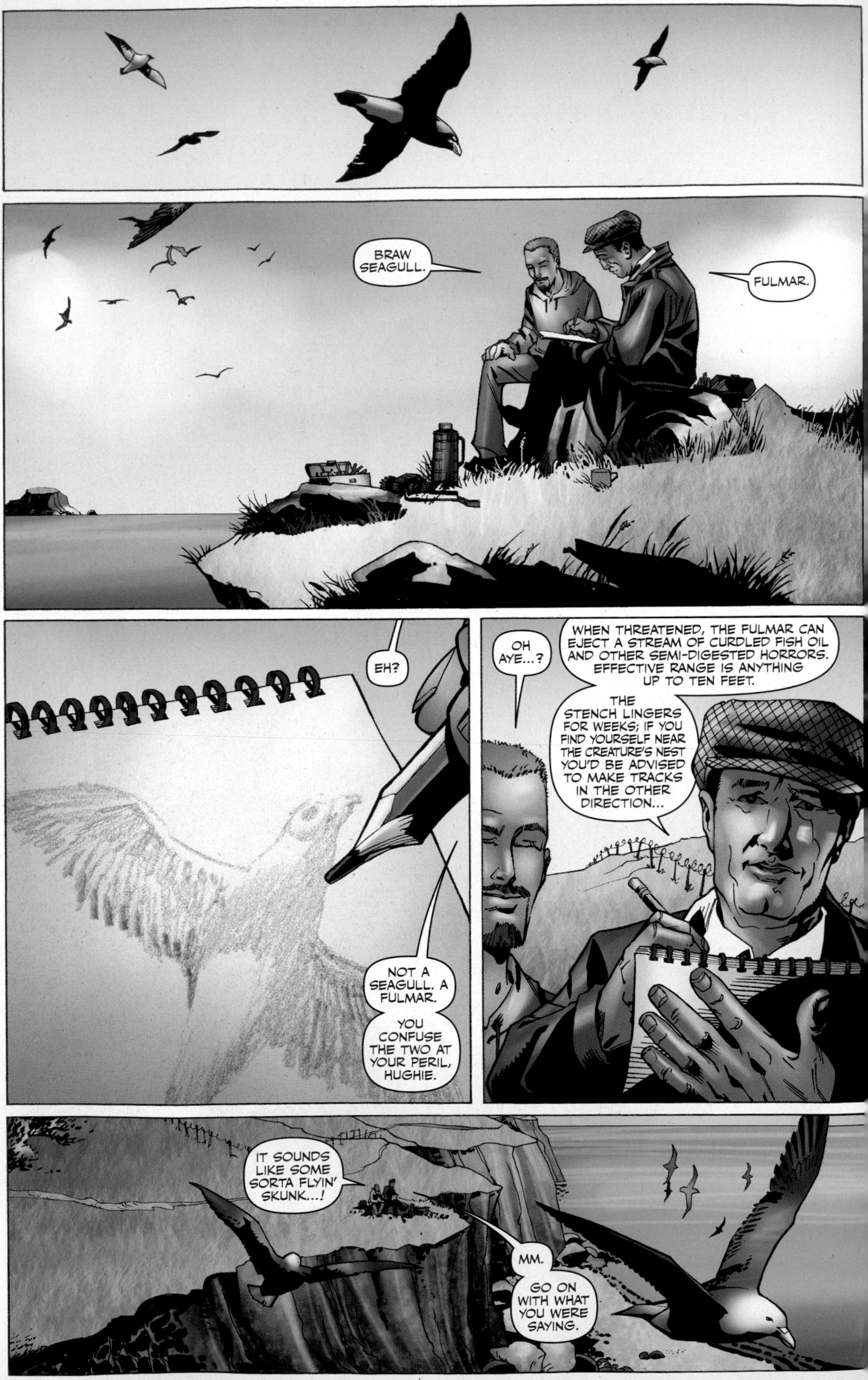
BRAW SEAGULL.
FULMAR.
EH?
NOT A SEAGULL. A FULMAR.
YOU CONFUSE THE TWO AT YOUR PERIL, HUGHIE.
OH AYE...?
WHEN THREATENED, THE FULMAR CAN EJECT A STREAM OF CURDLED FISH OIL AND OTHER SEMI-DIGESTED HORRORS. EFFECTIVE RANGE IS ANYTHING UP TO TEN FEET.
THE STENCH LINGERS FOR WEEKS; IF YOU FIND YOURSELF NEAR THE CREATURE'S NEST YOU'D BE ADVISED TO MAKE TRACKS IN THE OTHER DIRECTION...
IT SOUNDS LIKE SOME SORTA FLYIN' SKUNK...!
MM.
GO ON WITH WHAT YOU WERE SAYING.

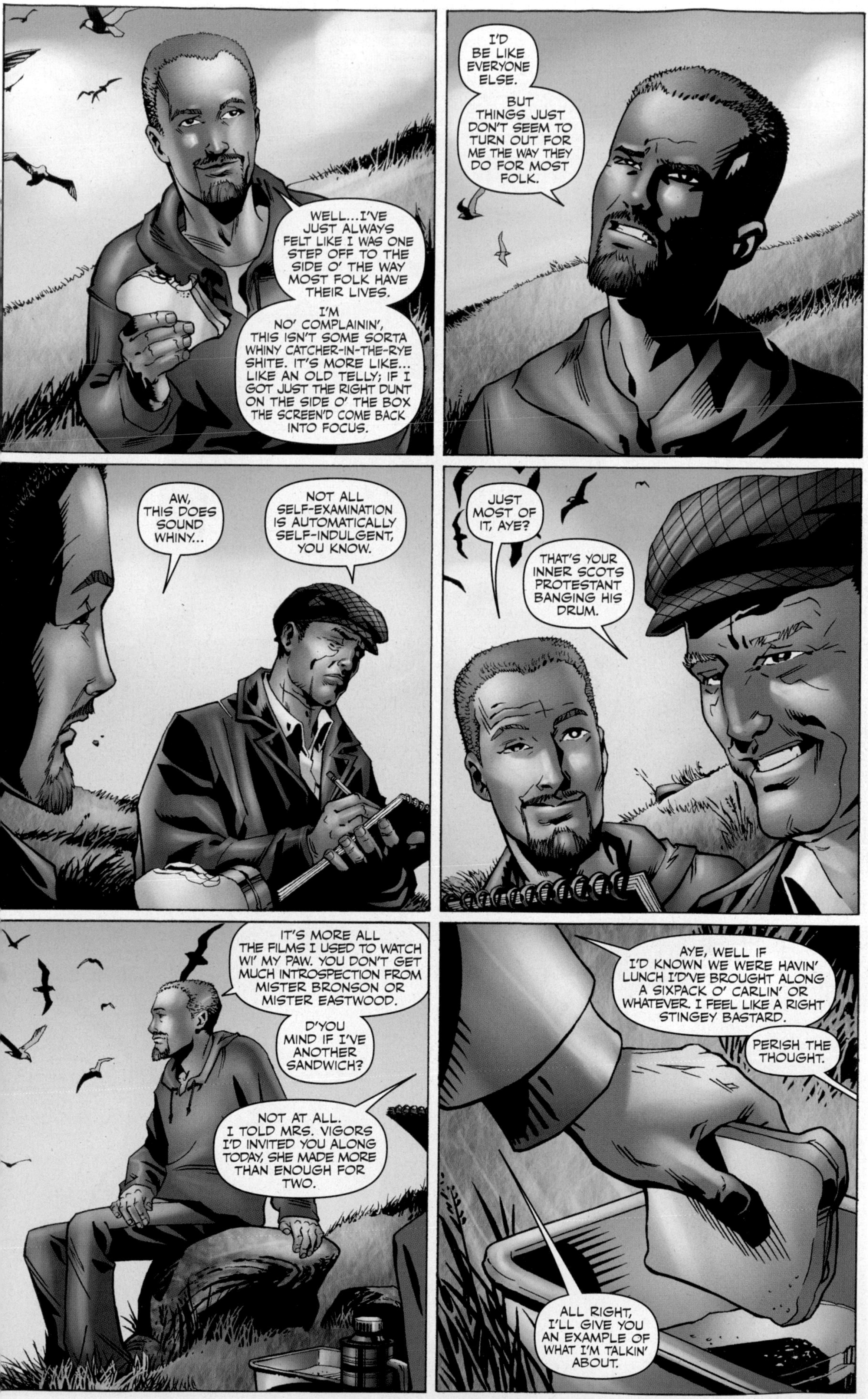
WELL...I'VE JUST ALWAYS FELT LIKE I WAS ONE STEP OFF TO THE SIDE O' THE WAY MOST FOLK HAVE THEIR LIVES.
I'M NO' COMPLAININ', THIS ISN'T SOME SORTA WHINY CATCHER-IN-THE-RYE SHITE. IT'S MORE LIKE... LIKE AN OLD TELLY; IF I GOT JUST THE RIGHT DUNT ON THE SIDE O' THE BOX THE SCREEN'D COME BACK INTO FOCUS.
I'D BE LIKE EVERYONE ELSE.
BUT THINGS JUST DON'T SEEM TO TURN OUT FOR ME THE WAY THEY DO FOR MOST FOLK.
AW, THIS DOES SOUND WHINY...
NOT ALL SELF-EXAMINATION IS AUTOMATICALLY SELF-INDULGENT, YOU KNOW.
JUST MOST OF IT, AYE?
THAT'S YOUR INNER SCOTS PROTESTANT BANGING HIS DRUM.
IT'S MORE ALL THE FILMS I USED TO WATCH WI' MY PAW. YOU DON'T GET MUCH INTROSPECTION FROM MISTER BRONSON OR MISTER EASTWOOD.
D'YOU MIND IF I'VE ANOTHER SANDWICH?
NOT AT ALL. I TOLD MRS. VIGORS I'D INVITED YOU ALONG TODAY, SHE MADE MORE THAN ENOUGH FOR TWO.
AYE, WELL IF I'D KNOWN WE WERE HAVIN' LUNCH I'D'VE BROUGHT ALONG A SIXPACK O' CARLIN' OR WHATEVER. I FEEL LIKE A RIGHT STINGEY BASTARD.
PERISH THE THOUGHT.
ALL RIGHT, I'LL GIVE YOU AN EXAMPLE OF WHAT I'M TALKIN' ABOUT.

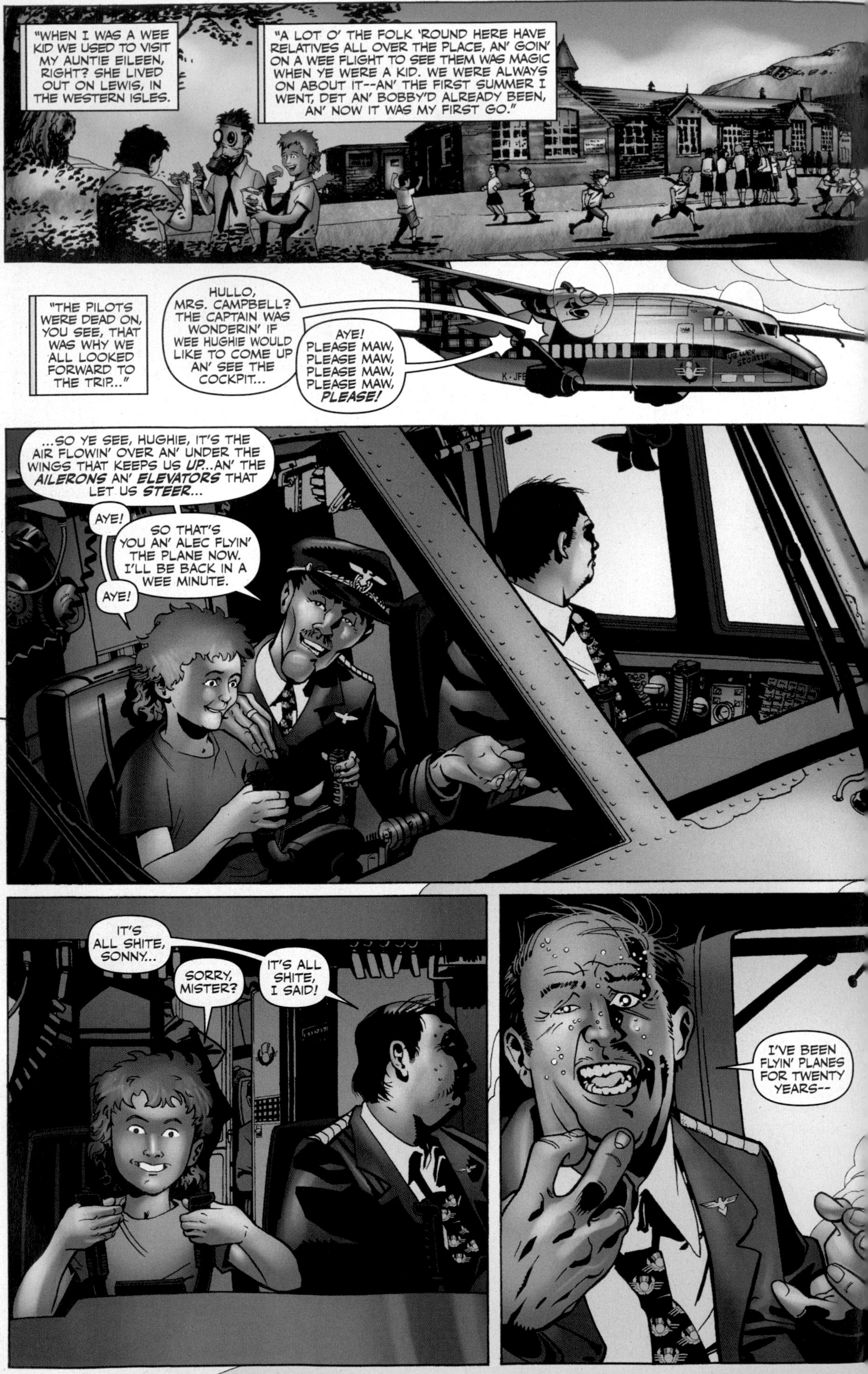
"WHEN I WAS A WEE KID WE USED TO VISIT MY AUNTIE EILEEN, RIGHT? SHE LIVED OUT ON LEWIS, IN THE WESTERN ISLES.
"A LOT O' THE FOLK 'ROUND HERE HAVE RELATIVES ALL OVER THE PLACE, AN' GOIN' ON A WEE FLIGHT TO SEE THEM WAS MAGIC WHEN YE WERE A KID. WE WERE ALWAYS ON ABOUT IT--AN' THE FIRST SUMMER I WENT, DET AN' BOBBY'D ALREADY BEEN, AN' NOW IT WAS MY FIRST GO."
"THE PILOTS WERE DEAD ON, YOU SEE, THAT WAS WHY WE ALL LOOKED FORWARD TO THE TRIP..."
HULLO, MRS. CAMPBELL? THE CAPTAIN WAS WONDERIN' IF WEE HUGHIE WOULD LIKE TO COME UP AN' SEE THE COCKPIT...
AYE! PLEASE MAW, PLEASE MAW, PLEASE MAW, PLEASE MAW, ***PLEASE!***
...SO YE SEE, HUGHIE, IT'S THE AIR FLOWIN' OVER AN' UNDER THE WINGS THAT KEEPS US ***UP***...AN' THE ***AILERONS*** AN' ***ELEVATORS*** THAT LET US ***STEER***...
AYE!
SO THAT'S YOU AN' ALEC FLYIN' THE PLANE NOW. I'LL BE BACK IN A WEE MINUTE.
AYE!
IT'S ALL SHITE, SONNY...
SORRY, MISTER?
IT'S ALL SHITE, I SAID!
I'VE BEEN FLYIN' PLANES FOR TWENTY YEARS--

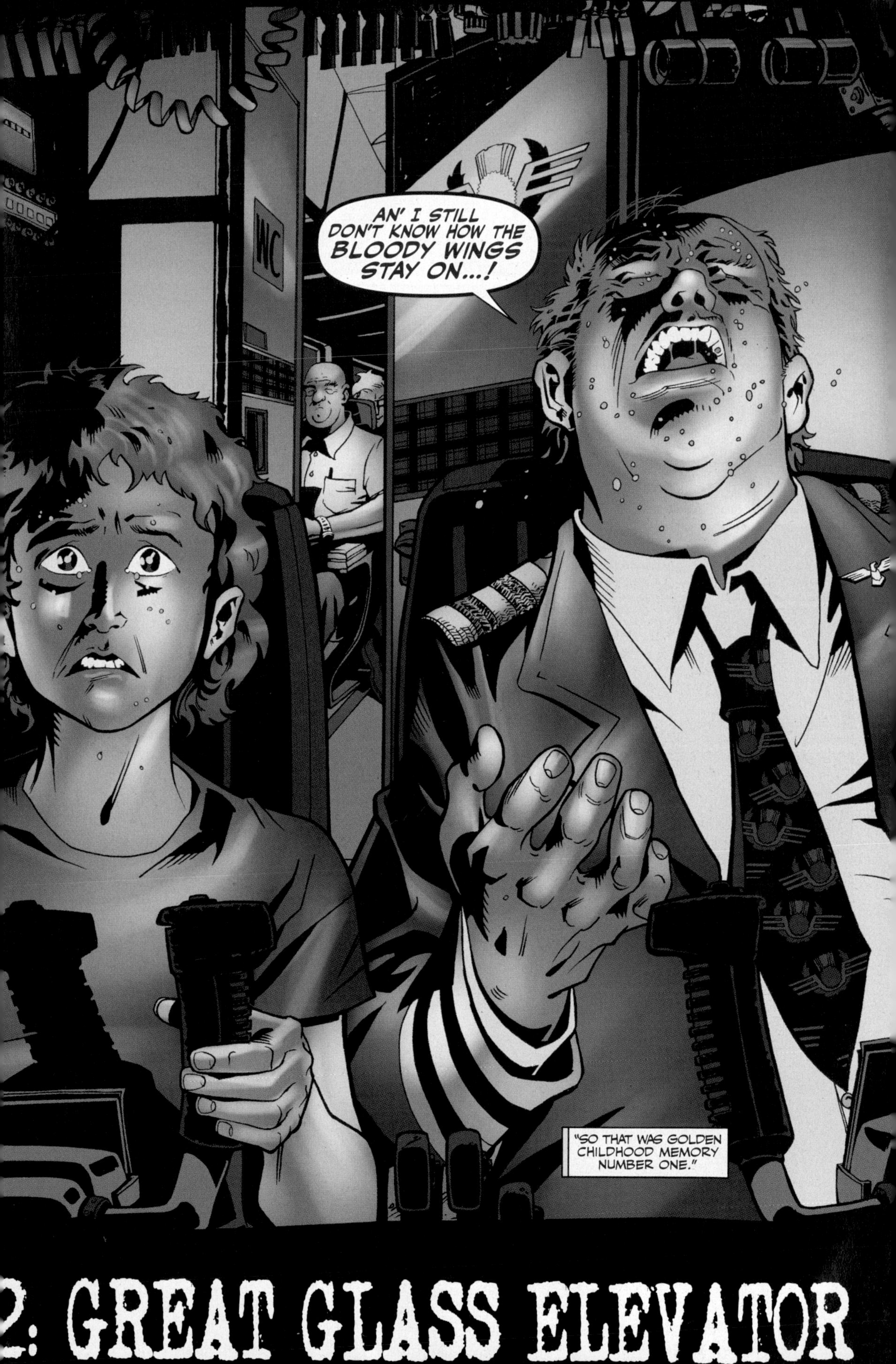
WC
AN' I STILL DON'T KNOW HOW THE BLOODY WINGS STAY ON...!
"SO THAT WAS GOLDEN CHILDHOOD MEMORY NUMBER ONE."

2: GREAT GLASS ELEVATOR

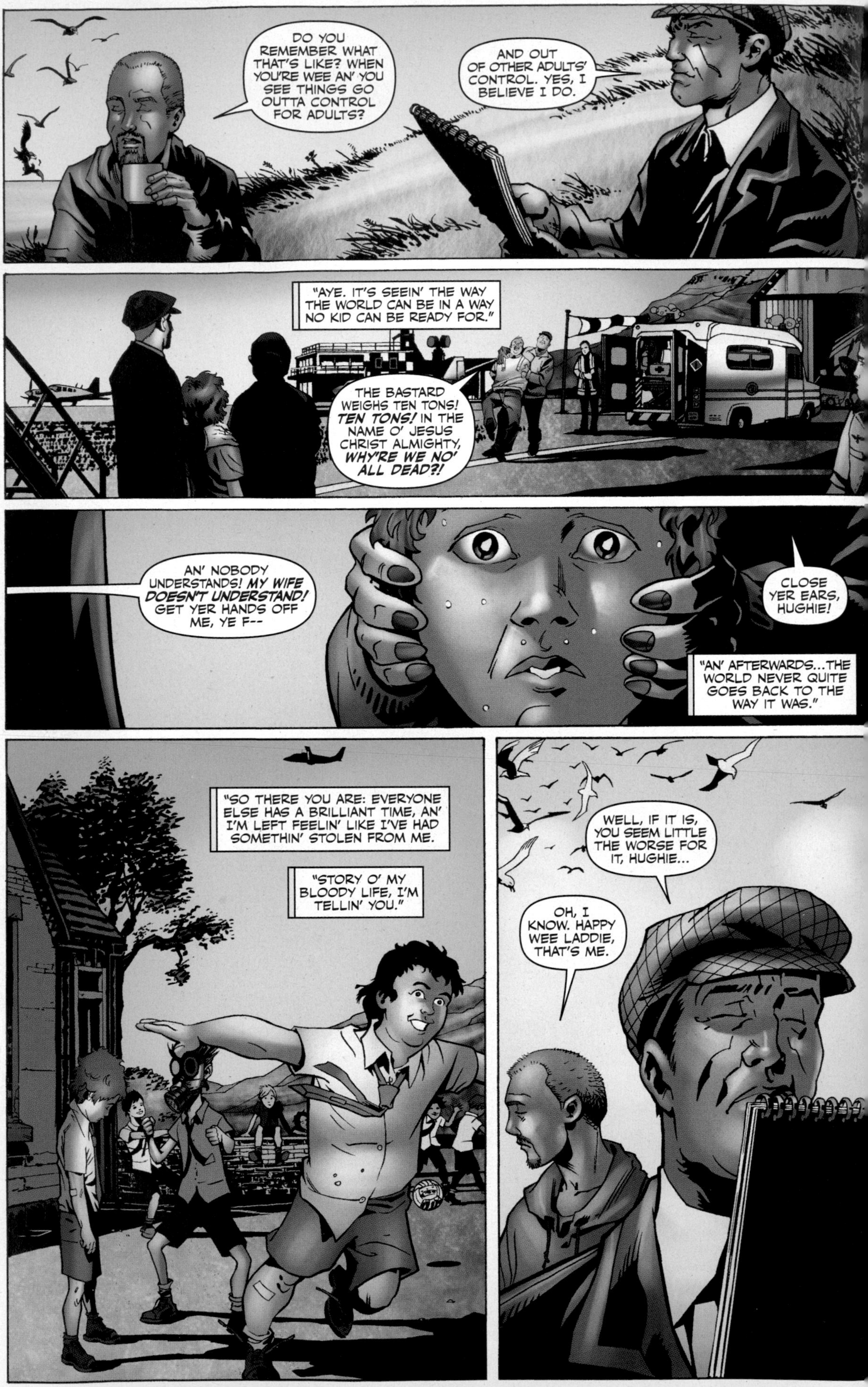
DO YOU REMEMBER WHAT THAT'S LIKE? WHEN YOU'RE WEE AN' YOU SEE THINGS GO OUTTA CONTROL FOR ADULTS?
AND OUT OF OTHER ADULTS' CONTROL. YES, I BELIEVE I DO.
"AYE. IT'S SEEIN' THE WAY THE WORLD CAN BE IN A WAY NO KID CAN BE READY FOR."
THE BASTARD WEIGHS TEN TONS! TEN TONS! IN THE NAME O' JESUS CHRIST ALMIGHTY, WHY'RE WE NO' ALL DEAD?!
AN' NOBODY UNDERSTANDS! MY WIFE DOESN'T UNDERSTAND! GET YER HANDS OFF ME, YE F--
CLOSE YER EARS, HUGHIE!
"AN' AFTERWARDS...THE WORLD NEVER QUITE GOES BACK TO THE WAY IT WAS."
"SO THERE YOU ARE: EVERYONE ELSE HAS A BRILLIANT TIME, AN' I'M LEFT FEELIN' LIKE I'VE HAD SOMETHIN' STOLEN FROM ME.
"STORY O' MY BLOODY LIFE, I'M TELLIN' YOU."
WELL, IF IT IS, YOU SEEM LITTLE THE WORSE FOR IT, HUGHIE...
OH, I KNOW. HAPPY WEE LADDIE, THAT'S ME.

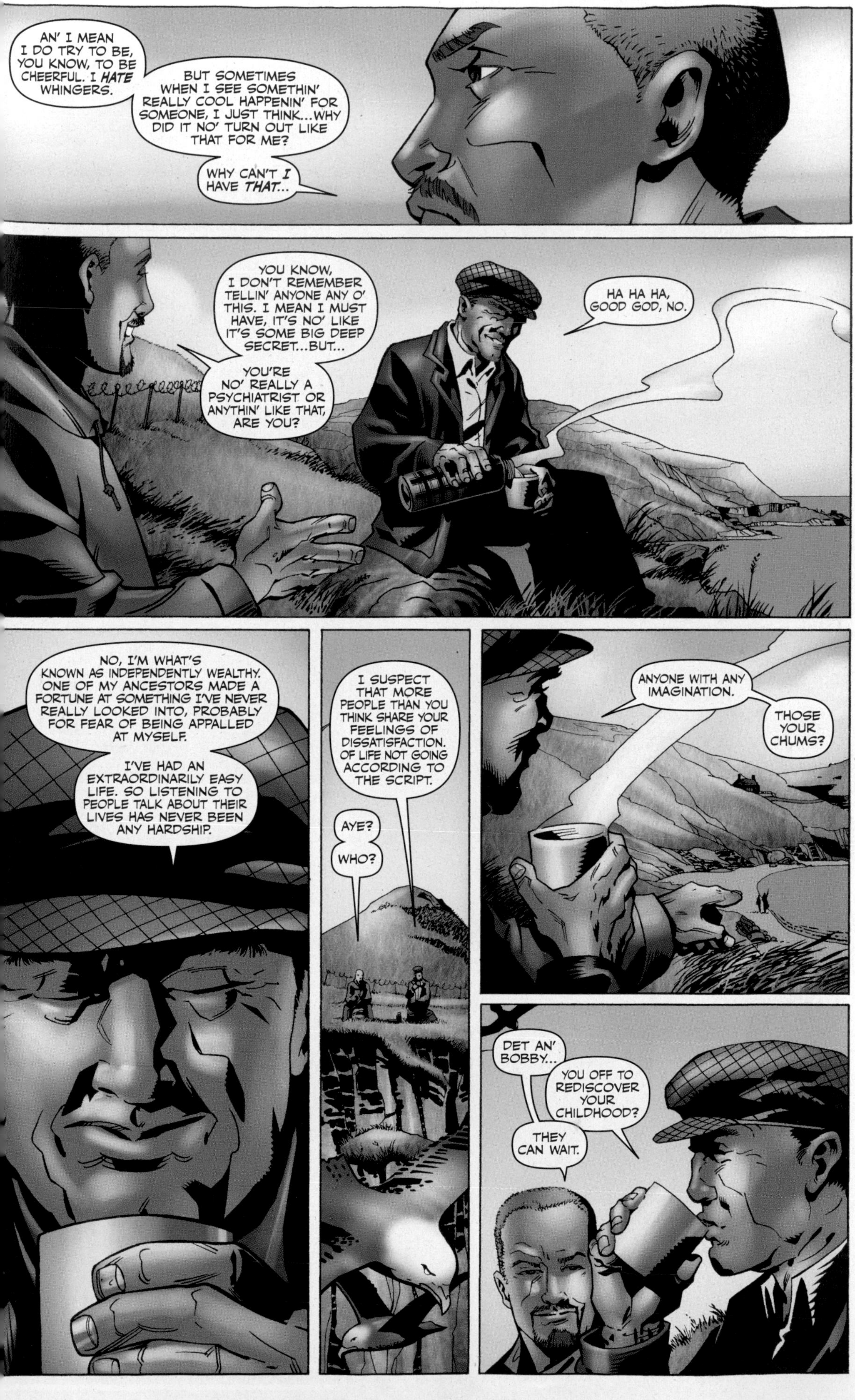
AN' I MEAN I DO TRY TO BE, YOU KNOW, TO BE CHEERFUL. I HATE WHINGERS.
BUT SOMETIMES WHEN I SEE SOMETHIN' REALLY COOL HAPPENIN' FOR SOMEONE, I JUST THINK...WHY DID IT NO' TURN OUT LIKE THAT FOR ME?
WHY CAN'T I HAVE THAT...
YOU KNOW, I DON'T REMEMBER TELLIN' ANYONE ANY O' THIS. I MEAN I MUST HAVE, IT'S NO' LIKE IT'S SOME BIG DEEP SECRET...BUT...
YOU'RE NO' REALLY A PSYCHIATRIST OR ANYTHIN' LIKE THAT, ARE YOU?
HA HA HA, GOOD GOD, NO.
NO, I'M WHAT'S KNOWN AS INDEPENDENTLY WEALTHY. ONE OF MY ANCESTORS MADE A FORTUNE AT SOMETHING I'VE NEVER REALLY LOOKED INTO, PROBABLY FOR FEAR OF BEING APPALLED AT MYSELF.
I'VE HAD AN EXTRAORDINARILY EASY LIFE. SO LISTENING TO PEOPLE TALK ABOUT THEIR LIVES HAS NEVER BEEN ANY HARDSHIP.
I SUSPECT THAT MORE PEOPLE THAN YOU THINK SHARE YOUR FEELINGS OF DISSATISFACTION. OF LIFE NOT GOING ACCORDING TO THE SCRIPT.
AYE?
WHO?
ANYONE WITH ANY IMAGINATION.
THOSE YOUR CHUMS?
DET AN' BOBBY...
YOU OFF TO REDISCOVER YOUR CHILDHOOD?
THEY CAN WAIT.

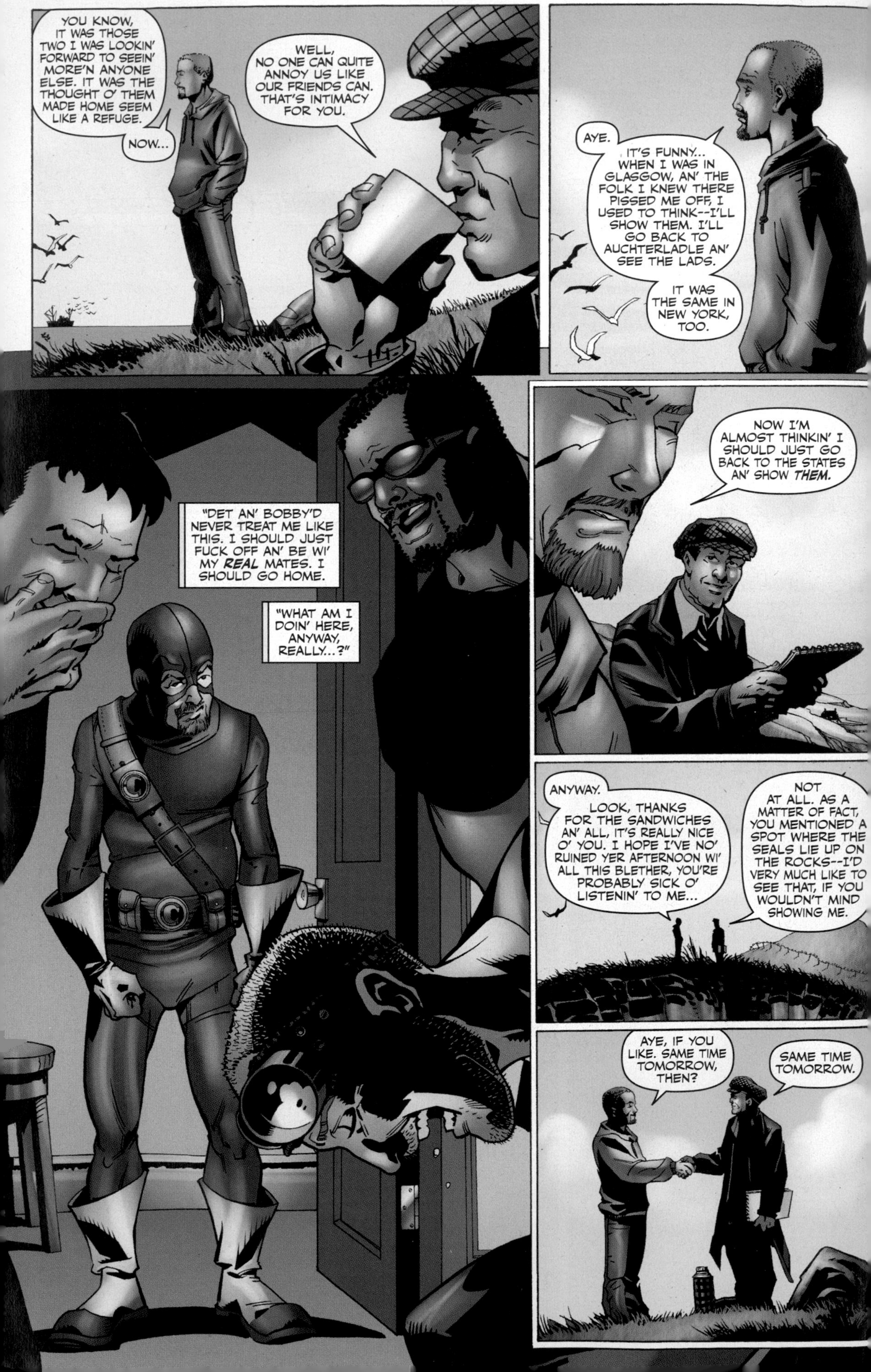
YOU KNOW, IT WAS THOSE TWO I WAS LOOKIN' FORWARD TO SEEIN' MORE'N ANYONE ELSE. IT WAS THE THOUGHT O' THEM MADE HOME SEEM LIKE A REFUGE.
NOW...
WELL, NO ONE CAN QUITE ANNOY US LIKE OUR FRIENDS CAN. THAT'S INTIMACY FOR YOU.
AYE.
IT'S FUNNY... WHEN I WAS IN GLASGOW, AN' THE FOLK I KNEW THERE PISSED ME OFF, I USED TO THINK--I'LL SHOW THEM. I'LL GO BACK TO AUCHTERLADLE AN' SEE THE LADS.
IT WAS THE SAME IN NEW YORK, TOO.
"DET AN' BOBBY'D NEVER TREAT ME LIKE THIS. I SHOULD JUST FUCK OFF AN' BE WI' MY REAL MATES. I SHOULD GO HOME.
"WHAT AM I DOIN' HERE, ANYWAY, REALLY...?"
NOW I'M ALMOST THINKIN' I SHOULD JUST GO BACK TO THE STATES AN' SHOW THEM.
ANYWAY.
LOOK, THANKS FOR THE SANDWICHES AN' ALL, IT'S REALLY NICE O' YOU. I HOPE I'VE NO' RUINED YER AFTERNOON WI' ALL THIS BLETHER, YOU'RE PROBABLY SICK O' LISTENIN' TO ME...
NOT AT ALL. AS A MATTER OF FACT, YOU MENTIONED A SPOT WHERE THE SEALS LIE UP ON THE ROCKS--I'D VERY MUCH LIKE TO SEE THAT, IF YOU WOULDN'T MIND SHOWING ME.
AYE, IF YOU LIKE. SAME TIME TOMORROW, THEN?
SAME TIME TOMORROW.

DOES THAT NO' LOOK A WEE BIT FUNNY TO YOU?

NO, IT LOOKS PERFECTLY FUCKIN' NORMAL--!

HUGHIE, IT'S AN INFLATABLE WOMAN IN THE SEA, PAL...

FOR CHRIST'S SAKE...!

AYE, BUT WHY'S IT NO' MOVING IN WI' THE WAVES? IS IT TETHERED THERE OR SOMETHIN'?

STICKS AN' STONES, WEE MAN. 'MON THEN, BOBBY, GIVE'S A WEE BLOWBACK THERE--

ARE YE HOPIN' IT'LL FLOAT IN AN' WE CAN GRAB IT, AYE?

ARE YE REALLY THAT DESPERATE TO GET YER HOLE?

AYE, WELL YOU'RE ONE TO FUCKIN' TALK THERE, AREN'T YOU?

WHY WOULD IT BE TETHERED...?

HFFFFF

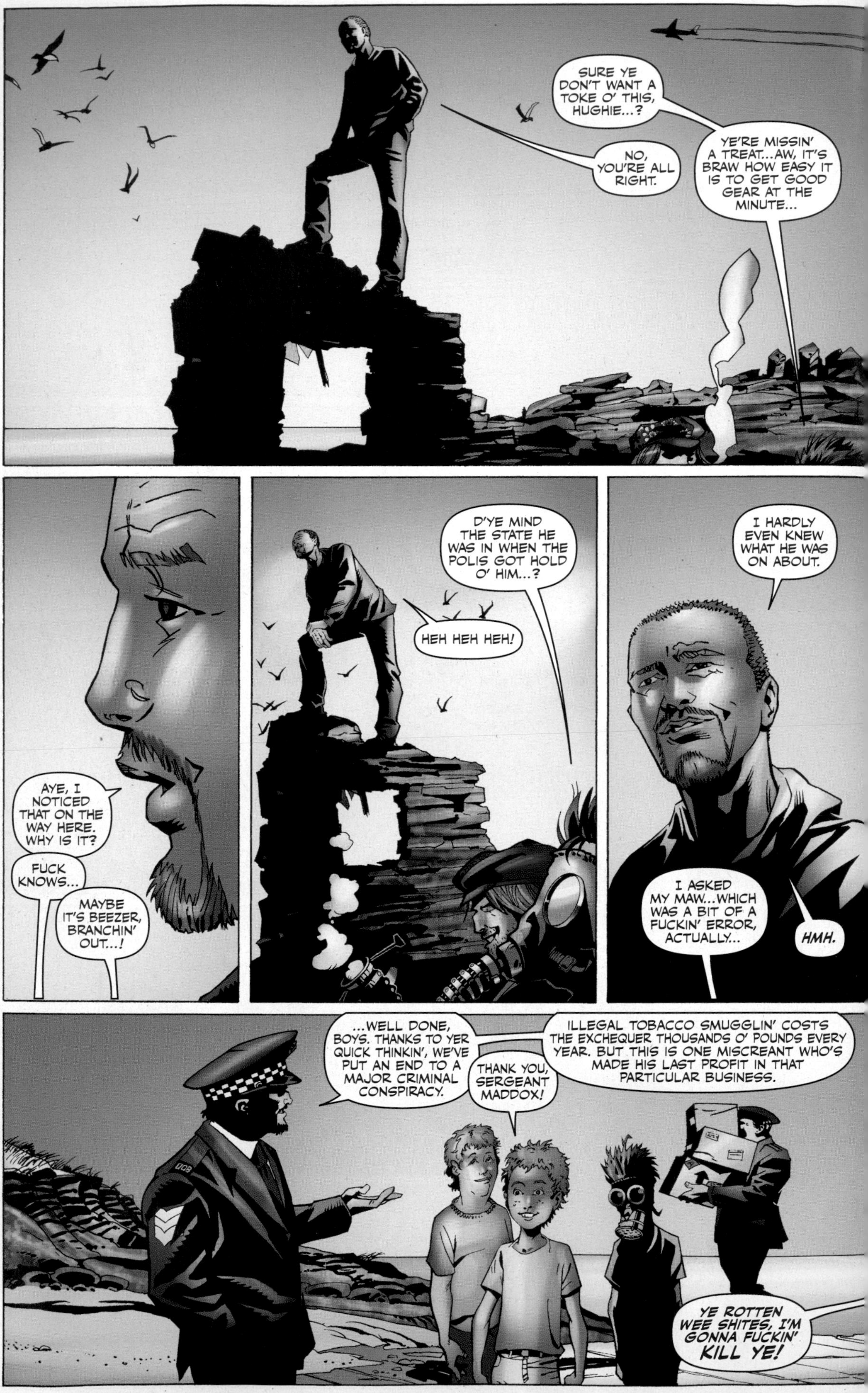
SURE YE DON'T WANT A TOKE O' THIS, HUGHIE...?
NO, YOU'RE ALL RIGHT.
YE'RE MISSIN' A TREAT...AW, IT'S BRAW HOW EASY IT IS TO GET GOOD GEAR AT THE MINUTE...
AYE, I NOTICED THAT ON THE WAY HERE. WHY IS IT?
FUCK KNOWS...
MAYBE IT'S BEEZER, BRANCHIN' OUT...!
D'YE MIND THE STATE HE WAS IN WHEN THE POLIS GOT HOLD O' HIM...?
HEH HEH HEH!
I HARDLY EVEN KNEW WHAT HE WAS ON ABOUT.
I ASKED MY MAW...WHICH WAS A BIT OF A FUCKIN' ERROR, ACTUALLY...
HMH.
...WELL DONE, BOYS. THANKS TO YER QUICK THINKIN', WE'VE PUT AN END TO A MAJOR CRIMINAL CONSPIRACY.
ILLEGAL TOBACCO SMUGGLIN' COSTS THE EXCHEQUER THOUSANDS O' POUNDS EVERY YEAR. BUT THIS IS ONE MISCREANT WHO'S MADE HIS LAST PROFIT IN THAT PARTICULAR BUSINESS.
THANK YOU, SERGEANT MADDOX!
YE ROTTEN WEE SHITES, I'M GONNA FUCKIN' KILL YE!

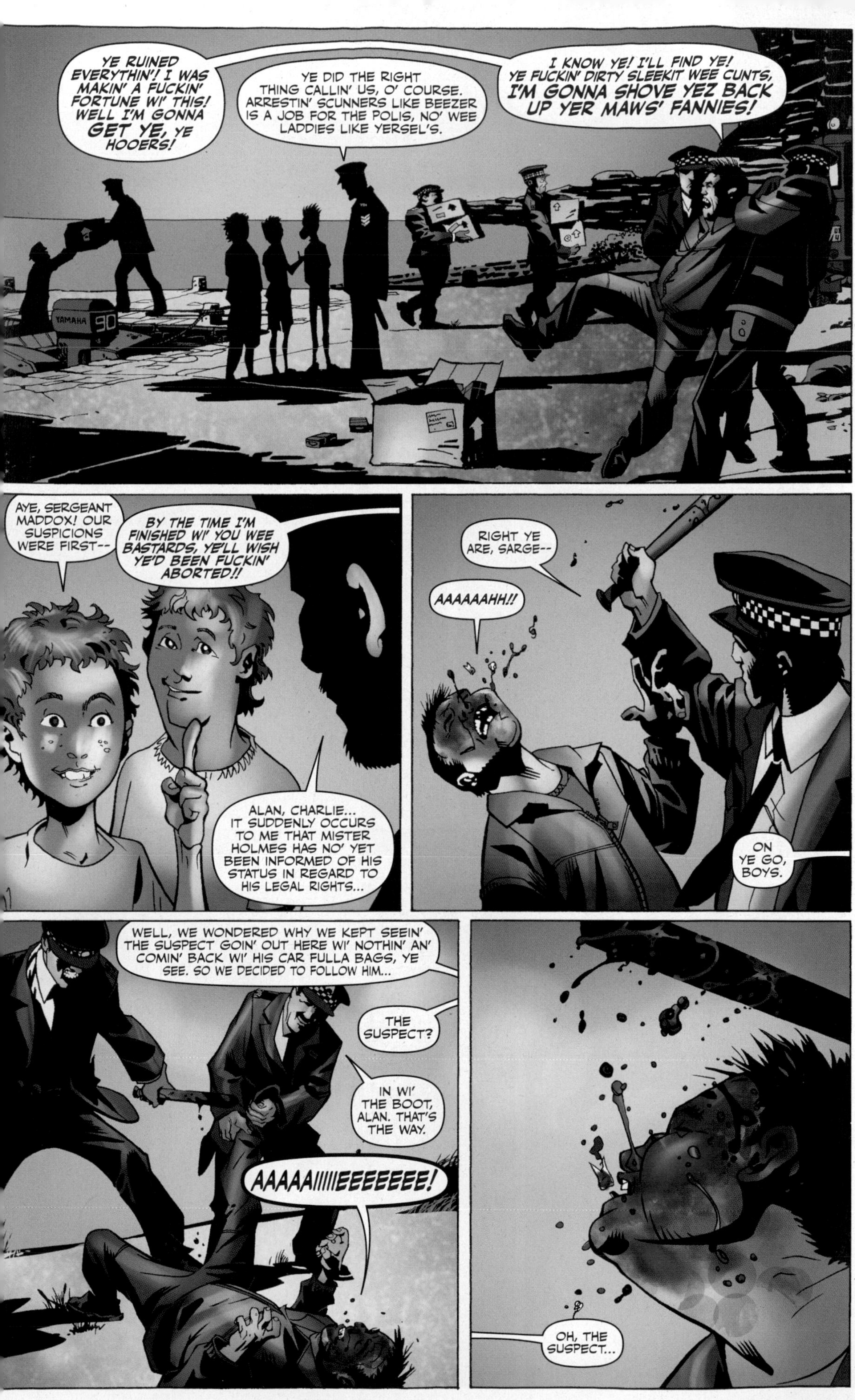
YE RUINED EVERYTHIN'! I WAS MAKIN' A FUCKIN' FORTUNE WI' THIS! WELL I'M GONNA GET YE, YE HOOERS!
YE DID THE RIGHT THING CALLIN' US, O' COURSE. ARRESTIN' SCUNNERS LIKE BEEZER IS A JOB FOR THE POLIS, NO' WEE LADDIES LIKE YERSEL'S.
I KNOW YE! I'LL FIND YE! YE FUCKIN' DIRTY SLEEKIT WEE CUNTS, I'M GONNA SHOVE YEZ BACK UP YER MAWS' FANNIES!
YAMAHA 90
AYE, SERGEANT MADDOX! OUR SUSPICIONS WERE FIRST--
BY THE TIME I'M FINISHED WI' YOU WEE BASTARDS, YE'LL WISH YE'D BEEN FUCKIN' ABORTED!!
ALAN, CHARLIE... IT SUDDENLY OCCURS TO ME THAT MISTER HOLMES HAS NO' YET BEEN INFORMED OF HIS STATUS IN REGARD TO HIS LEGAL RIGHTS...
RIGHT YE ARE, SARGE--
AAAAAAHH!!
ON YE GO, BOYS.
WELL, WE WONDERED WHY WE KEPT SEEIN' THE SUSPECT GOIN' OUT HERE WI' NOTHIN' AN' COMIN' BACK WI' HIS CAR FULLA BAGS, YE SEE. SO WE DECIDED TO FOLLOW HIM...
THE SUSPECT?
IN WI' THE BOOT, ALAN. THAT'S THE WAY.
AAAAAIIIIIEEEEEEE!
OH, THE SUSPECT...

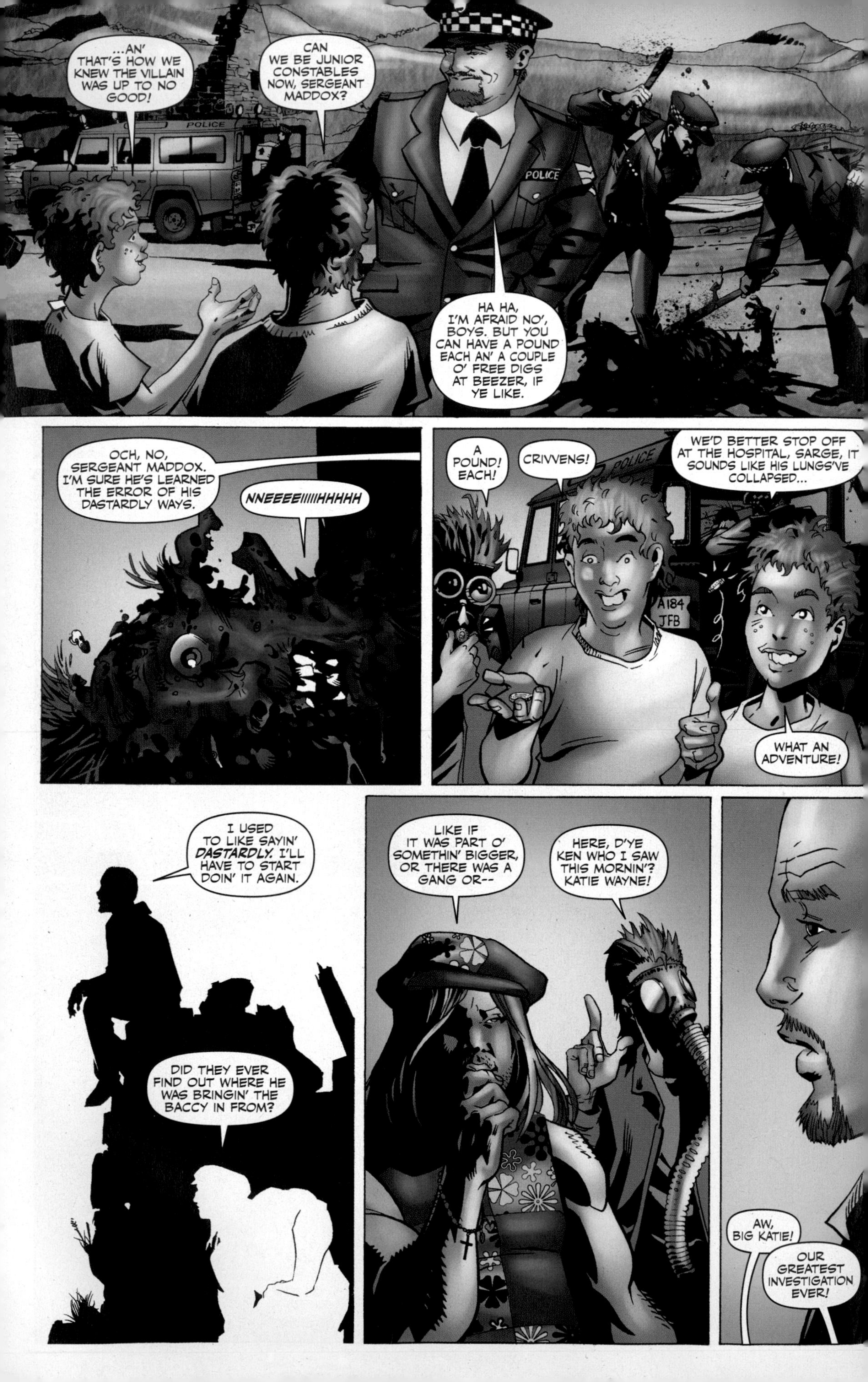
...AN' THAT'S HOW WE KNEW THE VILLAIN WAS UP TO NO GOOD!
CAN WE BE JUNIOR CONSTABLES NOW, SERGEANT MADDOX?
POLICE
HA HA, I'M AFRAID NO', BOYS. BUT YOU CAN HAVE A POUND EACH AN' A COUPLE O' FREE DIGS AT BEEZER, IF YE LIKE.
OCH, NO, SERGEANT MADDOX. I'M SURE HE'S LEARNED THE ERROR OF HIS DASTARDLY WAYS.
NNEEEEIIIIIIHHHHH
A POUND! EACH!
CRIVVENS!
WE'D BETTER STOP OFF AT THE HOSPITAL, SARGE, IT SOUNDS LIKE HIS LUNGS'VE COLLAPSED...
A184 JFB
WHAT AN ADVENTURE!
I USED TO LIKE SAYIN' *DASTARDLY.* I'LL HAVE TO START DOIN' IT AGAIN.
DID THEY EVER FIND OUT WHERE HE WAS BRINGIN' THE BACCY IN FROM?
LIKE IF IT WAS PART O' SOMETHIN' BIGGER, OR THERE WAS A GANG OR--
HERE, D'YE KEN WHO I SAW THIS MORNIN'? KATIE WAYNE!
AW, BIG KATIE!
OUR GREATEST INVESTIGATION EVER!

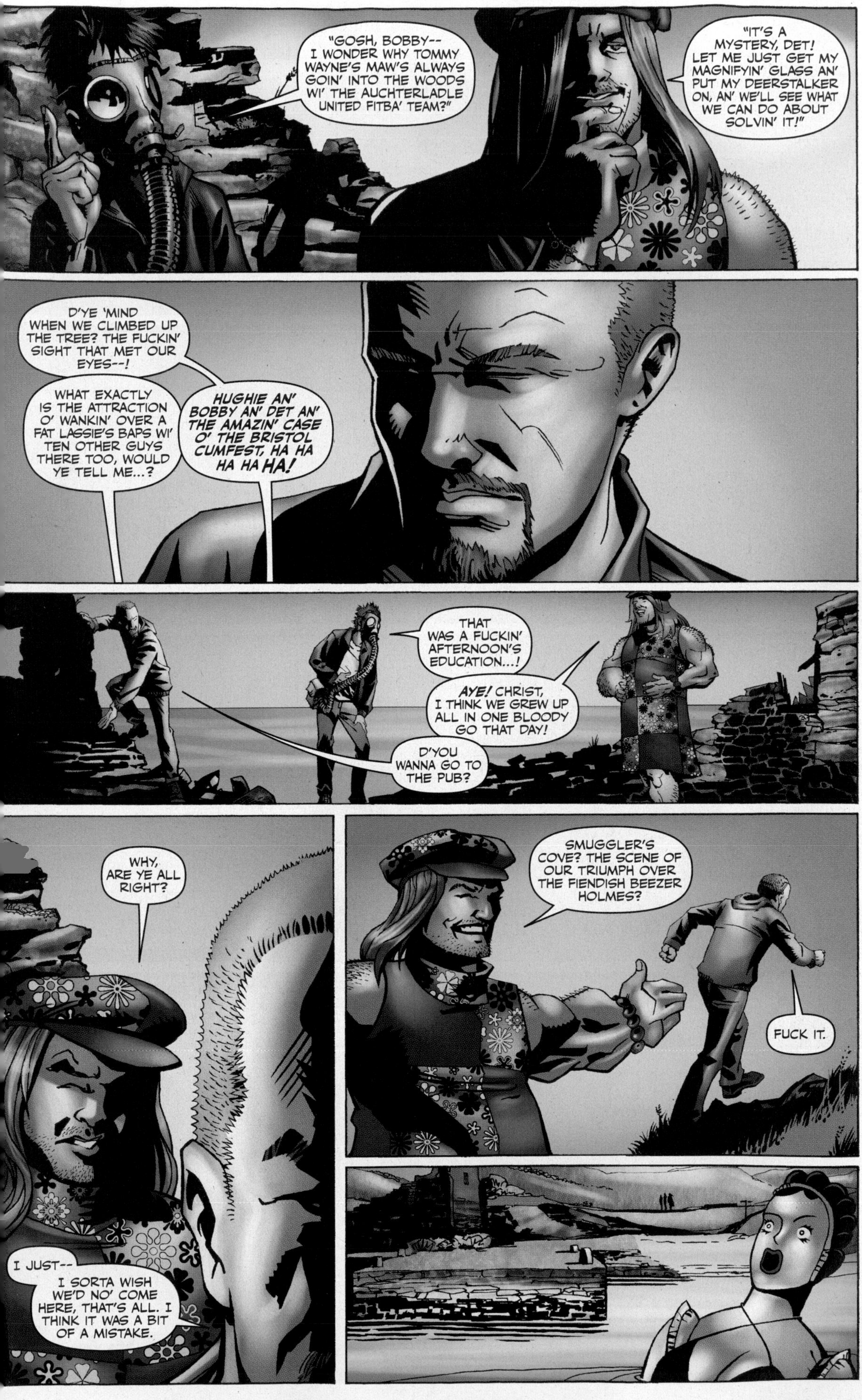
"GOSH, BOBBY-- I WONDER WHY TOMMY WAYNE'S MAW'S ALWAYS GOIN' INTO THE WOODS WI' THE AUCHTERLADLE UNITED FITBA' TEAM?"
"IT'S A MYSTERY, DET! LET ME JUST GET MY MAGNIFYIN' GLASS AN' PUT MY DEERSTALKER ON, AN' WE'LL SEE WHAT WE CAN DO ABOUT SOLVIN' IT!"
D'YE 'MIND WHEN WE CLIMBED UP THE TREE? THE FUCKIN' SIGHT THAT MET OUR EYES--!
WHAT EXACTLY IS THE ATTRACTION O' WANKIN' OVER A FAT LASSIE'S BAPS WI' TEN OTHER GUYS THERE TOO, WOULD YE TELL ME...?
HUGHIE AN' BOBBY AN' DET AN' THE AMAZIN' CASE O' THE BRISTOL CUMFEST, HA HA HA HA HA!
THAT WAS A FUCKIN' AFTERNOON'S EDUCATION...!
AYE! CHRIST, I THINK WE GREW UP ALL IN ONE BLOODY GO THAT DAY!
D'YOU WANNA GO TO THE PUB?
WHY, ARE YE ALL RIGHT?
I JUST--
I SORTA WISH WE'D NO' COME HERE, THAT'S ALL. I THINK IT WAS A BIT OF A MISTAKE.
SMUGGLER'S COVE? THE SCENE OF OUR TRIUMPH OVER THE FIENDISH BEEZER HOLMES?
FUCK IT.

YOU AIN'T HUNGRY?

AH...

OR YOU HAVIN' SECOND THOUGHTS?

NO, I'M GOIN'. I'M DEFINITELY GOIN'.

BUT YOU AIN'T GONNA TALK ABOUT THIS MYSTERY CHICK...

UH-UH. I WANNA TALK ABOUT OUR BOSS.

YEAH?

WE'RE MEANT TO BE A C.I.A. TEAM...A TEAM WI' C.I.A. BACKIN', ANYWAY...AN' IT'S OUR JOB TO KEEP AN EYE ON SUPERHEROES. THE WORD I ALWAYS USED TO HEAR WAS MANAGEMENT.

BUT I ASKED THE LEGEND ABOUT THAT, AN' HE TOLD ME THE SEVEN--THEM IN PARTICULAR--WERE REALLY A TARGET. HE SAID THEY WERE BUTCHER'S TARGET, HE ASKED ME IF I THOUGHT SOMEONE LIKE BUTCHER'D EVER BE INTERESTED IN MANAGIN' ANYTHIN'.

YOU ASK THE MAN HIMSELF ABOUT THIS?

OH, SHIT.

AYE, BUT I FUCKED UP THERE. I MENTIONED HIS WIFE.

I SORTA DID IT AGAIN RECENTLY THERE. I DUNNO WHAT'S THE MATTER WI' ME.

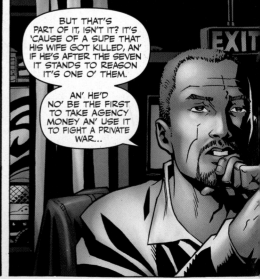

BUT THAT'S PART OF IT, ISN'T IT? IT'S 'CAUSE OF A SUPE THAT HIS WIFE GOT KILLED, AN' IF HE'S AFTER THE SEVEN IT STANDS TO REASON IT'S ONE O' THEM.

AN' HE'D NO' BE THE FIRST TO TAKE AGENCY MONEY AN' USE IT TO FIGHT A PRIVATE WAR...

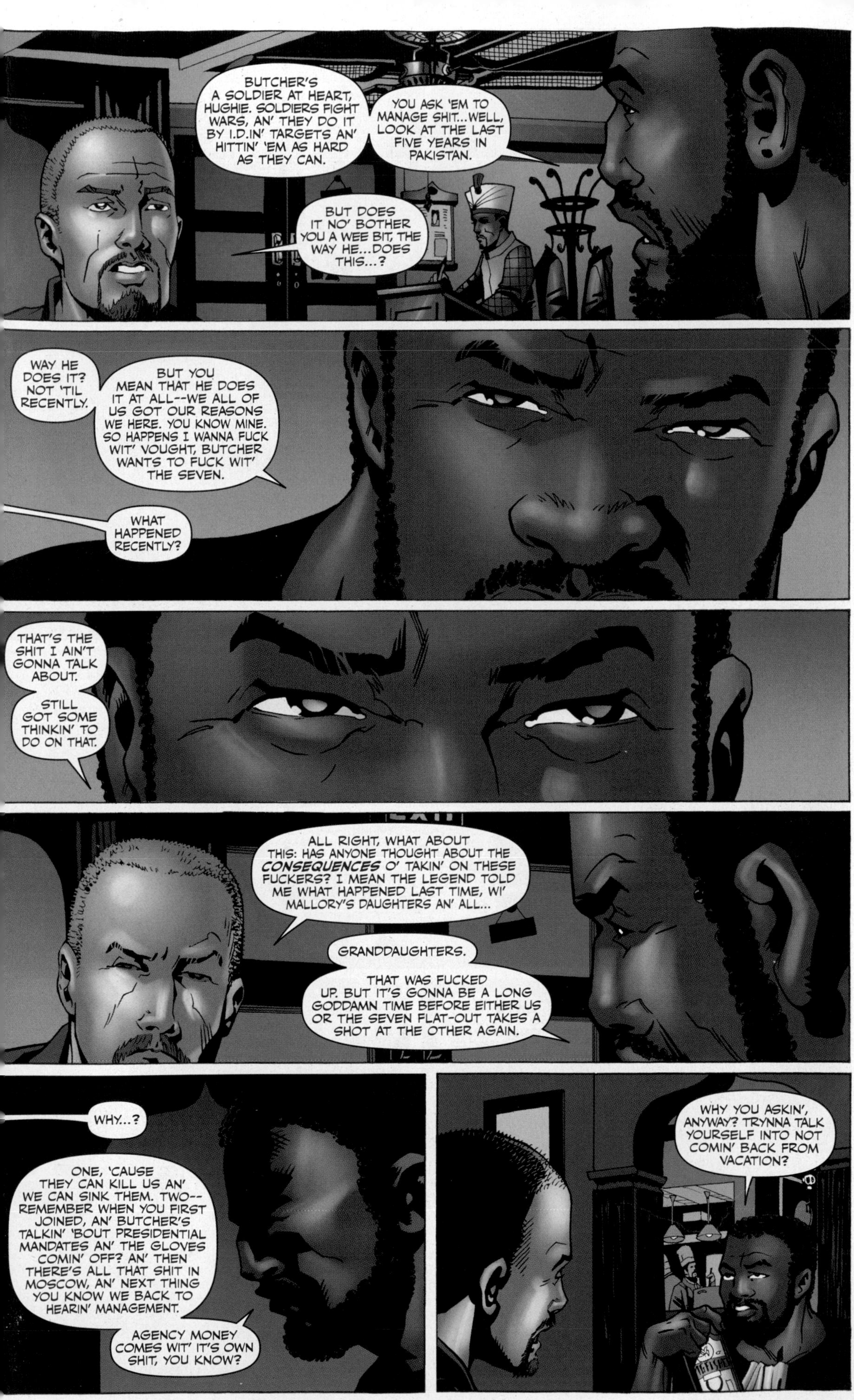
BUTCHER'S A SOLDIER AT HEART, HUGHIE. SOLDIERS FIGHT WARS, AN' THEY DO IT BY I.D.IN' TARGETS AN' HITTIN' 'EM AS HARD AS THEY CAN.
YOU ASK 'EM TO MANAGE SHIT...WELL, LOOK AT THE LAST FIVE YEARS IN PAKISTAN.
BUT DOES IT NO' BOTHER YOU A WEE BIT, THE WAY HE...DOES THIS...?
WAY HE DOES IT? NOT 'TIL RECENTLY.
BUT YOU MEAN THAT HE DOES IT AT ALL--WE ALL OF US GOT OUR REASONS WE HERE. YOU KNOW MINE. SO HAPPENS I WANNA FUCK WIT' VOUGHT, BUTCHER WANTS TO FUCK WIT' THE SEVEN.
WHAT HAPPENED RECENTLY?
THAT'S THE SHIT I AIN'T GONNA TALK ABOUT.
STILL GOT SOME THINKIN' TO DO ON THAT.
ALL RIGHT, WHAT ABOUT THIS: HAS ANYONE THOUGHT ABOUT THE CONSEQUENCES O' TAKIN' ON THESE FUCKERS? I MEAN THE LEGEND TOLD ME WHAT HAPPENED LAST TIME, WI' MALLORY'S DAUGHTERS AN' ALL...
GRANDDAUGHTERS.
THAT WAS FUCKED UP. BUT IT'S GONNA BE A LONG GODDAMN TIME BEFORE EITHER US OR THE SEVEN FLAT-OUT TAKES A SHOT AT THE OTHER AGAIN.
WHY...?
ONE, 'CAUSE THEY CAN KILL US AN' WE CAN SINK THEM. TWO--REMEMBER WHEN YOU FIRST JOINED, AN' BUTCHER'S TALKIN' 'BOUT PRESIDENTIAL MANDATES AN' THE GLOVES COMIN' OFF? AN' THEN THERE'S ALL THAT SHIT IN MOSCOW, AN' NEXT THING YOU KNOW WE BACK TO HEARIN' MANAGEMENT.
AGENCY MONEY COMES WIT' IT'S OWN SHIT, YOU KNOW?
WHY YOU ASKIN', ANYWAY? TRYNNA TALK YOURSELF INTO NOT COMIN' BACK FROM VACATION?

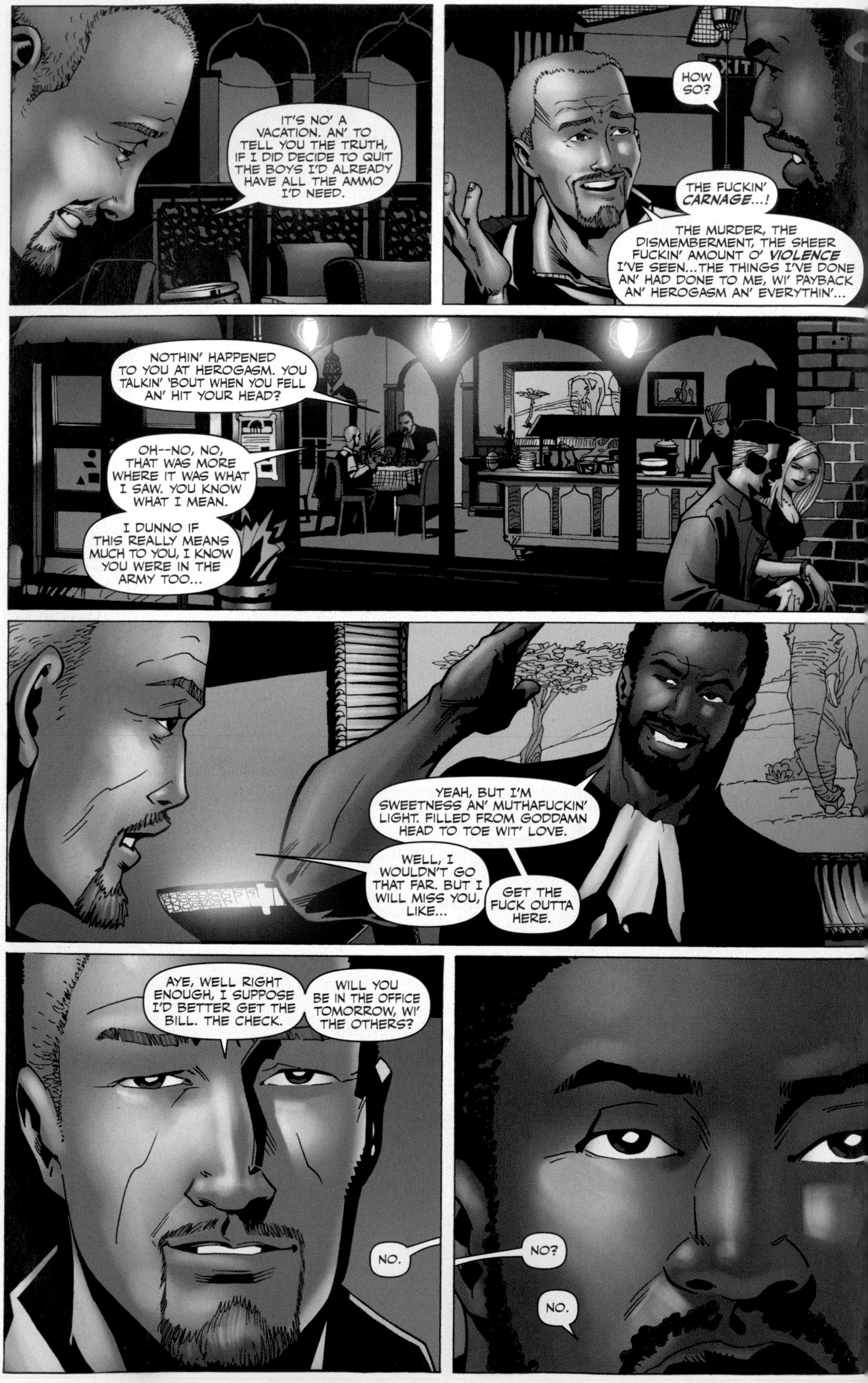
IT'S NO' A VACATION. AN' TO TELL YOU THE TRUTH, IF I DID DECIDE TO QUIT THE BOYS I'D ALREADY HAVE ALL THE AMMO I'D NEED.
HOW SO?
THE FUCKIN' CARNAGE...!
THE MURDER, THE DISMEMBERMENT, THE SHEER FUCKIN' AMOUNT O' VIOLENCE I'VE SEEN...THE THINGS I'VE DONE AN' HAD DONE TO ME, WI' PAYBACK AN' HEROGASM AN' EVERYTHIN'...
NOTHIN' HAPPENED TO YOU AT HEROGASM. YOU TALKIN' 'BOUT WHEN YOU FELL AN' HIT YOUR HEAD?
OH--NO, NO, THAT WAS MORE WHERE IT WAS WHAT I SAW. YOU KNOW WHAT I MEAN.
I DUNNO IF THIS REALLY MEANS MUCH TO YOU, I KNOW YOU WERE IN THE ARMY TOO...
YEAH, BUT I'M SWEETNESS AN' MUTHAFUCKIN' LIGHT. FILLED FROM GODDAMN HEAD TO TOE WIT' LOVE.
WELL, I WOULDN'T GO THAT FAR. BUT I WILL MISS YOU, LIKE...
GET THE FUCK OUTTA HERE.
AYE, WELL RIGHT ENOUGH, I SUPPOSE I'D BETTER GET THE BILL. THE CHECK.
WILL YOU BE IN THE OFFICE TOMORROW, WI' THE OTHERS?
NO.
NO?
NO.

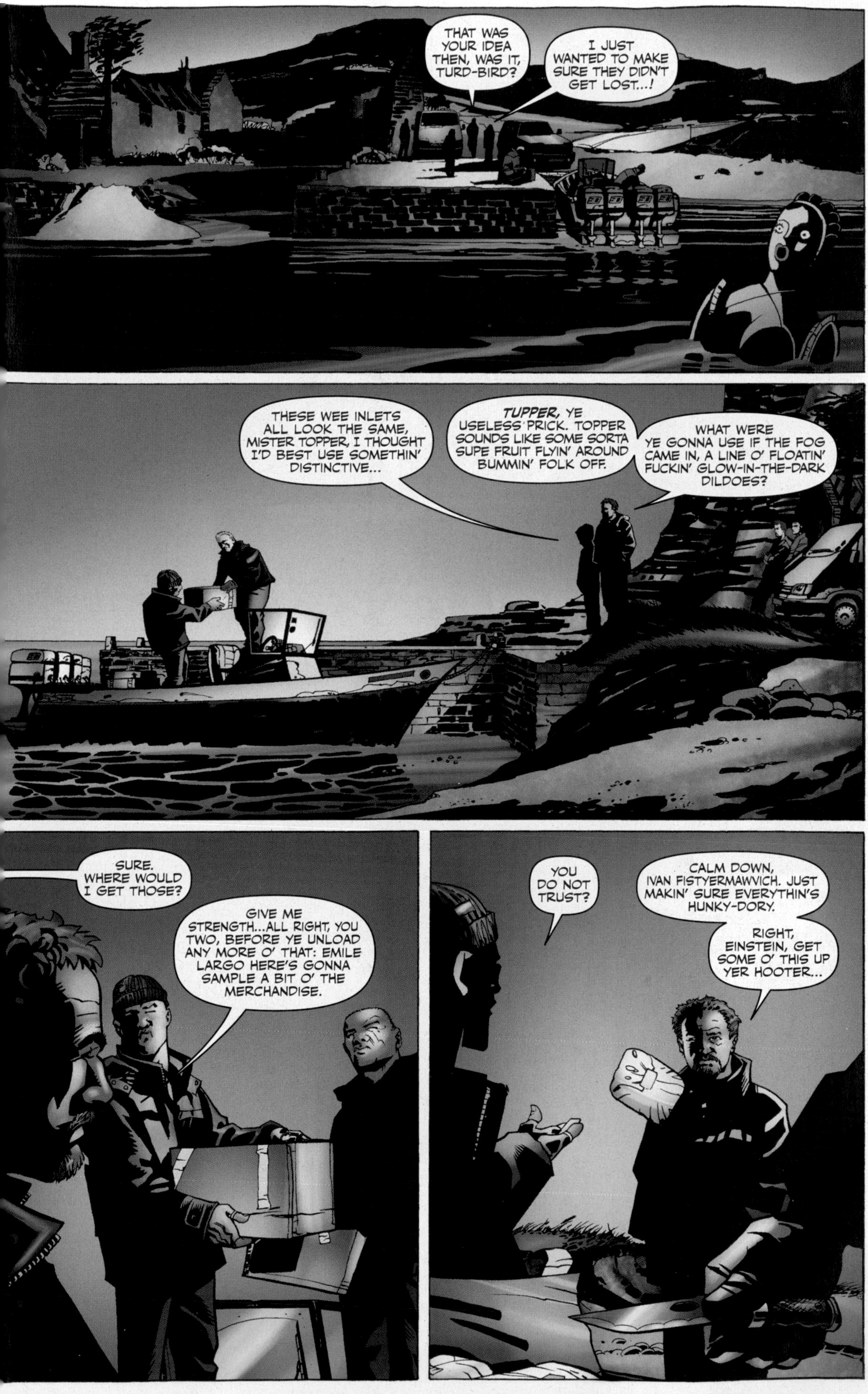
THAT WAS YOUR IDEA THEN, WAS IT, TURD-BIRD?
I JUST WANTED TO MAKE SURE THEY DIDN'T GET LOST...!
THESE WEE INLETS ALL LOOK THE SAME, MISTER TOPPER, I THOUGHT I'D BEST USE SOMETHIN' DISTINCTIVE...
TUPPER, YE USELESS PRICK. TOPPER SOUNDS LIKE SOME SORTA SUPE FRUIT FLYIN' AROUND BUMMIN' FOLK OFF.
WHAT WERE YE GONNA USE IF THE FOG CAME IN, A LINE O' FLOATIN' FUCKIN' GLOW-IN-THE-DARK DILDOES?
SURE. WHERE WOULD I GET THOSE?
GIVE ME STRENGTH...ALL RIGHT, YOU TWO, BEFORE YE UNLOAD ANY MORE O' THAT: EMILE LARGO HERE'S GONNA SAMPLE A BIT O' THE MERCHANDISE.
YOU DO NOT TRUST?
CALM DOWN, IVAN FISTYERMAWVICH. JUST MAKIN' SURE EVERYTHIN'S HUNKY-DORY.
RIGHT, EINSTEIN, GET SOME O' THIS UP YER HOOTER...

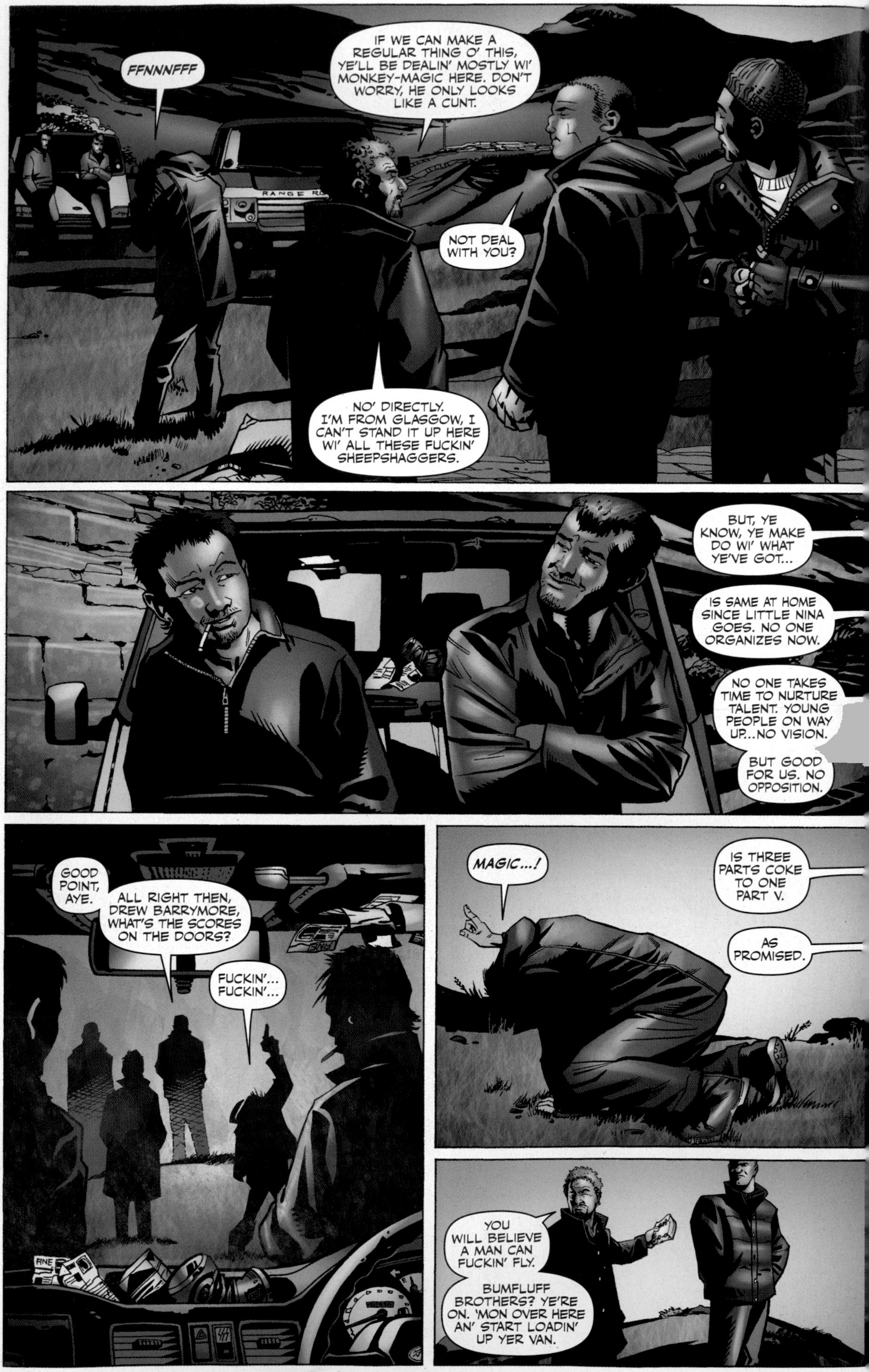
FFNNNFFF
IF WE CAN MAKE A REGULAR THING O' THIS, YE'LL BE DEALIN' MOSTLY WI' MONKEY-MAGIC HERE. DON'T WORRY, HE ONLY LOOKS LIKE A CUNT.
NOT DEAL WITH YOU?
NO' DIRECTLY. I'M FROM GLASGOW, I CAN'T STAND IT UP HERE WI' ALL THESE FUCKIN' SHEEPSHAGGERS.
BUT, YE KNOW, YE MAKE DO WI' WHAT YE'VE GOT...
IS SAME AT HOME SINCE LITTLE NINA GOES. NO ONE ORGANIZES NOW.
NO ONE TAKES TIME TO NURTURE TALENT. YOUNG PEOPLE ON WAY UP...NO VISION.
BUT GOOD FOR US. NO OPPOSITION.
GOOD POINT, AYE.
ALL RIGHT THEN, DREW BARRYMORE, WHAT'S THE SCORES ON THE DOORS?
FUCKIN'... FUCKIN'...
MAGIC...!
IS THREE PARTS COKE TO ONE PART V.
AS PROMISED.
YOU WILL BELIEVE A MAN CAN FUCKIN' FLY.
BUMFLUFF BROTHERS? YE'RE ON. 'MON OVER HERE AN' START LOADIN' UP YER VAN.

AYE, WELL, JUST A MINUTE THERE. WE WANTED A WEE WORD BEFORE WE WENT ANY FURTHER.

OH AYE?

AYE. WE WERE JUST LISTENIN' TO WHAT YE WERE SAYIN' TO THESE TWO BOYS HERE, YE KEN?

IT SOUNDS TO US LIKE YE'VE GOT QUITE A MAJOR OPERATION HERE. LIKE AN INTERNATIONAL SORTA THING.

AN' WE WERE THINKIN'...WELL, WE'RE THE ONES'VE GOTTA DRIVE THIS GEAR ALL OVER THE HIGHLANDS--NO' TO MENTION THE BIG DELIVERIES IN DUNDEE AN' GLASGOW...

SO WE THOUGHT, LIKE, WI' ALL THIS CASH YE'RE GONNA BE MAKIN', YE COULD AFFORD TO PAY US SOME PROPER--

AW, FOR FUCK'S SAKE...HERE, CUNTOSAURUS? I THOUGHT I TOLD YE TO HIRE SOMEONE RELIABLE?

MMMMMMM

BRILLIANT. OKAY THEN, WHAT IF I WAS TO OPEN THE NEGOTIATIONS BY TELLIN' YOU TWO FUDGE-MERCHANTS TO FUCK OFF?

WE COULD DO THAT. WE COULD FUCK OFF.

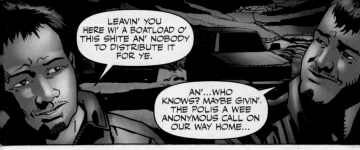

LEAVIN' YOU HERE WI' A BOATLOAD O' THIS SHITE AN' NOBODY TO DISTRIBUTE IT FOR YE.

AN'...WHO KNOWS? MAYBE GIVIN' THE POLIS A WEE ANONYMOUS CALL ON OUR WAY HOME...

SOME INTERESTIN' THOUGHTS THERE.

SARAH!

RANGE R

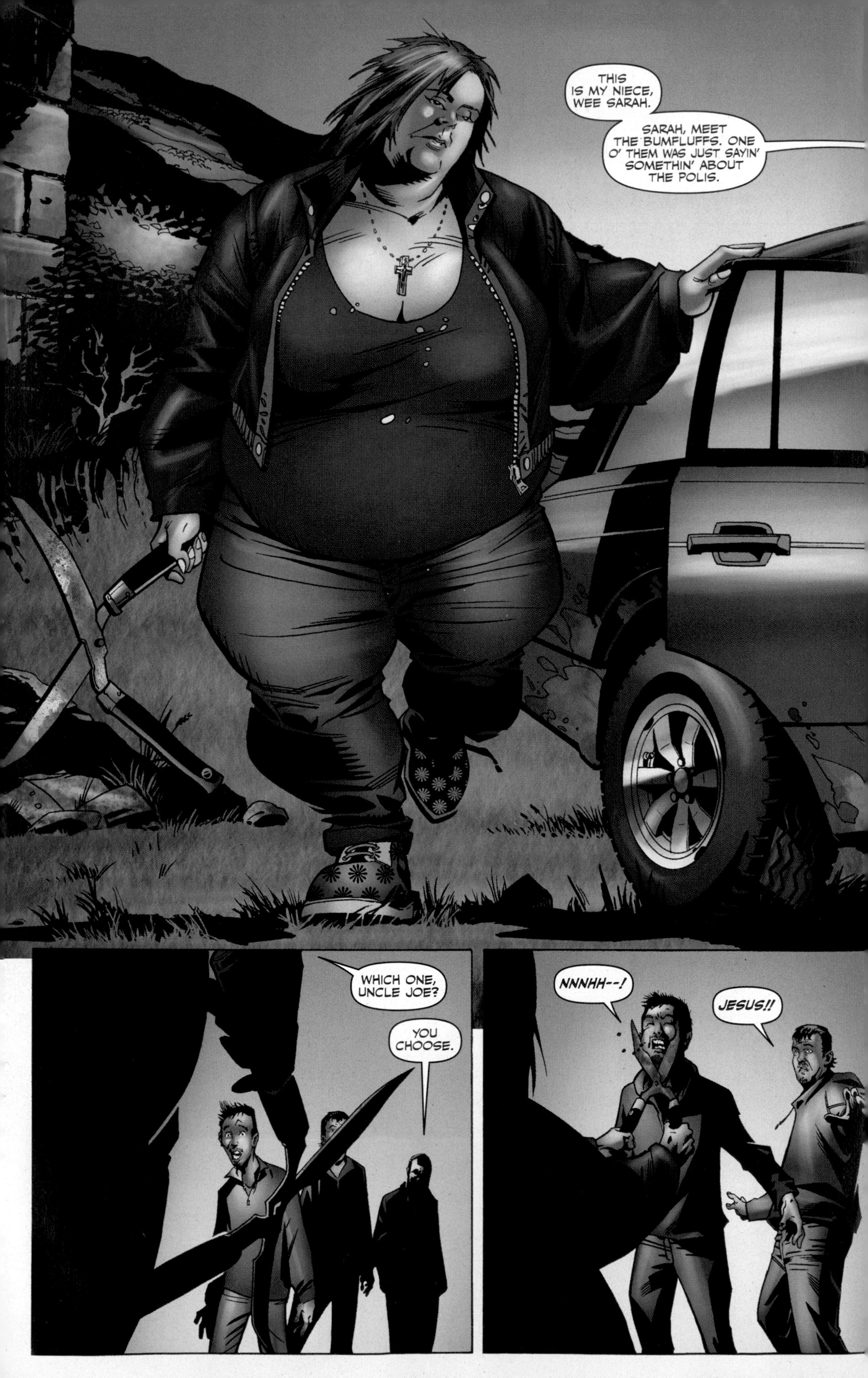
THIS IS MY NIECE, WEE SARAH.
SARAH, MEET THE BUMFLUFFS. ONE O' THEM WAS JUST SAYIN' SOMETHIN' ABOUT THE POLIS.
WHICH ONE, UNCLE JOE?
YOU CHOOSE.
NNNHH--!
JESUS!!

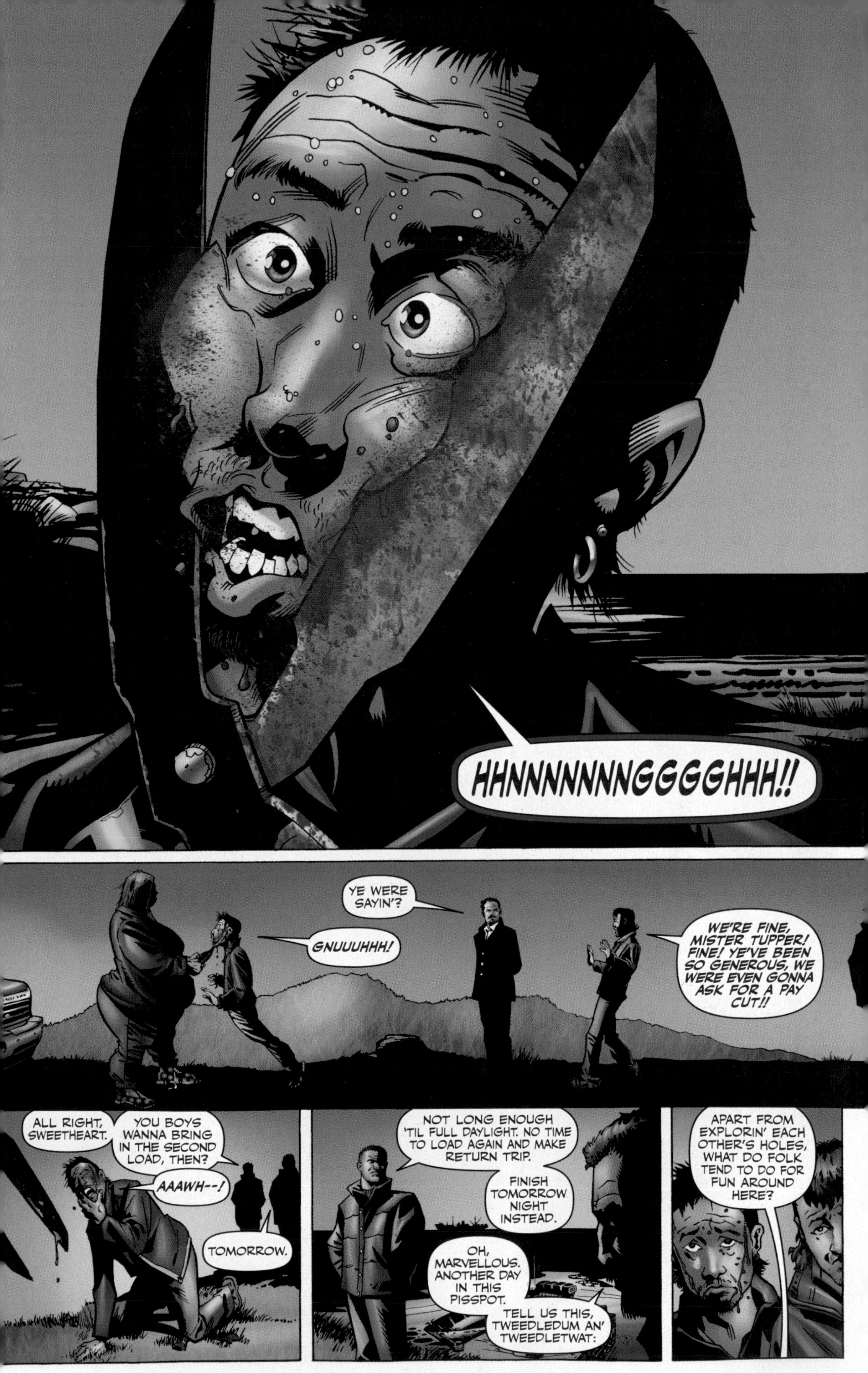
HHNNNNNNNGGGGHHH!!
YE WERE SAYIN'?
GNUUUHHH!
WE'RE FINE, MISTER TUPPER! FINE! YE'VE BEEN SO GENEROUS, WE WERE EVEN GONNA ASK FOR A PAY CUT!!
ALL RIGHT, SWEETHEART.
YOU BOYS WANNA BRING IN THE SECOND LOAD, THEN?
AAAWH--!
TOMORROW.
NOT LONG ENOUGH 'TIL FULL DAYLIGHT. NO TIME TO LOAD AGAIN AND MAKE RETURN TRIP.
FINISH TOMORROW NIGHT INSTEAD.
OH, MARVELLOUS. ANOTHER DAY IN THIS PISSPOT.
TELL US THIS, TWEEDLEDUM AN' TWEEDLETWAT:
APART FROM EXPLORIN' EACH OTHER'S HOLES, WHAT DO FOLK TEND TO DO FOR FUN AROUND HERE?

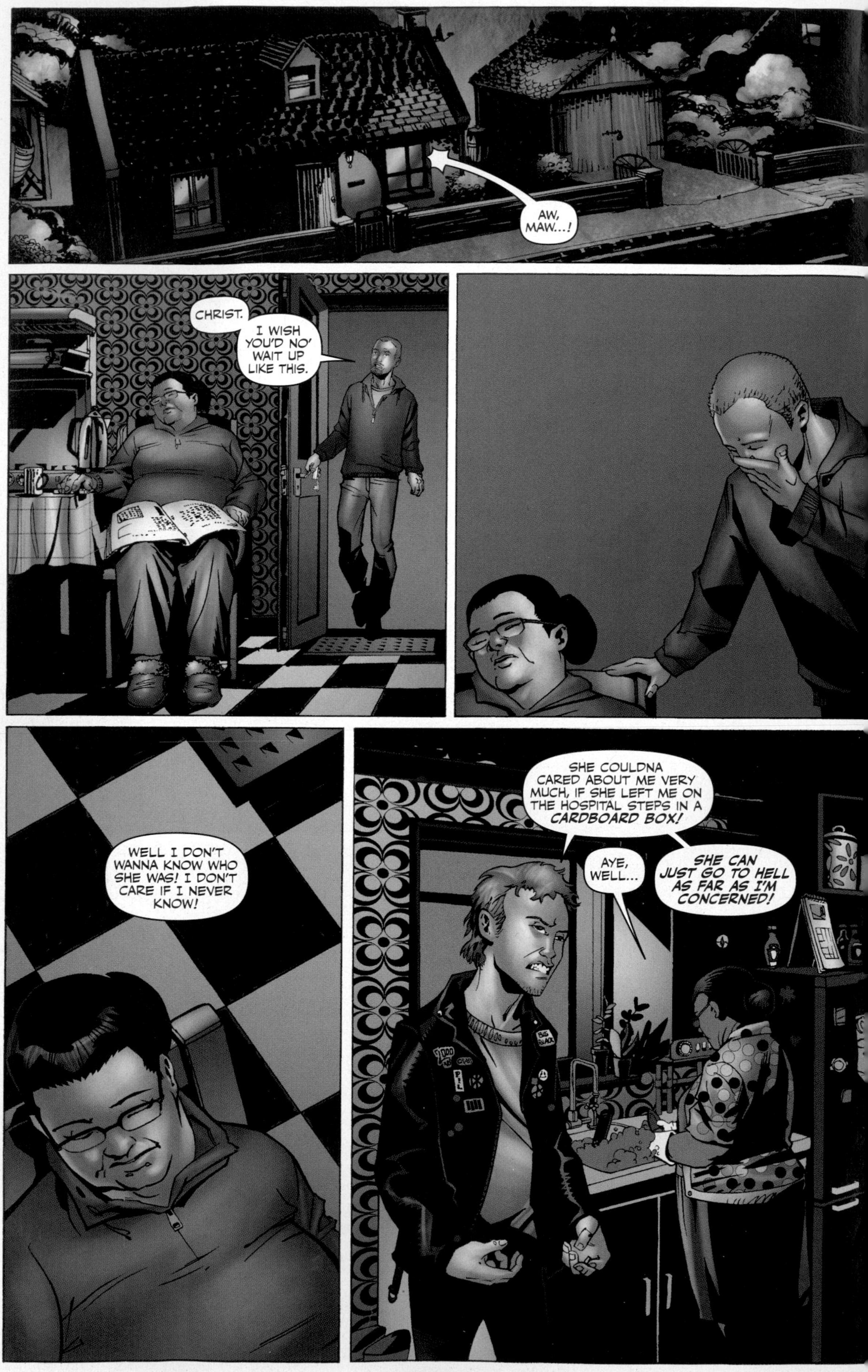
AW, MAW...!
CHRIST.
I WISH YOU'D NO' WAIT UP LIKE THIS.
WELL I DON'T WANNA KNOW WHO SHE WAS! I DON'T CARE IF I NEVER KNOW!
SHE COULDNA CARED ABOUT ME VERY MUCH, IF SHE LEFT ME ON THE HOSPITAL STEPS IN A CARDBOARD BOX!
AYE, WELL...
SHE CAN JUST GO TO HELL AS FAR AS I'M CONCERNED!

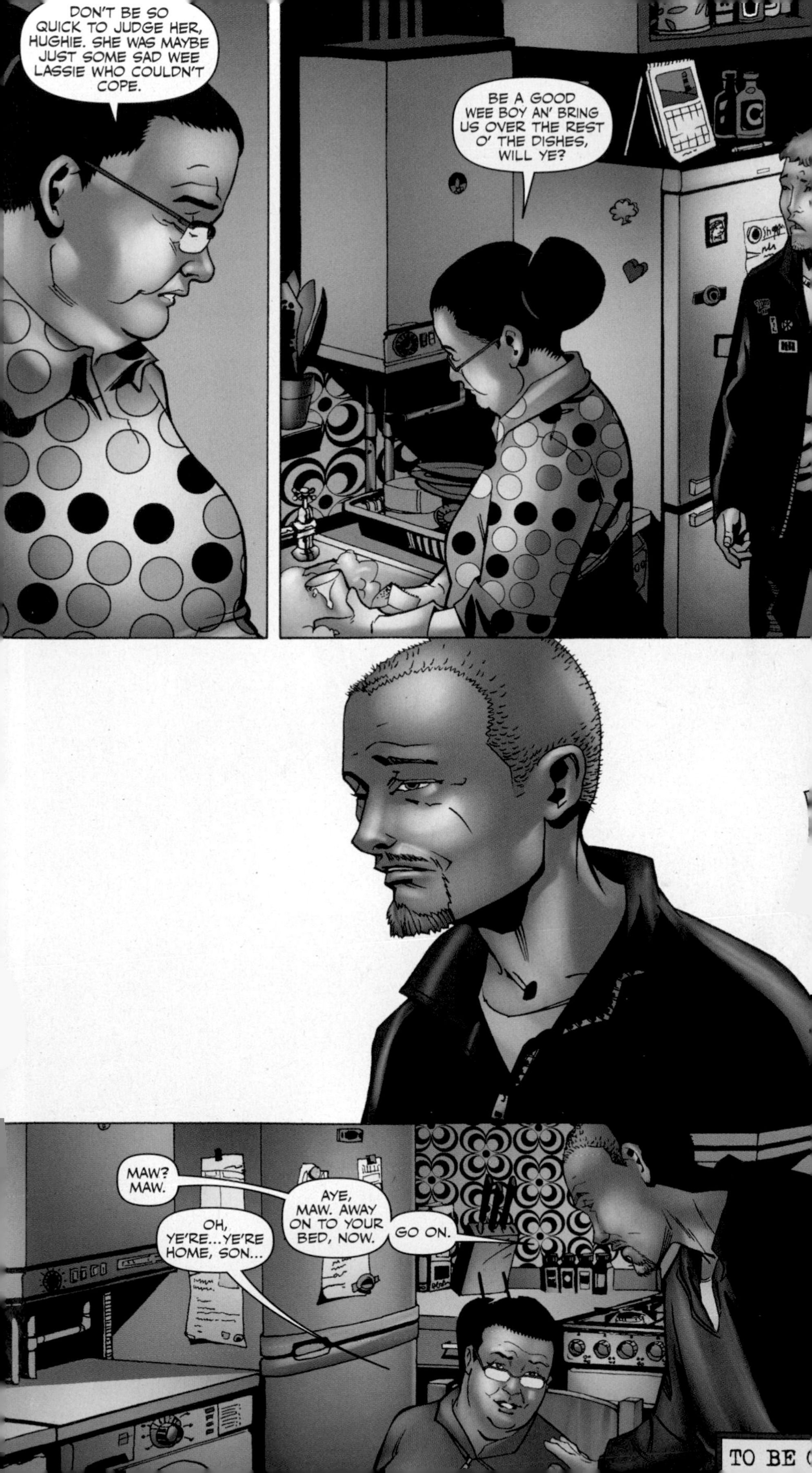
DON'T BE SO QUICK TO JUDGE HER, HUGHIE. SHE WAS MAYBE JUST SOME SAD WEE LASSIE WHO COULDN'T COPE.
BE A GOOD WEE BOY AN' BRING US OVER THE REST O' THE DISHES, WILL YE?
MAW? MAW.
OH, YE'RE...YE'RE HOME, SON...
AYE, MAW. AWAY ON TO YOUR BED, NOW.
GO ON.
TO BE C

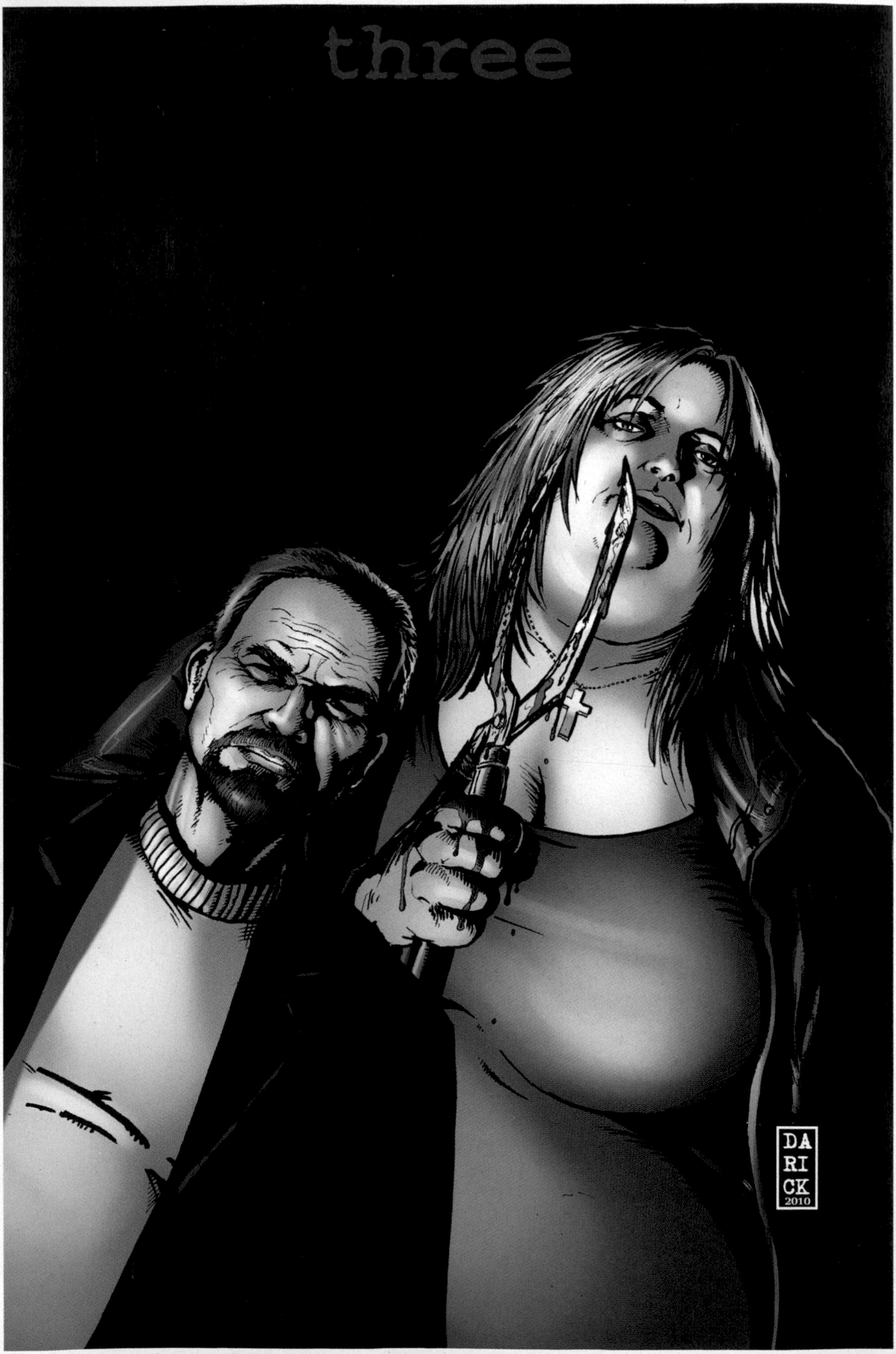
three
DA
RI
CK
2010

"AUNTIE MARY WAS...

"SHE WAS A FRAIL WEE WOMAN. SHE WAS NICE, BUT SHE WAS VAGUE. IT WASN'T SO MUCH THAT SHE'D LOSE TRACK O' WHERE SHE WAS, AS SHE'D FORGET THAT SHE WAS THERE AT ALL.

"ONE TIME SHE CAME TO STAY WI' US, AN' SHE GOT OUT O' THE BATH AN' WENT OUT THE BACK DOOR AN' KEPT GOIN'. SHE WENT LEFT INSTEAD O' RIGHT, OR SHE'D'VE JUST GONE BACK TO THE SPARE ROOM."

"IT WAS ONE IN THE MORNIN' BEFORE MAW AN' PAW TWIGGED SHE WAS GONE.

"SHE WOULDN'T SAY BOO TO A GOOSE, EITHER. NEVER ASKED FOR ANYTHIN'. THAT'S WHY SHE WAS SO THIN, MAW SAID, 'CAUSE SHE WOULDN'T ASK ANYONE FOR SOMETHIN' TO EAT AN' SHE KEPT FORGETTIN' TO FEED HERSELF.

"THAT'S WHAT WE THOUGHT IT WAS, AT LEAST."

"I LIKED AUNTIE MARY, I THOUGHT SHE WAS LOVELY. SHE WAS REALLY KIND, AN' IT WAS DEAD EASY BEATIN' HER AT MONOPOLY OR WHATEVER.

"YOU KEN WHAT IT'S LIKE AT THAT AGE, BUT YOU HAVEN'T A BLOODY CLUE."

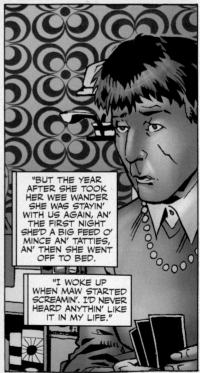

"BUT THE YEAR AFTER SHE TOOK HER WEE WANDER SHE WAS STAYIN' WITH US AGAIN, AN' THE FIRST NIGHT SHE'D A BIG FEED O' MINCE AN' TATTIES, AN' THEN SHE WENT OFF TO BED.

"I WOKE UP WHEN MAW STARTED SCREAMIN'. I'D NEVER HEARD ANYTHIN' LIKE IT IN MY LIFE."

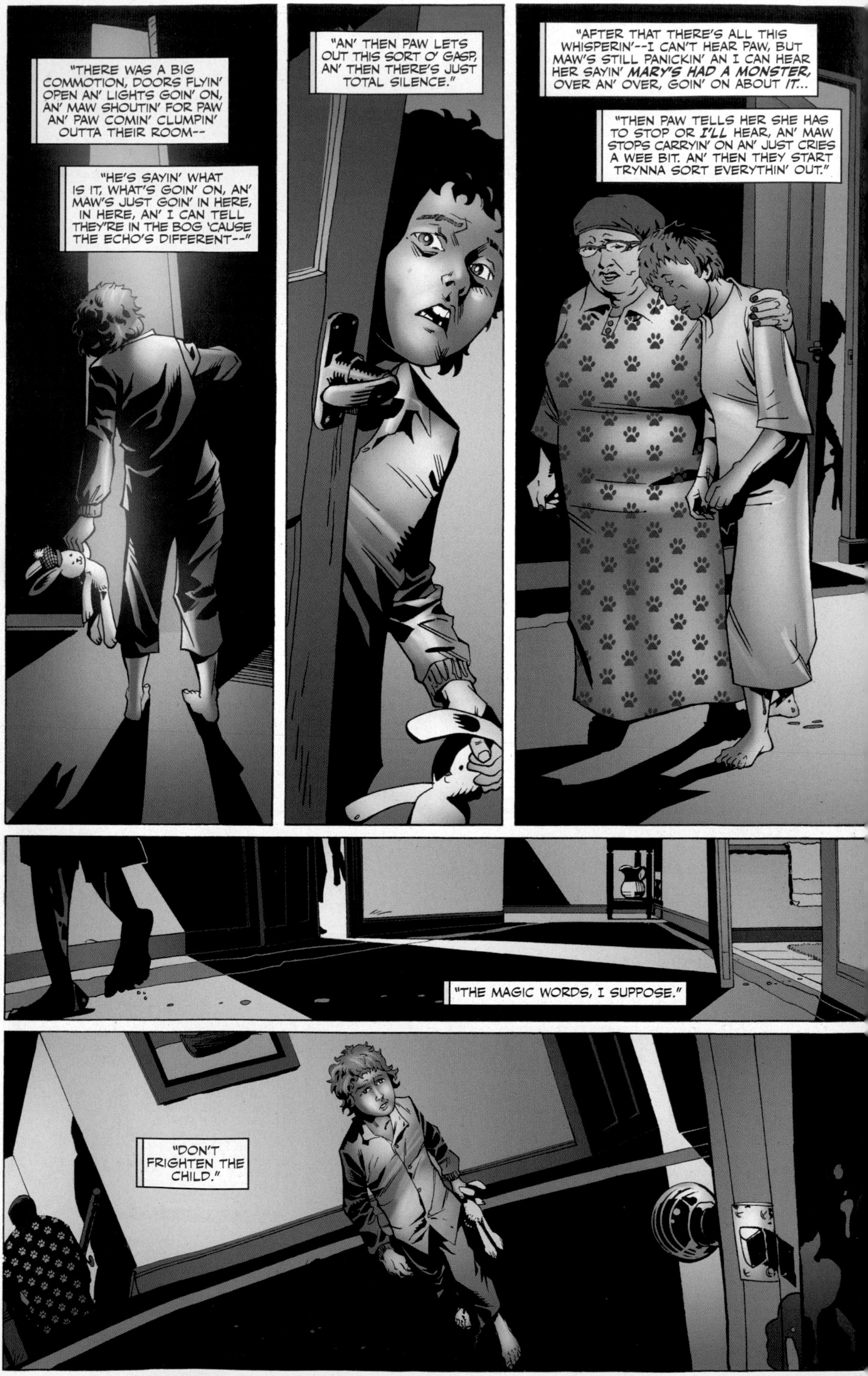
"THERE WAS A BIG COMMOTION, DOORS FLYIN' OPEN AN' LIGHTS GOIN' ON, AN' MAW SHOUTIN' FOR PAW AN' PAW COMIN' CLUMPIN' OUTTA THEIR ROOM--
"HE'S SAYIN' WHAT IS IT, WHAT'S GOIN' ON, AN' MAW'S JUST GOIN' IN HERE, IN HERE, AN' I CAN TELL THEY'RE IN THE BOG 'CAUSE THE ECHO'S DIFFERENT--"
"AN' THEN PAW LETS OUT THIS SORT O' GASP, AN' THEN THERE'S JUST TOTAL SILENCE."
"AFTER THAT THERE'S ALL THIS WHISPERIN'--I CAN'T HEAR PAW, BUT MAW'S STILL PANICKIN' AN I CAN HEAR HER SAYIN' *MARY'S HAD A MONSTER,* OVER AN' OVER, GOIN' ON ABOUT *IT*...
"THEN PAW TELLS HER SHE HAS TO STOP OR *I'LL* HEAR, AN' MAW STOPS CARRYIN' ON AN' JUST CRIES A WEE BIT. AN' THEN THEY START TRYNNA SORT EVERYTHIN' OUT."
"THE MAGIC WORDS, I SUPPOSE."
"DON'T FRIGHTEN THE CHILD."

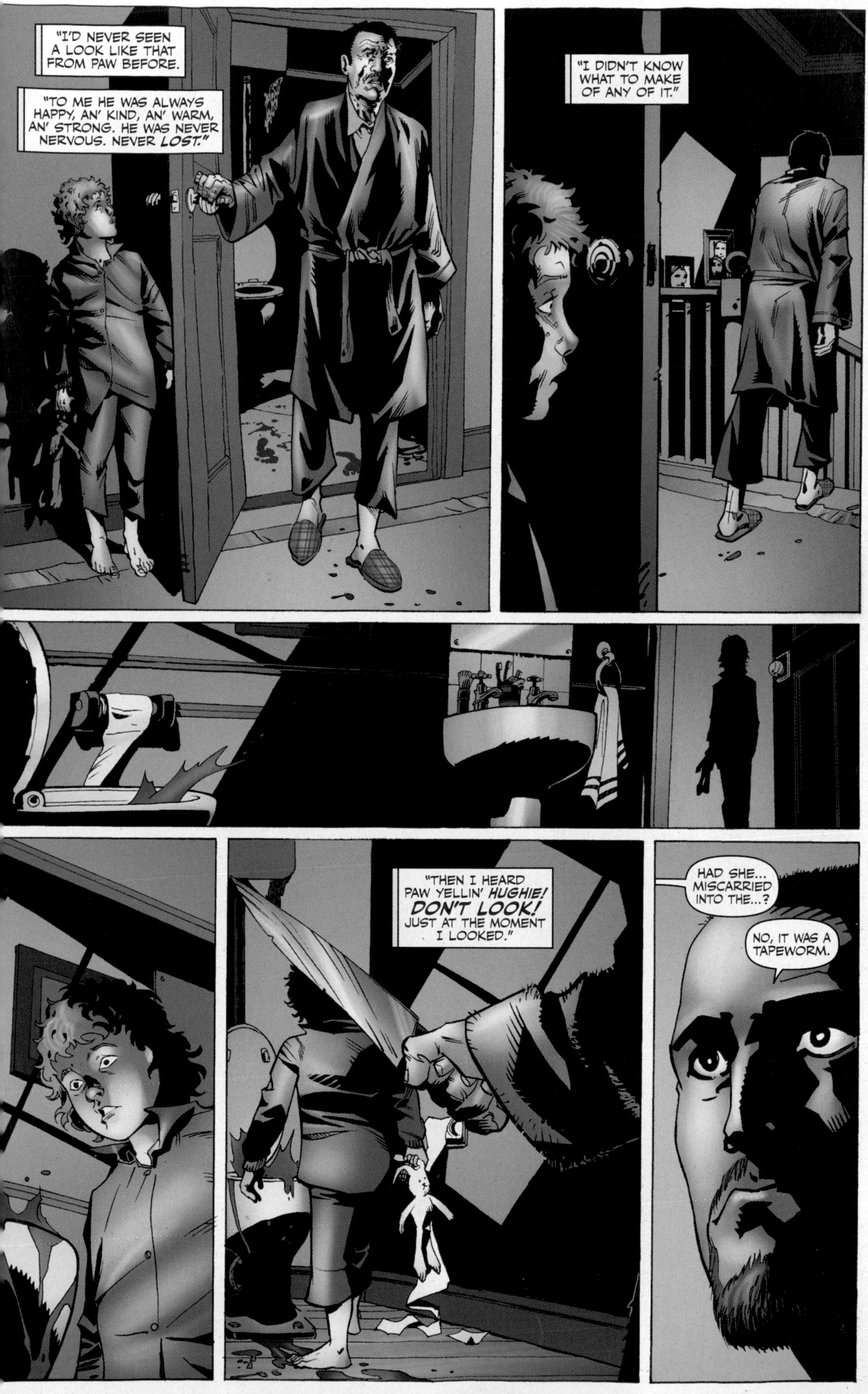
"I'D NEVER SEEN A LOOK LIKE THAT FROM PAW BEFORE.
"TO ME HE WAS ALWAYS HAPPY, AN' KIND, AN' WARM, AN' STRONG. HE WAS NEVER NERVOUS. NEVER *LOST.*"
"I DIDN'T KNOW WHAT TO MAKE OF ANY OF IT."
"THEN I HEARD PAW YELLIN' ***HUGHIE! DON'T LOOK!*** JUST AT THE MOMENT I LOOKED."
HAD SHE... MISCARRIED INTO THE...?
NO, IT WAS A TAPEWORM.

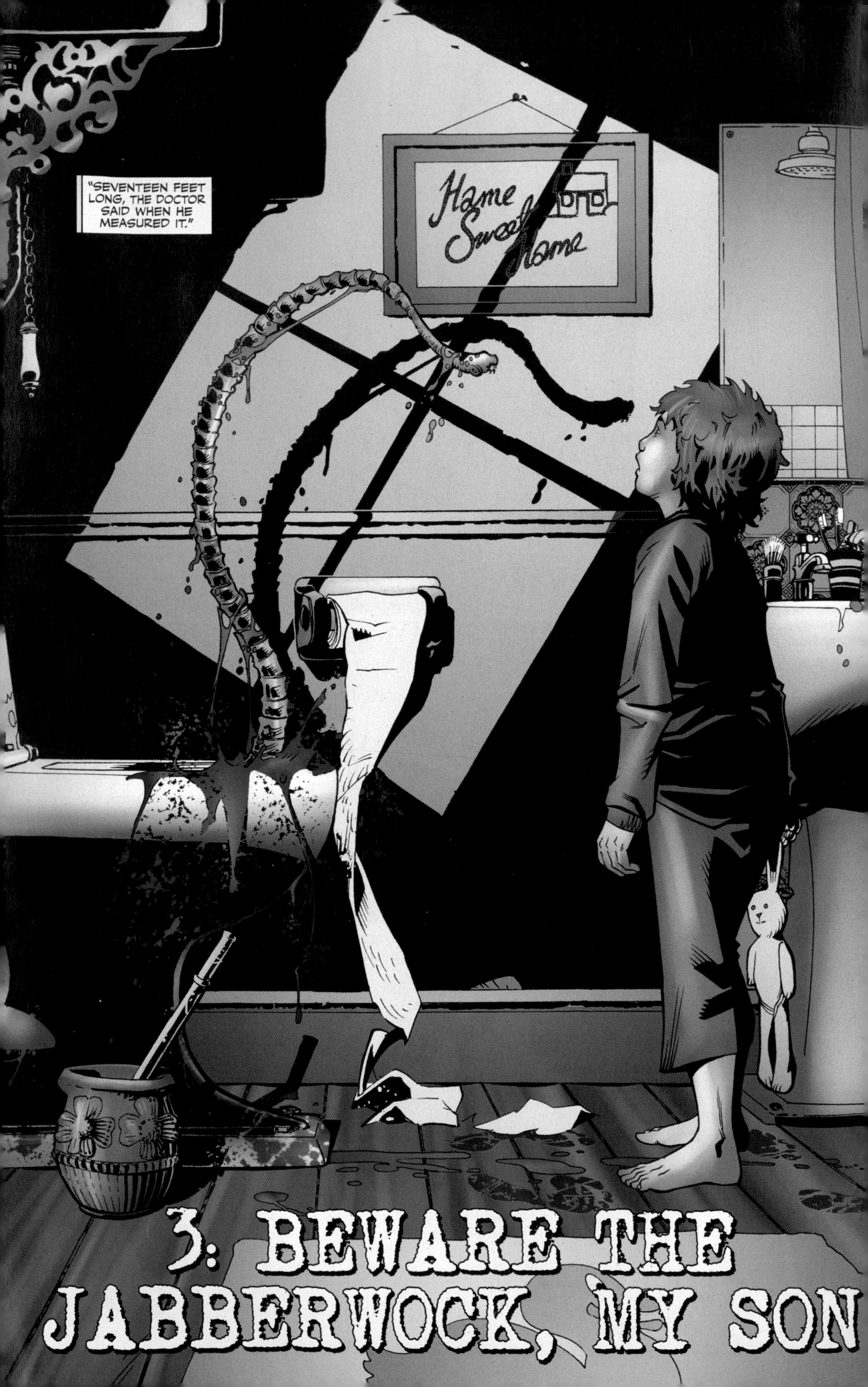
"SEVENTEEN FEET LONG, THE DOCTOR SAID WHEN HE MEASURED IT."
Home Sweet Home
3: BEWARE THE JABBERWOCK, MY SON

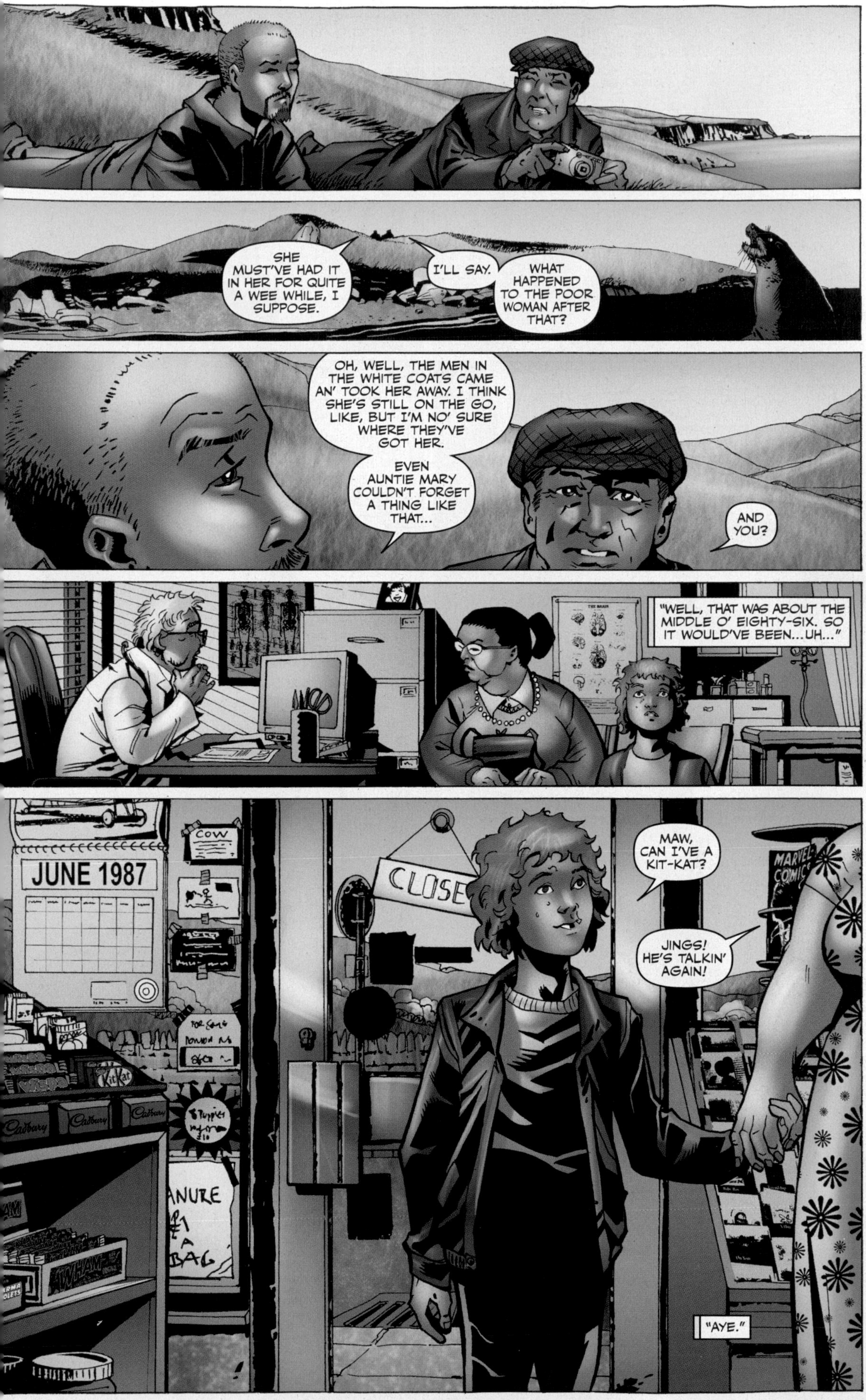
SHE MUST'VE HAD IT IN HER FOR QUITE A WEE WHILE, I SUPPOSE.
I'LL SAY.
WHAT HAPPENED TO THE POOR WOMAN AFTER THAT?
OH, WELL, THE MEN IN THE WHITE COATS CAME AN' TOOK HER AWAY. I THINK SHE'S STILL ON THE GO, LIKE, BUT I'M NO' SURE WHERE THEY'VE GOT HER.
EVEN AUNTIE MARY COULDN'T FORGET A THING LIKE THAT...
AND YOU?
"WELL, THAT WAS ABOUT THE MIDDLE O' EIGHTY-SIX. SO IT WOULD'VE BEEN...UH..."
JUNE 1987
COW
CLOSE
MAW, CAN I'VE A KIT-KAT?
JINGS! HE'S TALKIN' AGAIN!
Kit Kat
Cadbury
ANURE
BAG
"AYE."

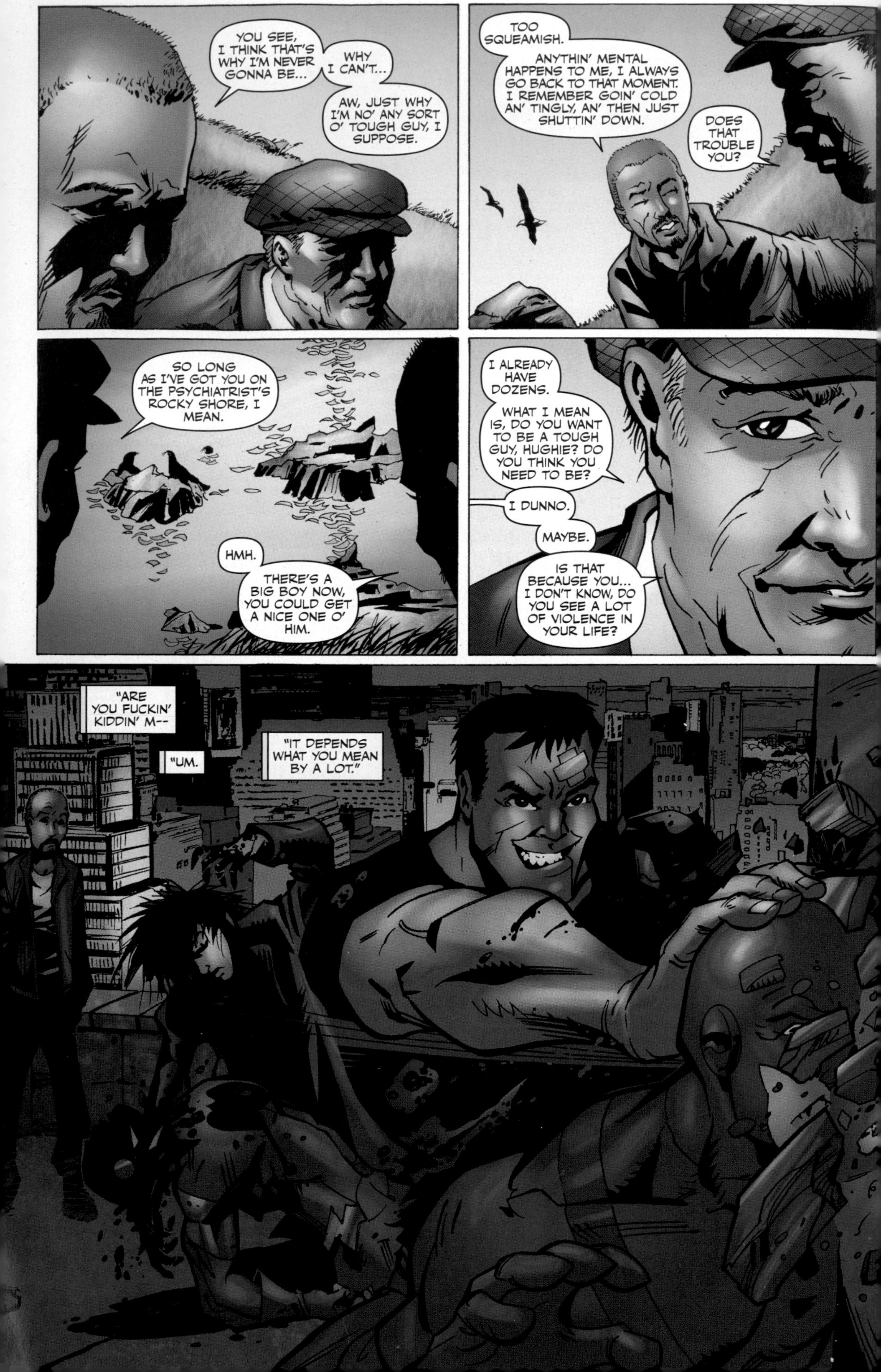
YOU SEE, I THINK THAT'S WHY I'M NEVER GONNA BE...
WHY I CAN'T...
AW, JUST WHY I'M NO' ANY SORT O' TOUGH GUY, I SUPPOSE.
TOO SQUEAMISH.
ANYTHIN' MENTAL HAPPENS TO ME, I ALWAYS GO BACK TO THAT MOMENT. I REMEMBER GOIN' COLD AN' TINGLY, AN' THEN JUST SHUTTIN' DOWN.
DOES THAT TROUBLE YOU?
SO LONG AS I'VE GOT YOU ON THE PSYCHIATRIST'S ROCKY SHORE, I MEAN.
HMH.
THERE'S A BIG BOY NOW, YOU COULD GET A NICE ONE O' HIM.
I ALREADY HAVE DOZENS.
WHAT I MEAN IS, DO YOU WANT TO BE A TOUGH GUY, HUGHIE? DO YOU THINK YOU NEED TO BE?
I DUNNO.
MAYBE.
IS THAT BECAUSE YOU... I DON'T KNOW, DO YOU SEE A LOT OF VIOLENCE IN YOUR LIFE?
"ARE YOU FUCKIN' KIDDIN' M--
"UM.
"IT DEPENDS WHAT YOU MEAN BY A LOT."

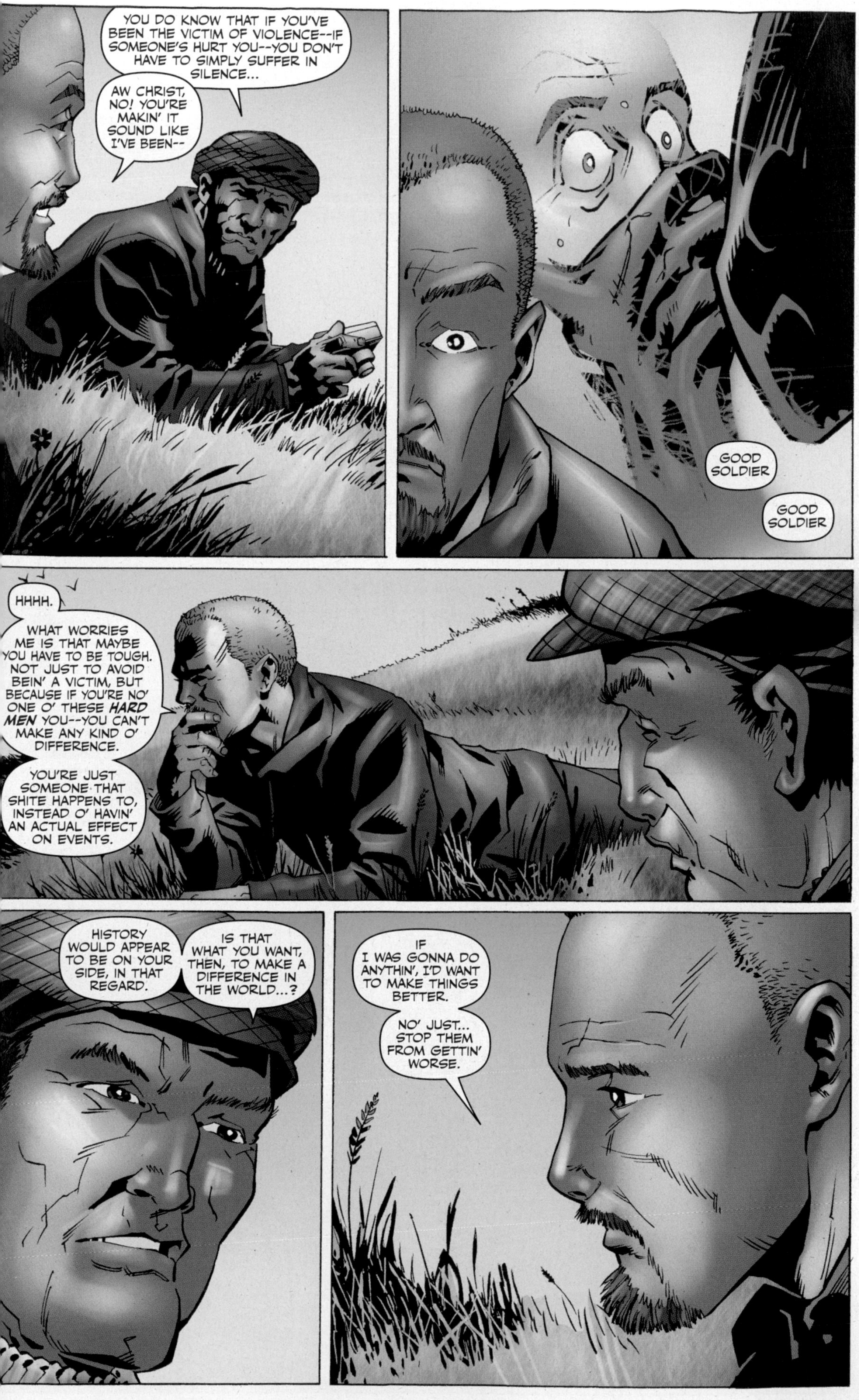
YOU DO KNOW THAT IF YOU'VE BEEN THE VICTIM OF VIOLENCE--IF SOMEONE'S HURT YOU--YOU DON'T HAVE TO SIMPLY SUFFER IN SILENCE...
AW CHRIST, NO! YOU'RE MAKIN' IT SOUND LIKE I'VE BEEN--
GOOD SOLDIER
GOOD SOLDIER
HHHH.
WHAT WORRIES ME IS THAT MAYBE YOU HAVE TO BE TOUGH. NOT JUST TO AVOID BEIN' A VICTIM, BUT BECAUSE IF YOU'RE NO' ONE O' THESE ***HARD MEN*** YOU--YOU CAN'T MAKE ANY KIND O' DIFFERENCE.
YOU'RE JUST SOMEONE THAT SHITE HAPPENS TO, INSTEAD O' HAVIN' AN ACTUAL EFFECT ON EVENTS.
HISTORY WOULD APPEAR TO BE ON YOUR SIDE, IN THAT REGARD.
IS THAT WHAT YOU WANT, THEN, TO MAKE A DIFFERENCE IN THE WORLD...?
IF I WAS GONNA DO ANYTHIN', I'D WANT TO MAKE THINGS BETTER.
NO' JUST... STOP THEM FROM GETTIN' WORSE.

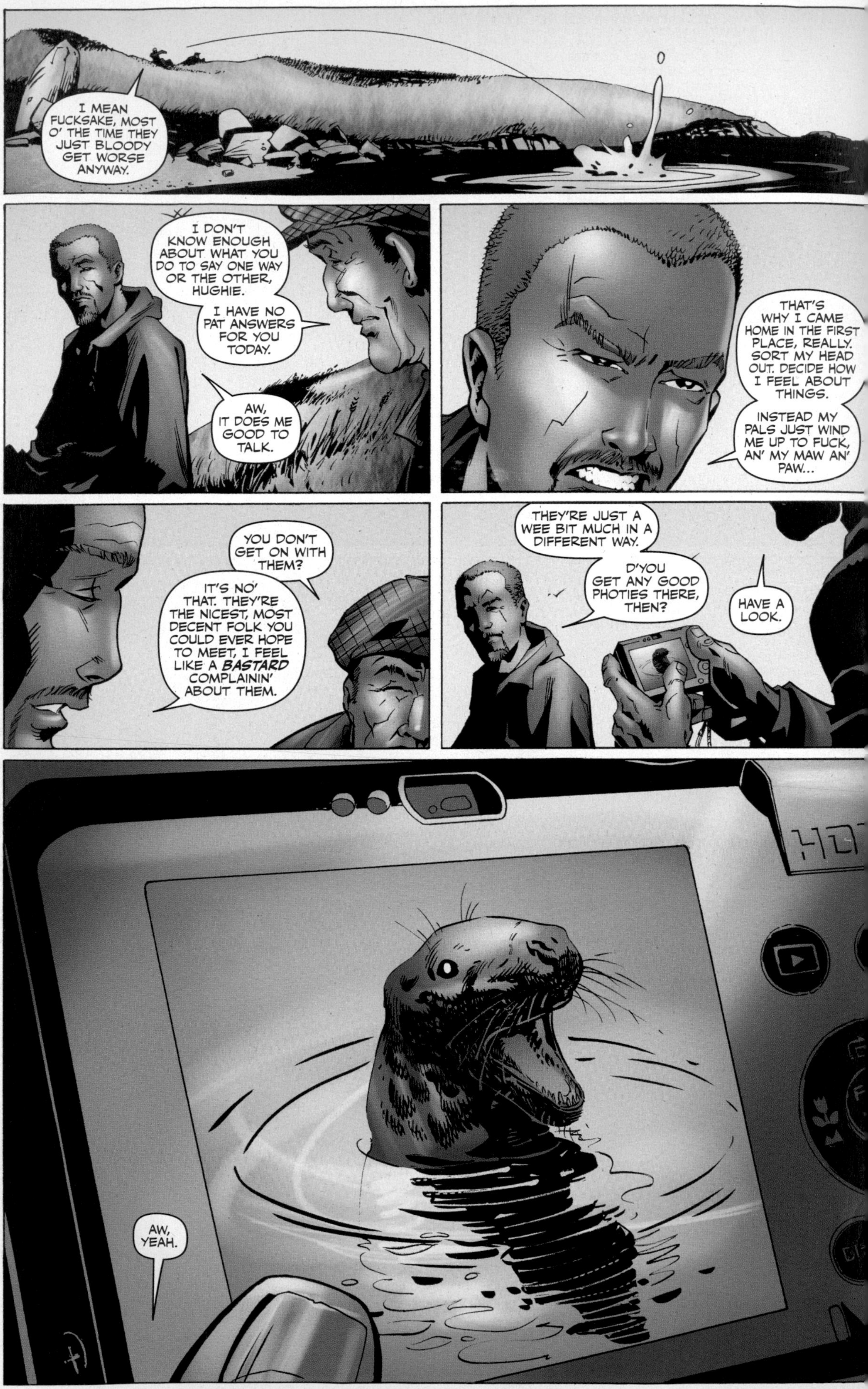
I MEAN FUCKSAKE, MOST O' THE TIME THEY JUST BLOODY GET WORSE ANYWAY.
I DON'T KNOW ENOUGH ABOUT WHAT YOU DO TO SAY ONE WAY OR THE OTHER, HUGHIE.
I HAVE NO PAT ANSWERS FOR YOU TODAY.
AW, IT DOES ME GOOD TO TALK.
THAT'S WHY I CAME HOME IN THE FIRST PLACE, REALLY. SORT MY HEAD OUT. DECIDE HOW I FEEL ABOUT THINGS.
INSTEAD MY PALS JUST WIND ME UP TO FUCK, AN' MY MAW AN' PAW...
YOU DON'T GET ON WITH THEM?
IT'S NO' THAT. THEY'RE THE NICEST, MOST DECENT FOLK YOU COULD EVER HOPE TO MEET, I FEEL LIKE A ***BASTARD*** COMPLAININ' ABOUT THEM.
THEY'RE JUST A WEE BIT MUCH IN A DIFFERENT WAY.
D'YOU GET ANY GOOD PHOTIES THERE, THEN?
HAVE A LOOK.
AW, YEAH.

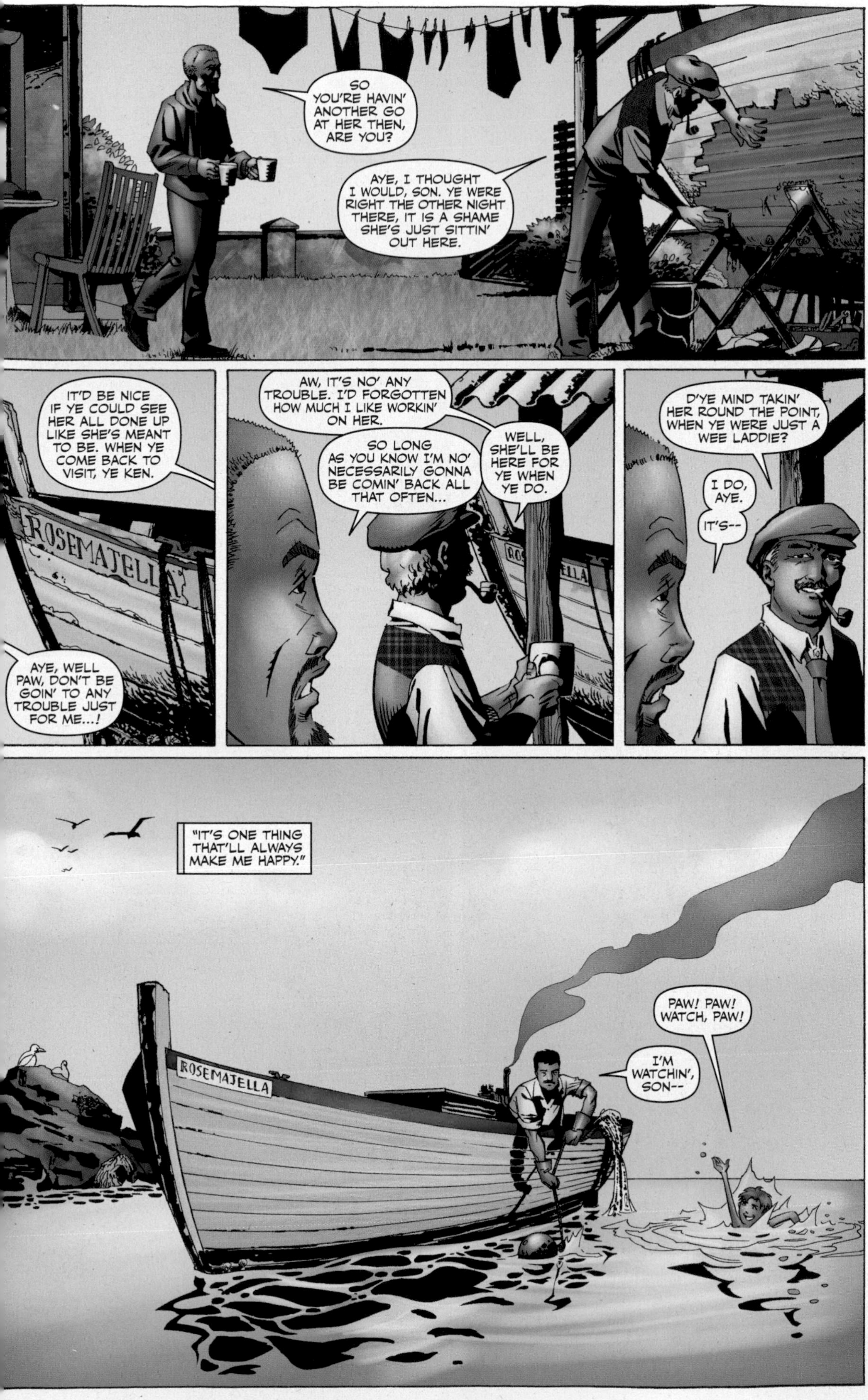
SO YOU'RE HAVIN' ANOTHER GO AT HER THEN, ARE YOU?
AYE, I THOUGHT I WOULD, SON. YE WERE RIGHT THE OTHER NIGHT THERE, IT IS A SHAME SHE'S JUST SITTIN' OUT HERE.
IT'D BE NICE IF YE COULD SEE HER ALL DONE UP LIKE SHE'S MEANT TO BE. WHEN YE COME BACK TO VISIT, YE KEN.
ROSEMAJELLA
AYE, WELL PAW, DON'T BE GOIN' TO ANY TROUBLE JUST FOR ME...!
AW, IT'S NO' ANY TROUBLE. I'D FORGOTTEN HOW MUCH I LIKE WORKIN' ON HER.
SO LONG AS YOU KNOW I'M NO' NECESSARILY GONNA BE COMIN' BACK ALL THAT OFTEN...
WELL, SHE'LL BE HERE FOR YE WHEN YE DO.
D'YE MIND TAKIN' HER ROUND THE POINT, WHEN YE WERE JUST A WEE LADDIE?
I DO, AYE.
IT'S--
"IT'S ONE THING THAT'LL ALWAYS MAKE ME HAPPY."
ROSEMAJELLA
PAW! PAW! WATCH, PAW!
I'M WATCHIN', SON--

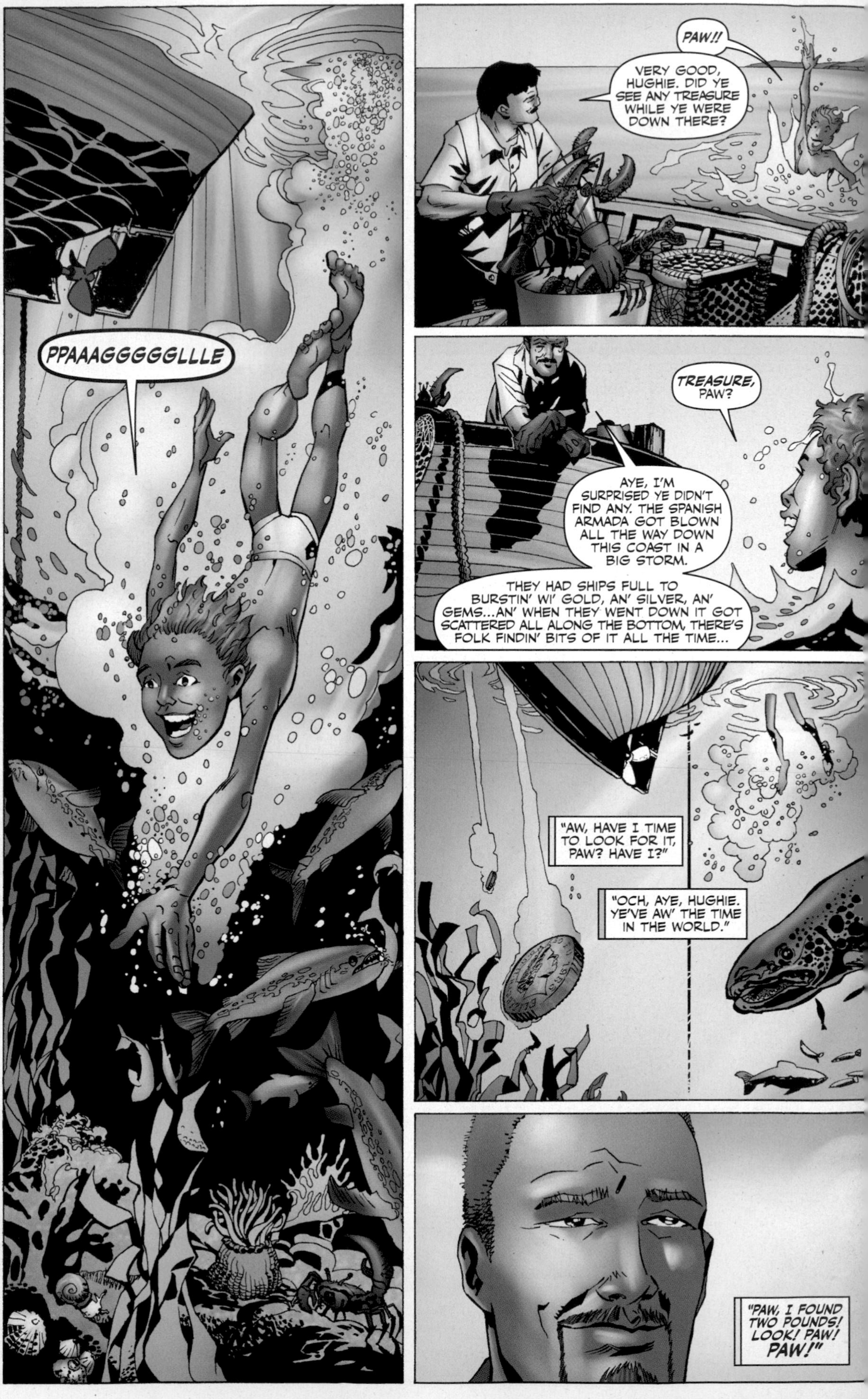
PPAAAGGGGGLLLE
PAW!!
VERY GOOD, HUGHIE. DID YE SEE ANY TREASURE WHILE YE WERE DOWN THERE?
TREASURE, PAW?
AYE, I'M SURPRISED YE DIDN'T FIND ANY. THE SPANISH ARMADA GOT BLOWN ALL THE WAY DOWN THIS COAST IN A BIG STORM.
THEY HAD SHIPS FULL TO BURSTIN' WI' GOLD, AN' SILVER, AN' GEMS...AN' WHEN THEY WENT DOWN IT GOT SCATTERED ALL ALONG THE BOTTOM, THERE'S FOLK FINDIN' BITS OF IT ALL THE TIME...
"AW, HAVE I TIME TO LOOK FOR IT, PAW? HAVE I?"
"OCH, AYE, HUGHIE. YE'VE AW' THE TIME IN THE WORLD."
"PAW, I FOUND TWO POUNDS! LOOK! PAW! PAW!"

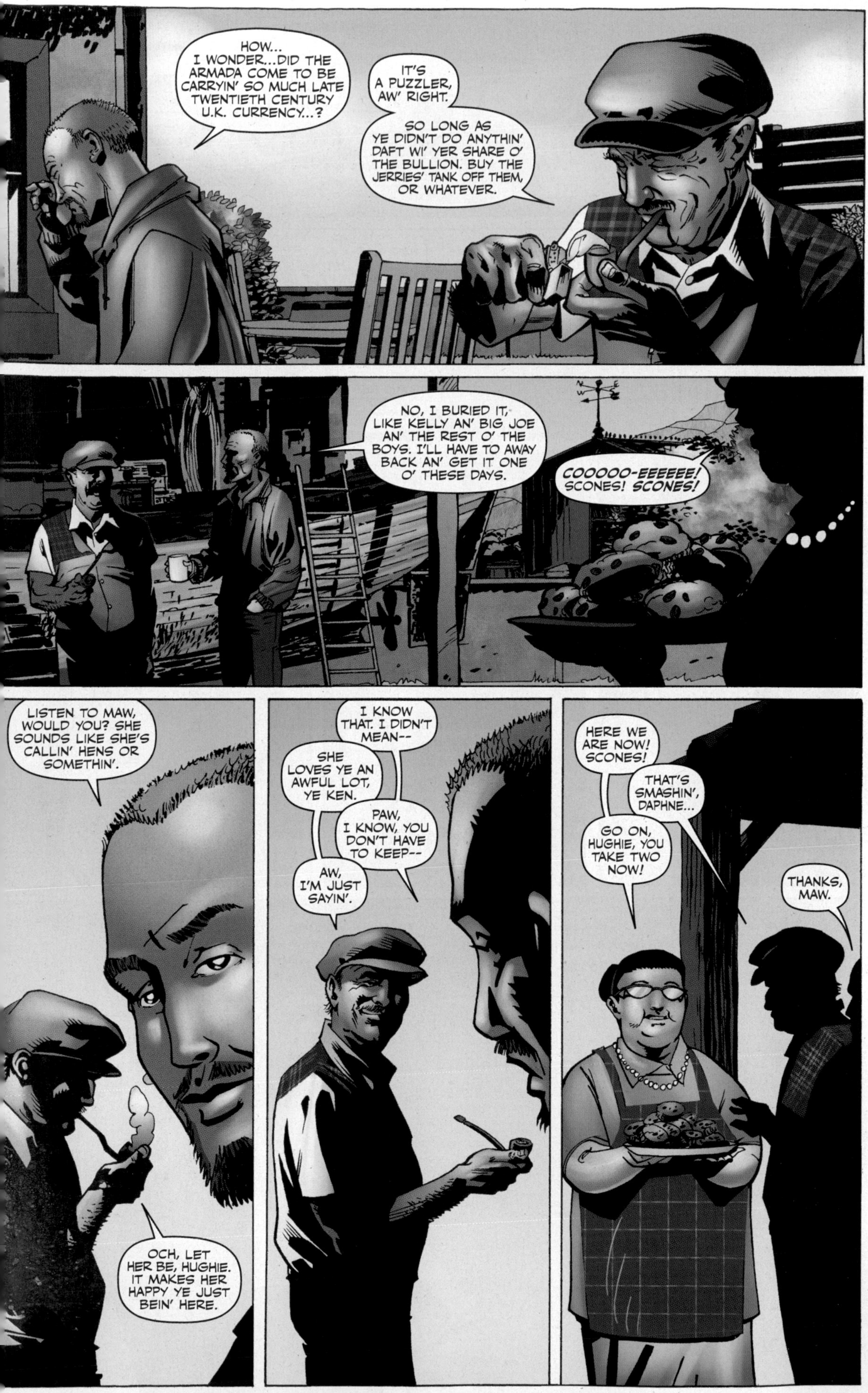
HOW... I WONDER...DID THE ARMADA COME TO BE CARRYIN' SO MUCH LATE TWENTIETH CENTURY U.K. CURRENCY...?
IT'S A PUZZLER, AW' RIGHT.
SO LONG AS YE DIDN'T DO ANYTHIN' DAFT WI' YER SHARE O' THE BULLION. BUY THE JERRIES' TANK OFF THEM, OR WHATEVER.
NO, I BURIED IT, LIKE KELLY AN' BIG JOE AN' THE REST O' THE BOYS. I'LL HAVE TO AWAY BACK AN' GET IT ONE O' THESE DAYS.
COOOOO-EEEEEE! SCONES! SCONES!
LISTEN TO MAW, WOULD YOU? SHE SOUNDS LIKE SHE'S CALLIN' HENS OR SOMETHIN'.
OCH, LET HER BE, HUGHIE. IT MAKES HER HAPPY YE JUST BEIN' HERE.
I KNOW THAT. I DIDN'T MEAN--
SHE LOVES YE AN AWFUL LOT, YE KEN.
PAW, I KNOW, YOU DON'T HAVE TO KEEP--
AW, I'M JUST SAYIN'.
HERE WE ARE NOW! SCONES!
THAT'S SMASHIN', DAPHNE...
GO ON, HUGHIE, YOU TAKE TWO NOW!
THANKS, MAW.

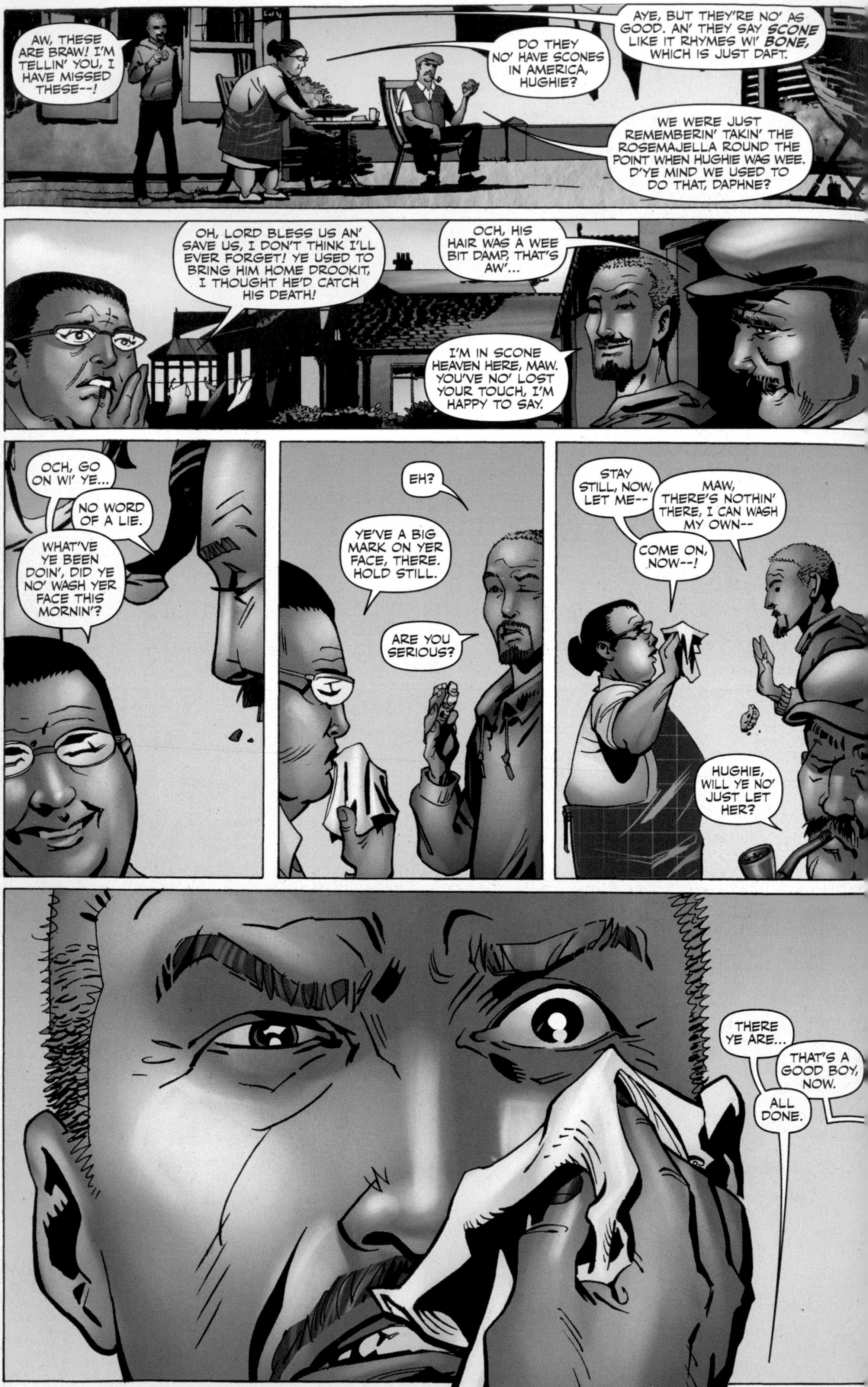
AW, THESE ARE BRAW! I'M TELLIN' YOU, I HAVE MISSED THESE--!
DO THEY NO' HAVE SCONES IN AMERICA, HUGHIE?
AYE, BUT THEY'RE NO' AS GOOD. AN' THEY SAY SCONE LIKE IT RHYMES WI' BONE, WHICH IS JUST DAFT.
WE WERE JUST REMEMBERIN' TAKIN' THE ROSEMAJELLA ROUND THE POINT WHEN HUGHIE WAS WEE. D'YE MIND WE USED TO DO THAT, DAPHNE?
OH, LORD BLESS US AN' SAVE US, I DON'T THINK I'LL EVER FORGET! YE USED TO BRING HIM HOME DROOKIT, I THOUGHT HE'D CATCH HIS DEATH!
OCH, HIS HAIR WAS A WEE BIT DAMP, THAT'S AW'...
I'M IN SCONE HEAVEN HERE, MAW. YOU'VE NO' LOST YOUR TOUCH, I'M HAPPY TO SAY.
OCH, GO ON WI' YE...
NO WORD OF A LIE.
WHAT'VE YE BEEN DOIN', DID YE NO' WASH YER FACE THIS MORNIN'?
EH?
YE'VE A BIG MARK ON YER FACE, THERE. HOLD STILL.
ARE YOU SERIOUS?
STAY STILL, NOW, LET ME--
MAW, THERE'S NOTHIN' THERE, I CAN WASH MY OWN--
COME ON, NOW--!
HUGHIE, WILL YE NO' JUST LET HER?
THERE YE ARE...
THAT'S A GOOD BOY, NOW.
ALL DONE.

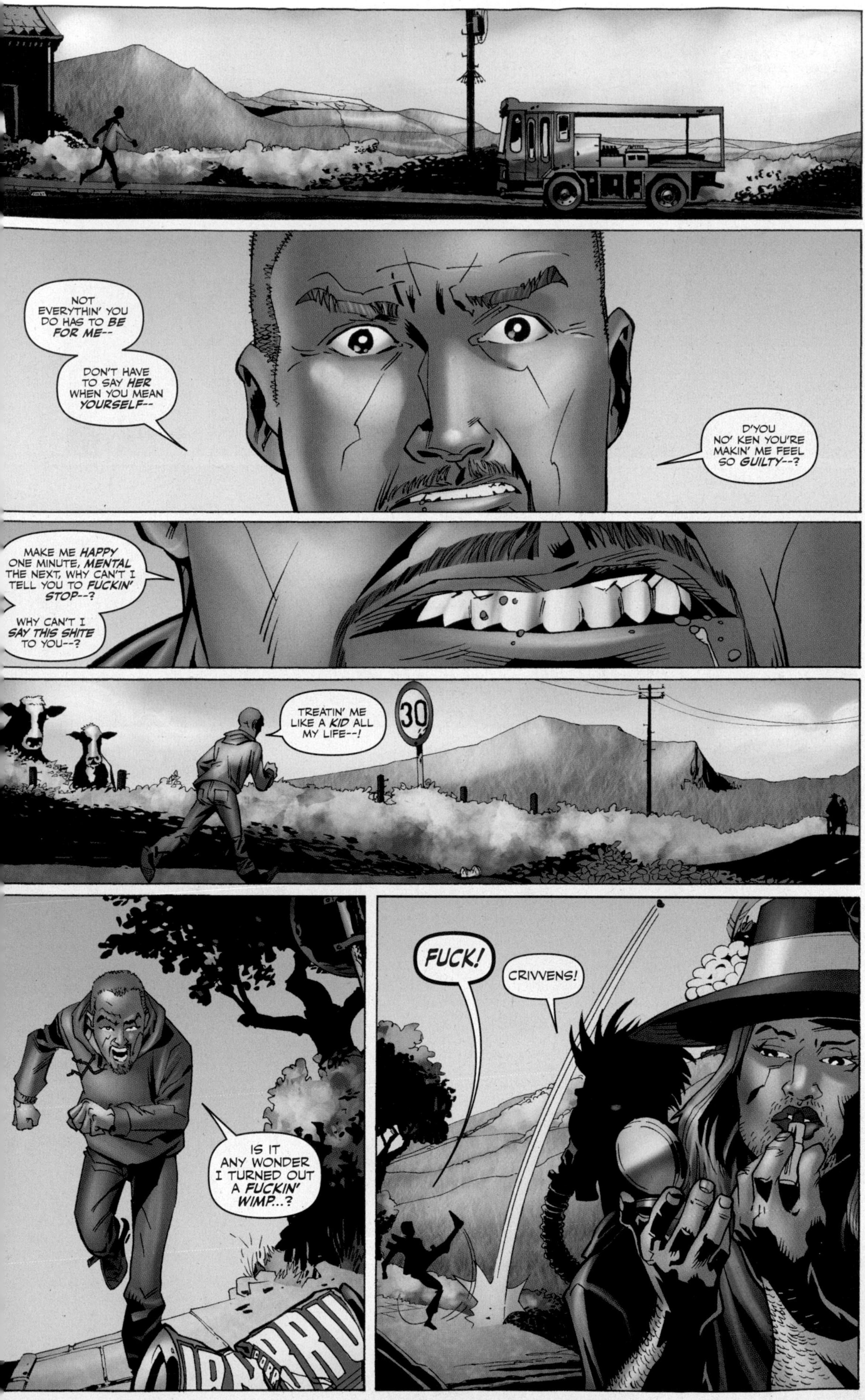

NOT EVERYTHIN' YOU DO HAS TO BE FOR ME--
DON'T HAVE TO SAY HER WHEN YOU MEAN YOURSELF--
D'YOU NO' KEN YOU'RE MAKIN' ME FEEL SO GUILTY--?
MAKE ME HAPPY ONE MINUTE, MENTAL THE NEXT, WHY CAN'T I TELL YOU TO FUCKIN' STOP--?
WHY CAN'T I SAY THIS SHITE TO YOU--?
TREATIN' ME LIKE A KID ALL MY LIFE--!
30
IS IT ANY WONDER I TURNED OUT A FUCKIN' WIMP...?
FUCK!
CRIVVENS!

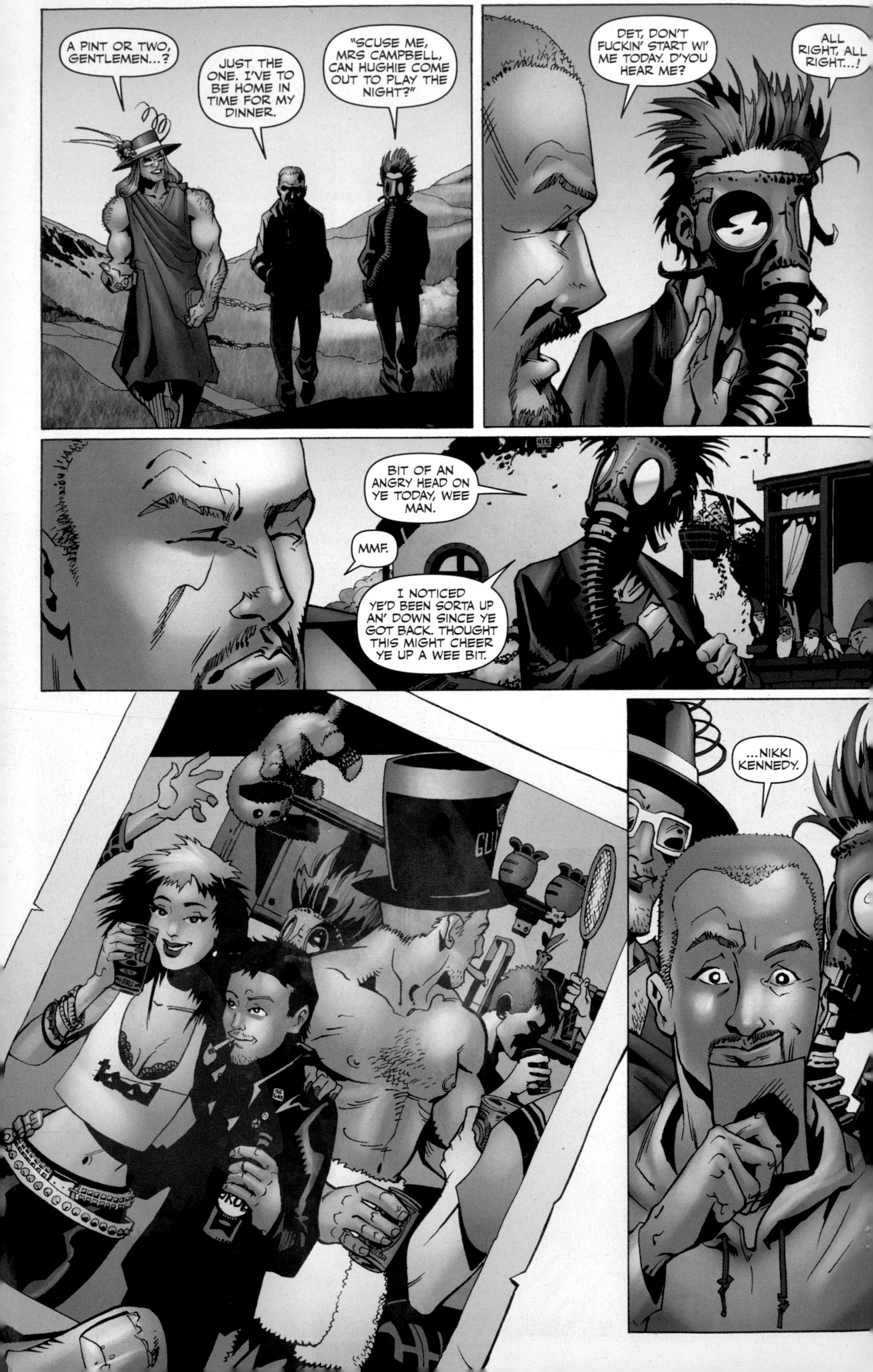
A PINT OR TWO, GENTLEMEN...?
JUST THE ONE. I'VE TO BE HOME IN TIME FOR MY DINNER.
"SCUSE ME, MRS CAMPBELL, CAN HUGHIE COME OUT TO PLAY THE NIGHT?"
DET, DON'T FUCKIN' START WI' ME TODAY. D'YOU HEAR ME?
ALL RIGHT, ALL RIGHT...!
BIT OF AN ANGRY HEAD ON YE TODAY, WEE MAN.
MMF.
I NOTICED YE'D BEEN SORTA UP AN' DOWN SINCE YE GOT BACK. THOUGHT THIS MIGHT CHEER YE UP A WEE BIT.
...NIKKI KENNEDY.

HOW...?

I FOUND IT LAST YEAR, I WAS HOKIN' THROUGH SOME STUFF FROM SCHOOL. HELD ONTO IT FOR THE NEXT TIME I SAW YE.

DID YOU EVER ACTUALLY SHAG HER?

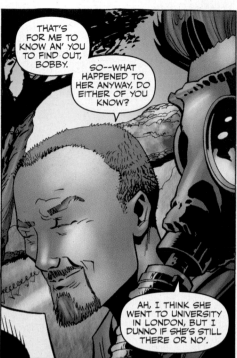

THAT'S FOR ME TO KNOW AN' YOU TO FIND OUT, BOBBY.

SO--WHAT HAPPENED TO HER ANYWAY, DO EITHER OF YOU KNOW?

AH, I THINK SHE WENT TO UNIVERSITY IN LONDON, BUT I DUNNO IF SHE'S STILL THERE OR NO'.

TRY FACEBOOK, OR FRIENDS REUNITED OR WHATEVER...

AW, THAT THING'S FOR WANKERS. WHY THE FUCK WOULD I WANNA BE REUNITED WI' SOME CUNT, AFTER I'VE GONE TO AW' THE TROUBLE O' LOSIN' TOUCH WI' THEM?

I'LL MAYBE DO THAT, DET. YOU NEVER KNOW.

WELL ANYONE REUNITED WI' YOU'S IN FOR A PRETTY MASSIVE FUCKIN' SHOCK, AREN'T THEY?

I'M SERIOUS. THE ONLY FOLK I CARE ABOUT, I KNOW EXACTLY HOW TO GET HOLD O' THEM.

FUCKSAKE, LOOK AT HUGHIE. THE FUTURE'S BRIGHT WI' GLITTERIN' POSSIBILITIES...

OCH, I DON'T BLAME HIM. SHE WAS A BONNY LASSIE.

SHE WAS, AYE.

SHE...

SHE WAS SOME GIRL.

THE BOYS...!

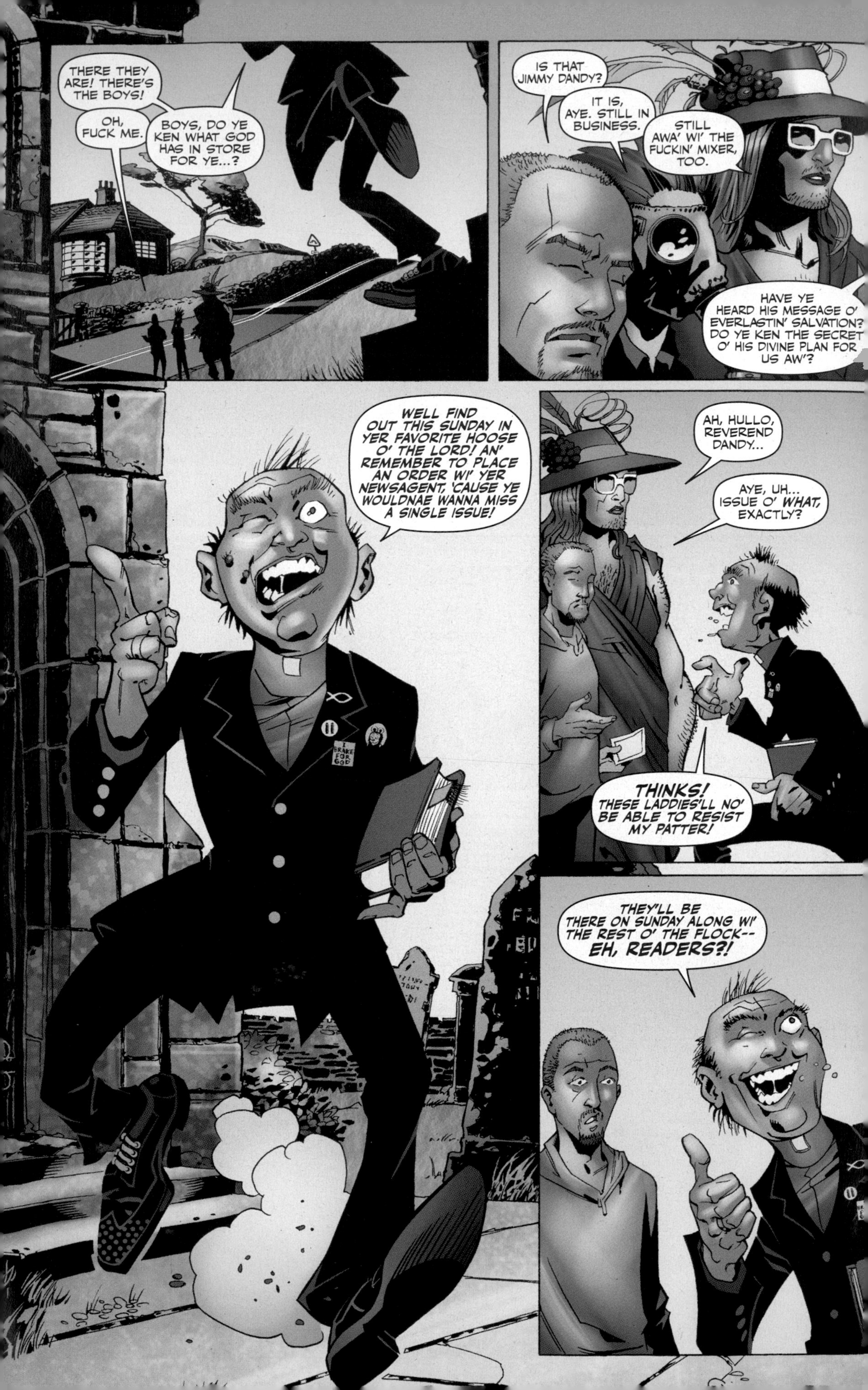
THERE THEY ARE! THERE'S THE BOYS!
OH, FUCK ME.
BOYS, DO YE KEN WHAT GOD HAS IN STORE FOR YE...?
IS THAT JIMMY DANDY?
IT IS, AYE. STILL IN BUSINESS.
STILL AWA' WI' THE FUCKIN' MIXER, TOO.
HAVE YE HEARD HIS MESSAGE O' EVERLASTIN' SALVATION? DO YE KEN THE SECRET O' HIS DIVINE PLAN FOR US AW'?
WELL FIND OUT THIS SUNDAY IN YER FAVORITE HOOSE O' THE LORD! AN' REMEMBER TO PLACE AN ORDER WI' YER NEWSAGENT, 'CAUSE YE WOULDNAE WANNA MISS A SINGLE ISSUE!
I BRAKE FOR GOD
AH, HULLO, REVEREND DANDY...
AYE, UH... ISSUE O' WHAT, EXACTLY?
THINKS! THESE LADDIES'LL NO' BE ABLE TO RESIST MY PATTER!
THEY'LL BE THERE ON SUNDAY ALONG WI' THE REST O' THE FLOCK-- EH, READERS?!

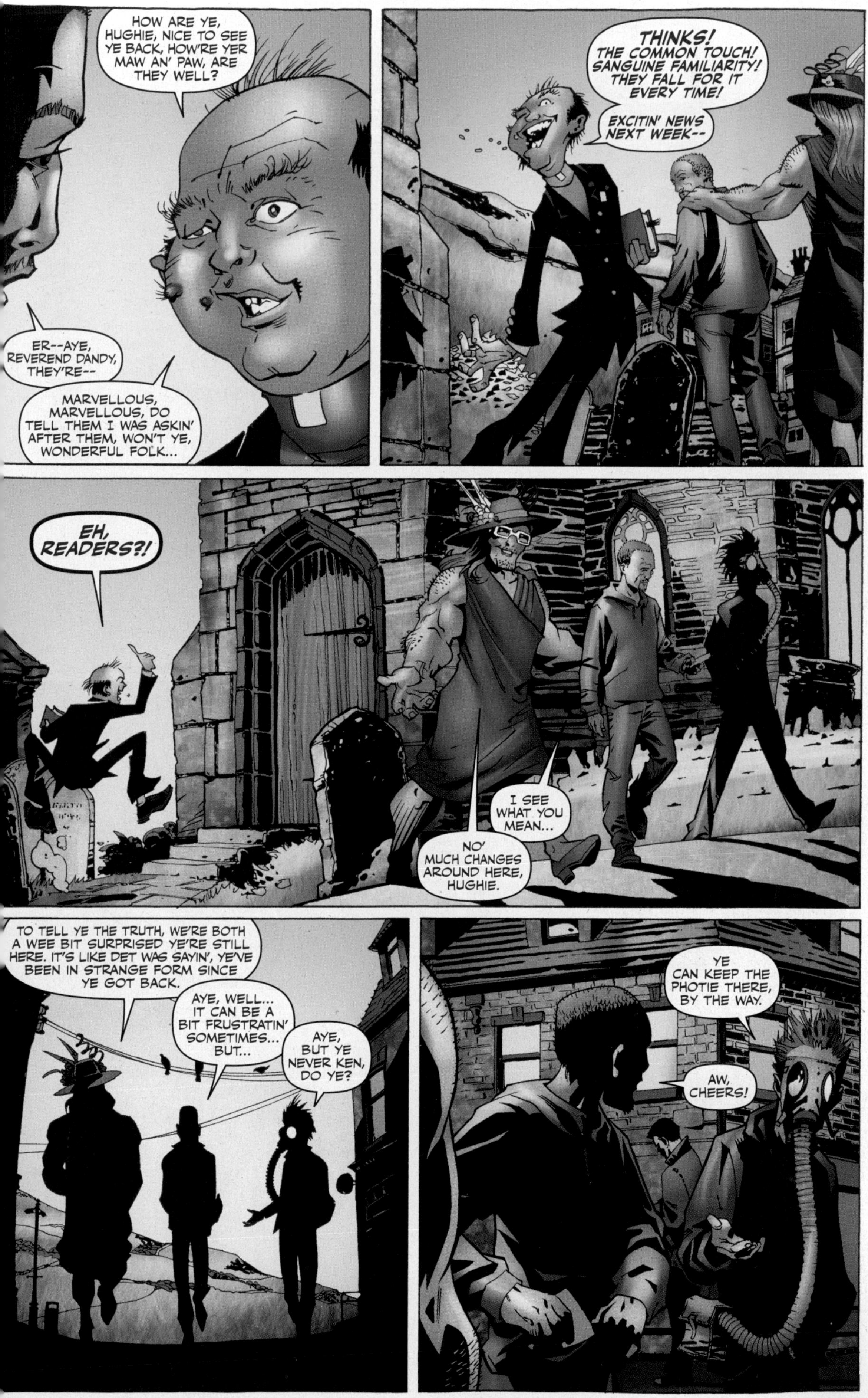
HOW ARE YE, HUGHIE, NICE TO SEE YE BACK, HOW'RE YER MAW AN' PAW, ARE THEY WELL?
ER--AYE, REVEREND DANDY, THEY'RE--
MARVELLOUS, MARVELLOUS, DO TELL THEM I WAS ASKIN' AFTER THEM, WON'T YE, WONDERFUL FOLK...
THINKS! THE COMMON TOUCH! SANGUINE FAMILIARITY! THEY FALL FOR IT EVERY TIME!
EXCITIN' NEWS NEXT WEEK--
EH, READERS?!
I SEE WHAT YOU MEAN...
NO' MUCH CHANGES AROUND HERE, HUGHIE.
TO TELL YE THE TRUTH, WE'RE BOTH A WEE BIT SURPRISED YE'RE STILL HERE. IT'S LIKE DET WAS SAYIN', YE'VE BEEN IN STRANGE FORM SINCE YE GOT BACK.
AYE, WELL... IT CAN BE A BIT FRUSTRATIN' SOMETIMES... BUT...
AYE, BUT YE NEVER KEN, DO YE?
YE CAN KEEP THE PHOTIE THERE, BY THE WAY.
AW, CHEERS!

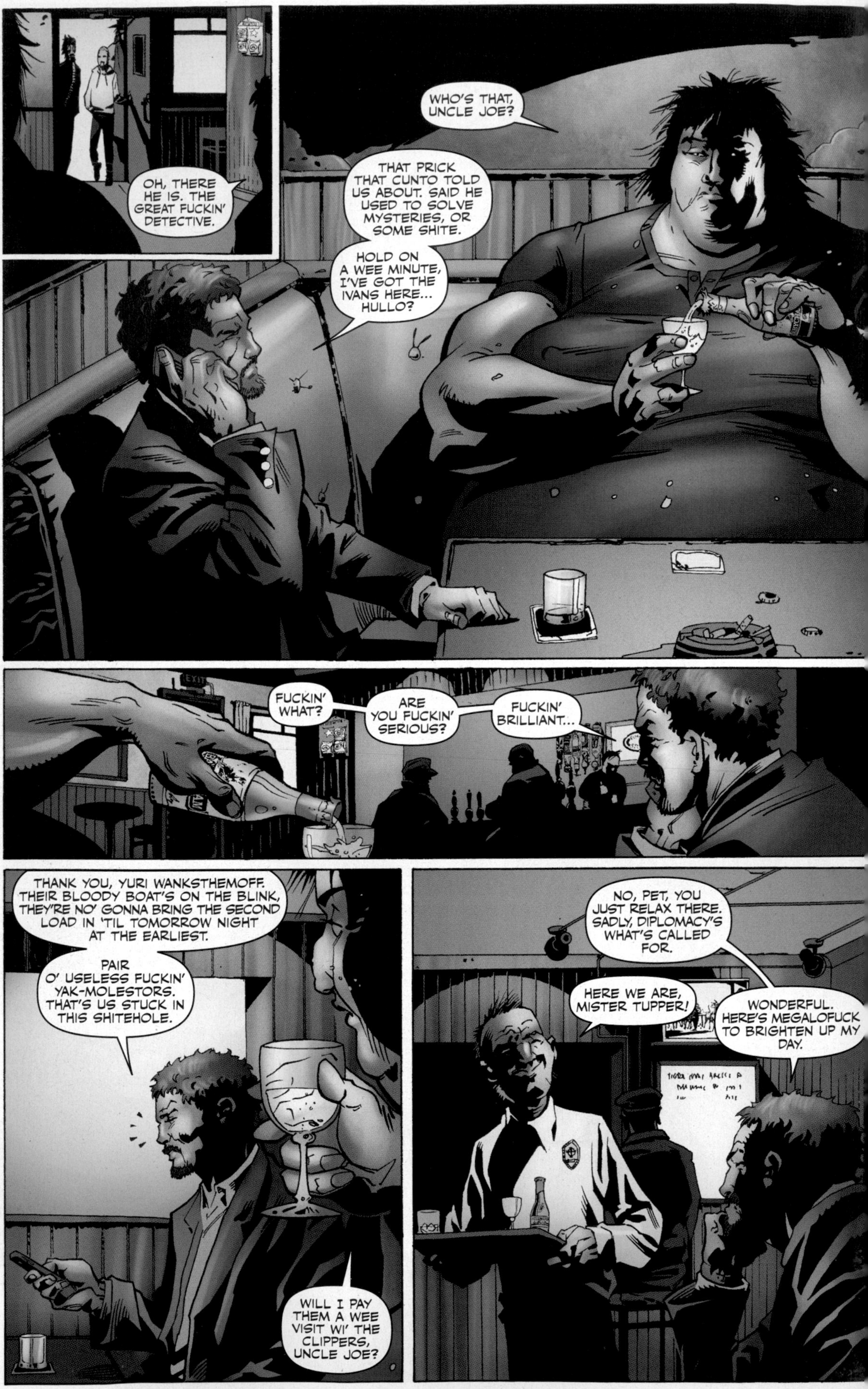
OH, THERE HE IS. THE GREAT FUCKIN' DETECTIVE.
WHO'S THAT, UNCLE JOE?
THAT PRICK THAT CUNTO TOLD US ABOUT. SAID HE USED TO SOLVE MYSTERIES, OR SOME SHITE.
HOLD ON A WEE MINUTE, I'VE GOT THE IVANS HERE... HULLO?
FUCKIN' WHAT?
ARE YOU FUCKIN' SERIOUS?
FUCKIN' BRILLIANT...
THANK YOU, YURI WANKSTHEMOFF. THEIR BLOODY BOAT'S ON THE BLINK, THEY'RE NO' GONNA BRING THE SECOND LOAD IN 'TIL TOMORROW NIGHT AT THE EARLIEST.
PAIR O' USELESS FUCKIN' YAK-MOLESTORS. THAT'S US STUCK IN THIS SHITEHOLE.
WILL I PAY THEM A WEE VISIT WI' THE CLIPPERS, UNCLE JOE?
NO, PET, YOU JUST RELAX THERE. SADLY, DIPLOMACY'S WHAT'S CALLED FOR.
HERE WE ARE, MISTER TUPPER!
WONDERFUL. HERE'S MEGALOFUCK TO BRIGHTEN UP MY DAY.

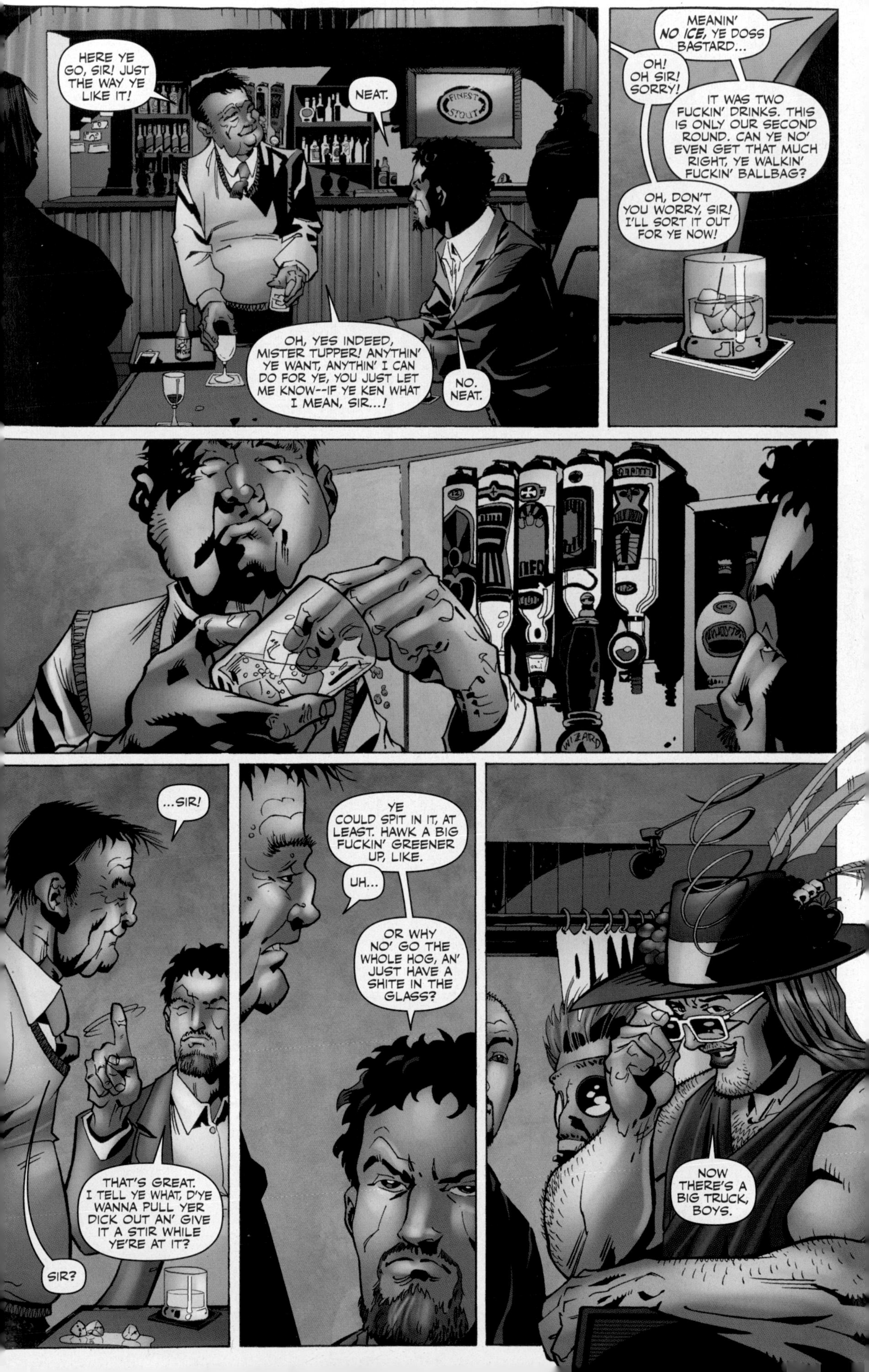
HERE YE GO, SIR! JUST THE WAY YE LIKE IT!
NEAT.
OH, YES INDEED, MISTER TUPPER! ANYTHIN' YE WANT, ANYTHIN' I CAN DO FOR YE, YOU JUST LET ME KNOW--IF YE KEN WHAT I MEAN, SIR...!
NO. NEAT.
FINEST STOUT
MEANIN' NO ICE, YE DOSS BASTARD...
OH! OH SIR! SORRY!
IT WAS TWO FUCKIN' DRINKS. THIS IS ONLY OUR SECOND ROUND. CAN YE NO' EVEN GET THAT MUCH RIGHT, YE WALKIN' FUCKIN' BALLBAG?
OH, DON'T YOU WORRY, SIR! I'LL SORT IT OUT FOR YE NOW!
WIZARD
...SIR!
THAT'S GREAT. I TELL YE WHAT, D'YE WANNA PULL YER DICK OUT AN' GIVE IT A STIR WHILE YE'RE AT IT?
SIR?
YE COULD SPIT IN IT, AT LEAST. HAWK A BIG FUCKIN' GREENER UP, LIKE.
UH...
OR WHY NO' GO THE WHOLE HOG, AN' JUST HAVE A SHITE IN THE GLASS?
NOW THERE'S A BIG TRUCK, BOYS.

WHO? *HER?*

THE FUCKIN' BRONTO WI' BEEZER'S PAL?

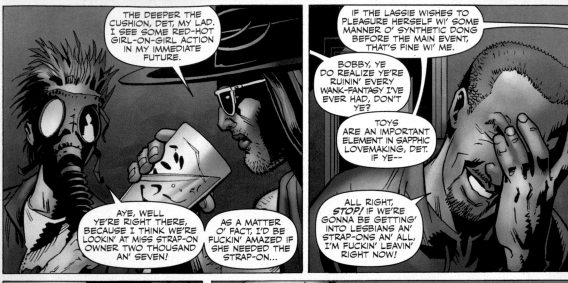

THE DEEPER THE CUSHION, DET, MY LAD. I SEE SOME RED-HOT GIRL-ON-GIRL ACTION IN MY IMMEDIATE FUTURE.

AYE, WELL YE'RE RIGHT THERE, BECAUSE I THINK WE'RE LOOKIN' AT MISS STRAP-ON OWNER TWO THOUSAND AN' SEVEN!

AS A MATTER O' FACT, I'D BE FUCKIN' AMAZED IF SHE NEEDED THE STRAP-ON...

IF THE LASSIE WISHES TO PLEASURE HERSELF WI' SOME MANNER O' SYNTHETIC DONG BEFORE THE MAIN EVENT, THAT'S FINE WI' ME.

BOBBY, YE DO REALIZE YE'RE RUININ' EVERY WANK-FANTASY I'VE EVER HAD, DON'T YE?

TOYS ARE AN IMPORTANT ELEMENT IN SAPPHIC LOVEMAKING, DET. IF YE--

ALL RIGHT, *STOP!* IF WE'RE GONNA BE GETTIN' INTO LESBIANS AN' STRAP-ONS AN' ALL, I'M FUCKIN' LEAVIN' RIGHT NOW!

"LINES YE DON'T HEAR VERY FUCKIN' OFTEN..."

HA!!

HA HA HA HA, YE PAIR O' WANKERS--!

ALL RIGHT, FUCK IT, I'M GETTIN' ANOTHER ROUND IN! DINNER CAN BLOODY WELL WAIT!

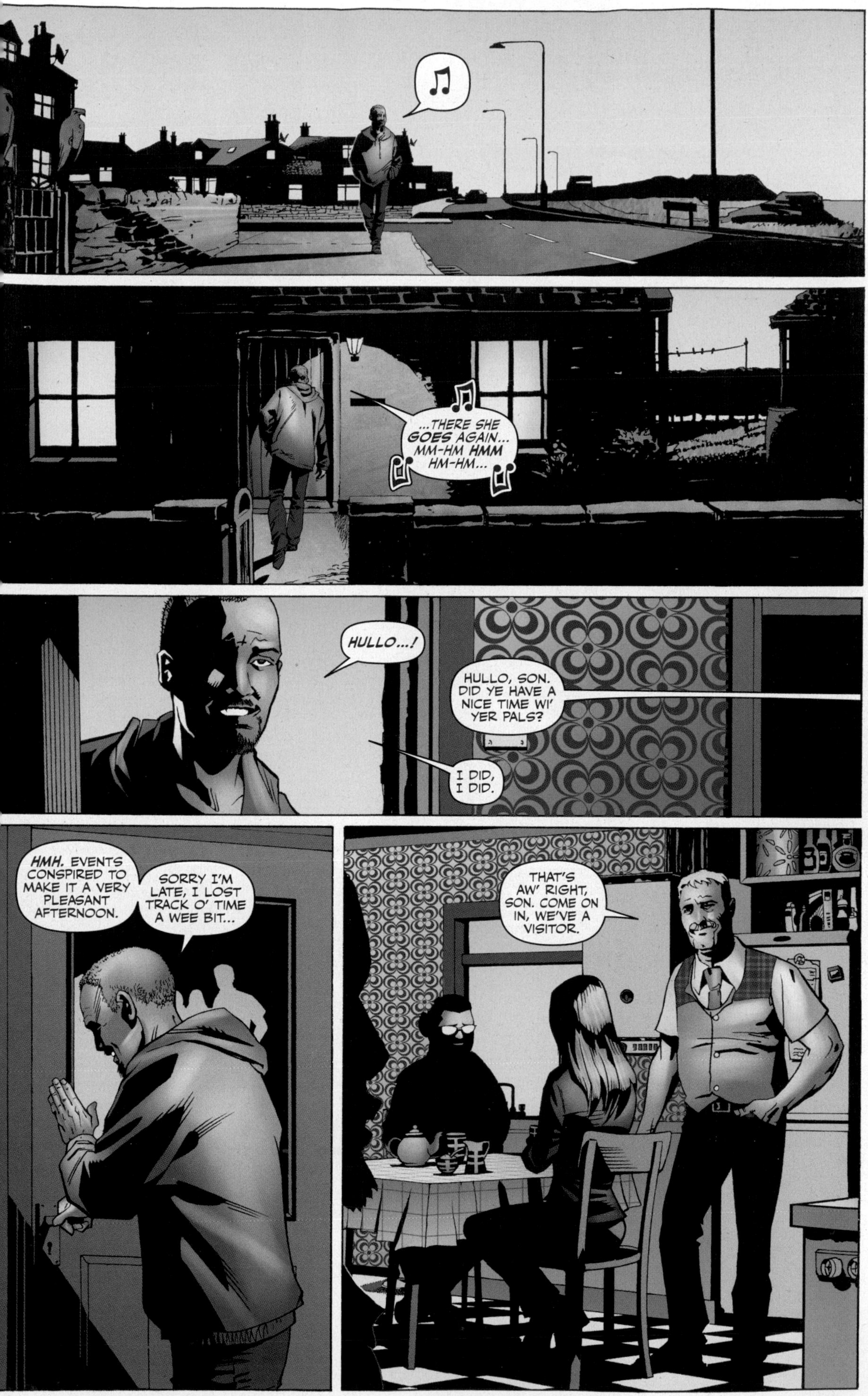
♫
...THERE SHE GOES AGAIN... MM-HM HMM HM-HM...
HULLO...!
HULLO, SON. DID YE HAVE A NICE TIME WI' YER PALS?
I DID, I DID.
HMH. EVENTS CONSPIRED TO MAKE IT A VERY PLEASANT AFTERNOON.
SORRY I'M LATE, I LOST TRACK O' TIME A WEE BIT...
THAT'S AW' RIGHT, SON. COME ON IN, WE'VE A VISITOR.

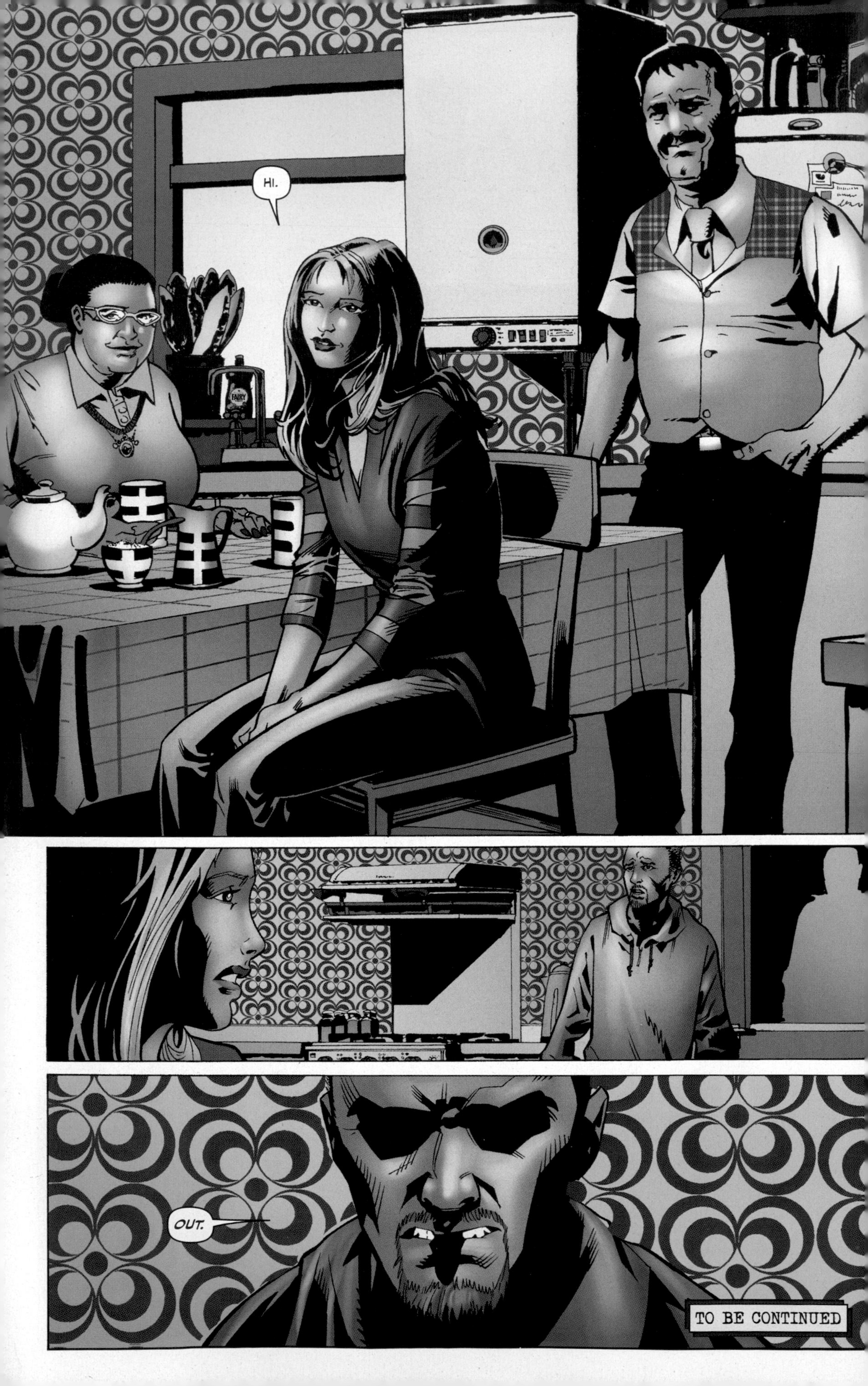
HI.
OUT.
TO BE CONTINUED

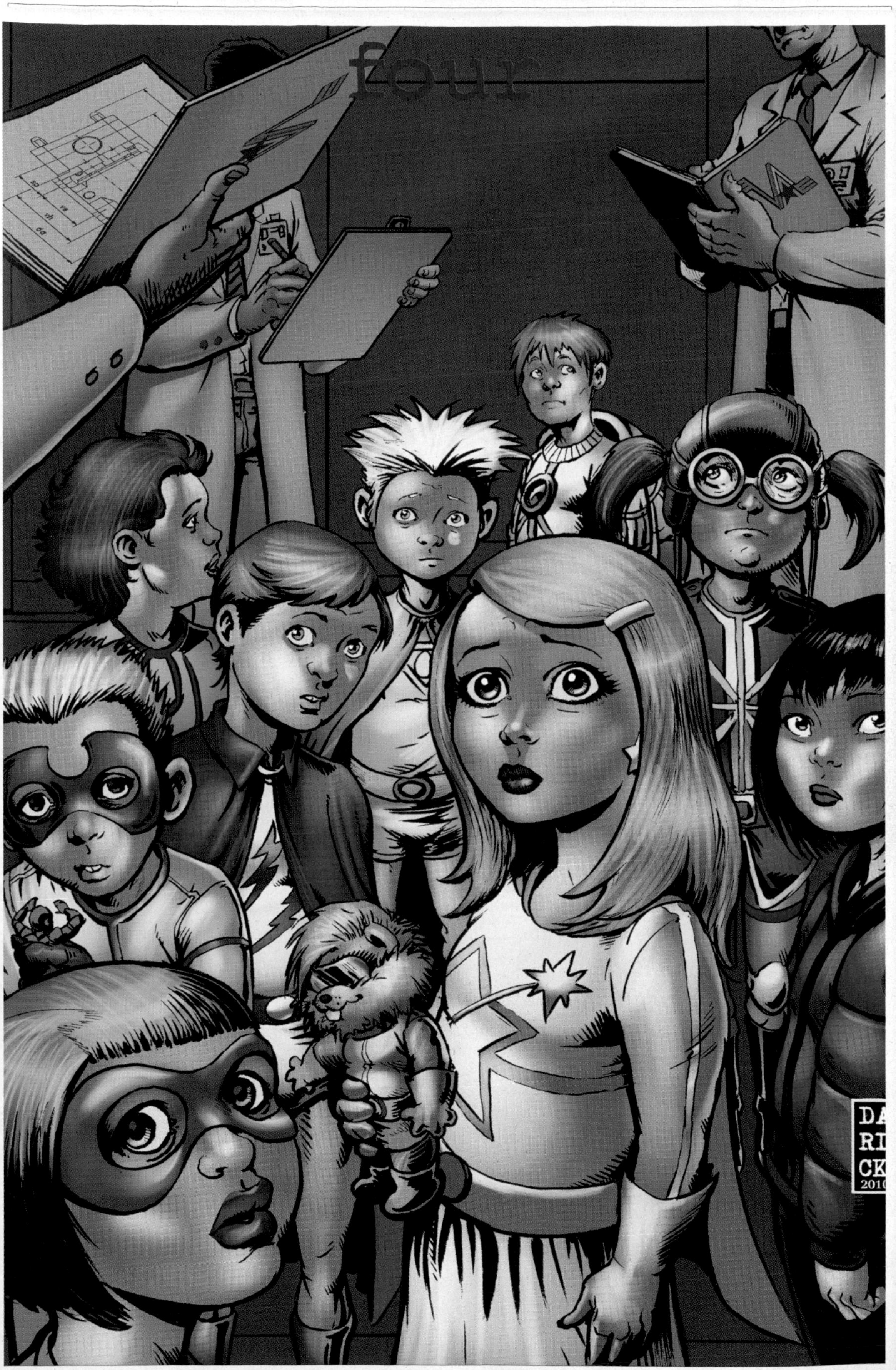
four
DA
RI
CK
2010

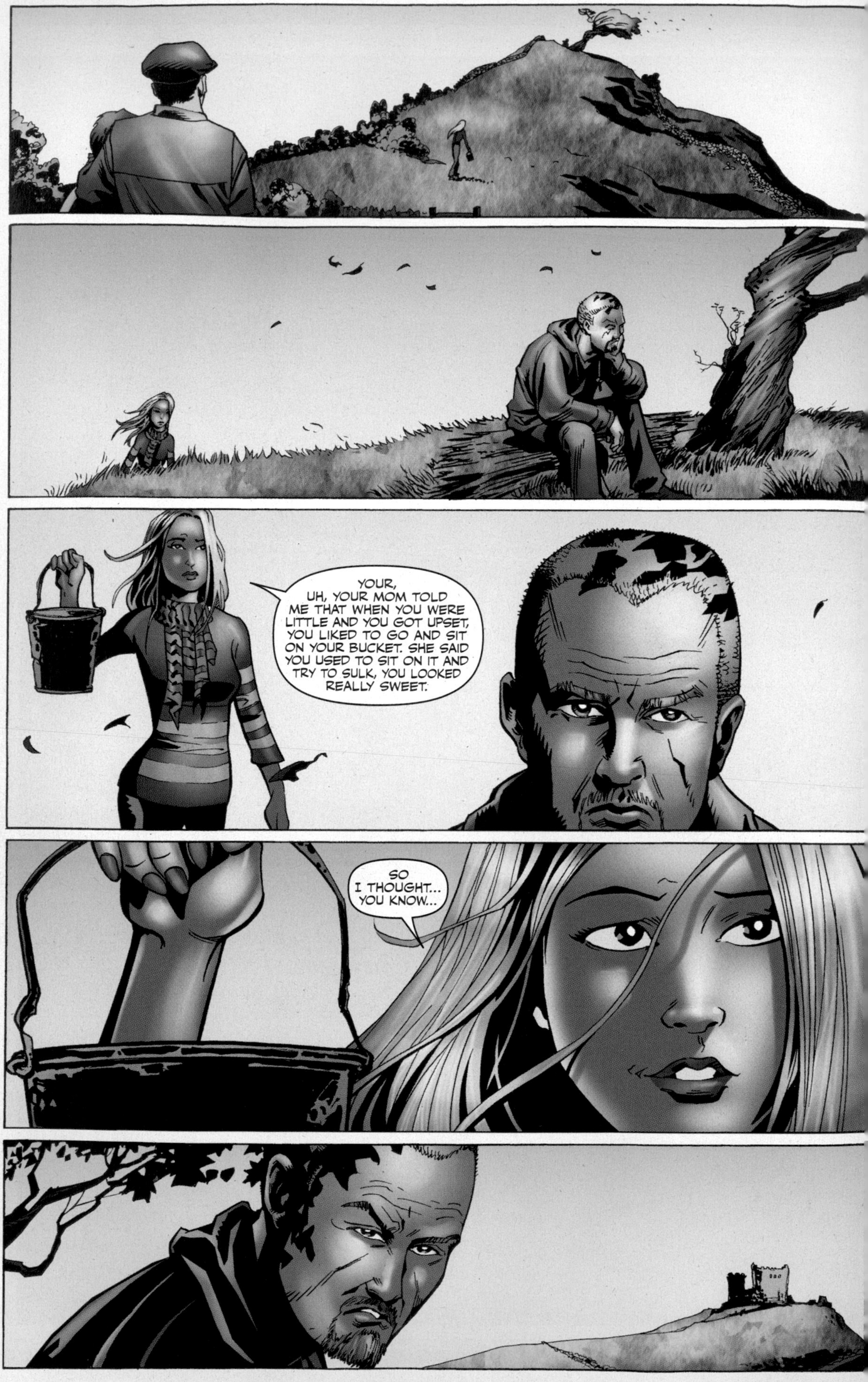
YOUR, UH, YOUR MOM TOLD ME THAT WHEN YOU WERE LITTLE AND YOU GOT UPSET, YOU LIKED TO GO AND SIT ON YOUR BUCKET. SHE SAID YOU USED TO SIT ON IT AND TRY TO SULK, YOU LOOKED REALLY SWEET.
SO I THOUGHT... YOU KNOW...

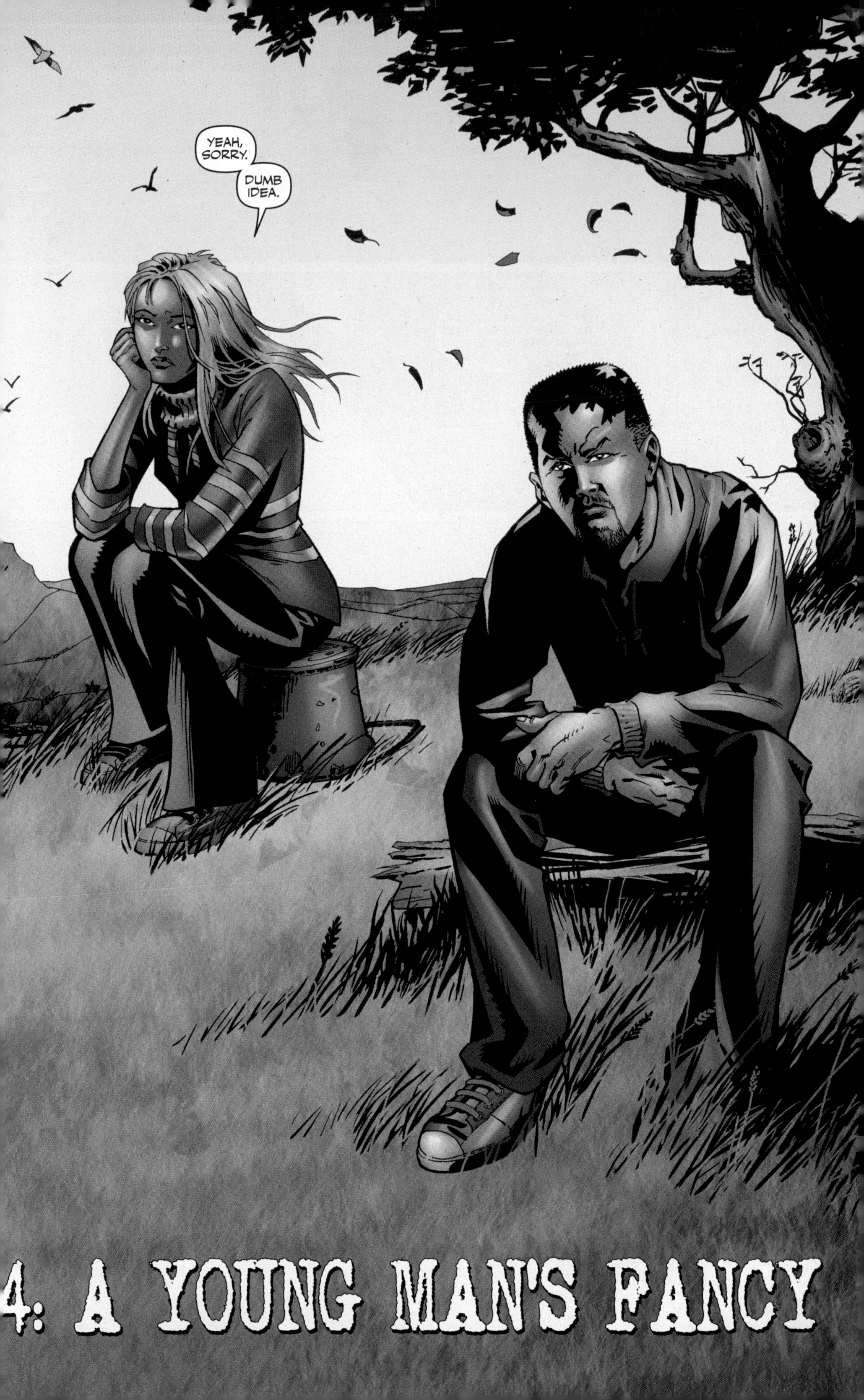
YEAH, SORRY.
DUMB IDEA.

4: A YOUNG MAN'S FANCY

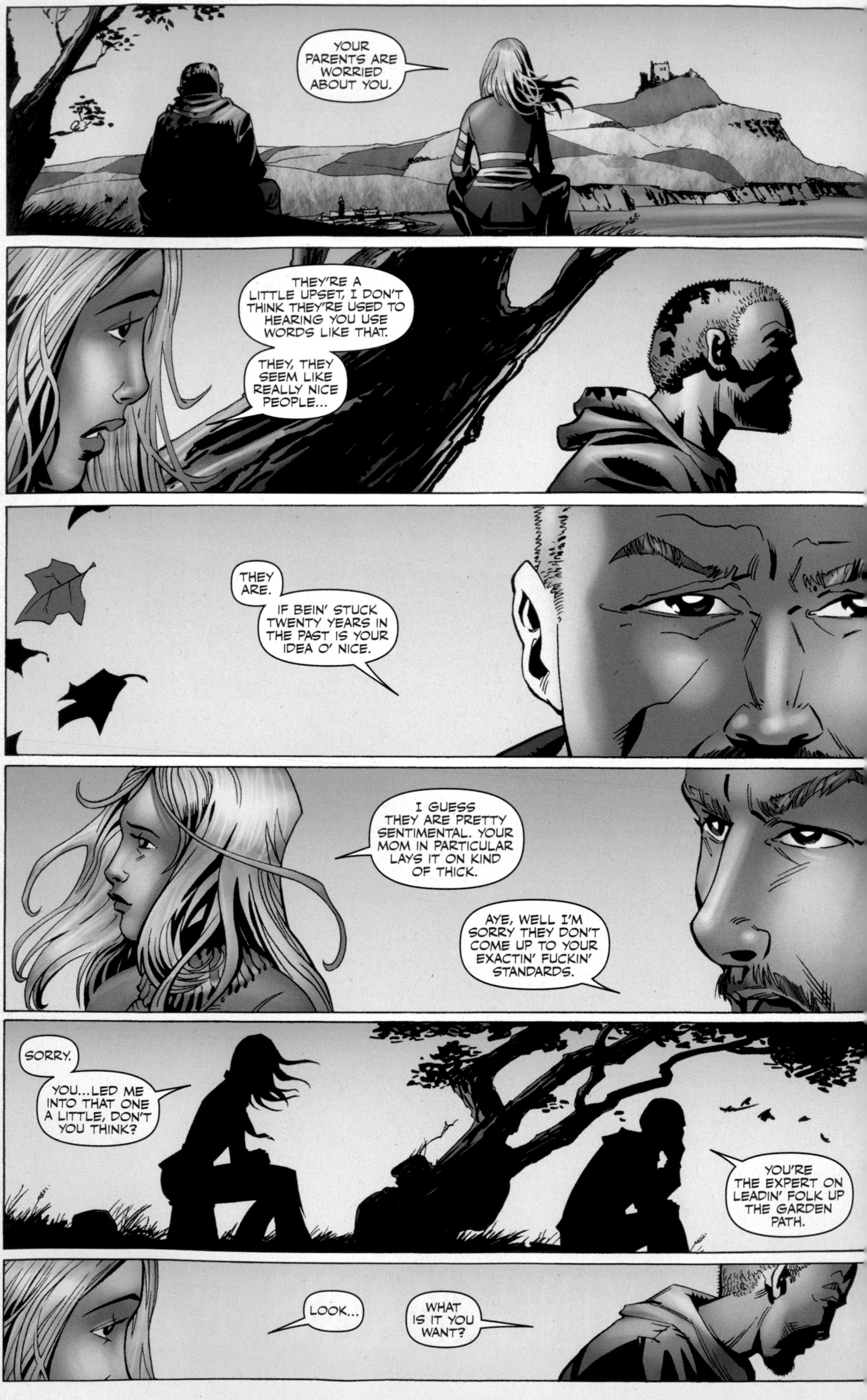
YOUR PARENTS ARE WORRIED ABOUT YOU.
THEY'RE A LITTLE UPSET, I DON'T THINK THEY'RE USED TO HEARING YOU USE WORDS LIKE THAT.
THEY, THEY SEEM LIKE REALLY NICE PEOPLE...
THEY ARE.
IF BEIN' STUCK TWENTY YEARS IN THE PAST IS YOUR IDEA O' NICE.
I GUESS THEY ARE PRETTY SENTIMENTAL. YOUR MOM IN PARTICULAR LAYS IT ON KIND OF THICK.
AYE, WELL I'M SORRY THEY DON'T COME UP TO YOUR EXACTIN' FUCKIN' STANDARDS.
SORRY.
YOU...LED ME INTO THAT ONE A LITTLE, DON'T YOU THINK?
YOU'RE THE EXPERT ON LEADIN' FOLK UP THE GARDEN PATH.
LOOK...
WHAT IS IT YOU WANT?

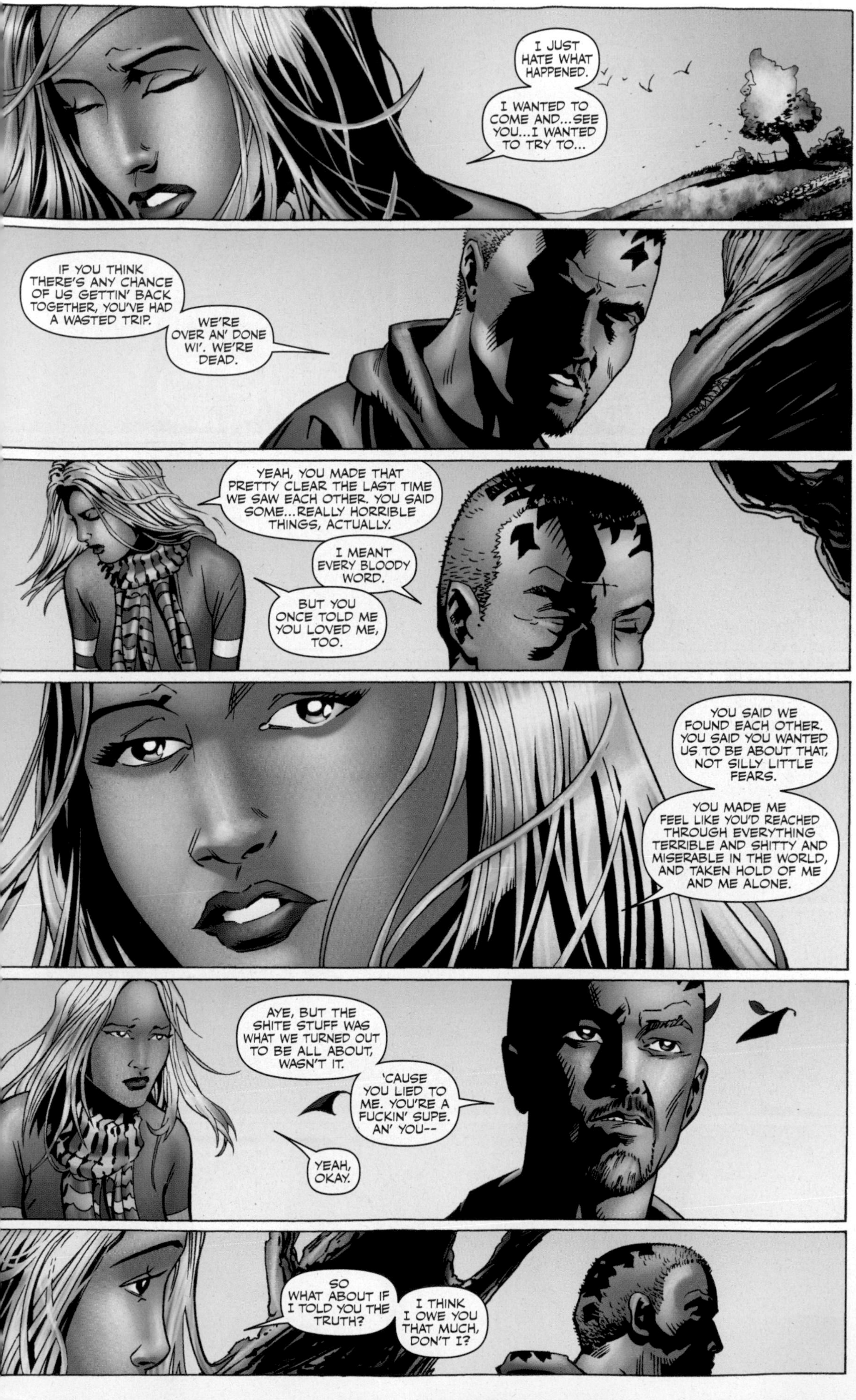
I JUST HATE WHAT HAPPENED.
I WANTED TO COME AND...SEE YOU...I WANTED TO TRY TO...
IF YOU THINK THERE'S ANY CHANCE OF US GETTIN' BACK TOGETHER, YOU'VE HAD A WASTED TRIP.
WE'RE OVER AN' DONE WI'. WE'RE DEAD.
YEAH, YOU MADE THAT PRETTY CLEAR THE LAST TIME WE SAW EACH OTHER. YOU SAID SOME...REALLY HORRIBLE THINGS, ACTUALLY.
I MEANT EVERY BLOODY WORD.
BUT YOU ONCE TOLD ME YOU LOVED ME, TOO.
YOU SAID WE FOUND EACH OTHER. YOU SAID YOU WANTED US TO BE ABOUT THAT, NOT SILLY LITTLE FEARS.
YOU MADE ME FEEL LIKE YOU'D REACHED THROUGH EVERYTHING TERRIBLE AND SHITTY AND MISERABLE IN THE WORLD, AND TAKEN HOLD OF ME AND ME ALONE.
AYE, BUT THE SHITE STUFF WAS WHAT WE TURNED OUT TO BE ALL ABOUT, WASN'T IT.
'CAUSE YOU LIED TO ME. YOU'RE A FUCKIN' SUPE. AN' YOU--
YEAH, OKAY.
SO WHAT ABOUT IF I TOLD YOU THE TRUTH?
I THINK I OWE YOU THAT MUCH, DON'T I?

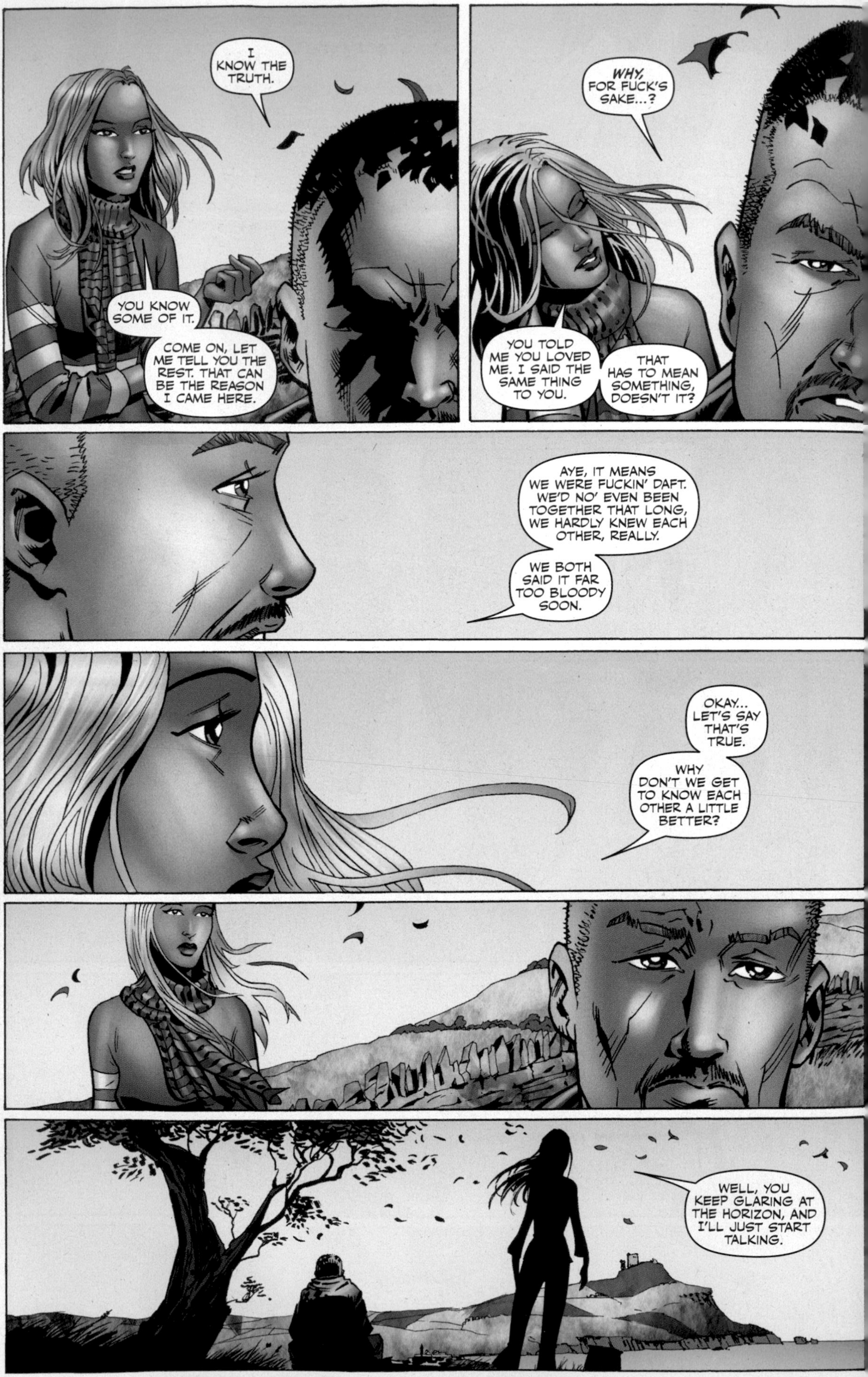
I KNOW THE TRUTH.
YOU KNOW SOME OF IT.
COME ON, LET ME TELL YOU THE REST. THAT CAN BE THE REASON I CAME HERE.
WHY, FOR FUCK'S SAKE...?
YOU TOLD ME YOU LOVED ME. I SAID THE SAME THING TO YOU.
THAT HAS TO MEAN SOMETHING, DOESN'T IT?
AYE, IT MEANS WE WERE FUCKIN' DAFT. WE'D NO' EVEN BEEN TOGETHER THAT LONG, WE HARDLY KNEW EACH OTHER, REALLY.
WE BOTH SAID IT FAR TOO BLOODY SOON.
OKAY... LET'S SAY THAT'S TRUE.
WHY DON'T WE GET TO KNOW EACH OTHER A LITTLE BETTER?
WELL, YOU KEEP GLARING AT THE HORIZON, AND I'LL JUST START TALKING.

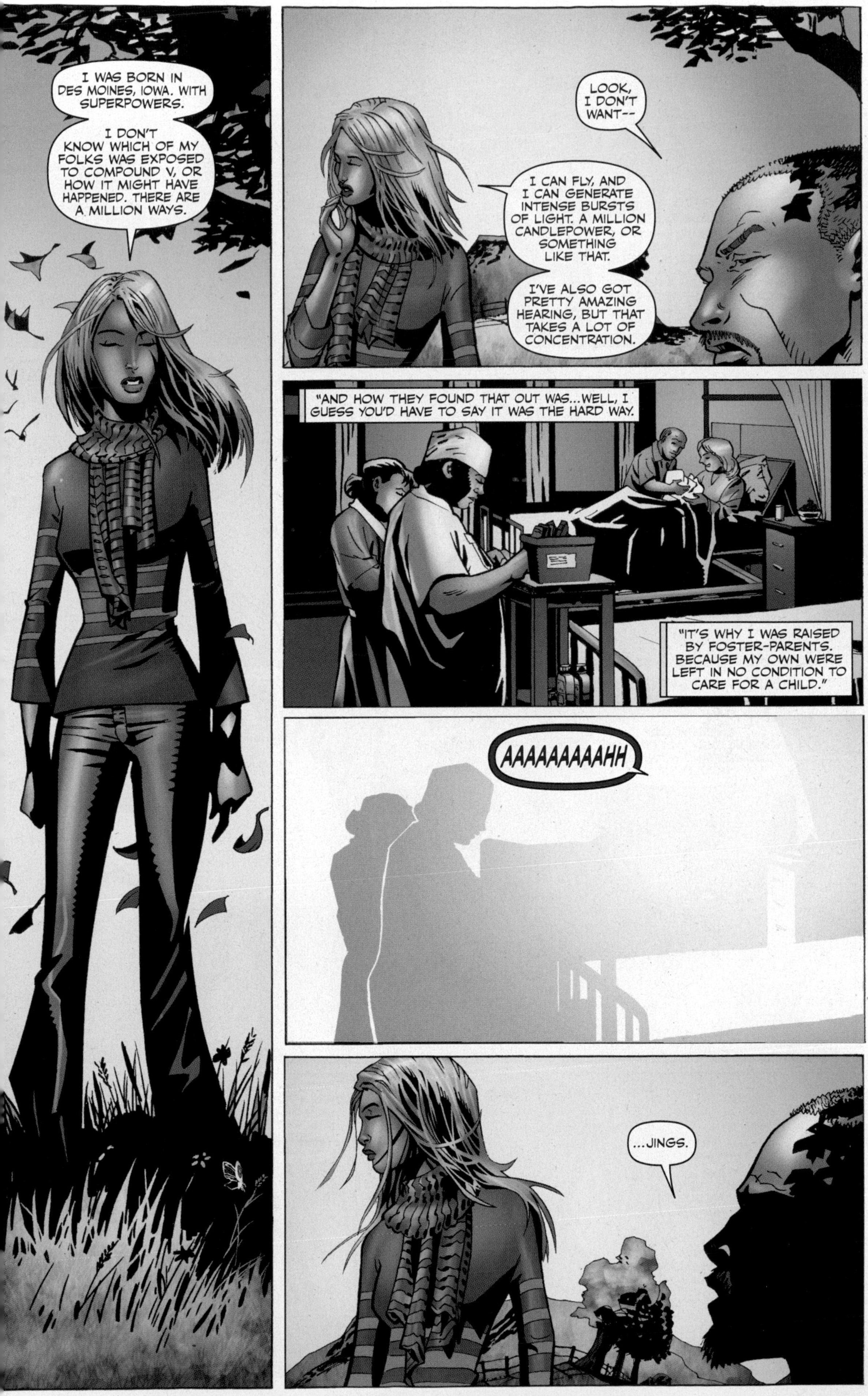
I WAS BORN IN DES MOINES, IOWA. WITH SUPERPOWERS.
I DON'T KNOW WHICH OF MY FOLKS WAS EXPOSED TO COMPOUND V, OR HOW IT MIGHT HAVE HAPPENED. THERE ARE A MILLION WAYS.
LOOK, I DON'T WANT--
I CAN FLY, AND I CAN GENERATE INTENSE BURSTS OF LIGHT. A MILLION CANDLEPOWER, OR SOMETHING LIKE THAT.
I'VE ALSO GOT PRETTY AMAZING HEARING, BUT THAT TAKES A LOT OF CONCENTRATION.
"AND HOW THEY FOUND THAT OUT WAS...WELL, I GUESS YOU'D HAVE TO SAY IT WAS THE HARD WAY.
"IT'S WHY I WAS RAISED BY FOSTER-PARENTS. BECAUSE MY OWN WERE LEFT IN NO CONDITION TO CARE FOR A CHILD."
AAAAAAAAAHH
...JINGS.

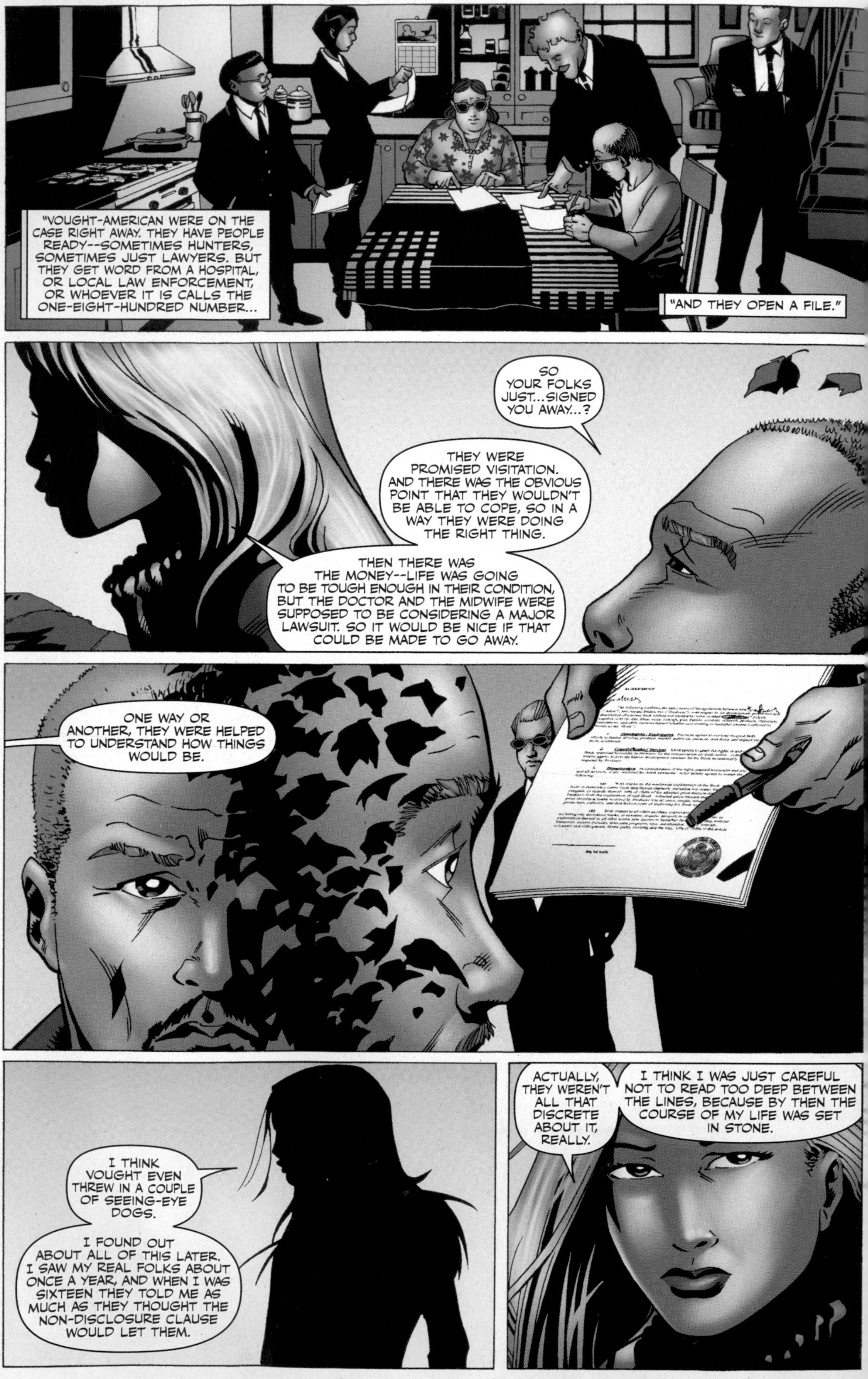
"VOUGHT-AMERICAN WERE ON THE CASE RIGHT AWAY. THEY HAVE PEOPLE READY--SOMETIMES HUNTERS, SOMETIMES JUST LAWYERS. BUT THEY GET WORD FROM A HOSPITAL, OR LOCAL LAW ENFORCEMENT, OR WHOEVER IT IS CALLS THE ONE-EIGHT-HUNDRED NUMBER...
"AND THEY OPEN A FILE."
SO YOUR FOLKS JUST...SIGNED YOU AWAY...?
THEY WERE PROMISED VISITATION. AND THERE WAS THE OBVIOUS POINT THAT THEY WOULDN'T BE ABLE TO COPE, SO IN A WAY THEY WERE DOING THE RIGHT THING.
THEN THERE WAS THE MONEY--LIFE WAS GOING TO BE TOUGH ENOUGH IN THEIR CONDITION, BUT THE DOCTOR AND THE MIDWIFE WERE SUPPOSED TO BE CONSIDERING A MAJOR LAWSUIT. SO IT WOULD BE NICE IF THAT COULD BE MADE TO GO AWAY.
ONE WAY OR ANOTHER, THEY WERE HELPED TO UNDERSTAND HOW THINGS WOULD BE.
I THINK VOUGHT EVEN THREW IN A COUPLE OF SEEING-EYE DOGS.
I FOUND OUT ABOUT ALL OF THIS LATER. I SAW MY REAL FOLKS ABOUT ONCE A YEAR, AND WHEN I WAS SIXTEEN THEY TOLD ME AS MUCH AS THEY THOUGHT THE NON-DISCLOSURE CLAUSE WOULD LET THEM.
ACTUALLY, THEY WEREN'T ALL THAT DISCRETE ABOUT IT, REALLY.
I THINK I WAS JUST CAREFUL NOT TO READ TOO DEEP BETWEEN THE LINES, BECAUSE BY THEN THE COURSE OF MY LIFE WAS SET IN STONE.

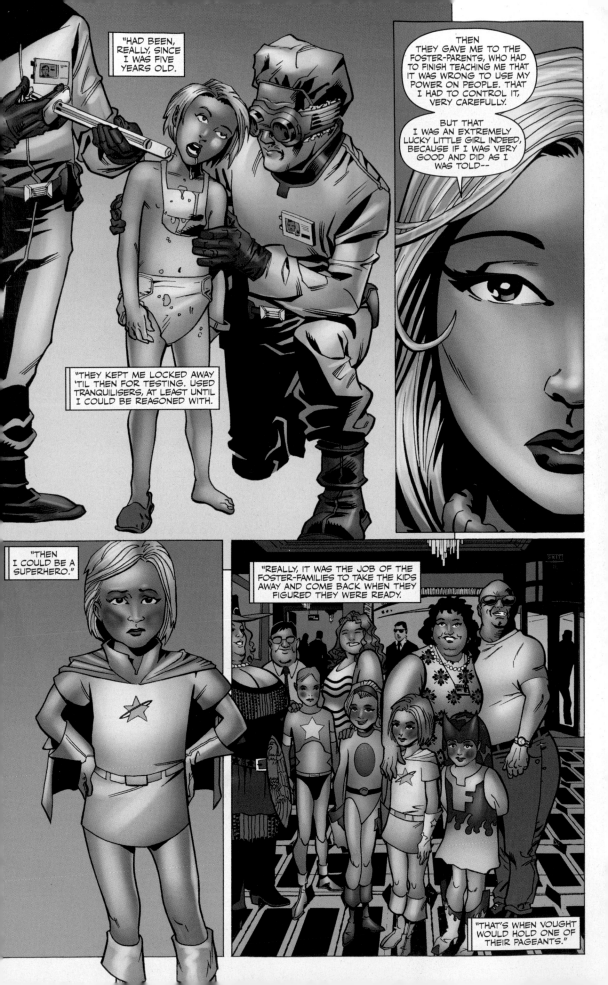

"HAD BEEN, REALLY, SINCE I WAS FIVE YEARS OLD.

THEN THEY GAVE ME TO THE FOSTER-PARENTS, WHO HAD TO FINISH TEACHING ME THAT IT WAS WRONG TO USE MY POWER ON PEOPLE. THAT I HAD TO CONTROL IT, VERY CAREFULLY.

BUT THAT I WAS AN EXTREMELY LUCKY LITTLE GIRL INDEED, BECAUSE IF I WAS VERY GOOD AND DID AS I WAS TOLD--

"THEY KEPT ME LOCKED AWAY 'TIL THEN FOR TESTING. USED TRANQUILISERS, AT LEAST UNTIL I COULD BE REASONED WITH.

"THEN I COULD BE A SUPERHERO."

"REALLY, IT WAS THE JOB OF THE FOSTER-FAMILIES TO TAKE THE KIDS AWAY AND COME BACK WHEN THEY FIGURED THEY WERE READY.

"THAT'S WHEN VOUGHT WOULD HOLD ONE OF THEIR PAGEANTS."

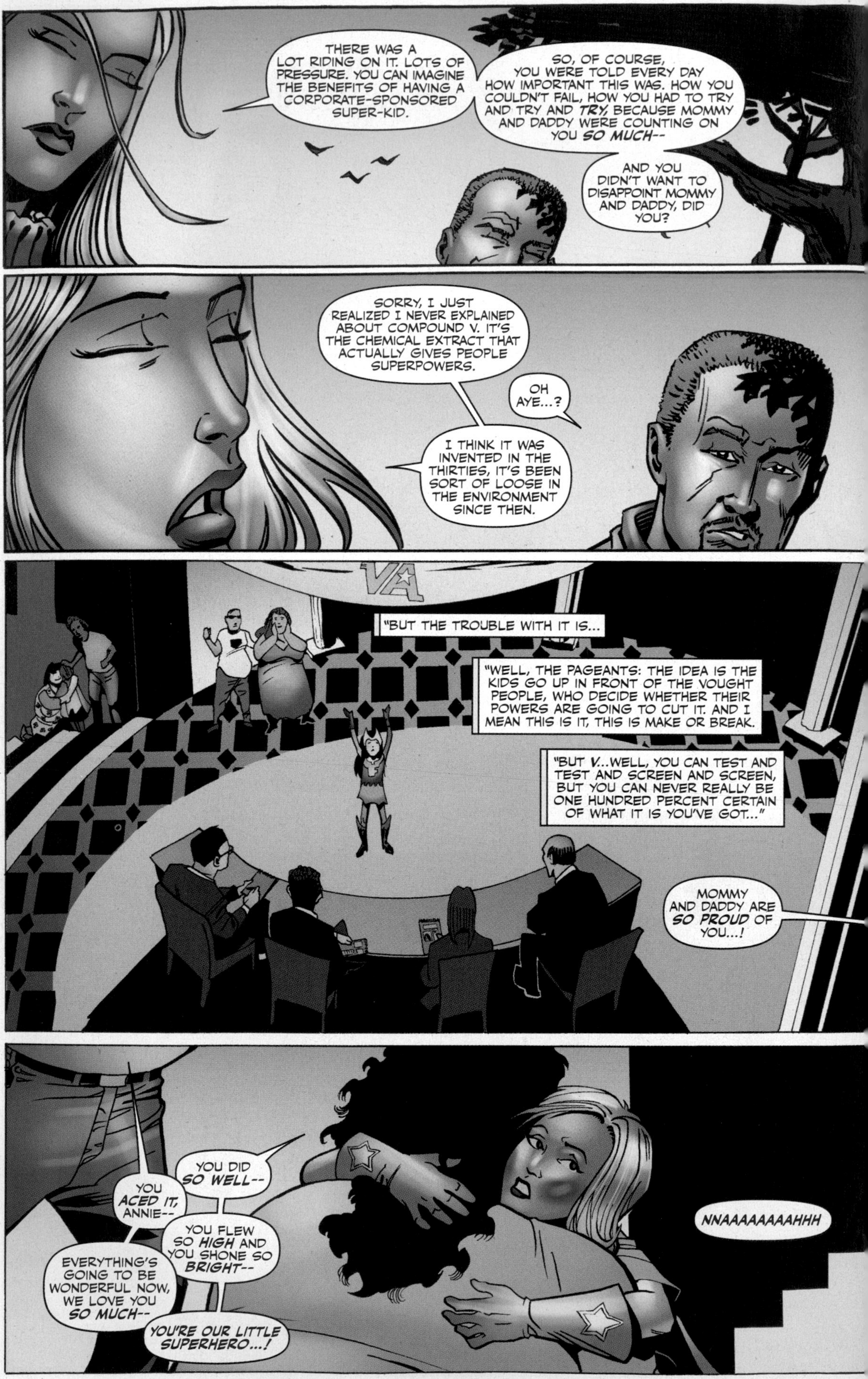
THERE WAS A LOT RIDING ON IT. LOTS OF PRESSURE. YOU CAN IMAGINE THE BENEFITS OF HAVING A CORPORATE-SPONSORED SUPER-KID.
SO, OF COURSE, YOU WERE TOLD EVERY DAY HOW IMPORTANT THIS WAS. HOW YOU COULDN'T FAIL, HOW YOU HAD TO TRY AND TRY AND *TRY,* BECAUSE MOMMY AND DADDY WERE COUNTING ON YOU *SO MUCH*--
AND YOU DIDN'T WANT TO DISAPPOINT MOMMY AND DADDY, DID YOU?
SORRY, I JUST REALIZED I NEVER EXPLAINED ABOUT COMPOUND V. IT'S THE CHEMICAL EXTRACT THAT ACTUALLY GIVES PEOPLE SUPERPOWERS.
OH AYE...?
I THINK IT WAS INVENTED IN THE THIRTIES, IT'S BEEN SORT OF LOOSE IN THE ENVIRONMENT SINCE THEN.
VA
"BUT THE TROUBLE WITH IT IS...
"WELL, THE PAGEANTS: THE IDEA IS THE KIDS GO UP IN FRONT OF THE VOUGHT PEOPLE, WHO DECIDE WHETHER THEIR POWERS ARE GOING TO CUT IT. AND I MEAN THIS IS IT, THIS IS MAKE OR BREAK.
"BUT *V*...WELL, YOU CAN TEST AND TEST AND SCREEN AND SCREEN, BUT YOU CAN NEVER REALLY BE ONE HUNDRED PERCENT CERTAIN OF WHAT IT IS YOU'VE GOT..."
MOMMY AND DADDY ARE *SO PROUD* OF YOU...!
YOU *ACED IT,* ANNIE--
YOU DID *SO WELL*--
YOU FLEW SO *HIGH* AND YOU SHONE SO *BRIGHT*--
EVERYTHING'S GOING TO BE WONDERFUL NOW, WE LOVE YOU *SO MUCH*--
YOU'RE OUR LITTLE SUPERHERO...!
NNAAAAAAAAHHH

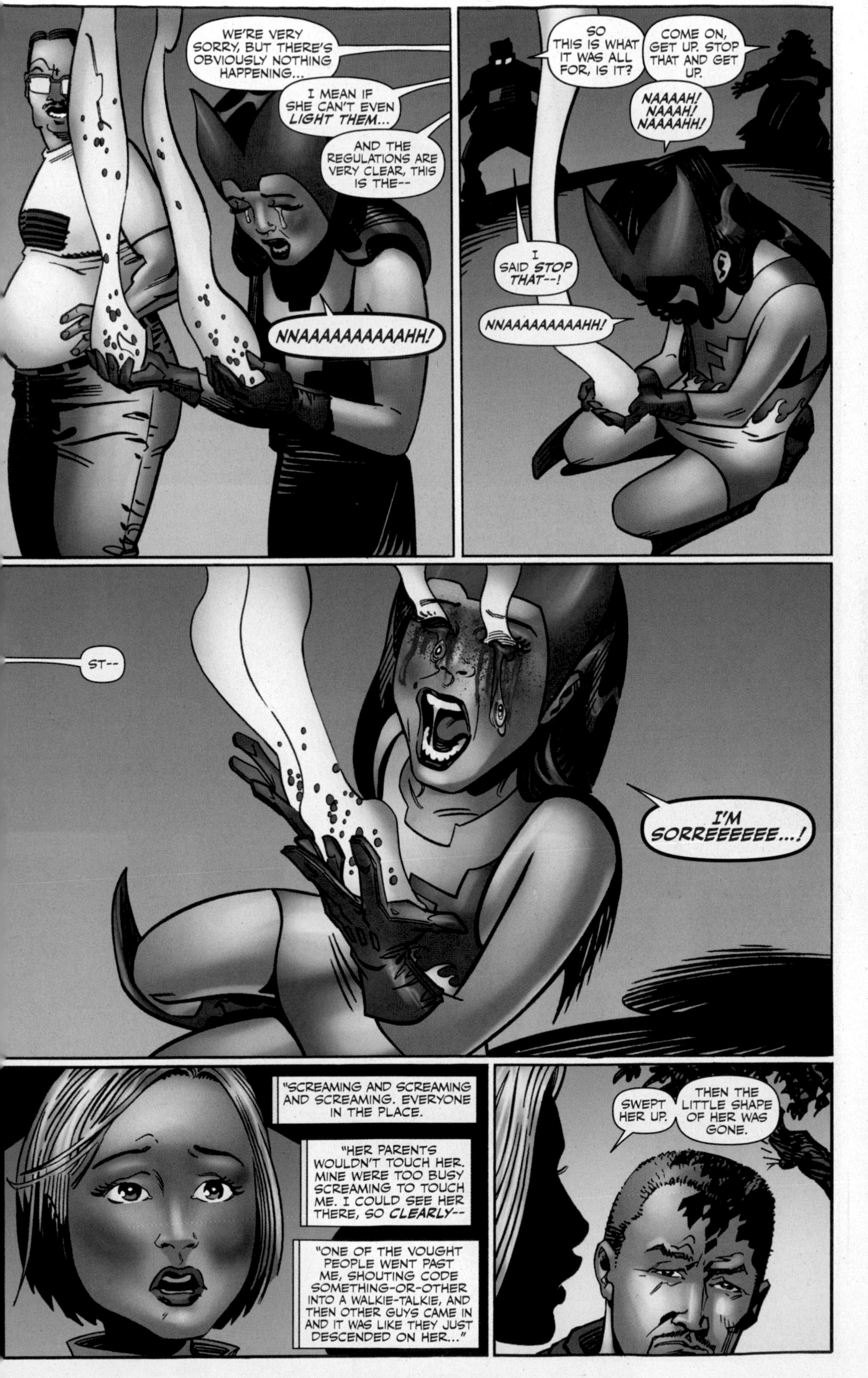
WE'RE VERY SORRY, BUT THERE'S OBVIOUSLY NOTHING HAPPENING...
I MEAN IF SHE CAN'T EVEN LIGHT THEM...
AND THE REGULATIONS ARE VERY CLEAR, THIS IS THE--
NNAAAAAAAAAAAHH!
SO THIS IS WHAT IT WAS ALL FOR, IS IT?
COME ON, GET UP. STOP THAT AND GET UP.
NAAAAH! NAAAH! NAAAAHH!
I SAID STOP THAT--!
NNAAAAAAAAAAHH!
ST--
I'M SORREEEEEE...!
"SCREAMING AND SCREAMING AND SCREAMING. EVERYONE IN THE PLACE.
"HER PARENTS WOULDN'T TOUCH HER. MINE WERE TOO BUSY SCREAMING TO TOUCH ME. I COULD SEE HER THERE, SO CLEARLY--
"ONE OF THE VOUGHT PEOPLE WENT PAST ME, SHOUTING CODE SOMETHING-OR-OTHER INTO A WALKIE-TALKIE, AND THEN OTHER GUYS CAME IN AND IT WAS LIKE THEY JUST DESCENDED ON HER..."
SWEPT HER UP.
THEN THE LITTLE SHAPE OF HER WAS GONE.

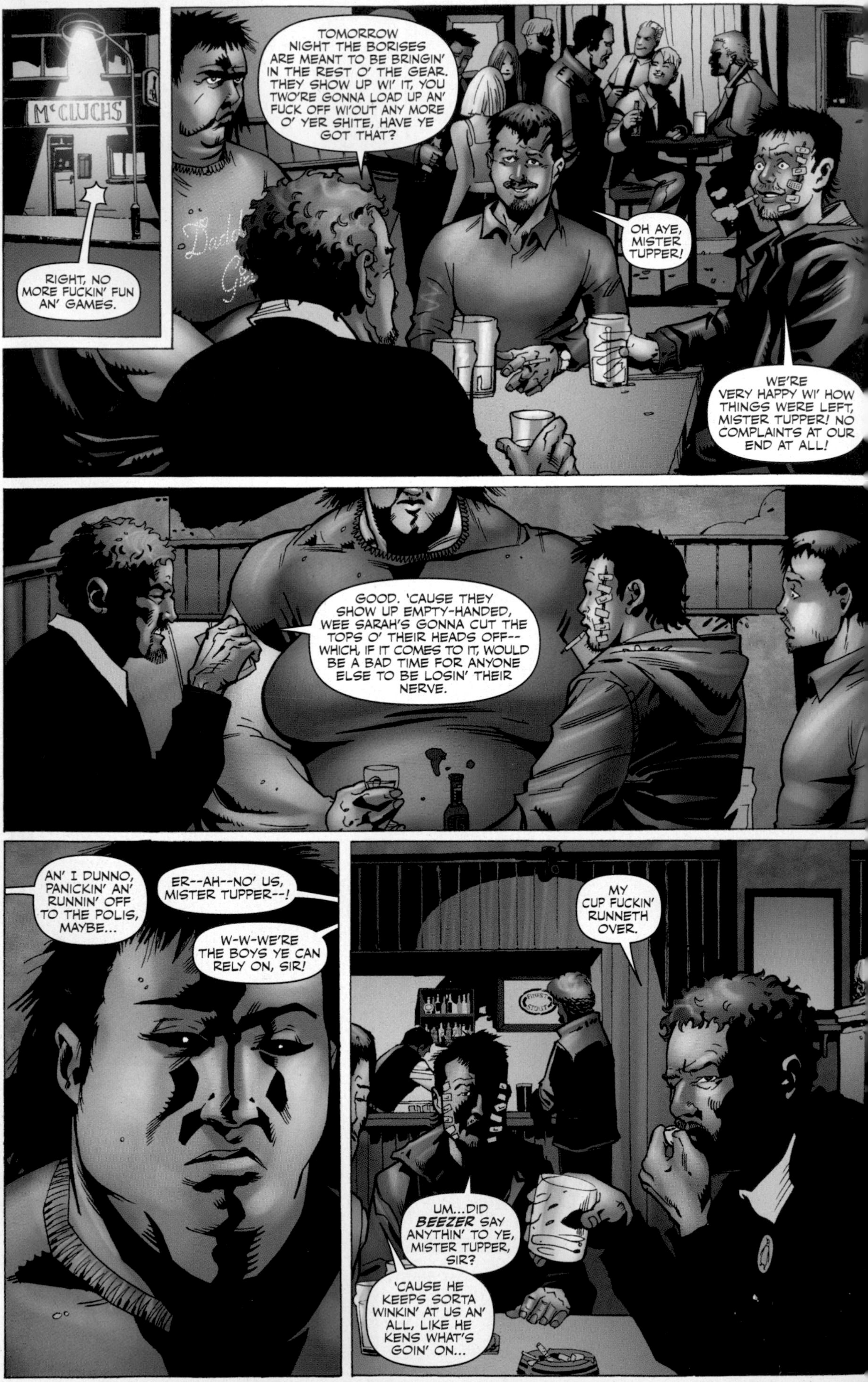
RIGHT, NO MORE FUCKIN' FUN AN' GAMES.
M'CLUCHS
TOMORROW NIGHT THE BORISES ARE MEANT TO BE BRINGIN' IN THE REST O' THE GEAR. THEY SHOW UP WI' IT, YOU TWO'RE GONNA LOAD UP AN' FUCK OFF WI'OUT ANY MORE O' YER SHITE, HAVE YE GOT THAT?
OH AYE, MISTER TUPPER!
WE'RE VERY HAPPY WI' HOW THINGS WERE LEFT, MISTER TUPPER! NO COMPLAINTS AT OUR END AT ALL!
GOOD. 'CAUSE THEY SHOW UP EMPTY-HANDED, WEE SARAH'S GONNA CUT THE TOPS O' THEIR HEADS OFF--WHICH, IF IT COMES TO IT, WOULD BE A BAD TIME FOR ANYONE ELSE TO BE LOSIN' THEIR NERVE.
AN' I DUNNO, PANICKIN' AN' RUNNIN' OFF TO THE POLIS, MAYBE...
ER--AH--NO' US, MISTER TUPPER--!
W-W-WE'RE THE BOYS YE CAN RELY ON, SIR!
MY CUP FUCKIN' RUNNETH OVER.
UM...DID BEEZER SAY ANYTHIN' TO YE, MISTER TUPPER, SIR?
'CAUSE HE KEEPS SORTA WINKIN' AT US AN' ALL, LIKE HE KENS WHAT'S GOIN' ON...

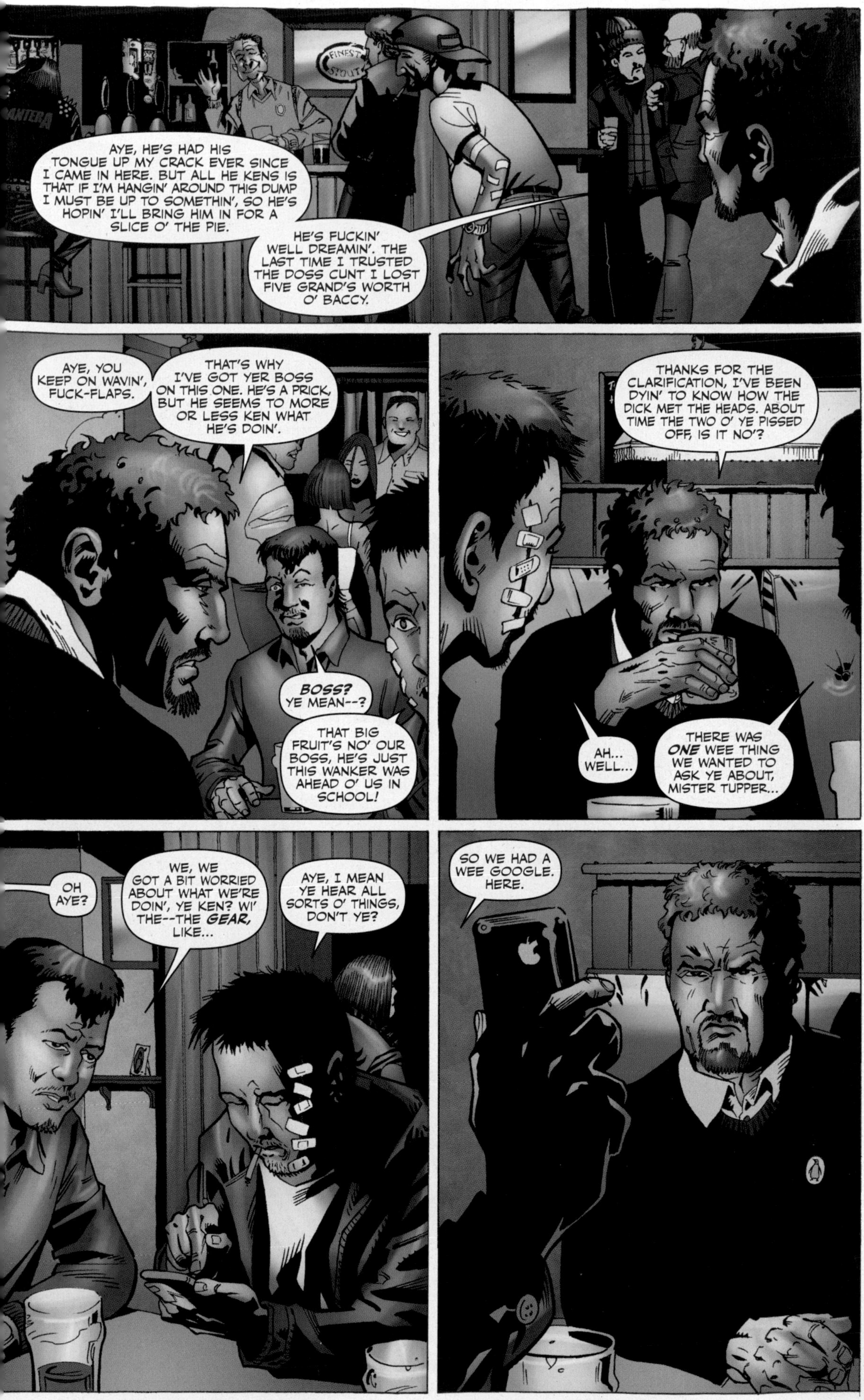
PANTERA
FINEST STOUT
AYE, HE'S HAD HIS TONGUE UP MY CRACK EVER SINCE I CAME IN HERE. BUT ALL HE KENS IS THAT IF I'M HANGIN' AROUND THIS DUMP I MUST BE UP TO SOMETHIN', SO HE'S HOPIN' I'LL BRING HIM IN FOR A SLICE O' THE PIE.
HE'S FUCKIN' WELL DREAMIN'. THE LAST TIME I TRUSTED THE DOSS CUNT I LOST FIVE GRAND'S WORTH O' BACCY.
AYE, YOU KEEP ON WAVIN', FUCK-FLAPS.
THAT'S WHY I'VE GOT YER BOSS ON THIS ONE. HE'S A PRICK, BUT HE SEEMS TO MORE OR LESS KEN WHAT HE'S DOIN'.
BOSS? YE MEAN--?
THAT BIG FRUIT'S NO' OUR BOSS, HE'S JUST THIS WANKER WAS AHEAD O' US IN SCHOOL!
THANKS FOR THE CLARIFICATION, I'VE BEEN DYIN' TO KNOW HOW THE DICK MET THE HEADS. ABOUT TIME THE TWO O' YE PISSED OFF, IS IT NO'?
AH... WELL...
THERE WAS ONE WEE THING WE WANTED TO ASK YE ABOUT, MISTER TUPPER...
OH AYE?
WE, WE GOT A BIT WORRIED ABOUT WHAT WE'RE DOIN', YE KEN? WI' THE--THE GEAR, LIKE...
AYE, I MEAN YE HEAR ALL SORTS O' THINGS, DON'T YE?
SO WE HAD A WEE GOOGLE. HERE.

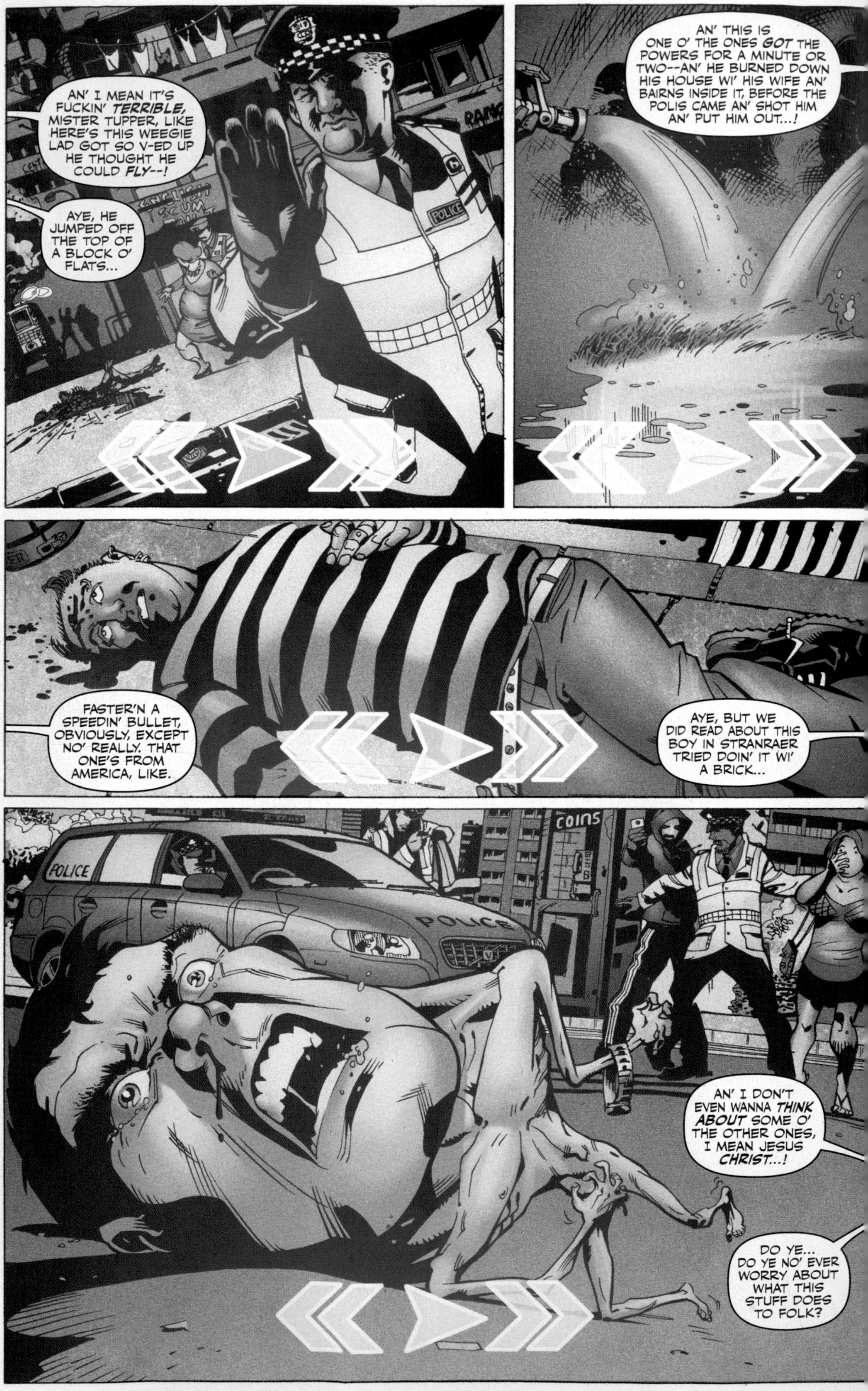
AN' I MEAN IT'S FUCKIN' TERRIBLE, MISTER TUPPER, LIKE HERE'S THIS WEEGIE LAD GOT SO V-ED UP HE THOUGHT HE COULD FLY--!
AYE, HE JUMPED OFF THE TOP OF A BLOCK O' FLATS...
AN' THIS IS ONE O' THE ONES GOT THE POWERS FOR A MINUTE OR TWO--AN' HE BURNED DOWN HIS HOUSE WI' HIS WIFE AN' BAIRNS INSIDE IT, BEFORE THE POLIS CAME AN' SHOT HIM AN' PUT HIM OUT...!
FASTER'N A SPEEDIN' BULLET, OBVIOUSLY, EXCEPT NO' REALLY. THAT ONE'S FROM AMERICA, LIKE.
AYE, BUT WE DID READ ABOUT THIS BOY IN STRANRAER TRIED DOIN' IT WI' A BRICK...
POLICE
COINS
AN' I DON'T EVEN WANNA THINK ABOUT SOME O' THE OTHER ONES, I MEAN JESUS CHRIST...!
DO YE... DO YE NO' EVER WORRY ABOUT WHAT THIS STUFF DOES TO FOLK?

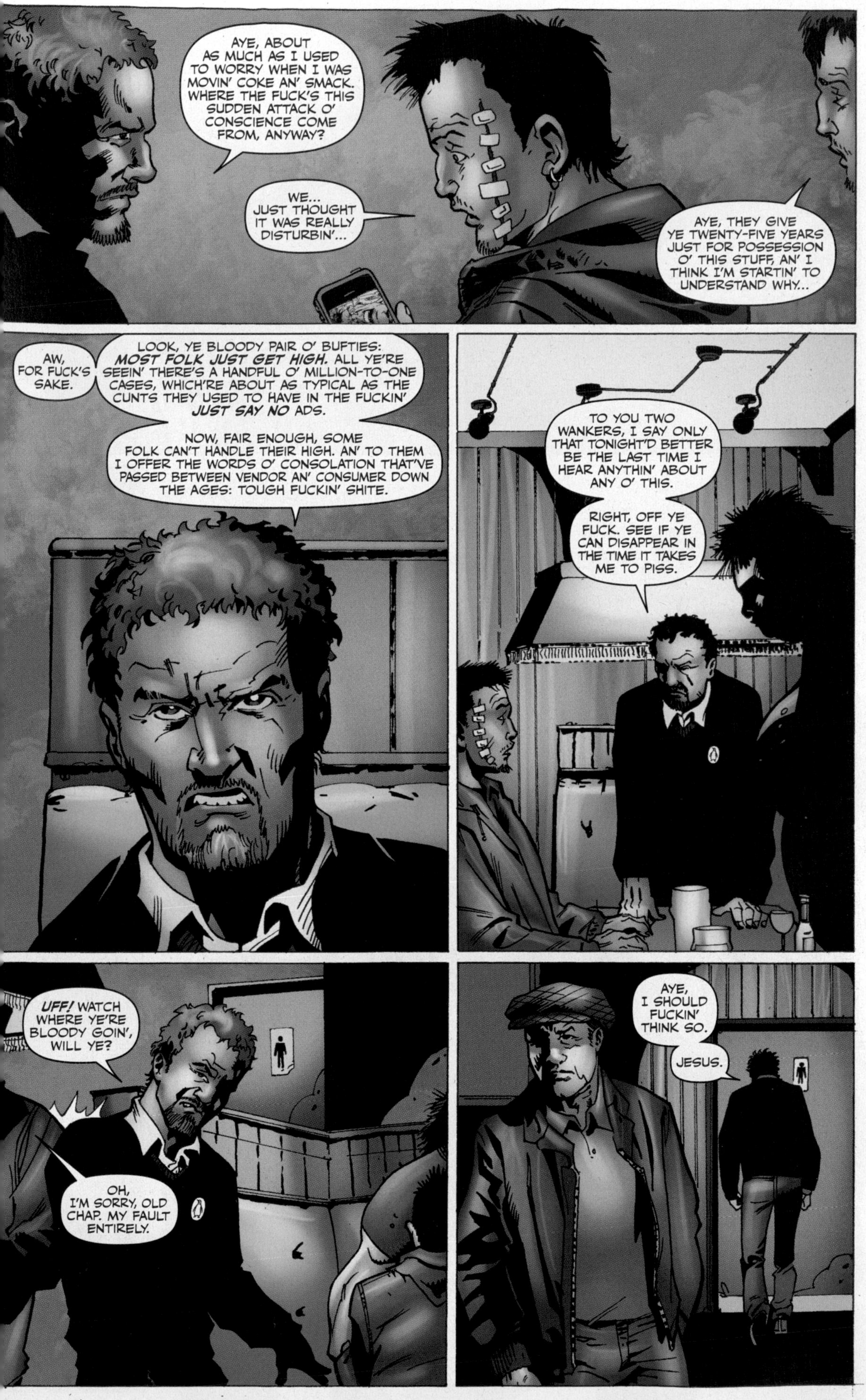
AYE, ABOUT AS MUCH AS I USED TO WORRY WHEN I WAS MOVIN' COKE AN' SMACK. WHERE THE FUCK'S THIS SUDDEN ATTACK O' CONSCIENCE COME FROM, ANYWAY?
WE... JUST THOUGHT IT WAS REALLY DISTURBIN'...
AYE, THEY GIVE YE TWENTY-FIVE YEARS JUST FOR POSSESSION O' THIS STUFF, AN' I THINK I'M STARTIN' TO UNDERSTAND WHY...
AW, FOR FUCK'S SAKE.
LOOK, YE BLOODY PAIR O' BUFTIES: MOST FOLK JUST GET HIGH. ALL YE'RE SEEIN' THERE'S A HANDFUL O' MILLION-TO-ONE CASES, WHICH'RE ABOUT AS TYPICAL AS THE CUNTS THEY USED TO HAVE IN THE FUCKIN' JUST SAY NO ADS.
NOW, FAIR ENOUGH, SOME FOLK CAN'T HANDLE THEIR HIGH. AN' TO THEM I OFFER THE WORDS O' CONSOLATION THAT'VE PASSED BETWEEN VENDOR AN' CONSUMER DOWN THE AGES: TOUGH FUCKIN' SHITE.
TO YOU TWO WANKERS, I SAY ONLY THAT TONIGHT'D BETTER BE THE LAST TIME I HEAR ANYTHIN' ABOUT ANY O' THIS.
RIGHT, OFF YE FUCK. SEE IF YE CAN DISAPPEAR IN THE TIME IT TAKES ME TO PISS.
UFF! WATCH WHERE YE'RE BLOODY GOIN', WILL YE?
OH, I'M SORRY, OLD CHAP. MY FAULT ENTIRELY.
AYE, I SHOULD FUCKIN' THINK SO.
JESUS.

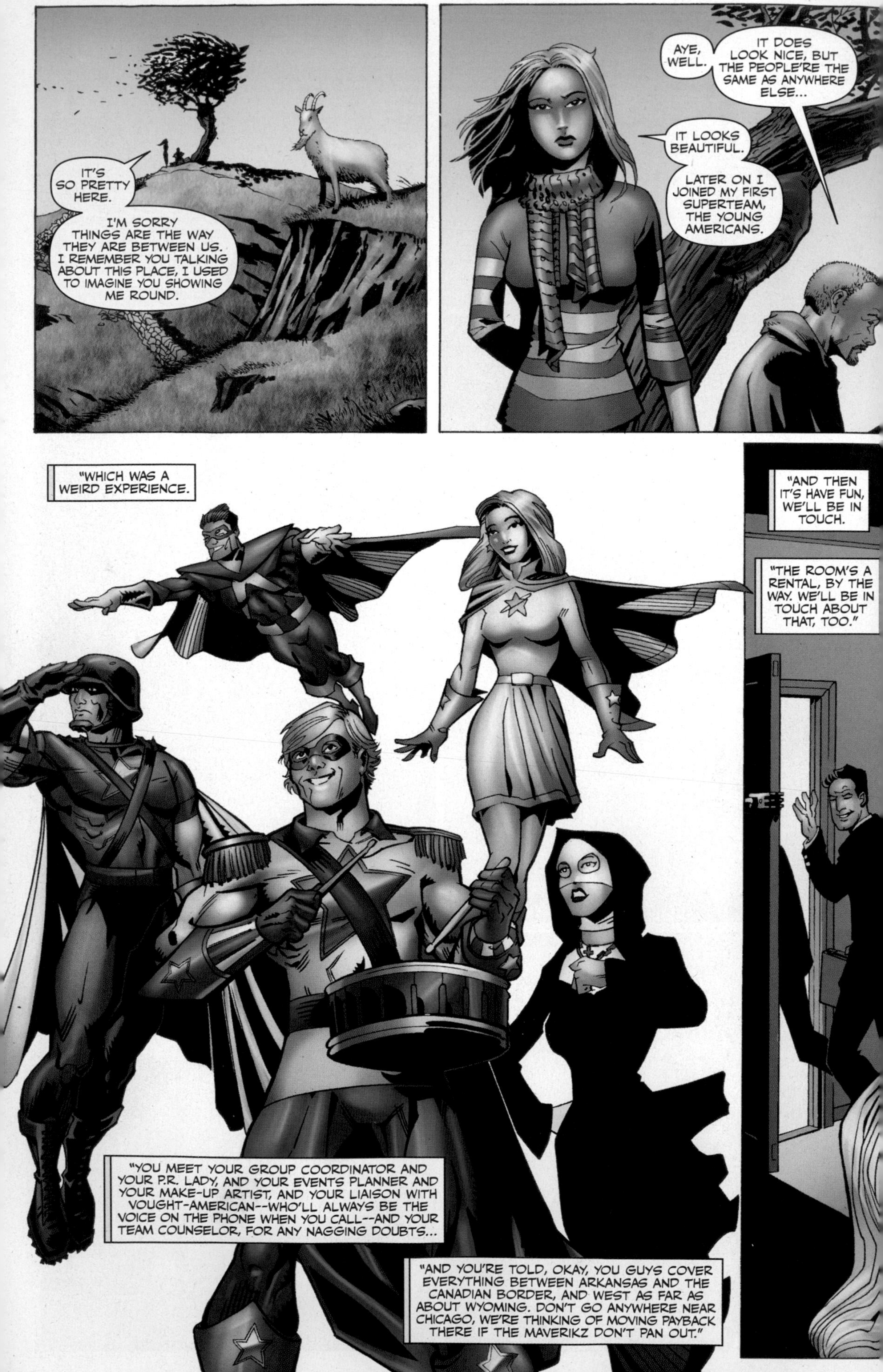
IT'S SO PRETTY HERE.
I'M SORRY THINGS ARE THE WAY THEY ARE BETWEEN US. I REMEMBER YOU TALKING ABOUT THIS PLACE, I USED TO IMAGINE YOU SHOWING ME ROUND.
AYE, WELL.
IT DOES LOOK NICE, BUT THE PEOPLE'RE THE SAME AS ANYWHERE ELSE...
IT LOOKS BEAUTIFUL.
LATER ON I JOINED MY FIRST SUPERTEAM, THE YOUNG AMERICANS.
"WHICH WAS A WEIRD EXPERIENCE.
"YOU MEET YOUR GROUP COORDINATOR AND YOUR P.R. LADY, AND YOUR EVENTS PLANNER AND YOUR MAKE-UP ARTIST, AND YOUR LIAISON WITH VOUGHT-AMERICAN--WHO'LL ALWAYS BE THE VOICE ON THE PHONE WHEN YOU CALL--AND YOUR TEAM COUNSELOR, FOR ANY NAGGING DOUBTS...
"AND YOU'RE TOLD, OKAY, YOU GUYS COVER EVERYTHING BETWEEN ARKANSAS AND THE CANADIAN BORDER, AND WEST AS FAR AS ABOUT WYOMING. DON'T GO ANYWHERE NEAR CHICAGO, WE'RE THINKING OF MOVING PAYBACK THERE IF THE MAVERIKZ DON'T PAN OUT."
"AND THEN IT'S HAVE FUN, WE'LL BE IN TOUCH.
"THE ROOM'S A RENTAL, BY THE WAY. WE'LL BE IN TOUCH ABOUT THAT, TOO."

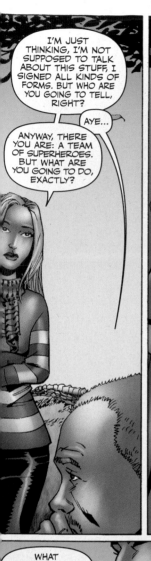

I'M JUST THINKING, I'M NOT SUPPOSED TO TALK ABOUT THIS STUFF, I SIGNED ALL KINDS OF FORMS. BUT WHO ARE YOU GOING TO TELL, RIGHT?

AYE...

ANYWAY, THERE YOU ARE: A TEAM OF SUPERHEROES. BUT WHAT ARE YOU GOING TO DO, EXACTLY?

"WELL, WE DIDN'T KNOW, SO WE ELECTED *THE STANDARD* AS OUR LEADER.

"THEN WE ASKED HIM, BUT HE HADN'T HAD ANY NEW IDEAS DURING THE ELECTION. IT WAS *GENERAL ISSUE* WHO SUGGESTED BUYING A POLICE SCANNER..."

WHAT SORT OF A NAME'S THE *STANDARD* MEANT TO BE--?

HE SAID IT WAS LIKE A FLAG, YOU KNOW, LIKE YOU CARRY INTO BATTLE? BUT I THINK IT'S MORE LIKELY THAT SOMEONE JUST RAN OUT OF INSPIRATION AT SOME POINT.

WE GOT A LOT OF STUFF OFF THE SCANNER, BUT IT WAS MOSTLY TRAFFIC ACCIDENTS OR BAR FIGHTS RATHER THAN LOCATIONS OF SHADY WATERFRONT DENS. AND WHEN WE DID GET SOMETHING WE THOUGHT WE COULD HELP WITH, WHICH WAS A FACTORY FIRE, WE REALIZED THE NEXT THING WE NEEDED WAS A STREET MAP.

AYE, YOU SEE, THAT'S THE THING THAT'S ALWAYS BOTHERED ME ABOUT SUPES...OR MAYBE JUST THE IDEA O' SUPES...

ALL RIGHT, SO YOU'VE GOT YOUR POWERS, BUT YOU'VE NO IDEA HOW TO DO WHAT YOU'RE DOIN', HAVE YOU? SO WHY DO YOU JUST-- DRESS UP LIKE A LOAD O' BAMS AN' START IN?

I MEAN IF YOU WANNA HELP FOLK, WHY D'YOU NO' GO ALONG TO A HOSPITAL AN' SAY-- I COULD WORK HERE, I COULD FLY CASUALTIES IN AFTER AN ACCIDENT. OR OFFER TO KICK DOORS DOWN FOR THE FIREMEN, OR WHATEVER.

I MEAN THEY COULD AT LEAST TRAIN YOU PROPERLY, COULDN'T THEY...?

GOOD QUESTION.

IT NEVER CAME UP FOR US, BUT...WITH HINDSIGHT, I'D GUESS THAT VOUGHT DON'T WANT SUPERPOWER ANYWHERE NEAR FEDERAL HANDS. OR LOCAL SERVICES EITHER.

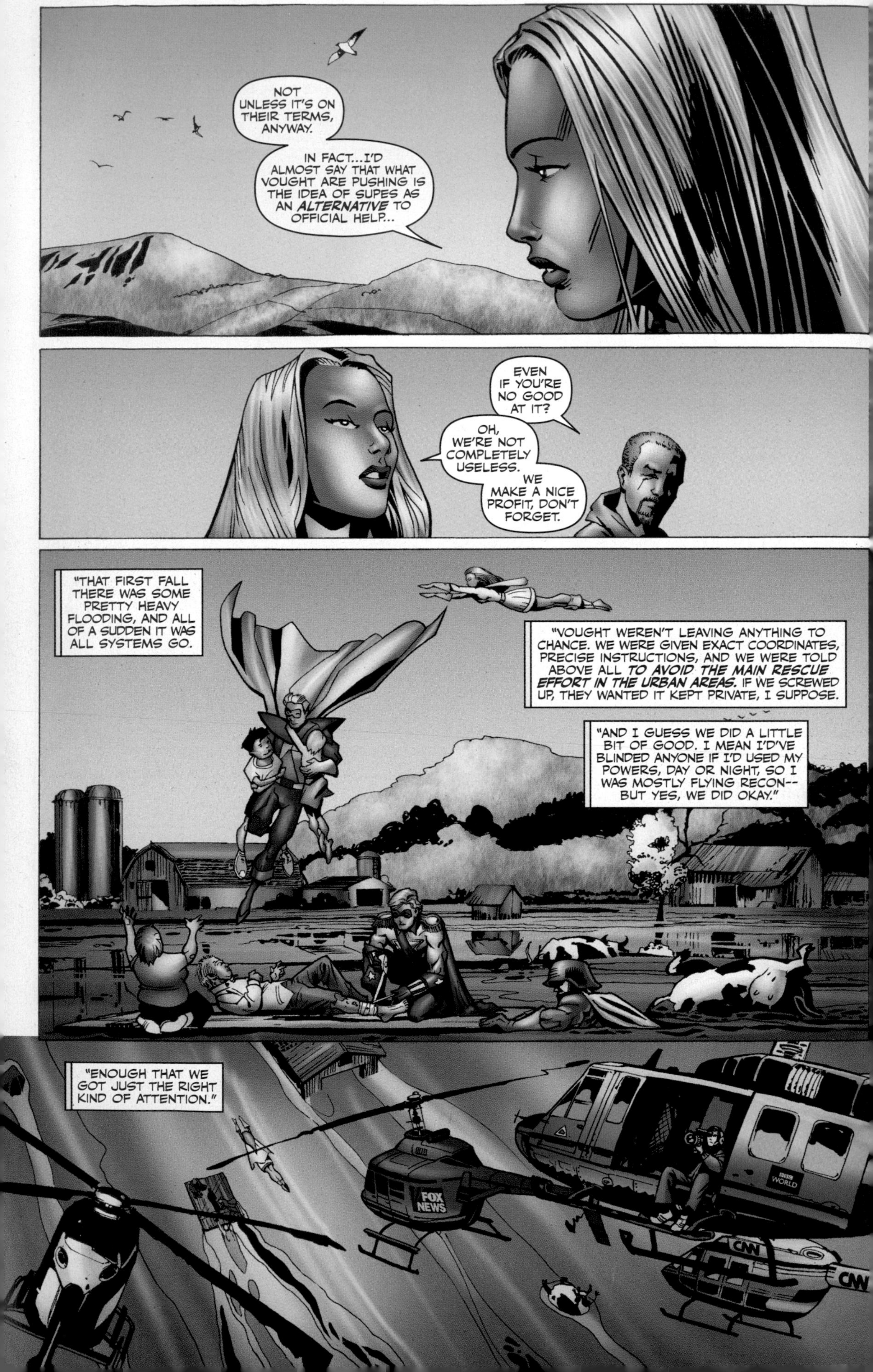
NOT UNLESS IT'S ON THEIR TERMS, ANYWAY.
IN FACT...I'D ALMOST SAY THAT WHAT VOUGHT ARE PUSHING IS THE IDEA OF SUPES AS AN *ALTERNATIVE* TO OFFICIAL HELP...
EVEN IF YOU'RE NO GOOD AT IT?
OH, WE'RE NOT COMPLETELY USELESS.
WE MAKE A NICE PROFIT, DON'T FORGET.
"THAT FIRST FALL THERE WAS SOME PRETTY HEAVY FLOODING, AND ALL OF A SUDDEN IT WAS ALL SYSTEMS GO.
"VOUGHT WEREN'T LEAVING ANYTHING TO CHANCE. WE WERE GIVEN EXACT COORDINATES, PRECISE INSTRUCTIONS, AND WE WERE TOLD ABOVE ALL ***TO AVOID THE MAIN RESCUE EFFORT IN THE URBAN AREAS.*** IF WE SCREWED UP, THEY WANTED IT KEPT PRIVATE, I SUPPOSE.
"AND I GUESS WE DID A LITTLE BIT OF GOOD. I MEAN I'D'VE BLINDED ANYONE IF I'D USED MY POWERS, DAY OR NIGHT, SO I WAS MOSTLY FLYING RECON-- BUT YES, WE DID OKAY."
"ENOUGH THAT WE GOT JUST THE RIGHT KIND OF ATTENTION."
FOX NEWS
BBC WORLD
CNN
CNN

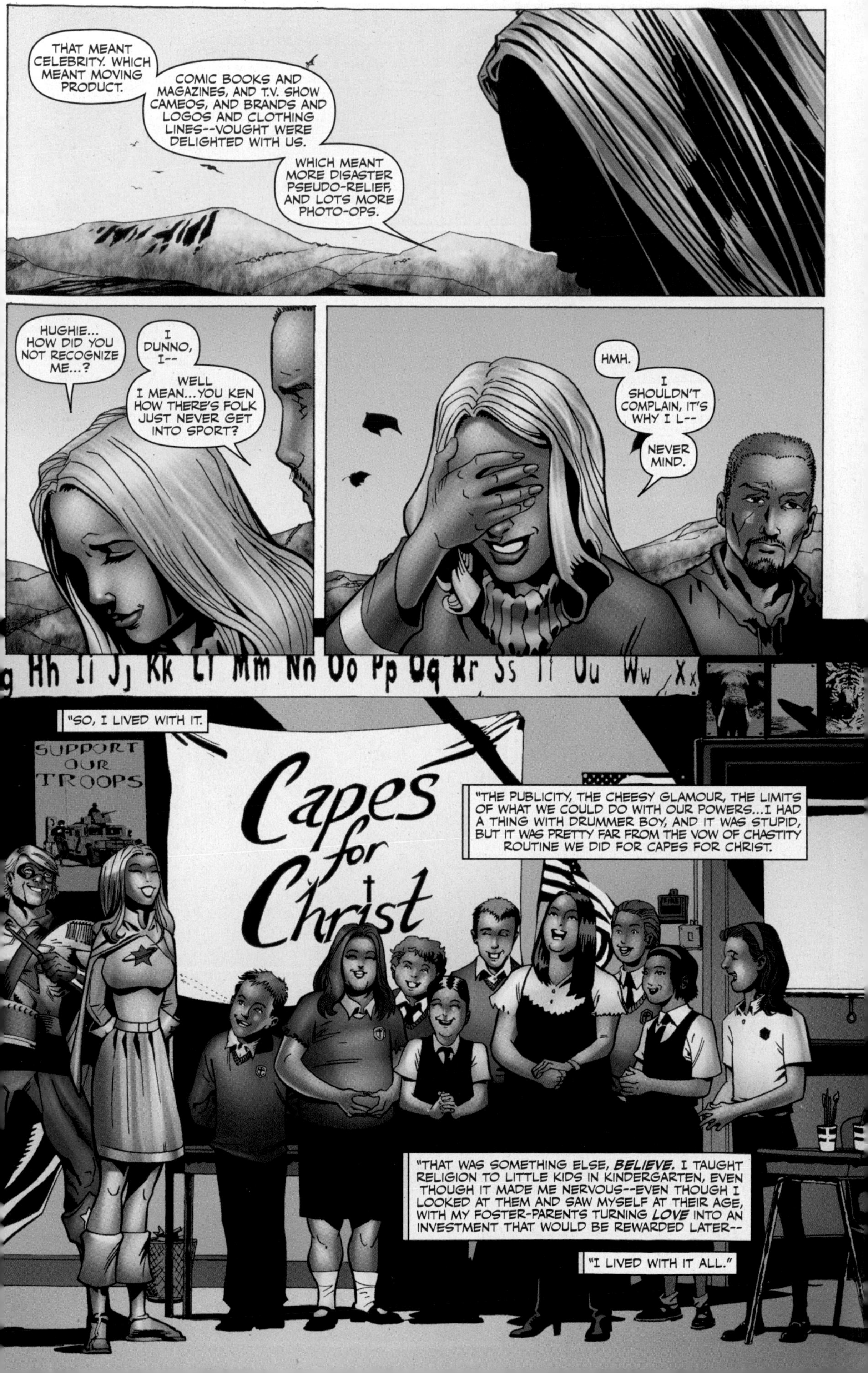
THAT MEANT CELEBRITY. WHICH MEANT MOVING PRODUCT.
COMIC BOOKS AND MAGAZINES, AND T.V. SHOW CAMEOS, AND BRANDS AND LOGOS AND CLOTHING LINES--VOUGHT WERE DELIGHTED WITH US.
WHICH MEANT MORE DISASTER PSEUDO-RELIEF, AND LOTS MORE PHOTO-OPS.
HUGHIE... HOW DID YOU NOT RECOGNIZE ME...?
I DUNNO, I--
WELL I MEAN...YOU KEN HOW THERE'S FOLK JUST NEVER GET INTO SPORT?
HMH.
I SHOULDN'T COMPLAIN, IT'S WHY I L--
NEVER MIND.
"SO, I LIVED WITH IT.
SUPPORT OUR TROOPS
Capes for Christ
"THE PUBLICITY, THE CHEESY GLAMOUR, THE LIMITS OF WHAT WE COULD DO WITH OUR POWERS...I HAD A THING WITH DRUMMER BOY, AND IT WAS STUPID, BUT IT WAS PRETTY FAR FROM THE VOW OF CHASTITY ROUTINE WE DID FOR CAPES FOR CHRIST.
"THAT WAS SOMETHING ELSE, BELIEVE. I TAUGHT RELIGION TO LITTLE KIDS IN KINDERGARTEN, EVEN THOUGH IT MADE ME NERVOUS--EVEN THOUGH I LOOKED AT THEM AND SAW MYSELF AT THEIR AGE, WITH MY FOSTER-PARENTS TURNING LOVE INTO AN INVESTMENT THAT WOULD BE REWARDED LATER--
"I LIVED WITH IT ALL."

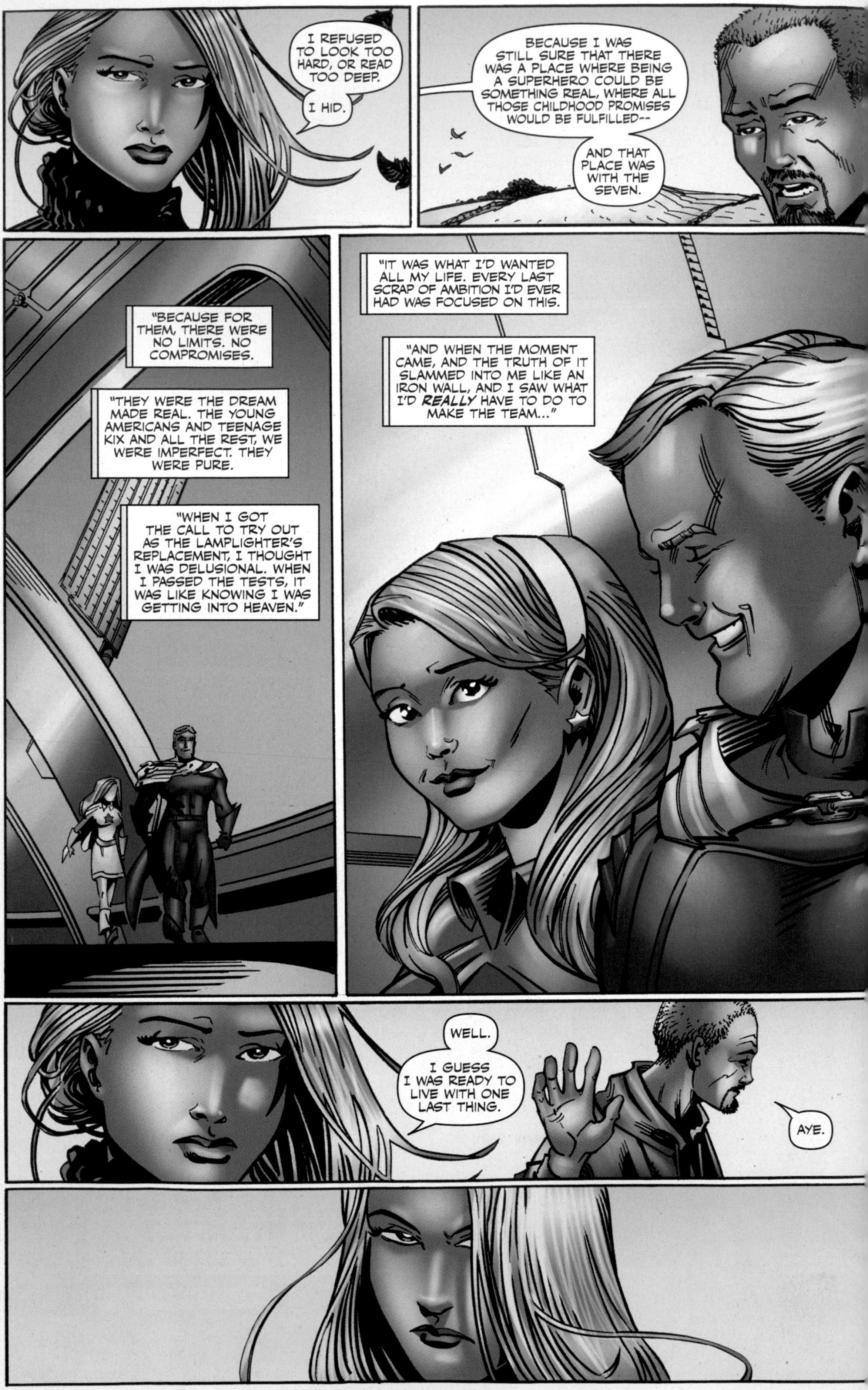
I REFUSED TO LOOK TOO HARD, OR READ TOO DEEP.
I HID.
BECAUSE I WAS STILL SURE THAT THERE WAS A PLACE WHERE BEING A SUPERHERO COULD BE SOMETHING REAL, WHERE ALL THOSE CHILDHOOD PROMISES WOULD BE FULFILLED--
AND THAT PLACE WAS WITH THE SEVEN.
"BECAUSE FOR THEM, THERE WERE NO LIMITS. NO COMPROMISES.
"THEY WERE THE DREAM MADE REAL. THE YOUNG AMERICANS AND TEENAGE KIX AND ALL THE REST, WE WERE IMPERFECT. THEY WERE PURE.
"WHEN I GOT THE CALL TO TRY OUT AS THE LAMPLIGHTER'S REPLACEMENT, I THOUGHT I WAS DELUSIONAL. WHEN I PASSED THE TESTS, IT WAS LIKE KNOWING I WAS GETTING INTO HEAVEN."
"IT WAS WHAT I'D WANTED ALL MY LIFE. EVERY LAST SCRAP OF AMBITION I'D EVER HAD WAS FOCUSED ON THIS.
"AND WHEN THE MOMENT CAME, AND THE TRUTH OF IT SLAMMED INTO ME LIKE AN IRON WALL, AND I SAW WHAT I'D *REALLY* HAVE TO DO TO MAKE THE TEAM..."
WELL.
I GUESS I WAS READY TO LIVE WITH ONE LAST THING.
AYE.

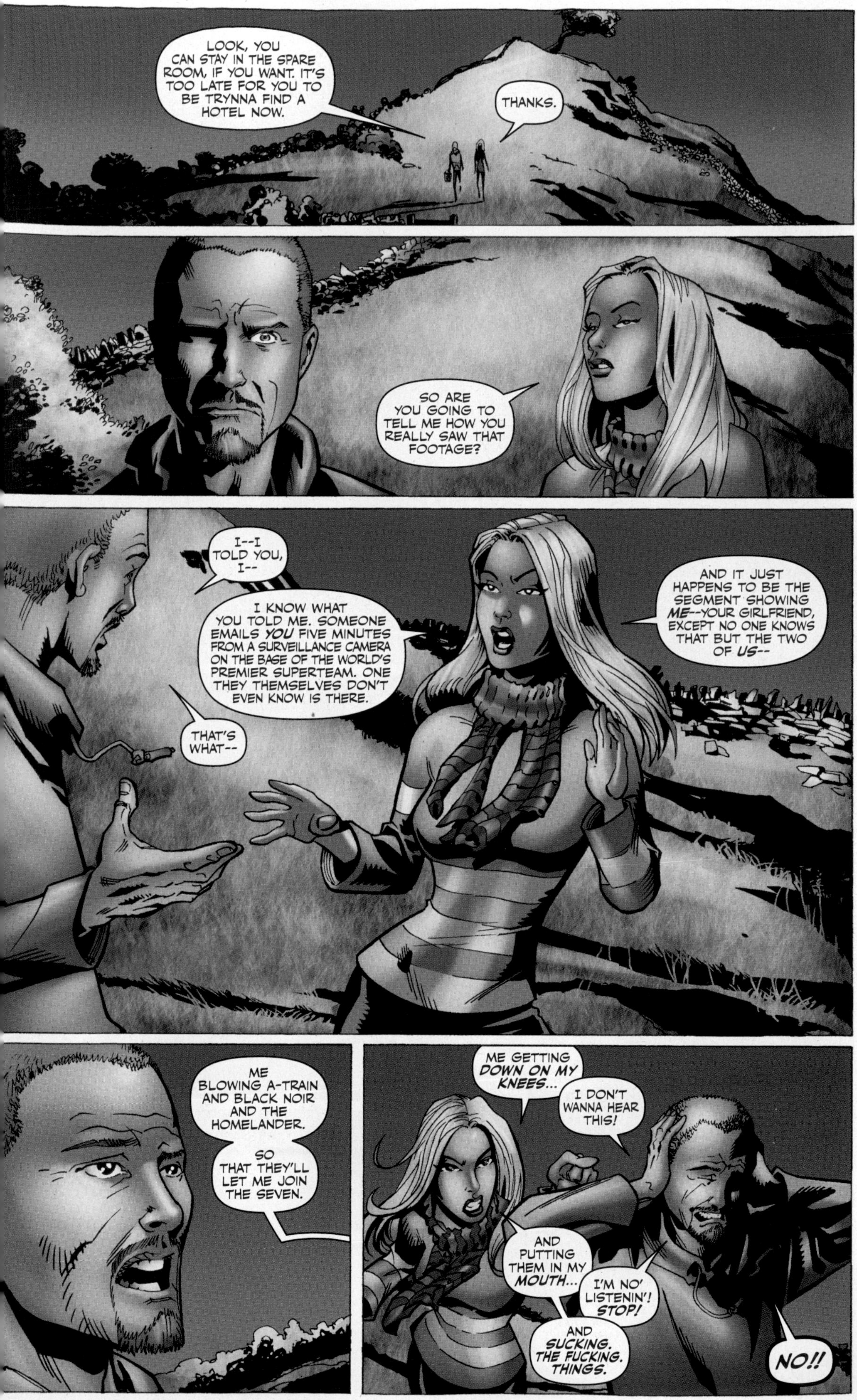
LOOK, YOU CAN STAY IN THE SPARE ROOM, IF YOU WANT. IT'S TOO LATE FOR YOU TO BE TRYNNA FIND A HOTEL NOW.
THANKS.
SO ARE YOU GOING TO TELL ME HOW YOU REALLY SAW THAT FOOTAGE?
I--I TOLD YOU, I--
I KNOW WHAT YOU TOLD ME. SOMEONE EMAILS *YOU* FIVE MINUTES FROM A SURVEILLANCE CAMERA ON THE BASE OF THE WORLD'S PREMIER SUPERTEAM. ONE THEY THEMSELVES DON'T EVEN KNOW IS THERE.
THAT'S WHAT--
AND IT JUST HAPPENS TO BE THE SEGMENT SHOWING *ME*--YOUR GIRLFRIEND, EXCEPT NO ONE KNOWS THAT BUT THE TWO OF *US*--
ME BLOWING A-TRAIN AND BLACK NOIR AND THE HOMELANDER.
SO THAT THEY'LL LET ME JOIN THE SEVEN.
ME GETTING *DOWN ON MY KNEES*...
I DON'T WANNA HEAR THIS!
AND PUTTING THEM IN MY *MOUTH*...
I'M NO' LISTENIN'! *STOP!*
AND *SUCKING. THE FUCKING. THINGS.*
NO!!

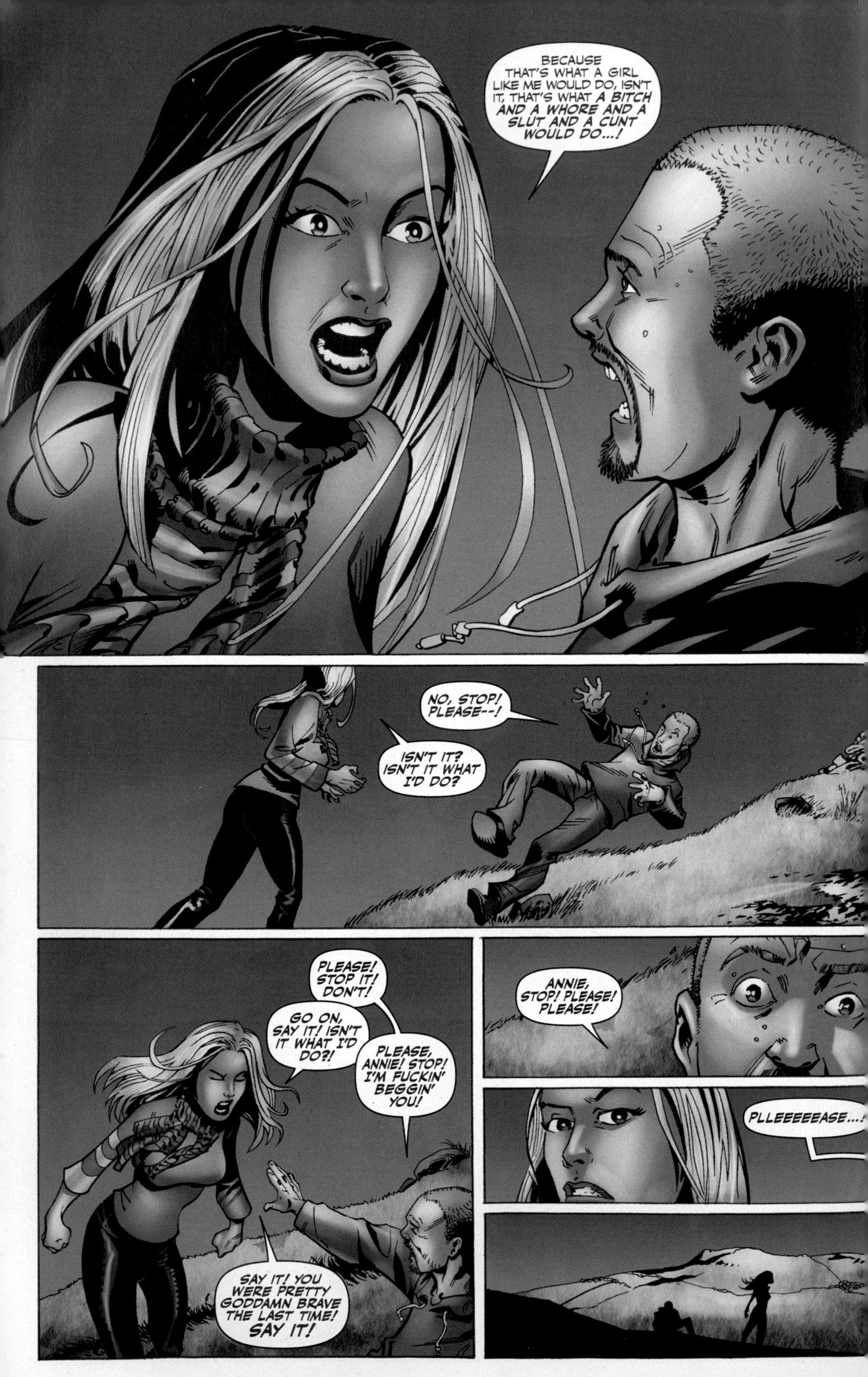
BECAUSE THAT'S WHAT A GIRL LIKE ME WOULD DO, ISN'T IT, THAT'S WHAT A BITCH AND A WHORE AND A SLUT AND A CUNT WOULD DO...!
NO, STOP! PLEASE--!
ISN'T IT? ISN'T IT WHAT I'D DO?
PLEASE! STOP IT! DON'T!
GO ON, SAY IT! ISN'T IT WHAT I'D DO?!
PLEASE, ANNIE! STOP! I'M FUCKIN' BEGGIN' YOU!
SAY IT! YOU WERE PRETTY GODDAMN BRAVE THE LAST TIME! SAY IT!
ANNIE, STOP! PLEASE! PLEASE!
PLLEEEEEASE...!

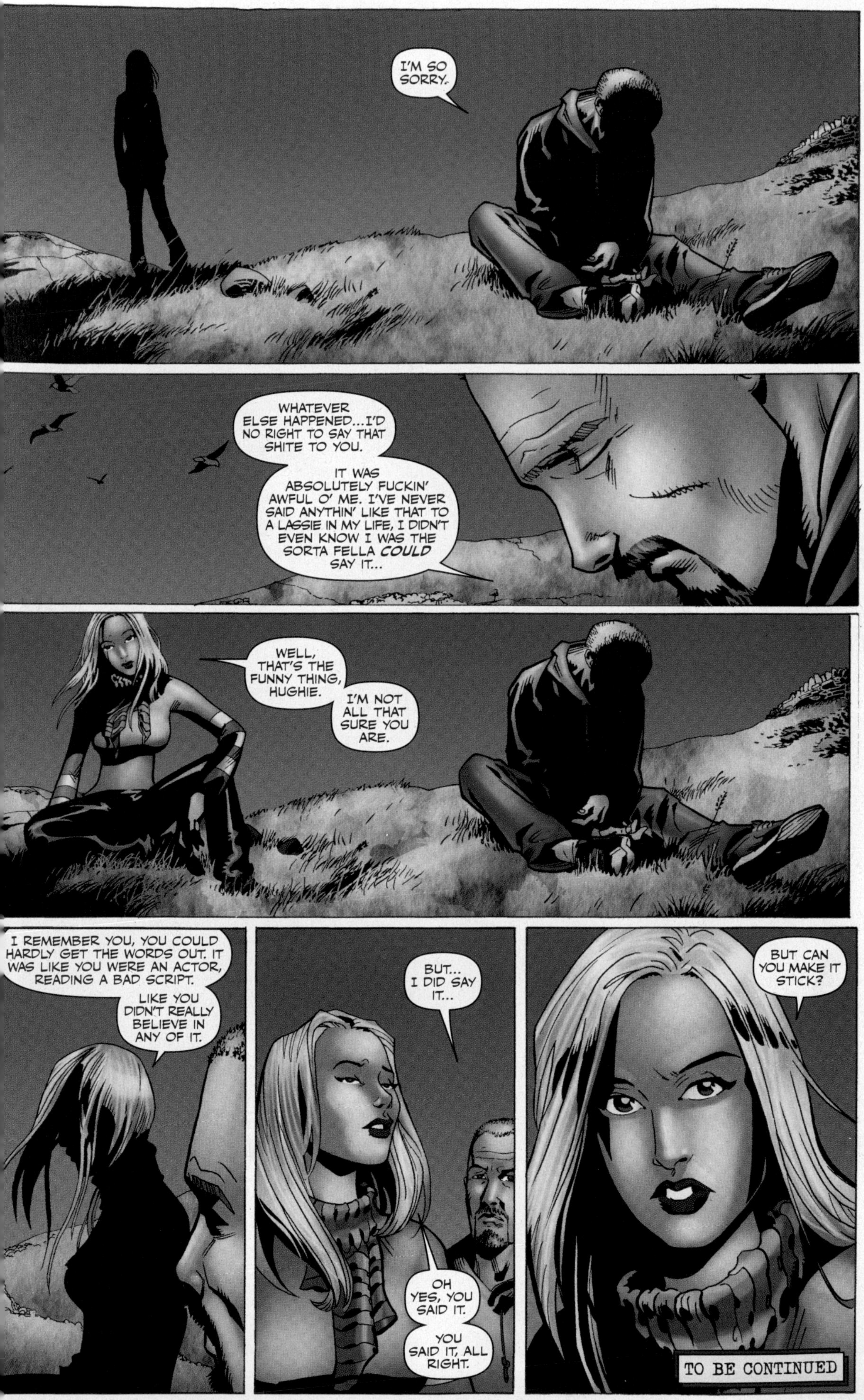
I'M SO SORRY.
WHATEVER ELSE HAPPENED...I'D NO RIGHT TO SAY THAT SHITE TO YOU.
IT WAS ABSOLUTELY FUCKIN' AWFUL O' ME. I'VE NEVER SAID ANYTHIN' LIKE THAT TO A LASSIE IN MY LIFE, I DIDN'T EVEN KNOW I WAS THE SORTA FELLA *COULD* SAY IT...
WELL, THAT'S THE FUNNY THING, HUGHIE.
I'M NOT ALL THAT SURE YOU ARE.
I REMEMBER YOU, YOU COULD HARDLY GET THE WORDS OUT. IT WAS LIKE YOU WERE AN ACTOR, READING A BAD SCRIPT.
LIKE YOU DIDN'T REALLY BELIEVE IN ANY OF IT.
BUT... I DID SAY IT...
OH YES, YOU SAID IT.
YOU SAID IT, ALL RIGHT.
BUT CAN YOU MAKE IT STICK?
TO BE CONTINUED

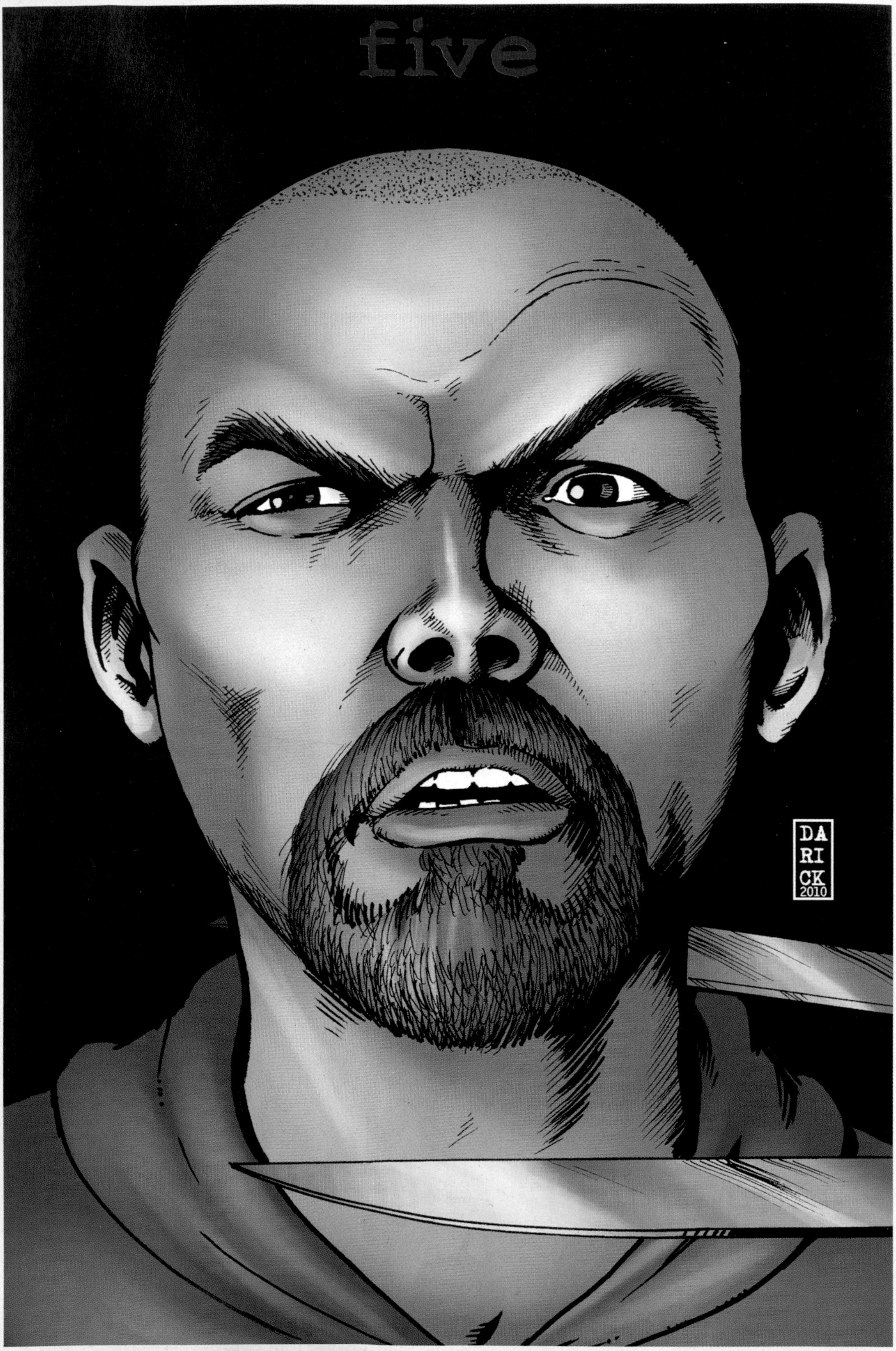
five
DA
RI
CK
2010

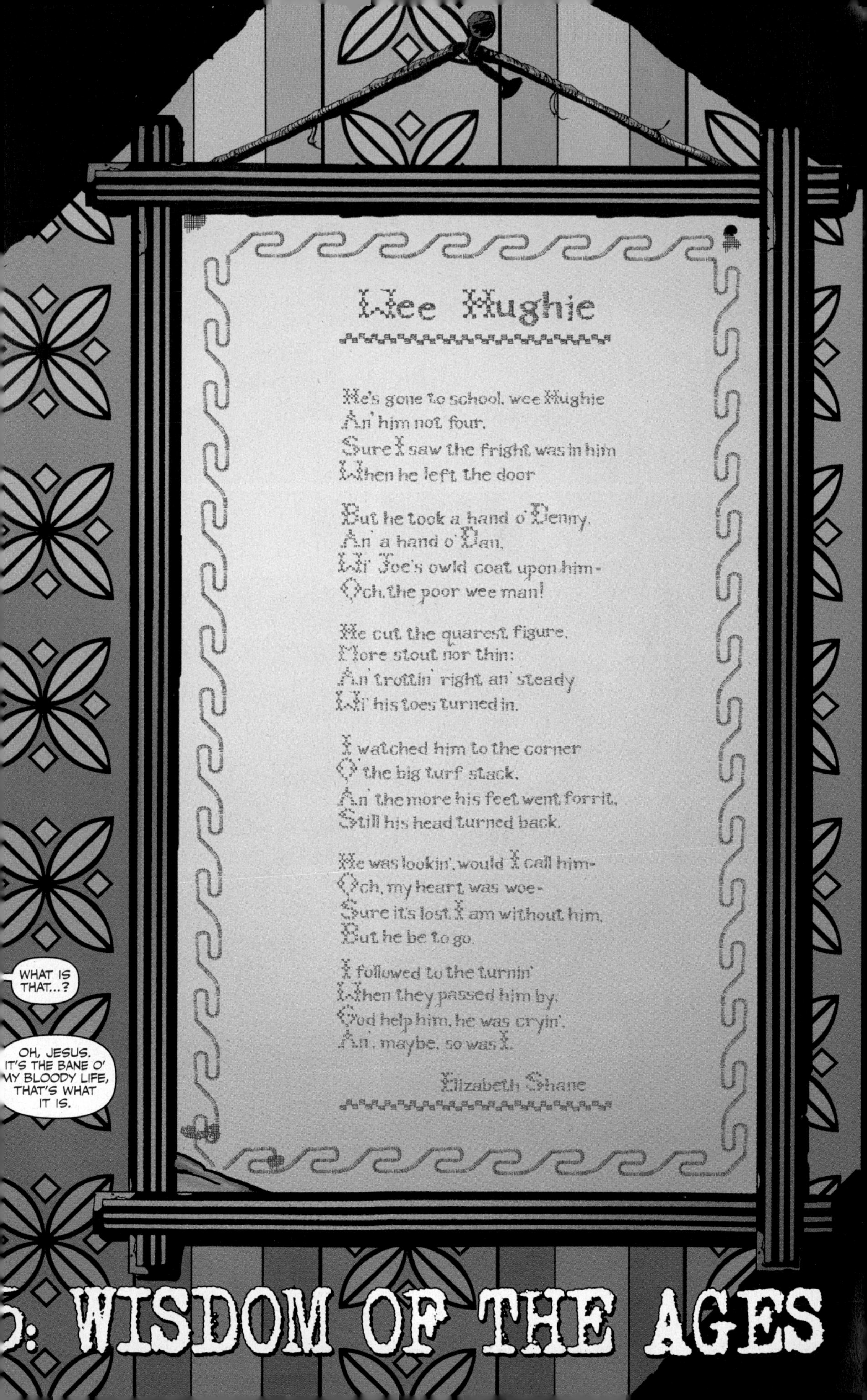

Wee Hughie
He's gone to school, wee Hughie
An' him not four.
Sure I saw the fright was in him
When he left the door
But he took a hand o' Denny,
An' a hand o' Dan,
Wi' Joe's owld coat upon him-
Och, the poor wee man!
He cut the quarest figure,
More stout nor thin:
An' trottin' right an' steady
Wi' his toes turned in.
I watched him to the corner
O' the big turf stack,
An' the more his feet went forrit,
Still his head turned back.
He was lookin', would I call him-
Och, my heart was woe-
Sure it's lost I am without him,
But he be to go.
I followed to the turnin'
When they passed him by,
God help him, he was cryin',
An', maybe, so was I.
Elizabeth Shane
WHAT IS THAT...?
OH, JESUS. IT'S THE BANE O' MY BLOODY LIFE, THAT'S WHAT IT IS.
WISDOM OF THE AGES

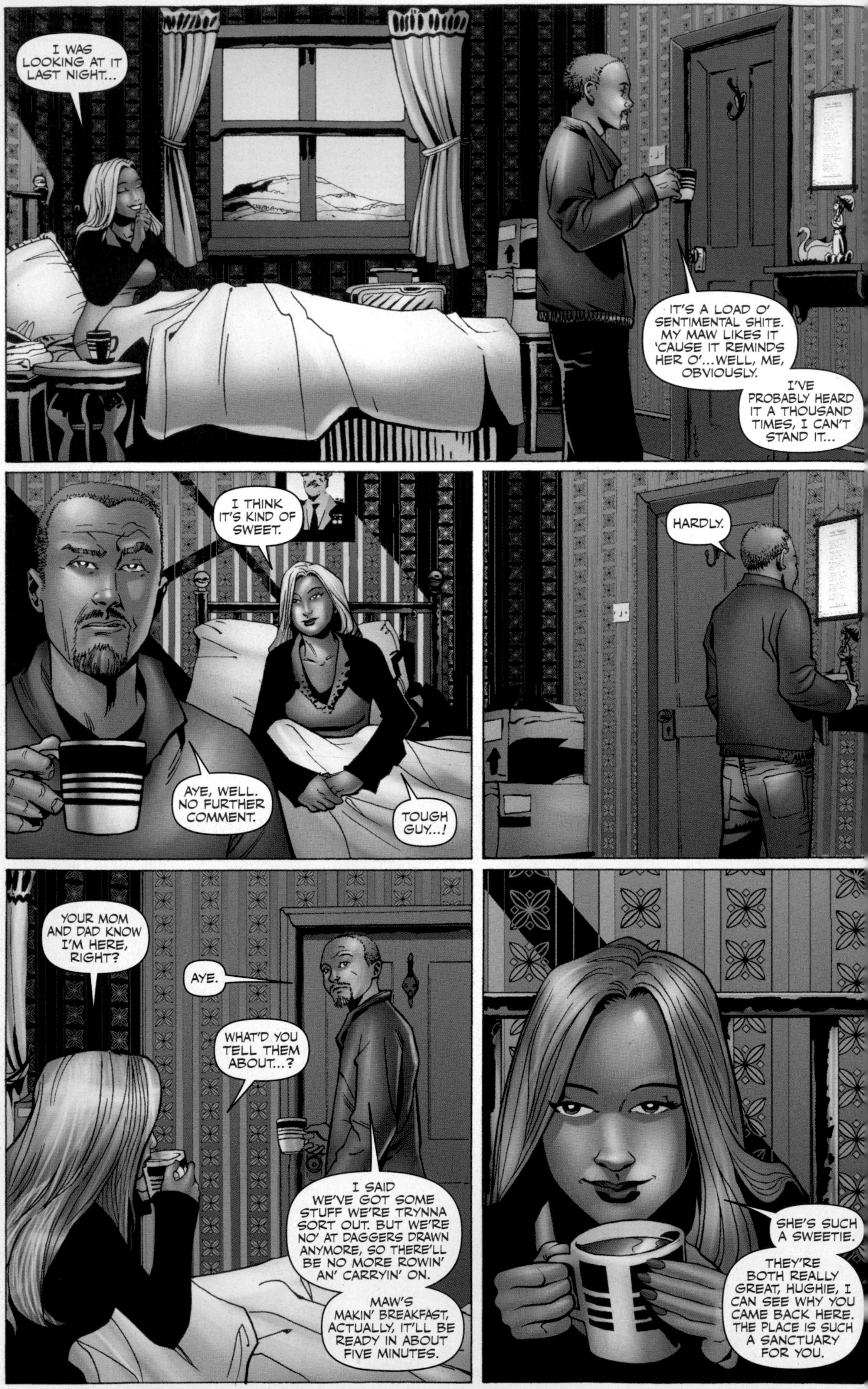

I WAS LOOKING AT IT LAST NIGHT...
IT'S A LOAD O' SENTIMENTAL SHITE. MY MAW LIKES IT 'CAUSE IT REMINDS HER O'...WELL, ME, OBVIOUSLY.
I'VE PROBABLY HEARD IT A THOUSAND TIMES, I CAN'T STAND IT...
I THINK IT'S KIND OF SWEET.
AYE, WELL. NO FURTHER COMMENT.
TOUGH GUY...!
HARDLY.
YOUR MOM AND DAD KNOW I'M HERE, RIGHT?
AYE.
WHAT'D YOU TELL THEM ABOUT...?
I SAID WE'VE GOT SOME STUFF WE'RE TRYNNA SORT OUT. BUT WE'RE NO' AT DAGGERS DRAWN ANYMORE, SO THERE'LL BE NO MORE ROWIN' AN' CARRYIN' ON.
MAW'S MAKIN' BREAKFAST, ACTUALLY, IT'LL BE READY IN ABOUT FIVE MINUTES.
SHE'S SUCH A SWEETIE.
THEY'RE BOTH REALLY GREAT, HUGHIE, I CAN SEE WHY YOU CAME BACK HERE. THE PLACE IS SUCH A SANCTUARY FOR YOU.

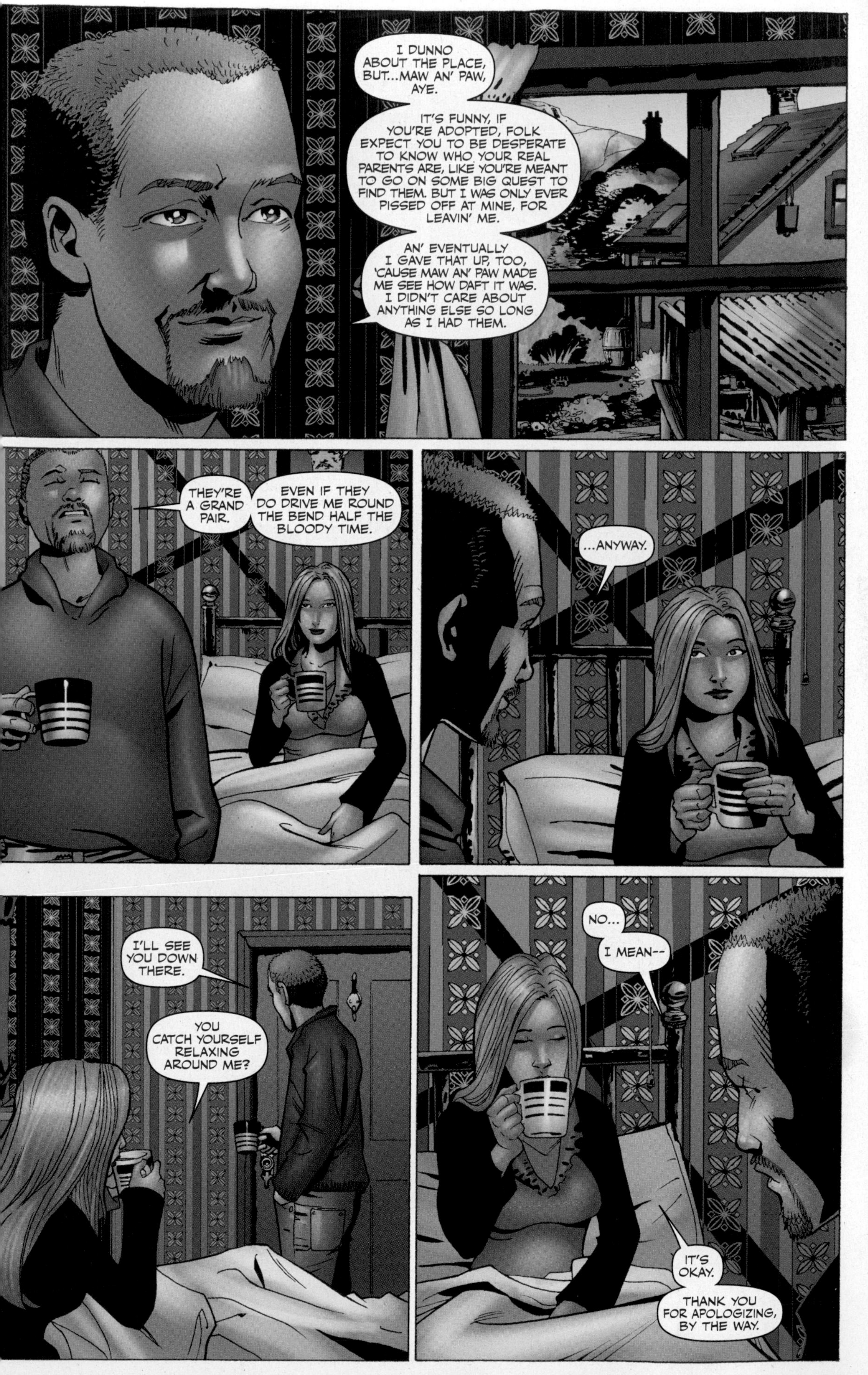
I DUNNO ABOUT THE PLACE, BUT...MAW AN' PAW, AYE.
IT'S FUNNY, IF YOU'RE ADOPTED, FOLK EXPECT YOU TO BE DESPERATE TO KNOW WHO YOUR REAL PARENTS ARE, LIKE YOU'RE MEANT TO GO ON SOME BIG QUEST TO FIND THEM. BUT I WAS ONLY EVER PISSED OFF AT MINE, FOR LEAVIN' ME.
AN' EVENTUALLY I GAVE THAT UP, TOO, 'CAUSE MAW AN' PAW MADE ME SEE HOW DAFT IT WAS. I DIDN'T CARE ABOUT ANYTHING ELSE SO LONG AS I HAD THEM.
THEY'RE A GRAND PAIR.
EVEN IF THEY DO DRIVE ME ROUND THE BEND HALF THE BLOODY TIME.
...ANYWAY.
I'LL SEE YOU DOWN THERE.
YOU CATCH YOURSELF RELAXING AROUND ME?
NO...
I MEAN--
IT'S OKAY.
THANK YOU FOR APOLOGIZING, BY THE WAY.

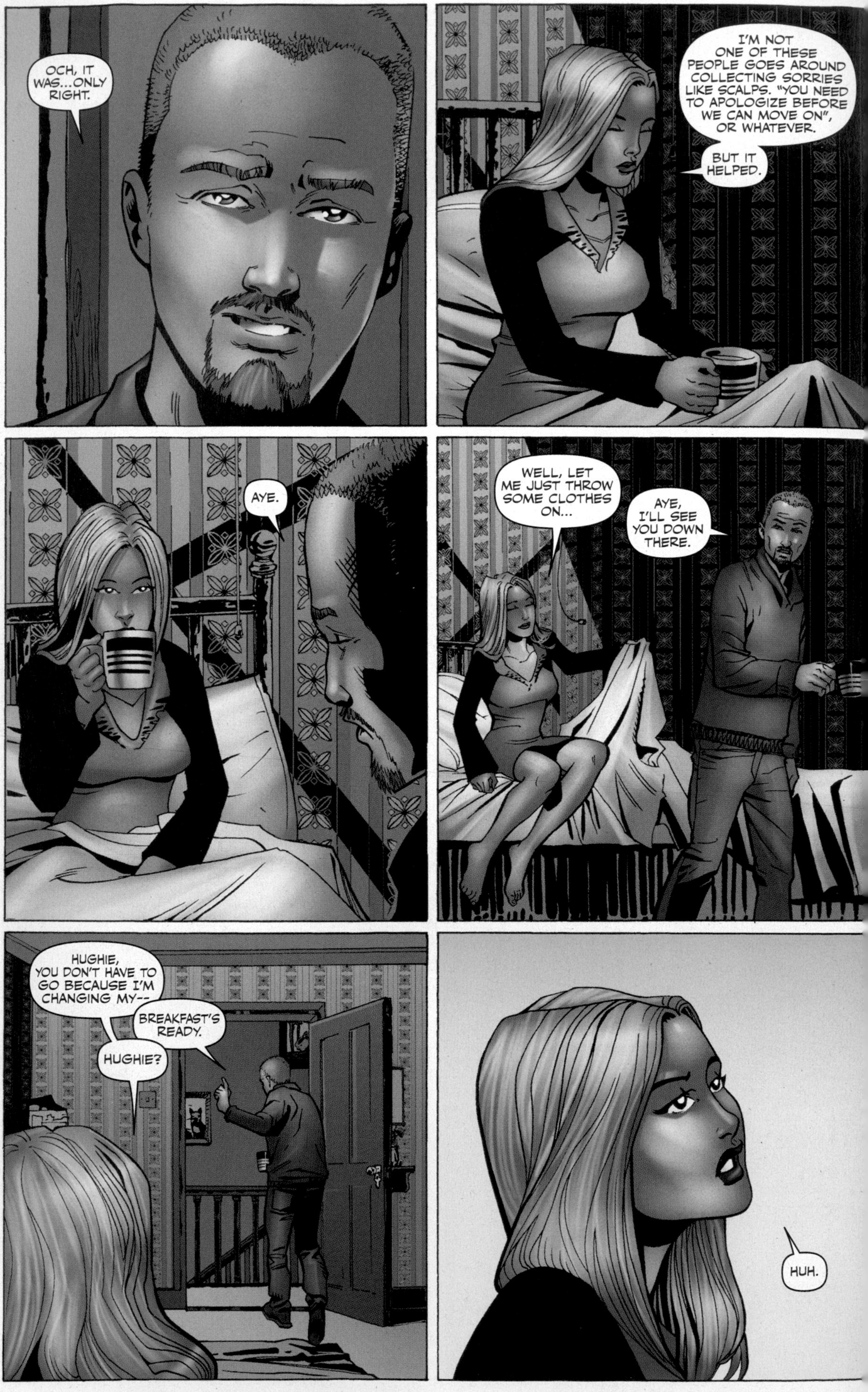
OCH, IT WAS...ONLY RIGHT.
I'M NOT ONE OF THESE PEOPLE GOES AROUND COLLECTING SORRIES LIKE SCALPS. "YOU NEED TO APOLOGIZE BEFORE WE CAN MOVE ON", OR WHATEVER.
BUT IT HELPED.
AYE.
WELL, LET ME JUST THROW SOME CLOTHES ON...
AYE, I'LL SEE YOU DOWN THERE.
HUGHIE, YOU DON'T HAVE TO GO BECAUSE I'M CHANGING MY--
BREAKFAST'S READY.
HUGHIE?
HUH.

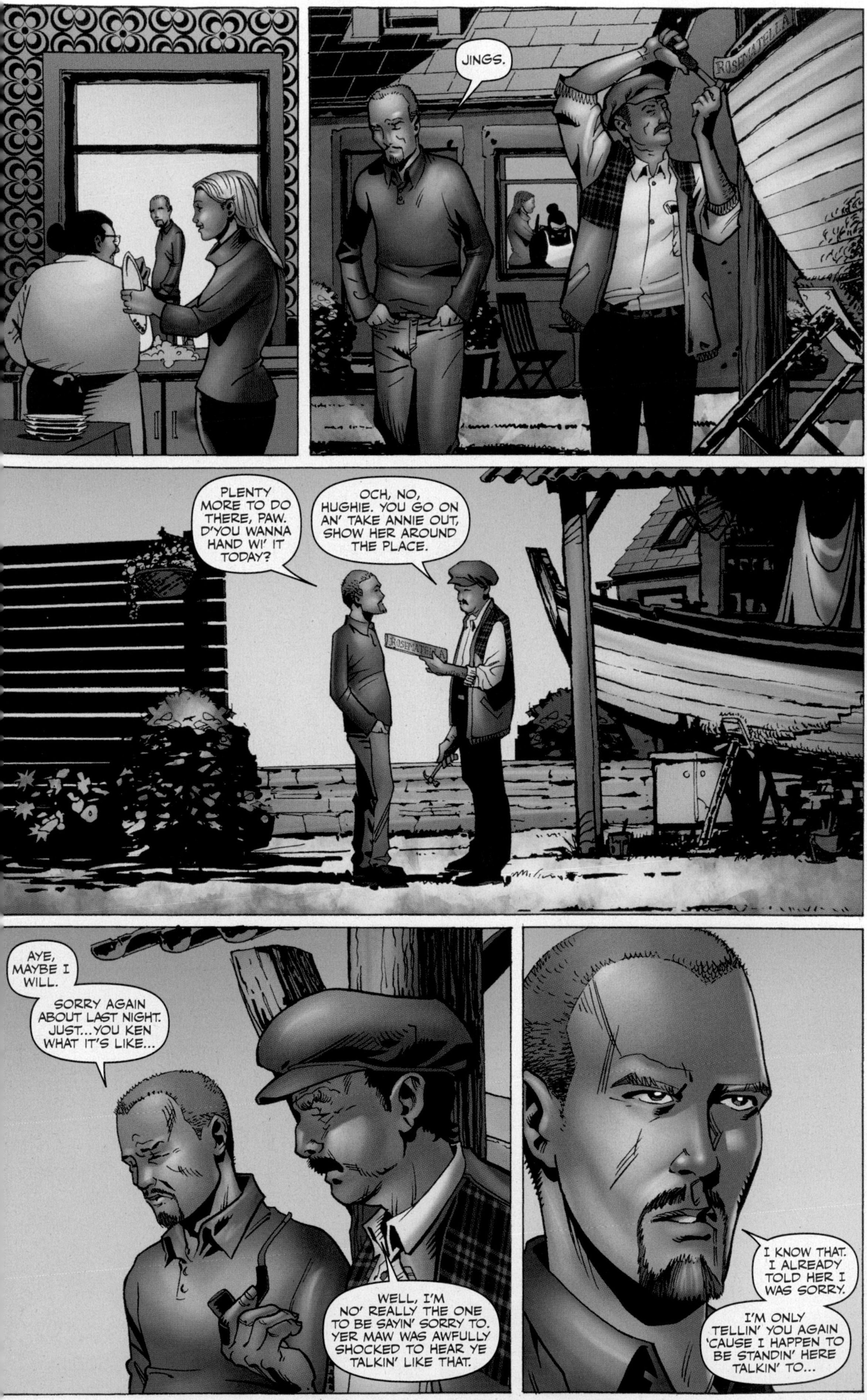
JINGS.
ROSEMATELLA
PLENTY MORE TO DO THERE, PAW. D'YOU WANNA HAND WI' IT TODAY?
OCH, NO, HUGHIE. YOU GO ON AN' TAKE ANNIE OUT, SHOW HER AROUND THE PLACE.
AYE, MAYBE I WILL.
SORRY AGAIN ABOUT LAST NIGHT. JUST...YOU KEN WHAT IT'S LIKE...
WELL, I'M NO' REALLY THE ONE TO BE SAYIN' SORRY TO. YER MAW WAS AWFULLY SHOCKED TO HEAR YE TALKIN' LIKE THAT.
I KNOW THAT. I ALREADY TOLD HER I WAS SORRY.
I'M ONLY TELLIN' YOU AGAIN 'CAUSE I HAPPEN TO BE STANDIN' HERE TALKIN' TO...

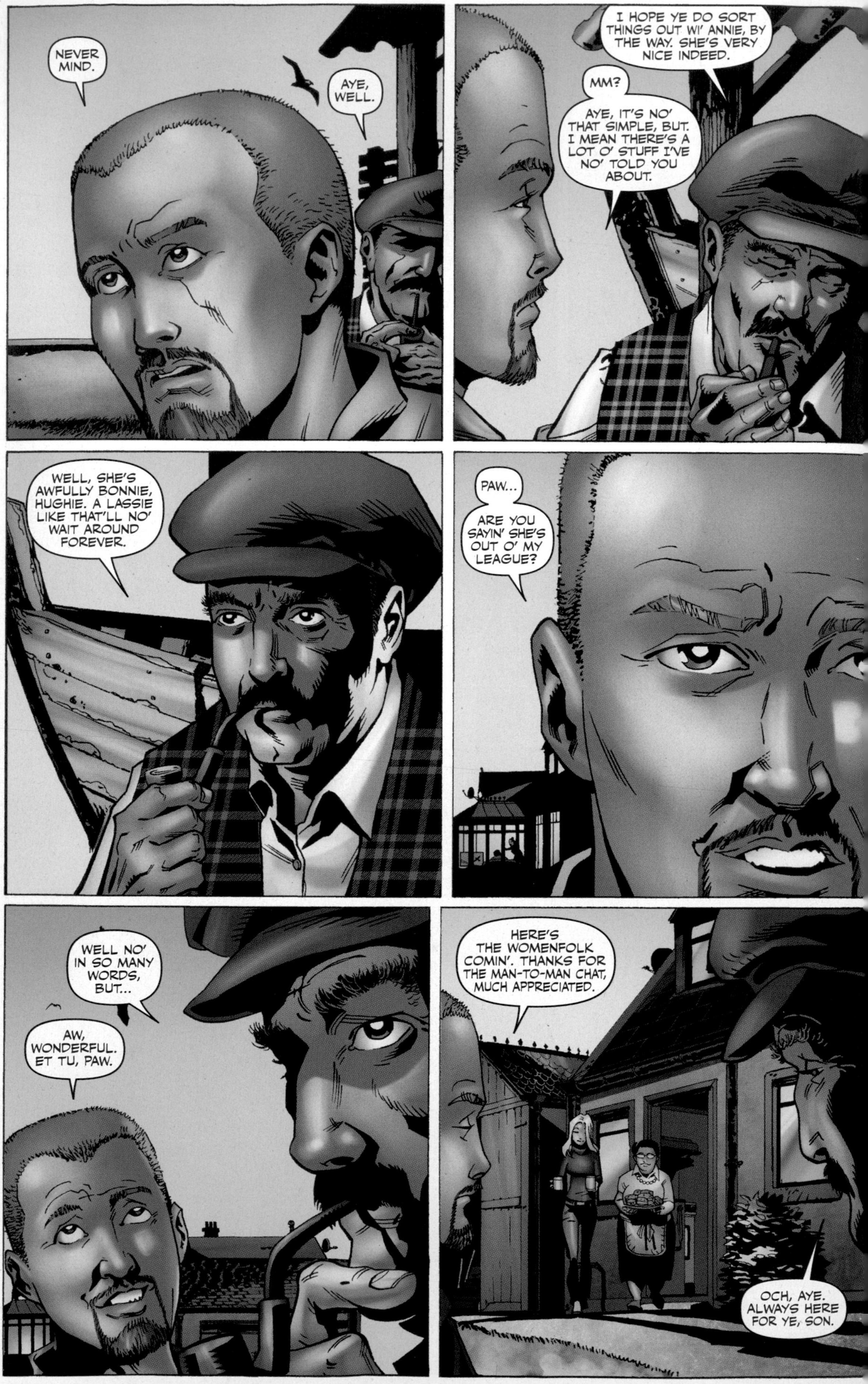
NEVER MIND.
AYE, WELL.
I HOPE YE DO SORT THINGS OUT WI' ANNIE, BY THE WAY. SHE'S VERY NICE INDEED.
MM?
AYE, IT'S NO' THAT SIMPLE, BUT. I MEAN THERE'S A LOT O' STUFF I'VE NO' TOLD YOU ABOUT.
WELL, SHE'S AWFULLY BONNIE, HUGHIE. A LASSIE LIKE THAT'LL NO' WAIT AROUND FOREVER.
PAW...
ARE YOU SAYIN' SHE'S OUT O' MY LEAGUE?
WELL NO' IN SO MANY WORDS, BUT...
AW, WONDERFUL. ET TU, PAW.
HERE'S THE WOMENFOLK COMIN'. THANKS FOR THE MAN-TO-MAN CHAT, MUCH APPRECIATED.
OCH, AYE. ALWAYS HERE FOR YE, SON.

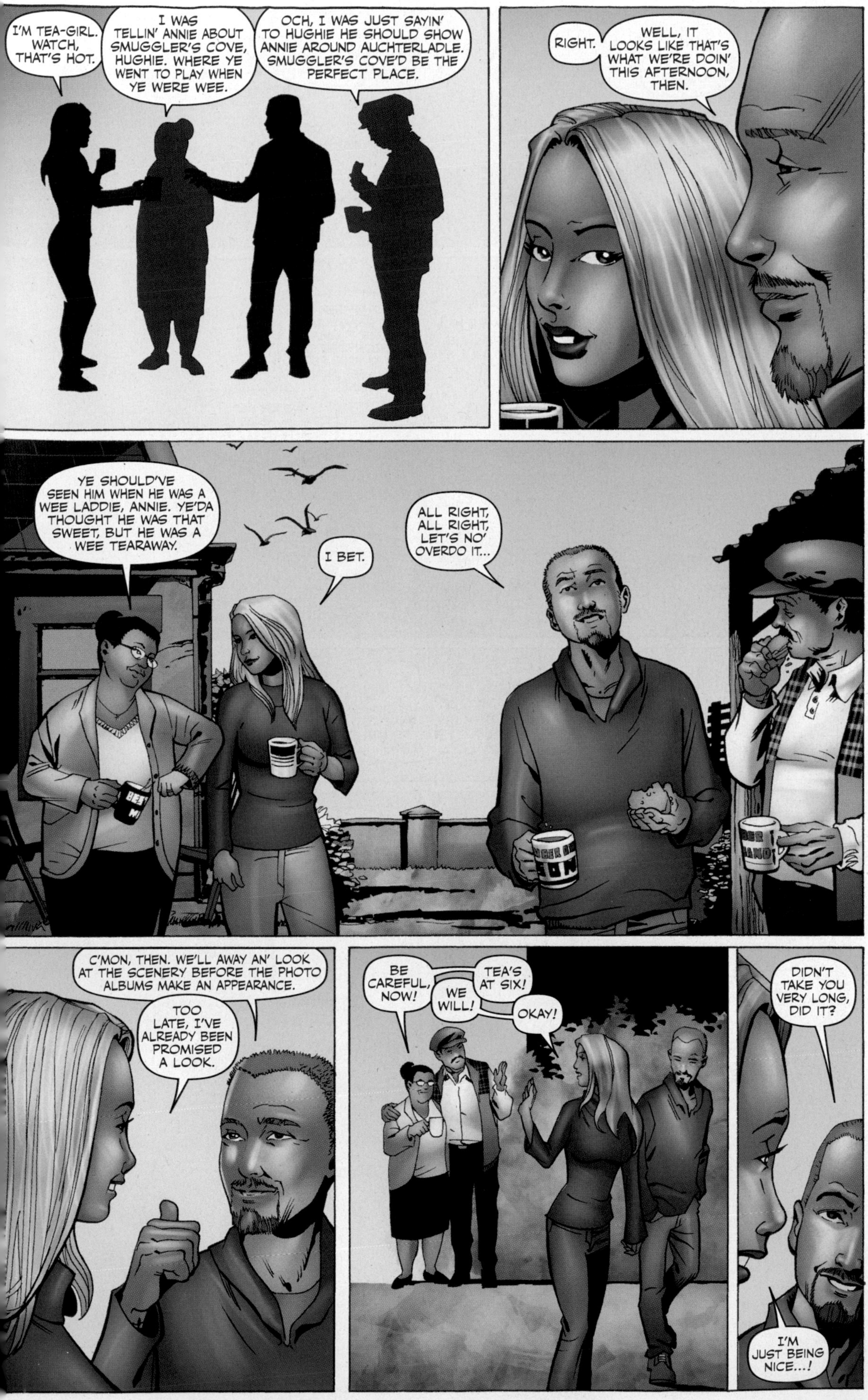
I'M TEA-GIRL. WATCH, THAT'S HOT.
I WAS TELLIN' ANNIE ABOUT SMUGGLER'S COVE, HUGHIE. WHERE YE WENT TO PLAY WHEN YE WERE WEE.
OCH, I WAS JUST SAYIN' TO HUGHIE HE SHOULD SHOW ANNIE AROUND AUCHTERLADLE. SMUGGLER'S COVE'D BE THE PERFECT PLACE.
RIGHT.
WELL, IT LOOKS LIKE THAT'S WHAT WE'RE DOIN' THIS AFTERNOON, THEN.
YE SHOULD'VE SEEN HIM WHEN HE WAS A WEE LADDIE, ANNIE. YE'DA THOUGHT HE WAS THAT SWEET, BUT HE WAS A WEE TEARAWAY.
I BET.
ALL RIGHT, ALL RIGHT, LET'S NO' OVERDO IT...
C'MON, THEN. WE'LL AWAY AN' LOOK AT THE SCENERY BEFORE THE PHOTO ALBUMS MAKE AN APPEARANCE.
TOO LATE, I'VE ALREADY BEEN PROMISED A LOOK.
BE CAREFUL, NOW!
WE WILL!
TEA'S AT SIX!
OKAY!
DIDN'T TAKE YOU VERY LONG, DID IT?
I'M JUST BEING NICE...!

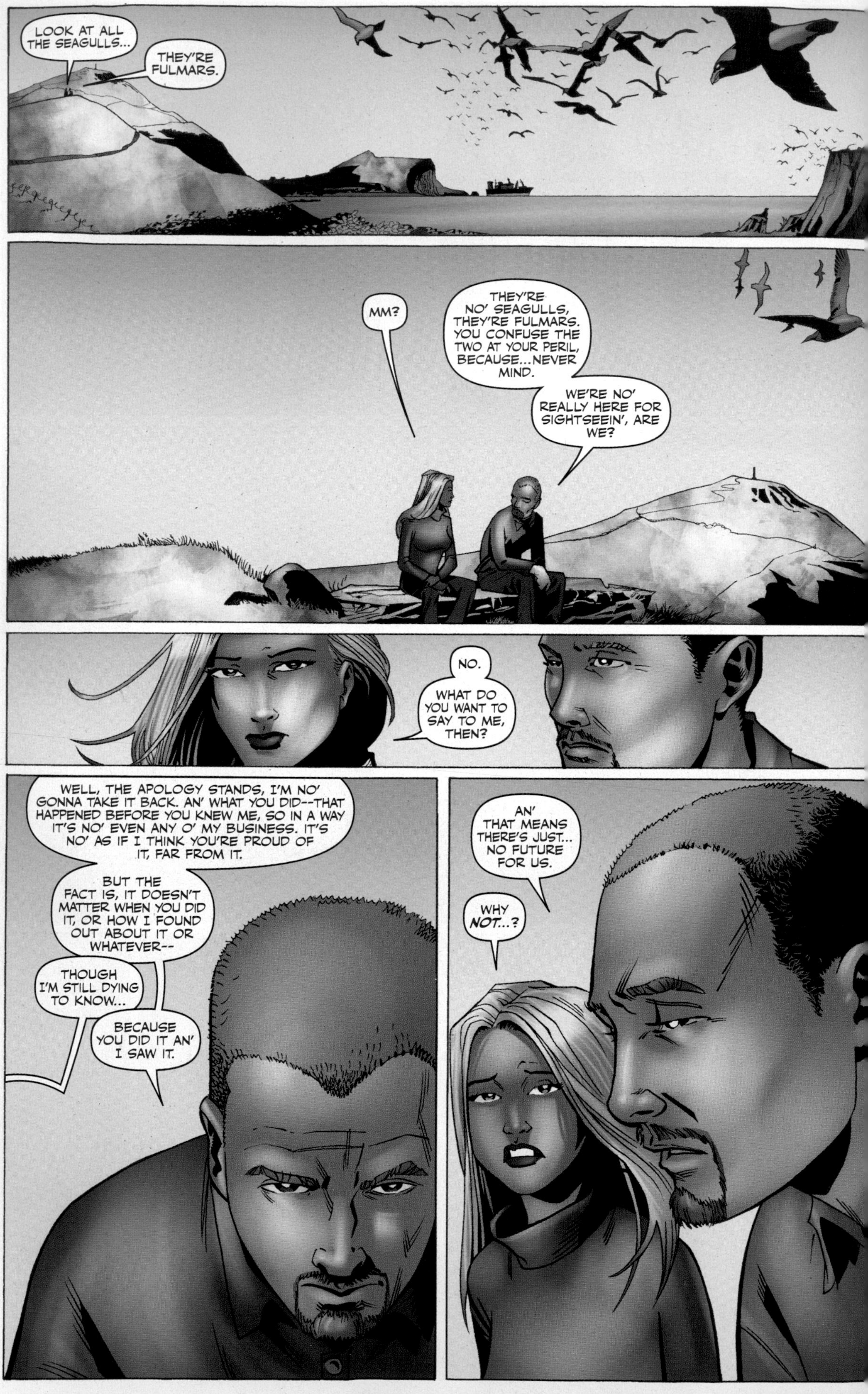

LOOK AT ALL THE SEAGULLS...
THEY'RE FULMARS.
MM?
THEY'RE NO' SEAGULLS, THEY'RE FULMARS. YOU CONFUSE THE TWO AT YOUR PERIL, BECAUSE...NEVER MIND.
WE'RE NO' REALLY HERE FOR SIGHTSEEIN', ARE WE?
NO.
WHAT DO YOU WANT TO SAY TO ME, THEN?
WELL, THE APOLOGY STANDS, I'M NO' GONNA TAKE IT BACK. AN' WHAT YOU DID--THAT HAPPENED BEFORE YOU KNEW ME, SO IN A WAY IT'S NO' EVEN ANY O' MY BUSINESS. IT'S NO' AS IF I THINK YOU'RE PROUD OF IT, FAR FROM IT.
BUT THE FACT IS, IT DOESN'T MATTER WHEN YOU DID IT, OR HOW I FOUND OUT ABOUT IT OR WHATEVER--
THOUGH I'M STILL DYING TO KNOW...
BECAUSE YOU DID IT AN' I SAW IT.
AN' THAT MEANS THERE'S JUST... NO FUTURE FOR US.
WHY *NOT*...?

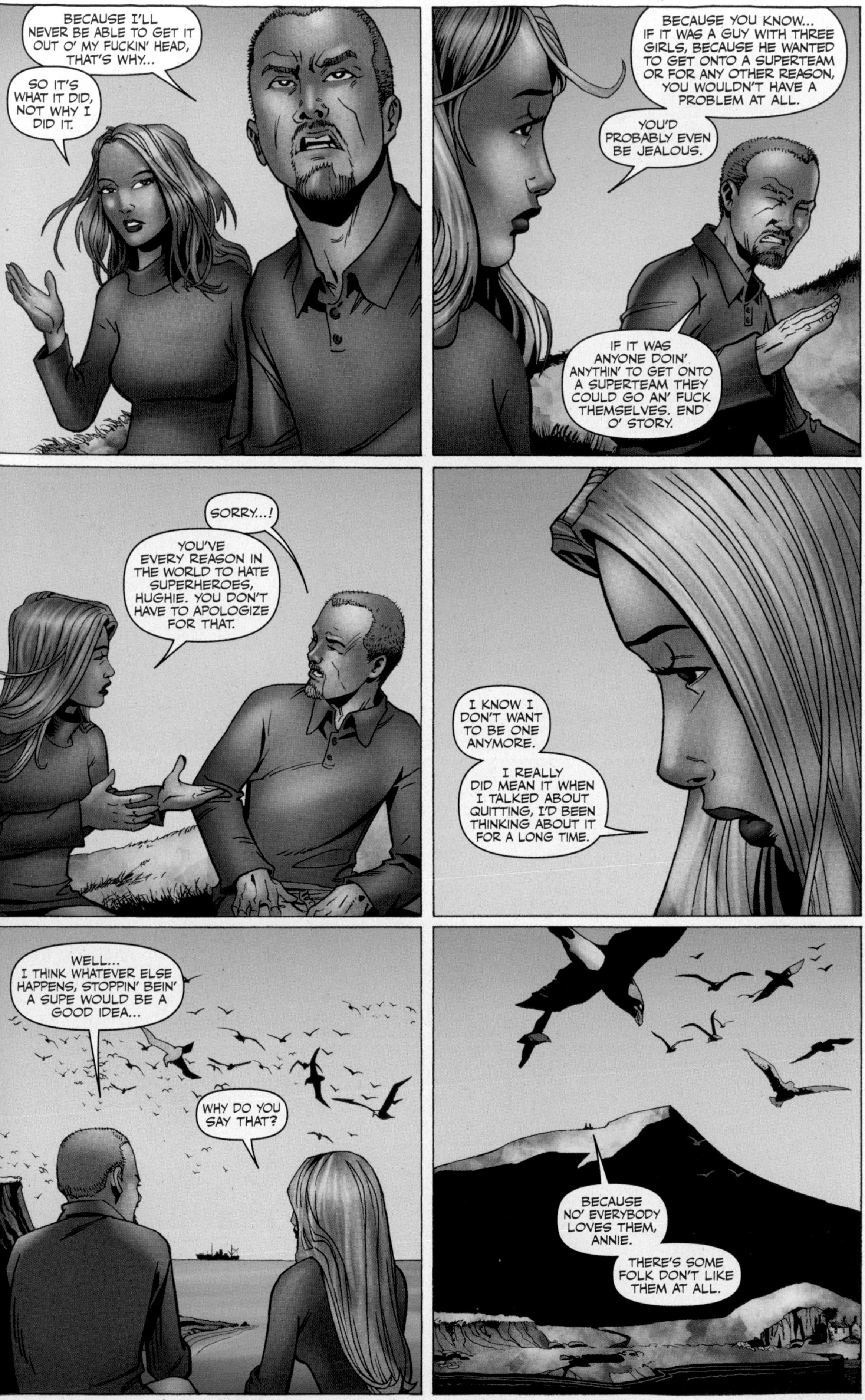
BECAUSE I'LL NEVER BE ABLE TO GET IT OUT O' MY FUCKIN' HEAD, THAT'S WHY...
SO IT'S WHAT IT DID, NOT WHY I DID IT.
BECAUSE YOU KNOW... IF IT WAS A GUY WITH THREE GIRLS, BECAUSE HE WANTED TO GET ONTO A SUPERTEAM OR FOR ANY OTHER REASON, YOU WOULDN'T HAVE A PROBLEM AT ALL.
YOU'D PROBABLY EVEN BE JEALOUS.
IF IT WAS ANYONE DOIN' ANYTHIN' TO GET ONTO A SUPERTEAM THEY COULD GO AN' FUCK THEMSELVES. END O' STORY.
SORRY...!
YOU'VE EVERY REASON IN THE WORLD TO HATE SUPERHEROES, HUGHIE. YOU DON'T HAVE TO APOLOGIZE FOR THAT.
I KNOW I DON'T WANT TO BE ONE ANYMORE.
I REALLY DID MEAN IT WHEN I TALKED ABOUT QUITTING, I'D BEEN THINKING ABOUT IT FOR A LONG TIME.
WELL... I THINK WHATEVER ELSE HAPPENS, STOPPIN' BEIN' A SUPE WOULD BE A GOOD IDEA...
WHY DO YOU SAY THAT?
BECAUSE NO' EVERYBODY LOVES THEM, ANNIE.
THERE'S SOME FOLK DON'T LIKE THEM AT ALL.

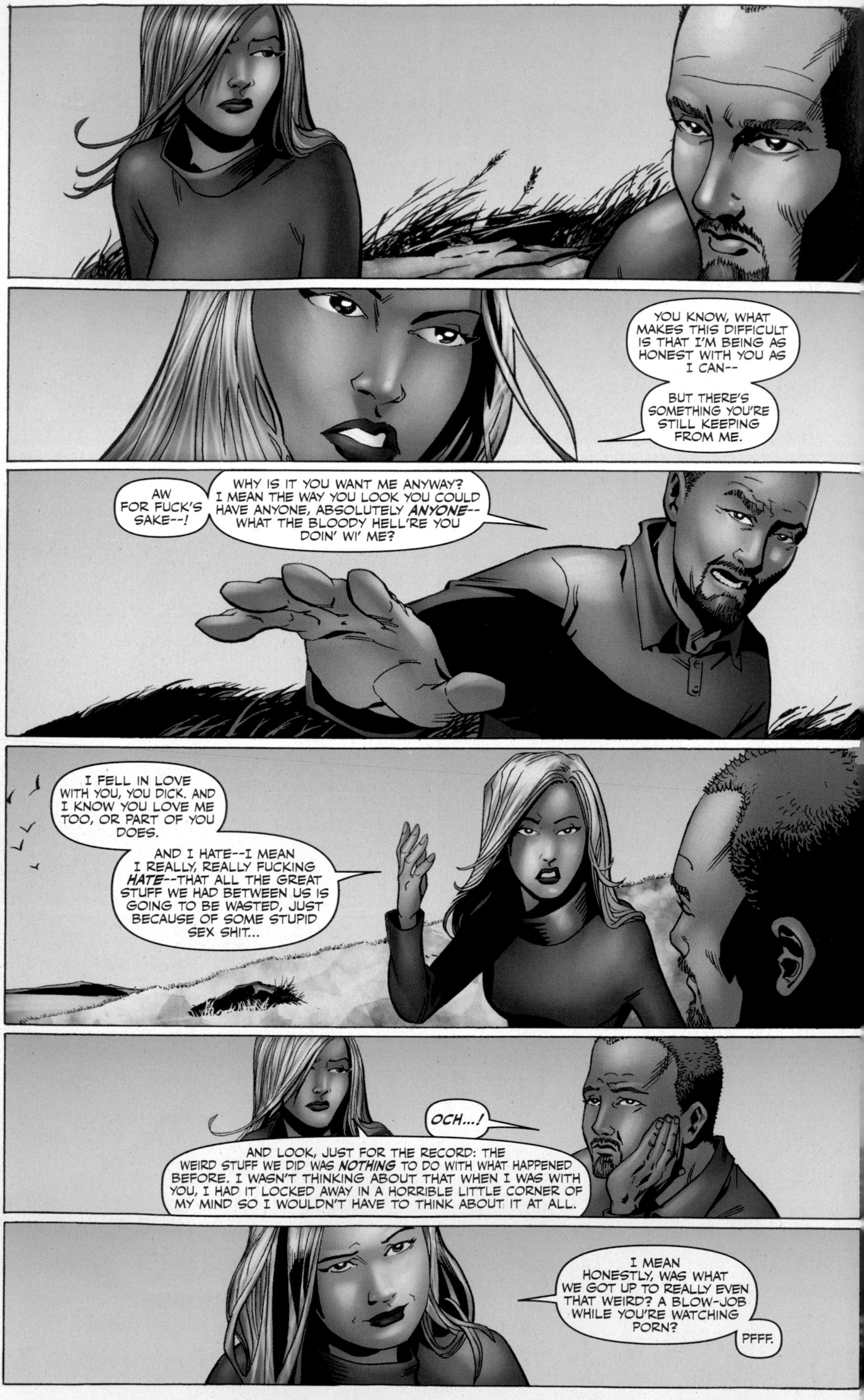

YOU KNOW, WHAT MAKES THIS DIFFICULT IS THAT I'M BEING AS HONEST WITH YOU AS I CAN--
BUT THERE'S SOMETHING YOU'RE STILL KEEPING FROM ME.
AW FOR FUCK'S SAKE--!
WHY IS IT YOU WANT ME ANYWAY? I MEAN THE WAY YOU LOOK YOU COULD HAVE ANYONE, ABSOLUTELY *ANYONE*-- WHAT THE BLOODY HELL'RE YOU DOIN' WI' ME?
I FELL IN LOVE WITH YOU, YOU DICK. AND I KNOW YOU LOVE ME TOO, OR PART OF YOU DOES.
AND I HATE--I MEAN I REALLY, REALLY FUCKING *HATE*--THAT ALL THE GREAT STUFF WE HAD BETWEEN US IS GOING TO BE WASTED, JUST BECAUSE OF SOME STUPID SEX SHIT...
OCH...!
AND LOOK, JUST FOR THE RECORD: THE WEIRD STUFF WE DID WAS *NOTHING* TO DO WITH WHAT HAPPENED BEFORE. I WASN'T THINKING ABOUT THAT WHEN I WAS WITH YOU, I HAD IT LOCKED AWAY IN A HORRIBLE LITTLE CORNER OF MY MIND SO I WOULDN'T HAVE TO THINK ABOUT IT AT ALL.
I MEAN HONESTLY, WAS WHAT WE GOT UP TO REALLY EVEN THAT WEIRD? A BLOW-JOB WHILE YOU'RE WATCHING PORN?
PFFF.

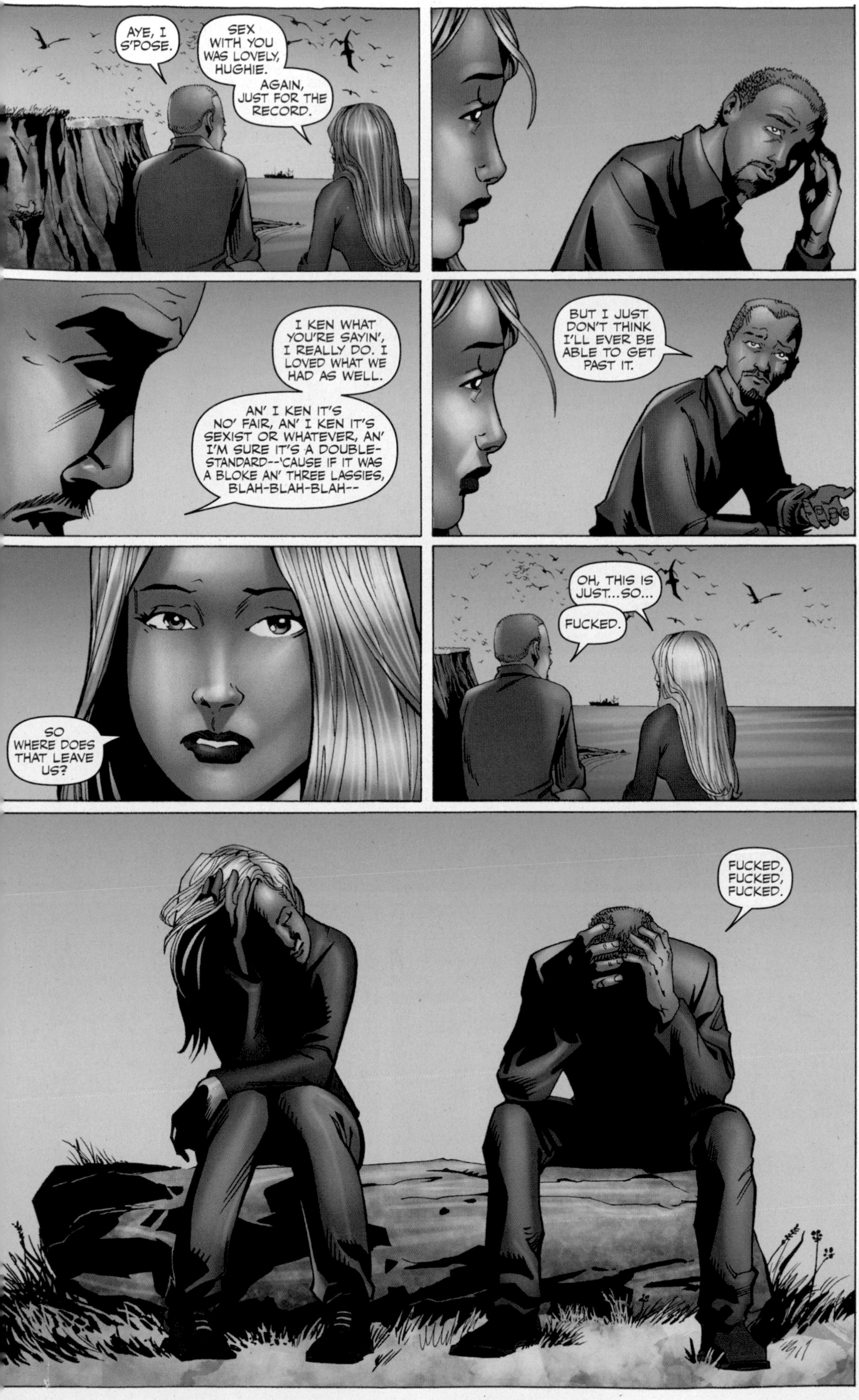
AYE, I S'POSE.
SEX WITH YOU WAS LOVELY, HUGHIE.
AGAIN, JUST FOR THE RECORD.
I KEN WHAT YOU'RE SAYIN', I REALLY DO. I LOVED WHAT WE HAD AS WELL.
AN' I KEN IT'S NO' FAIR, AN' I KEN IT'S SEXIST OR WHATEVER, AN' I'M SURE IT'S A DOUBLE-STANDARD--'CAUSE IF IT WAS A BLOKE AN' THREE LASSIES, BLAH-BLAH-BLAH--
BUT I JUST DON'T THINK I'LL EVER BE ABLE TO GET PAST IT.
SO WHERE DOES THAT LEAVE US?
OH, THIS IS JUST...SO...
FUCKED.
FUCKED, FUCKED, FUCKED.

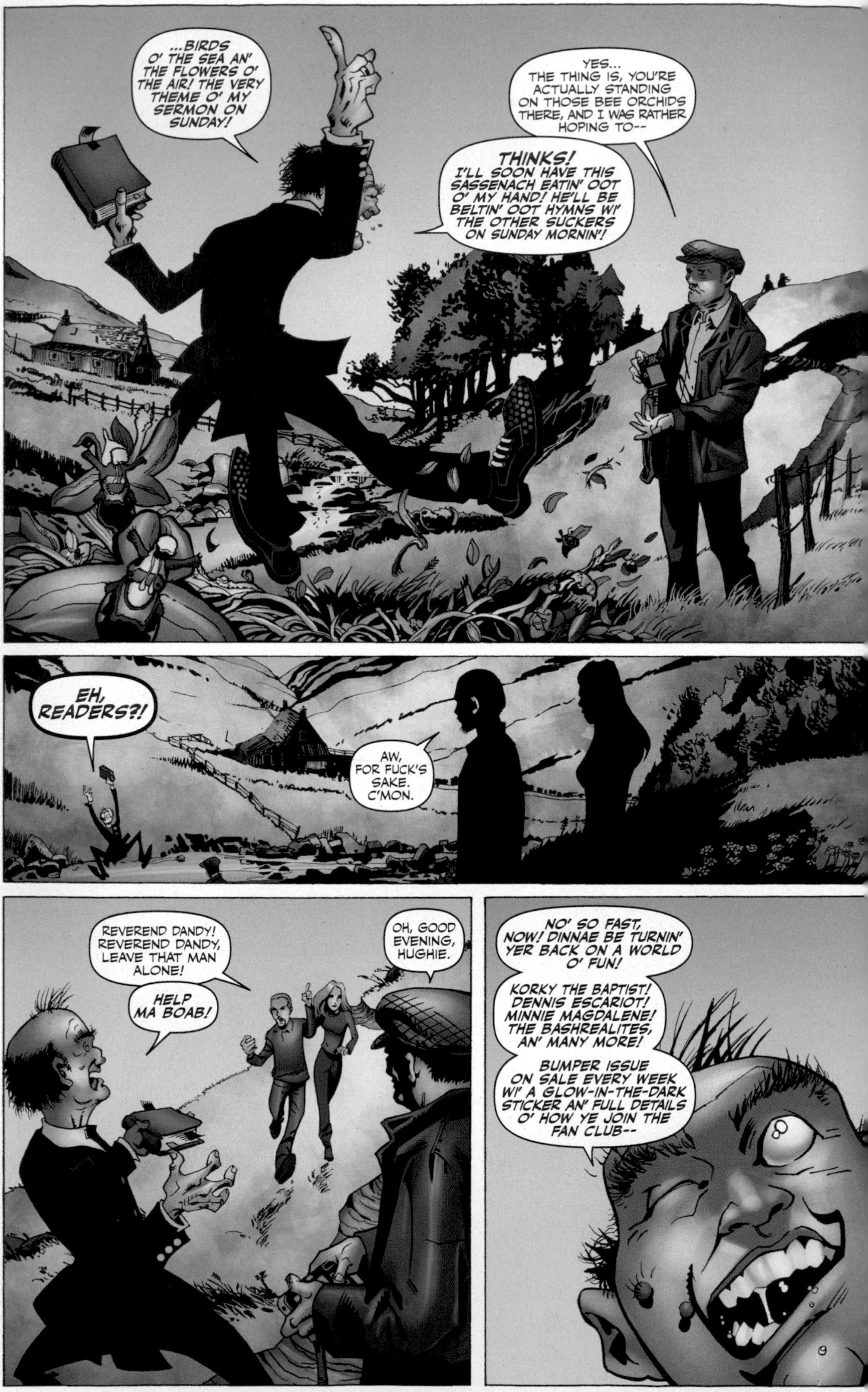
...BIRDS O' THE SEA AN' THE FLOWERS O' THE AIR! THE VERY THEME O' MY SERMON ON SUNDAY!
YES... THE THING IS, YOU'RE ACTUALLY STANDING ON THOSE BEE ORCHIDS THERE, AND I WAS RATHER HOPING TO--
THINKS! I'LL SOON HAVE THIS SASSENACH EATIN' OOT O' MY HAND! HE'LL BE BELTIN' OOT HYMNS WI' THE OTHER SUCKERS ON SUNDAY MORNIN'!
EH, READERS?!
AW, FOR FUCK'S SAKE. C'MON.
REVEREND DANDY! REVEREND DANDY, LEAVE THAT MAN ALONE!
HELP MA BOAB!
OH, GOOD EVENING, HUGHIE.
NO' SO FAST, NOW! DINNAE BE TURNIN' YER BACK ON A WORLD O' FUN!
KORKY THE BAPTIST! DENNIS ESCARIOT! MINNIE MAGDALENE! THE BASHREALITES, AN' MANY MORE!
BUMPER ISSUE ON SALE EVERY WEEK WI' A GLOW-IN-THE-DARK STICKER AN' FULL DETAILS O' HOW YE JOIN THE FAN CLUB--

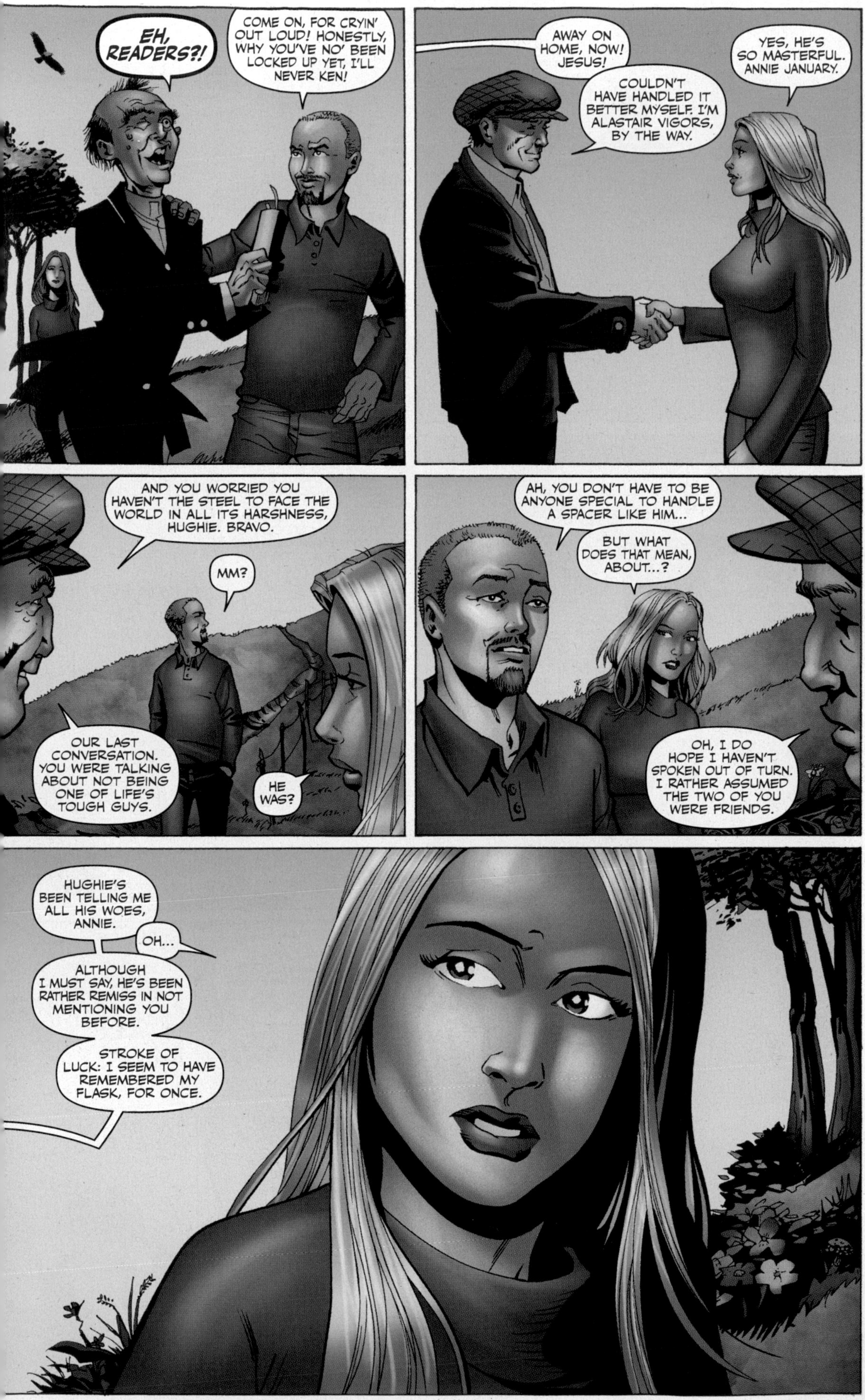
EH, READERS?!
COME ON, FOR CRYIN' OUT LOUD! HONESTLY, WHY YOU'VE NO' BEEN LOCKED UP YET, I'LL NEVER KEN!
AWAY ON HOME, NOW! JESUS!
COULDN'T HAVE HANDLED IT BETTER MYSELF. I'M ALASTAIR VIGORS, BY THE WAY.
YES, HE'S SO MASTERFUL. ANNIE JANUARY.
AND YOU WORRIED YOU HAVEN'T THE STEEL TO FACE THE WORLD IN ALL ITS HARSHNESS, HUGHIE. BRAVO.
MM?
OUR LAST CONVERSATION. YOU WERE TALKING ABOUT NOT BEING ONE OF LIFE'S TOUGH GUYS.
HE WAS?
AH, YOU DON'T HAVE TO BE ANYONE SPECIAL TO HANDLE A SPACER LIKE HIM...
BUT WHAT DOES THAT MEAN, ABOUT...?
OH, I DO HOPE I HAVEN'T SPOKEN OUT OF TURN. I RATHER ASSUMED THE TWO OF YOU WERE FRIENDS.
HUGHIE'S BEEN TELLING ME ALL HIS WOES, ANNIE.
OH...
ALTHOUGH I MUST SAY, HE'S BEEN RATHER REMISS IN NOT MENTIONING YOU BEFORE.
STROKE OF LUCK: I SEEM TO HAVE REMEMBERED MY FLASK, FOR ONCE.

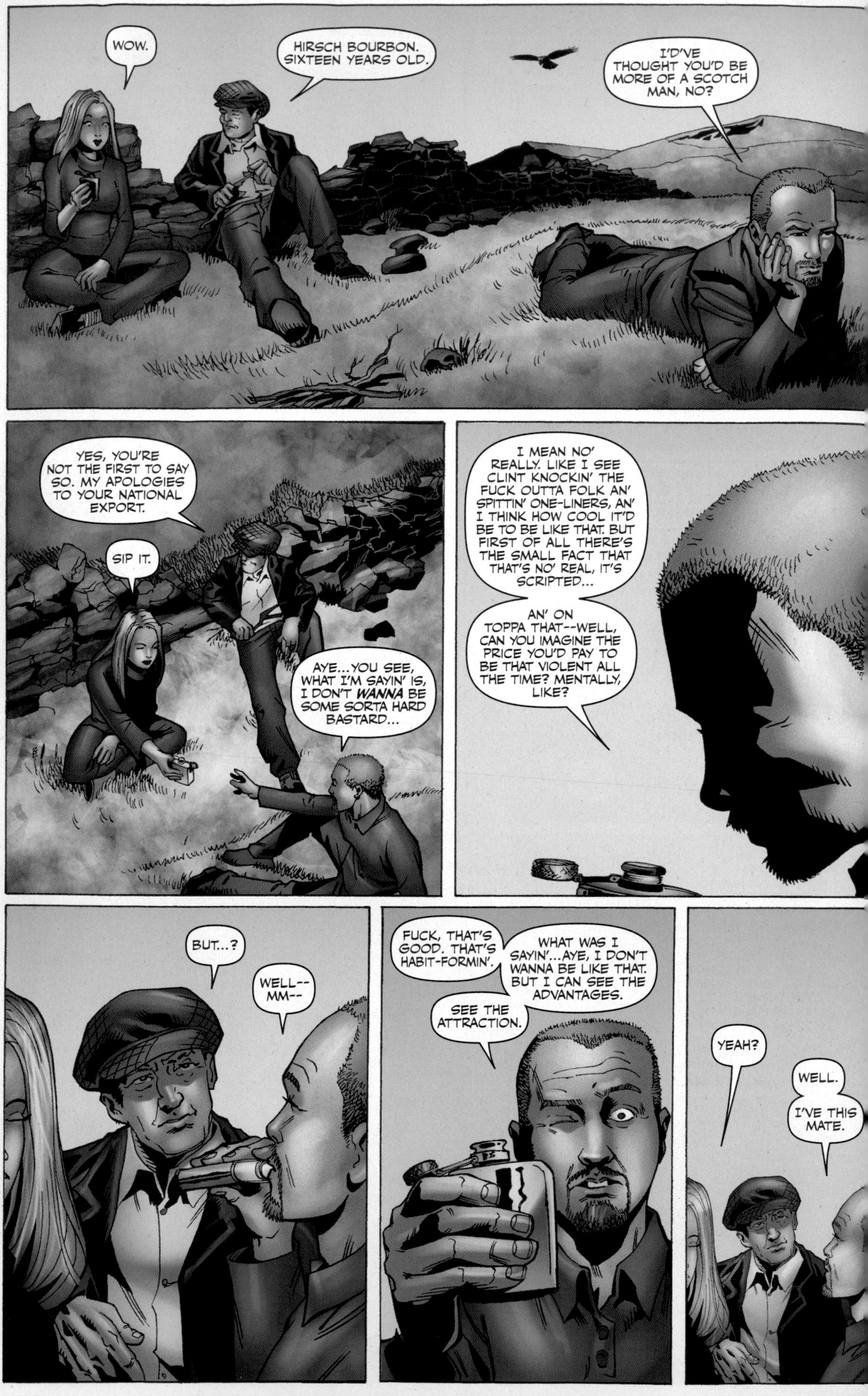
WOW.
HIRSCH BOURBON. SIXTEEN YEARS OLD.
I'D'VE THOUGHT YOU'D BE MORE OF A SCOTCH MAN, NO?
YES, YOU'RE NOT THE FIRST TO SAY SO. MY APOLOGIES TO YOUR NATIONAL EXPORT.
SIP IT.
AYE...YOU SEE, WHAT I'M SAYIN' IS, I DON'T WANNA BE SOME SORTA HARD BASTARD...
I MEAN NO' REALLY. LIKE I SEE CLINT KNOCKIN' THE FUCK OUTTA FOLK AN' SPITTIN' ONE-LINERS, AN' I THINK HOW COOL IT'D BE TO BE LIKE THAT. BUT FIRST OF ALL THERE'S THE SMALL FACT THAT THAT'S NO' REAL, IT'S SCRIPTED...
AN' ON TOPPA THAT--WELL, CAN YOU IMAGINE THE PRICE YOU'D PAY TO BE THAT VIOLENT ALL THE TIME? MENTALLY, LIKE?
BUT...?
WELL-- MM--
FUCK, THAT'S GOOD. THAT'S HABIT-FORMIN'.
WHAT WAS I SAYIN'...AYE, I DON'T WANNA BE LIKE THAT. BUT I CAN SEE THE ADVANTAGES.
SEE THE ATTRACTION.
YEAH?
WELL.
I'VE THIS MATE.

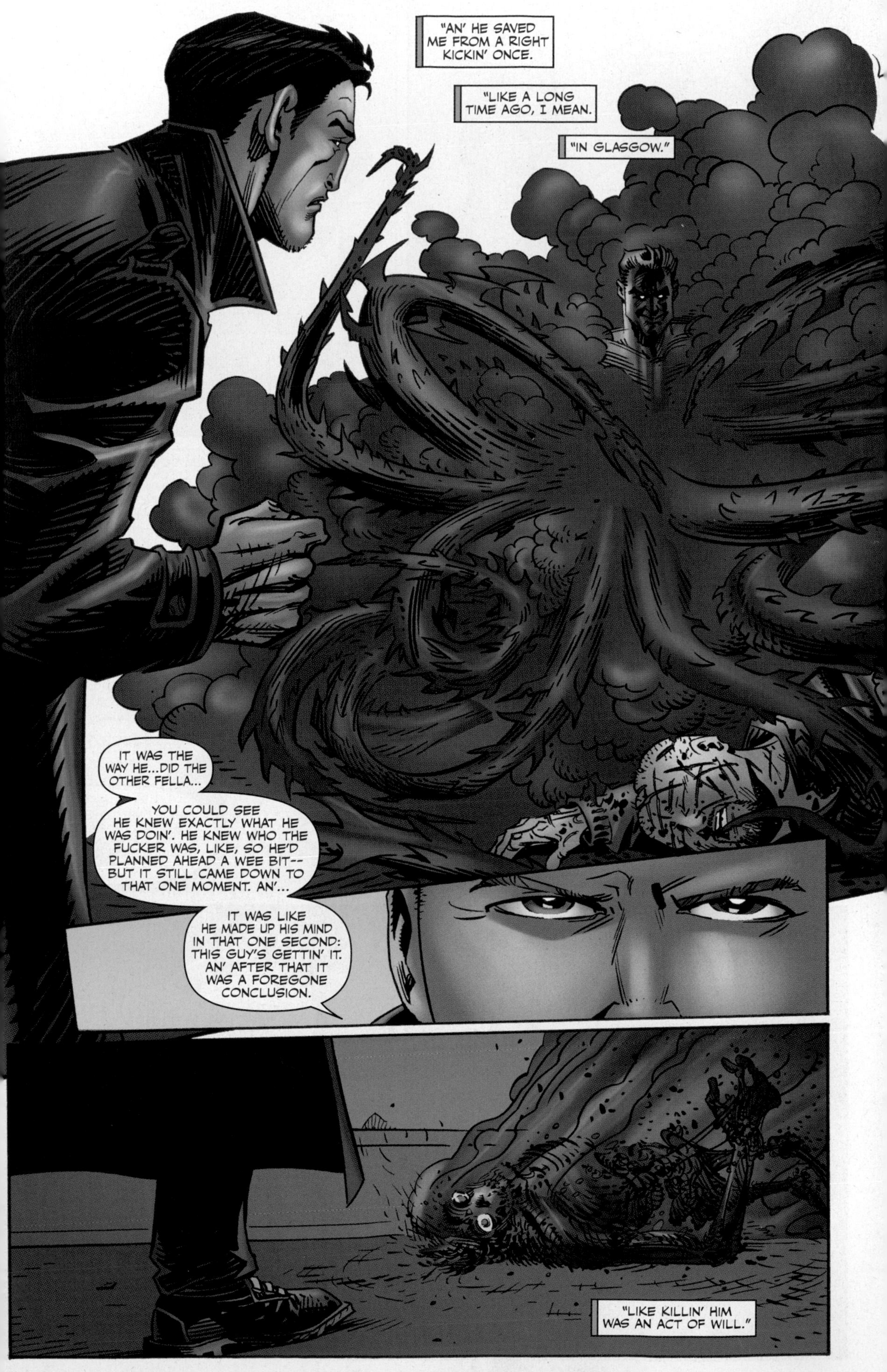
"AN' HE SAVED ME FROM A RIGHT KICKIN' ONCE.
"LIKE A LONG TIME AGO, I MEAN.
"IN GLASGOW."
IT WAS THE WAY HE...DID THE OTHER FELLA...
YOU COULD SEE HE KNEW EXACTLY WHAT HE WAS DOIN'. HE KNEW WHO THE FUCKER WAS, LIKE, SO HE'D PLANNED AHEAD A WEE BIT--BUT IT STILL CAME DOWN TO THAT ONE MOMENT. AN'...
IT WAS LIKE HE MADE UP HIS MIND IN THAT ONE SECOND: THIS GUY'S GETTIN' IT. AN' AFTER THAT IT WAS A FOREGONE CONCLUSION.
"LIKE KILLIN' HIM WAS AN ACT OF WILL."

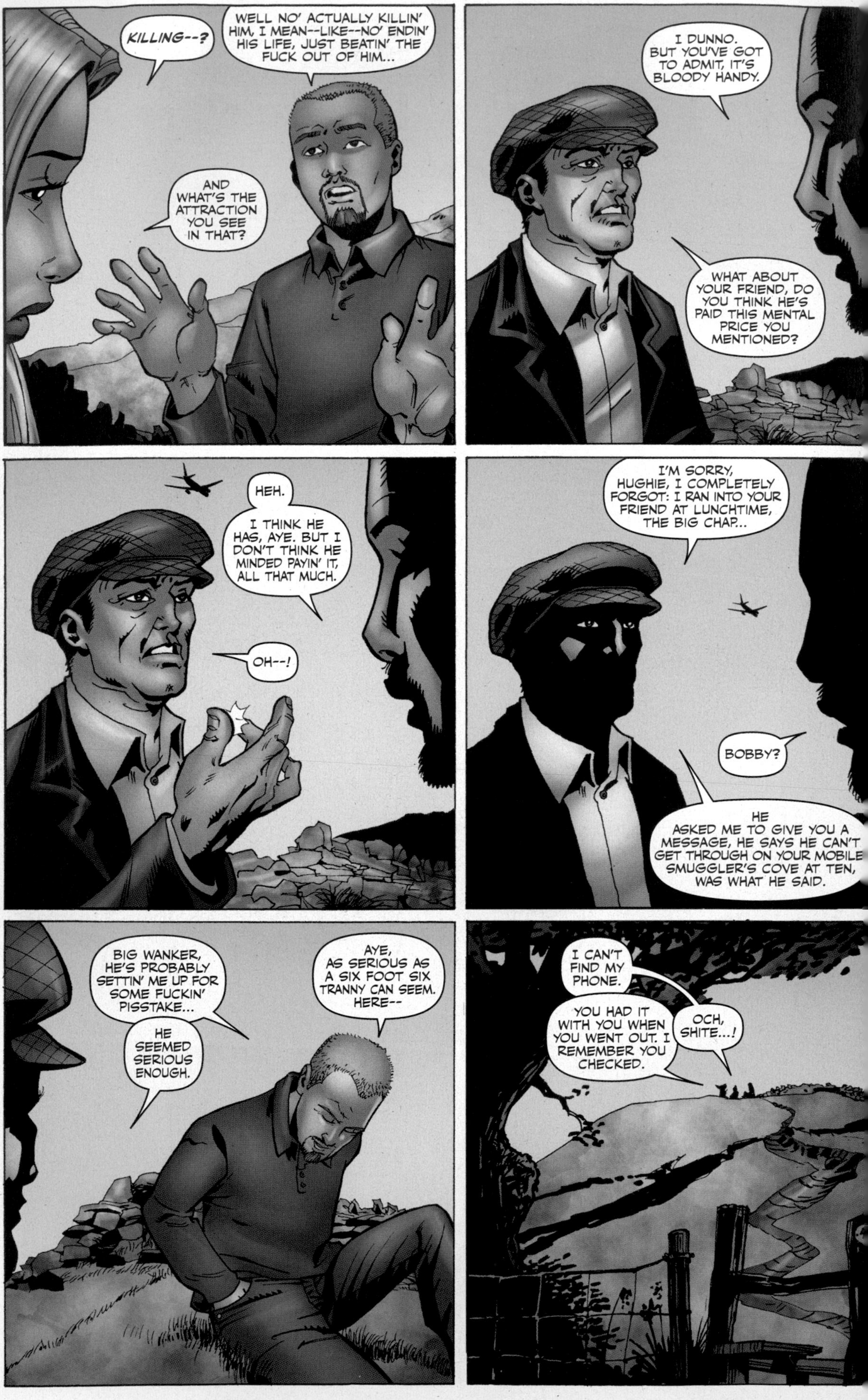
KILLING--?
WELL NO' ACTUALLY KILLIN' HIM, I MEAN--LIKE--NO' ENDIN' HIS LIFE, JUST BEATIN' THE FUCK OUT OF HIM...
AND WHAT'S THE ATTRACTION YOU SEE IN THAT?
I DUNNO. BUT YOU'VE GOT TO ADMIT, IT'S BLOODY HANDY.
WHAT ABOUT YOUR FRIEND, DO YOU THINK HE'S PAID THIS MENTAL PRICE YOU MENTIONED?
HEH.
I THINK HE HAS, AYE. BUT I DON'T THINK HE MINDED PAYIN' IT, ALL THAT MUCH.
OH--!
I'M SORRY, HUGHIE, I COMPLETELY FORGOT: I RAN INTO YOUR FRIEND AT LUNCHTIME, THE BIG CHAP...
BOBBY?
HE ASKED ME TO GIVE YOU A MESSAGE, HE SAYS HE CAN'T GET THROUGH ON YOUR MOBILE. SMUGGLER'S COVE AT TEN, WAS WHAT HE SAID.
BIG WANKER, HE'S PROBABLY SETTIN' ME UP FOR SOME FUCKIN' PISSTAKE...
HE SEEMED SERIOUS ENOUGH.
AYE, AS SERIOUS AS A SIX FOOT SIX TRANNY CAN SEEM. HERE--
I CAN'T FIND MY PHONE.
YOU HAD IT WITH YOU WHEN YOU WENT OUT. I REMEMBER YOU CHECKED.
OCH, SHITE...!

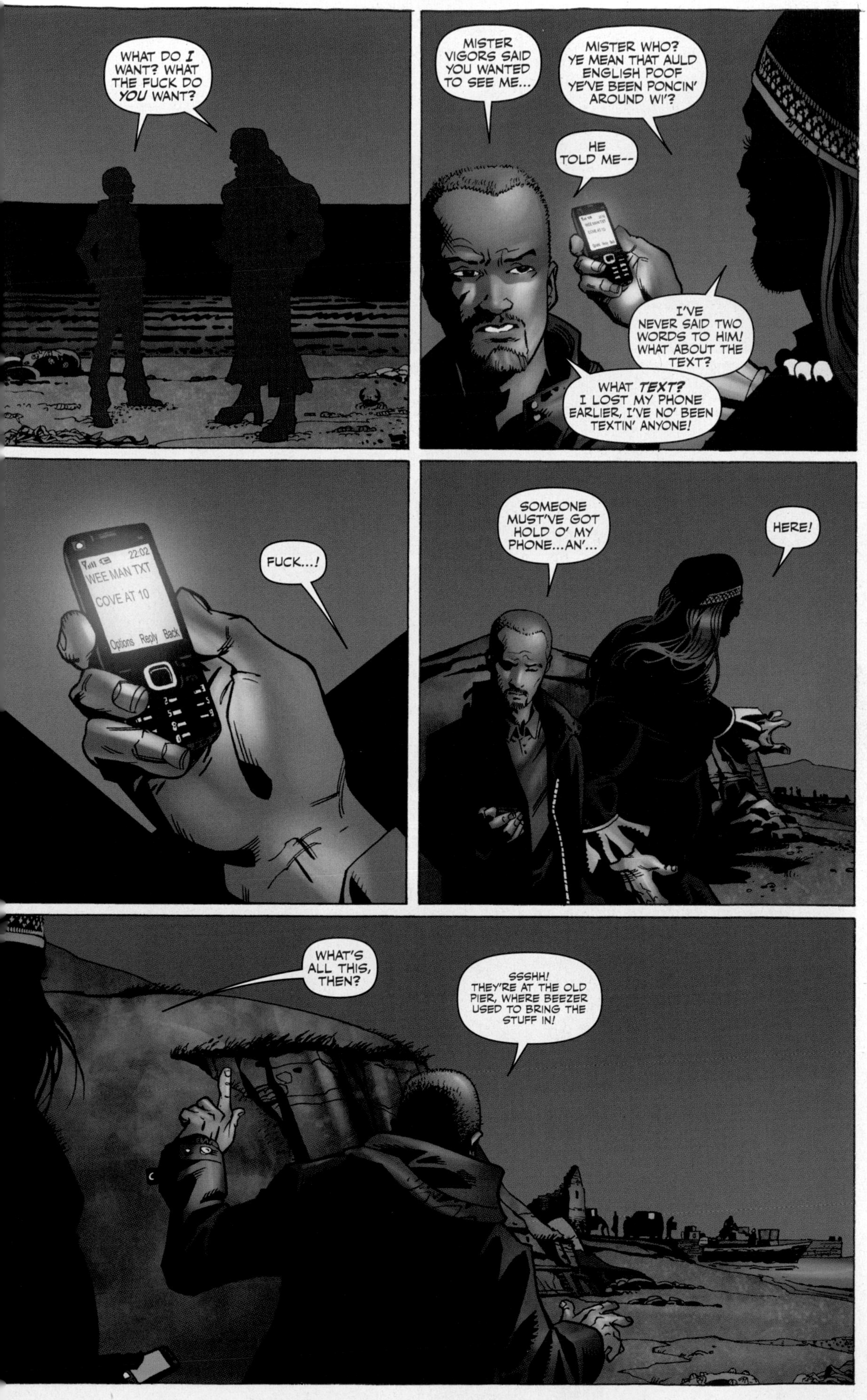
WHAT DO *I* WANT? WHAT THE FUCK DO *YOU* WANT?
MISTER VIGORS SAID YOU WANTED TO SEE ME...
MISTER WHO? YE MEAN THAT AULD ENGLISH POOF YE'VE BEEN PONCIN' AROUND WI'?
HE TOLD ME--
I'VE NEVER SAID TWO WORDS TO HIM! WHAT ABOUT THE TEXT?
WHAT *TEXT?* I LOST MY PHONE EARLIER, I'VE NO' BEEN TEXTIN' ANYONE!
22:02
WEE MAN TXT
COVE AT 10
Options Reply Back
FUCK...!
SOMEONE MUST'VE GOT HOLD O' MY PHONE...AN'...
HERE!
WHAT'S ALL THIS, THEN?
SSSHH! THEY'RE AT THE OLD PIER, WHERE BEEZER USED TO BRING THE STUFF IN!

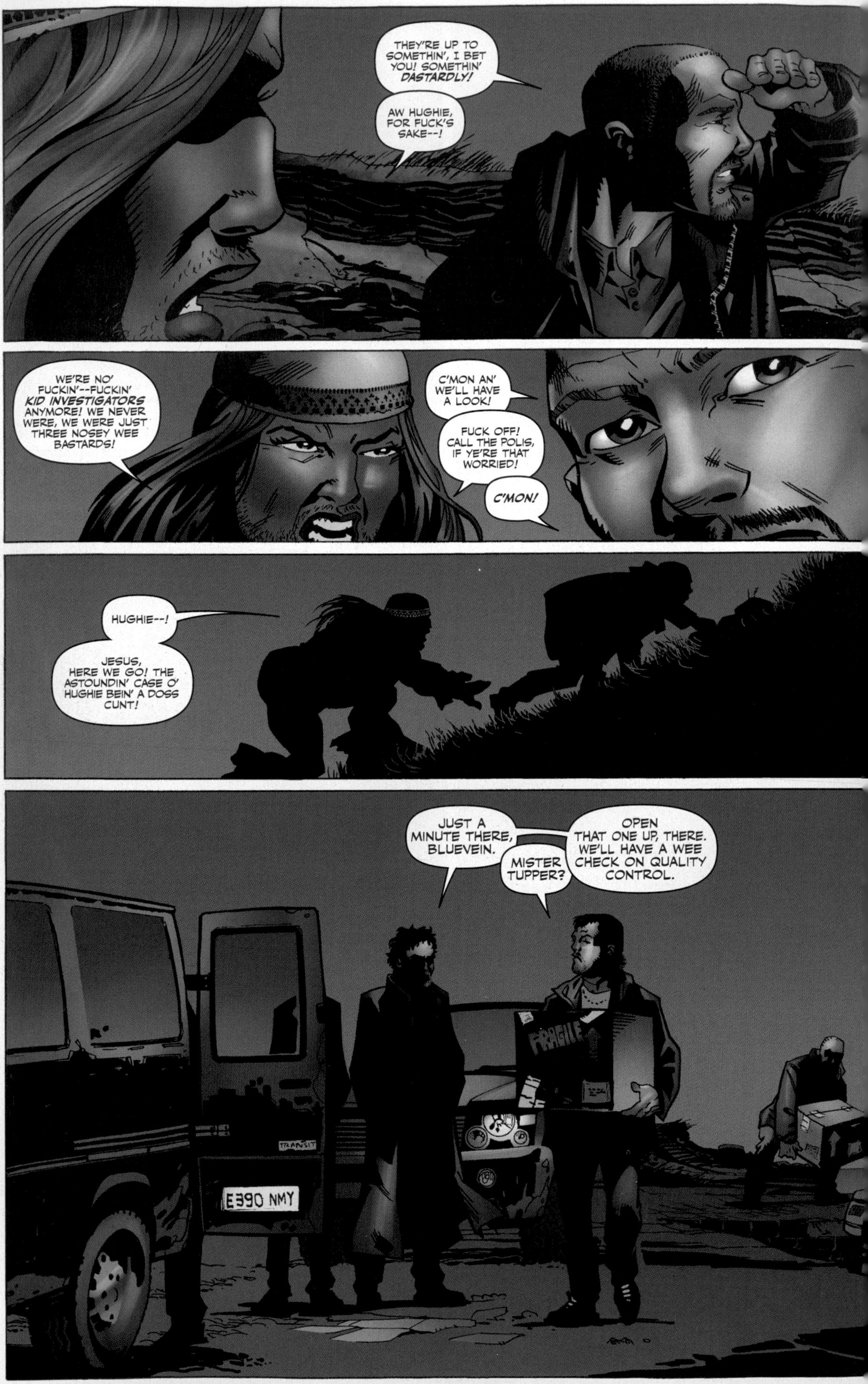
THEY'RE UP TO SOMETHIN', I BET YOU! SOMETHIN' DASTARDLY!
AW HUGHIE, FOR FUCK'S SAKE--!
WE'RE NO' FUCKIN'--FUCKIN' KID INVESTIGATORS ANYMORE! WE NEVER WERE, WE WERE JUST THREE NOSEY WEE BASTARDS!
C'MON AN' WE'LL HAVE A LOOK!
FUCK OFF! CALL THE POLIS, IF YE'RE THAT WORRIED!
C'MON!
HUGHIE--!
JESUS, HERE WE GO! THE ASTOUNDIN' CASE O' HUGHIE BEIN' A DOSS CUNT!
JUST A MINUTE THERE, BLUEVEIN.
MISTER TUPPER?
OPEN THAT ONE UP, THERE. WE'LL HAVE A WEE CHECK ON QUALITY CONTROL.
FRAGILE
TRANSIT
E390 NMY

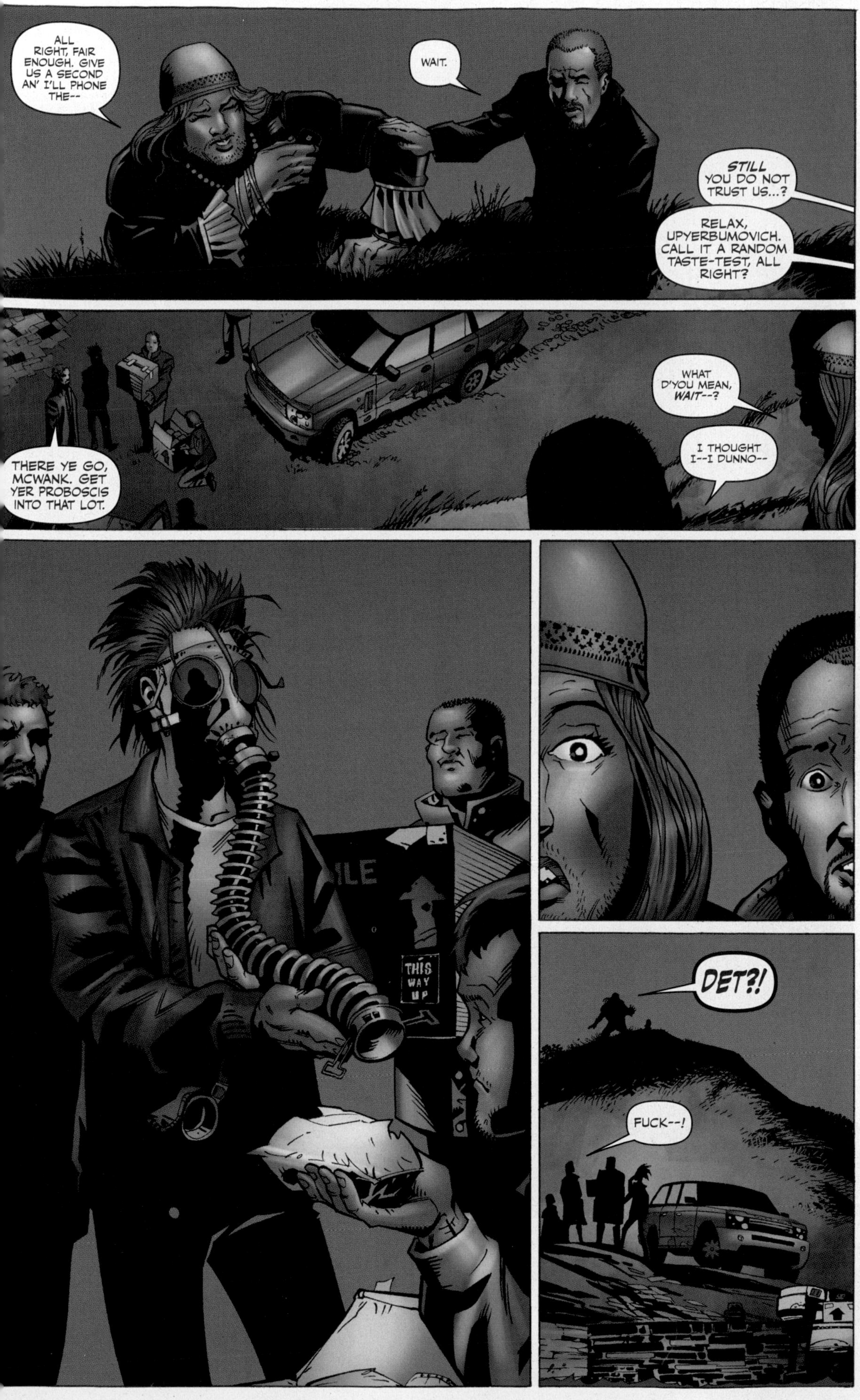
ALL RIGHT, FAIR ENOUGH. GIVE US A SECOND AN' I'LL PHONE THE--
WAIT.
STILL YOU DO NOT TRUST US...?
RELAX, UPYERBUMOVICH. CALL IT A RANDOM TASTE-TEST, ALL RIGHT?
WHAT D'YOU MEAN, WAIT--?
I THOUGHT I--I DUNNO--
THERE YE GO, MCWANK. GET YER PROBOSCIS INTO THAT LOT.
THIS WAY UP
DET?!
FUCK--!

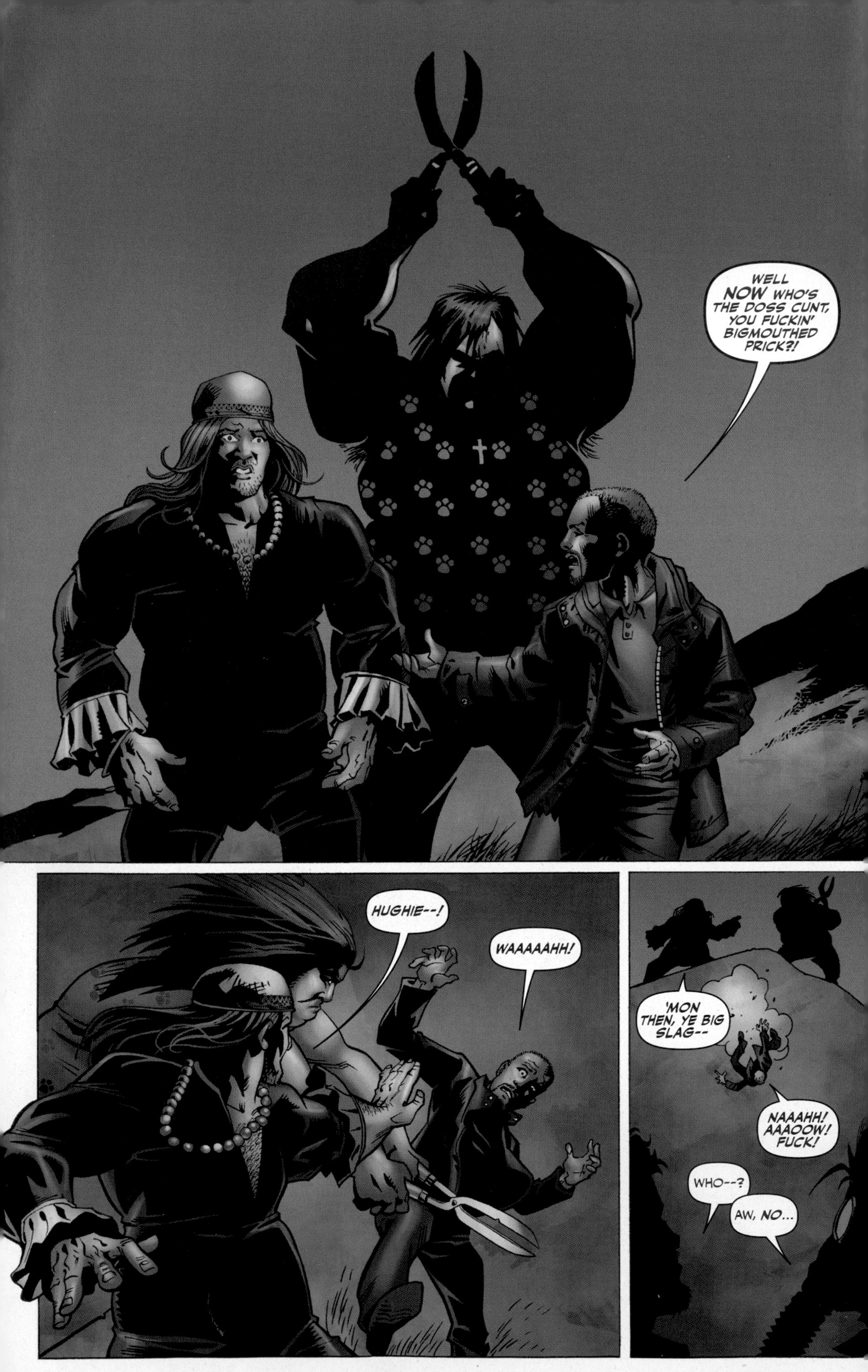
WELL NOW WHO'S THE DOSS CUNT, YOU FUCKIN' BIGMOUTHED PRICK?!
HUGHIE--!
WAAAAAAHH!
'MON THEN, YE BIG SLAG--
NAAAHH! AAAOOW! FUCK!
WHO--?
AW, NO...

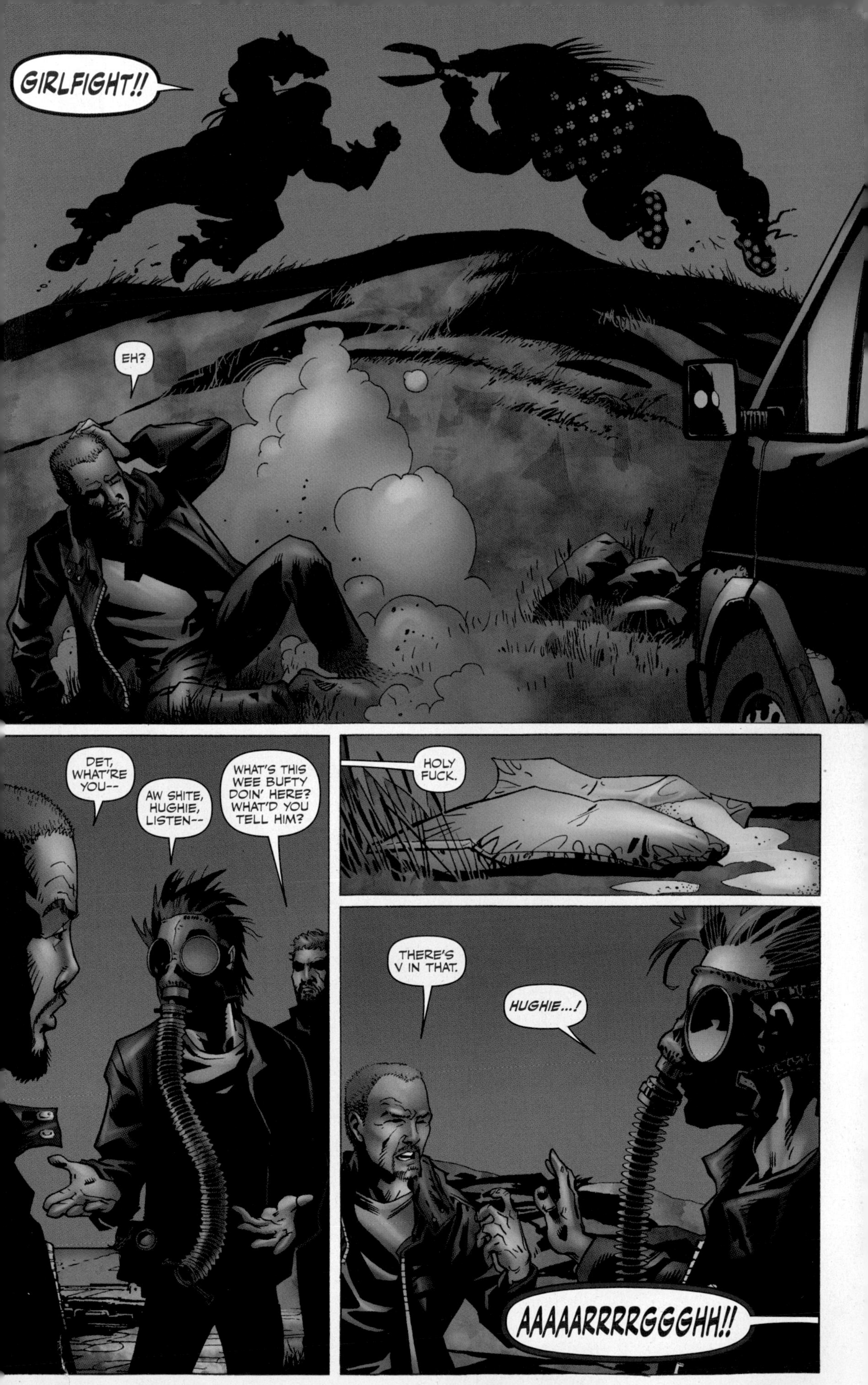
GIRLFIGHT!!
EH?
DET, WHAT'RE YOU--
AW SHITE, HUGHIE, LISTEN--
WHAT'S THIS WEE BUFTY DOIN' HERE? WHAT'D YOU TELL HIM?
HOLY FUCK.
THERE'S V IN THAT.
HUGHIE...!
AAAAARRRRGGGHH!!

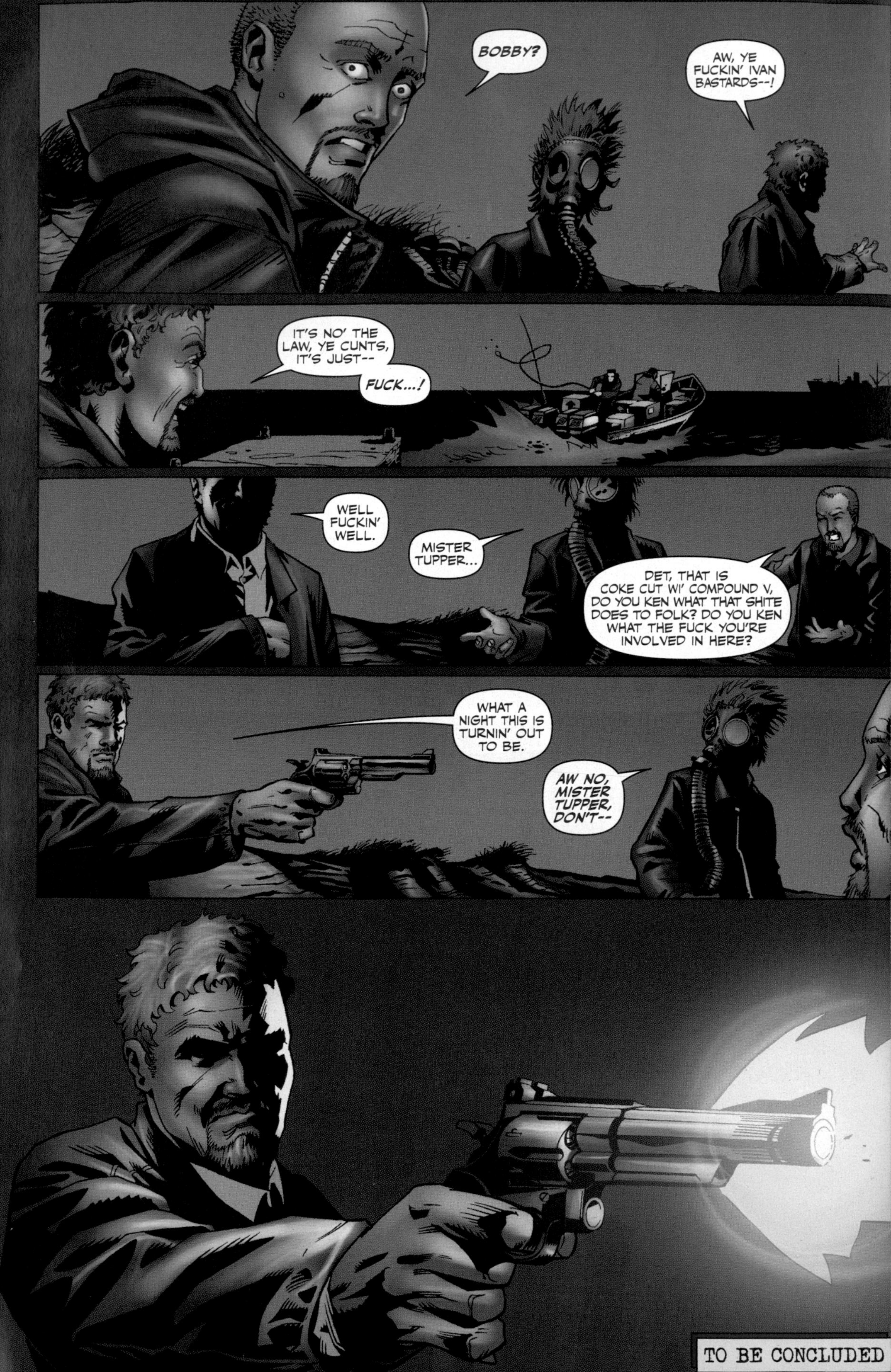
BOBBY?
AW, YE FUCKIN' IVAN BASTARDS--!
IT'S NO' THE LAW, YE CUNTS, IT'S JUST--
FUCK...!
WELL FUCKIN' WELL.
MISTER TUPPER...
DET, THAT IS COKE CUT WI' COMPOUND V, DO YOU KEN WHAT THAT SHITE DOES TO FOLK? DO YOU KEN WHAT THE FUCK YOU'RE INVOLVED IN HERE?
WHAT A NIGHT THIS IS TURNIN' OUT TO BE.
AW NO, MISTER TUPPER, DON'T--
TO BE CONCLUDED

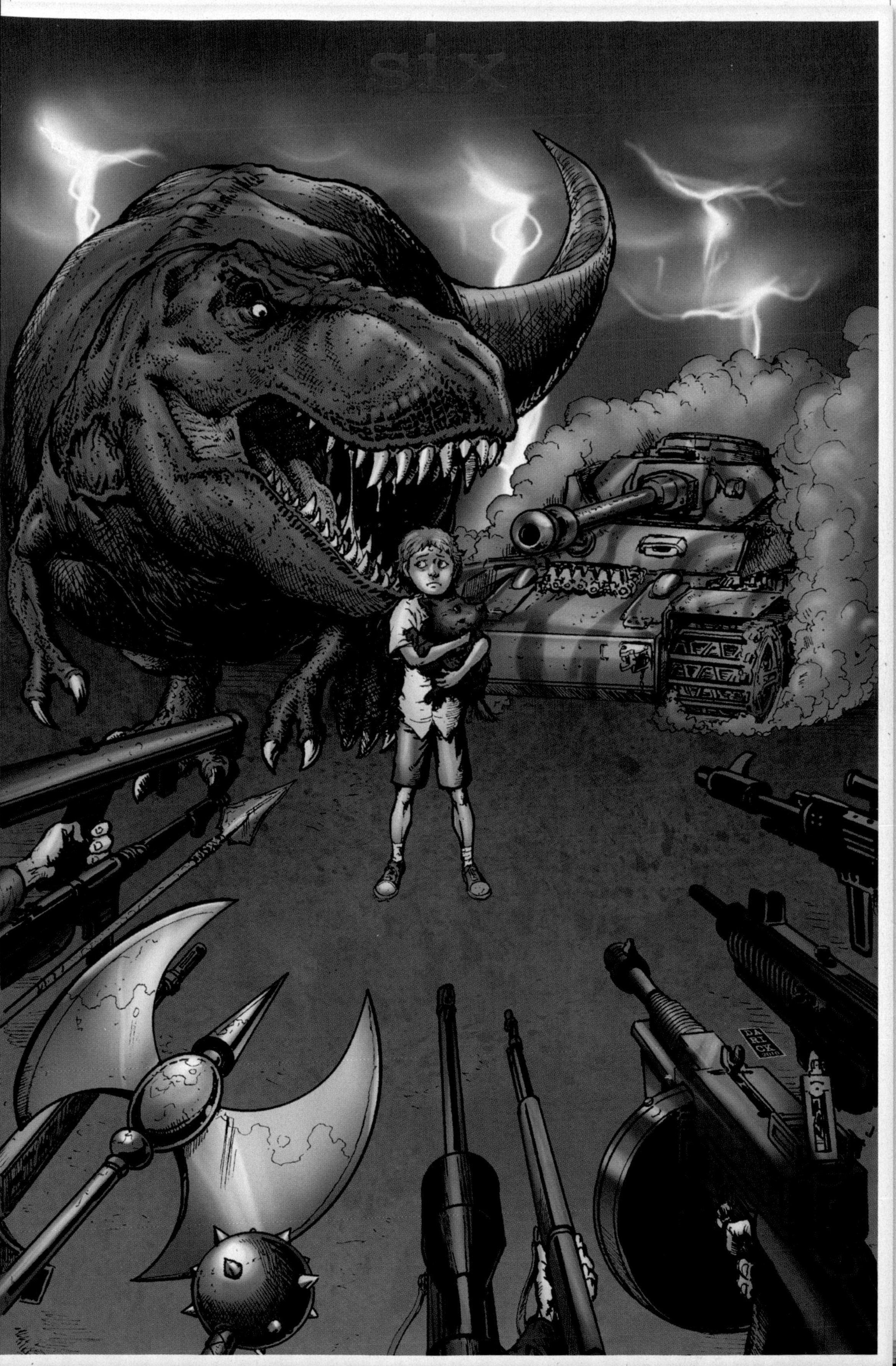
six

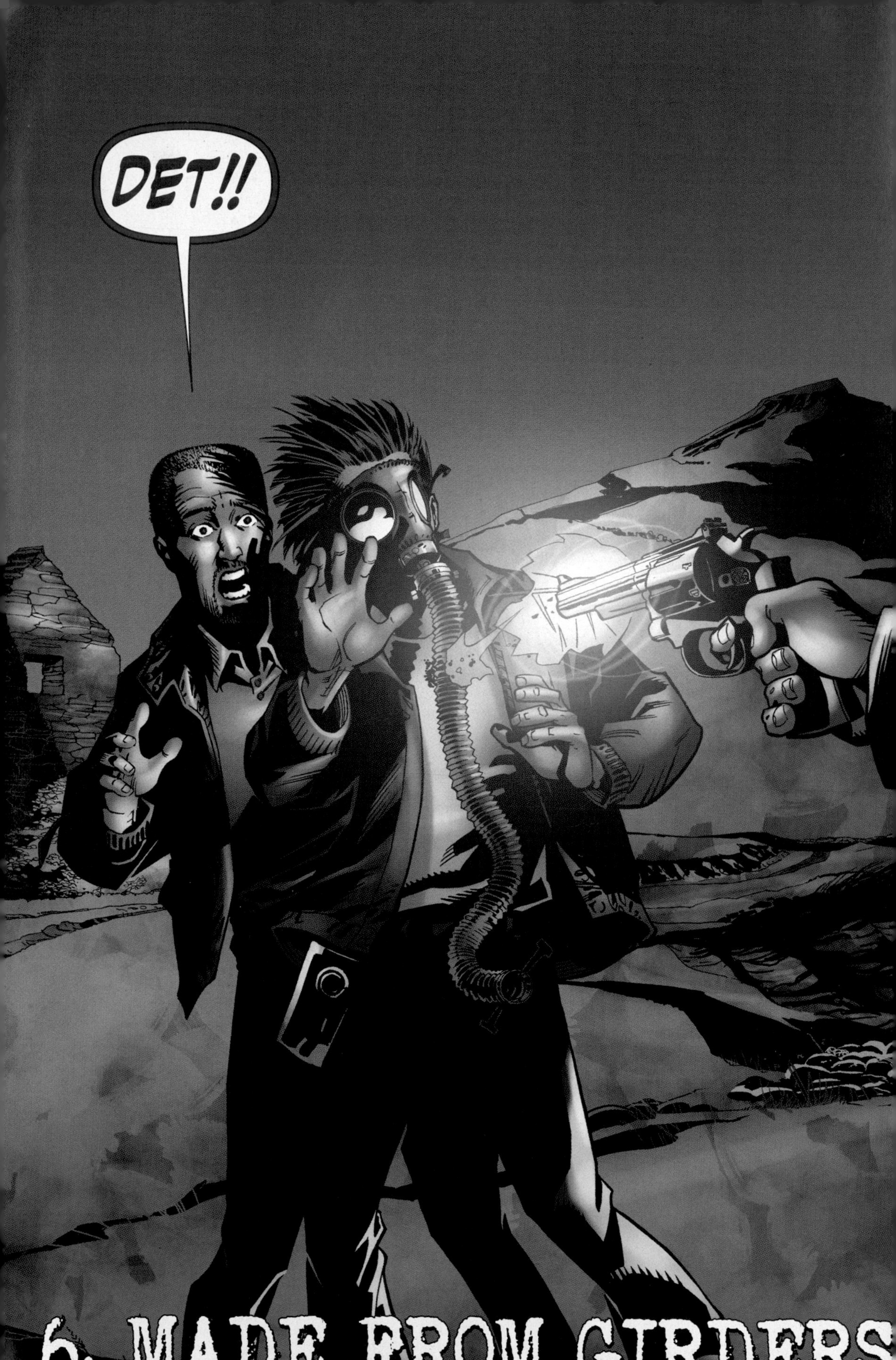
DET!!

6: MADE FROM GIRDERS

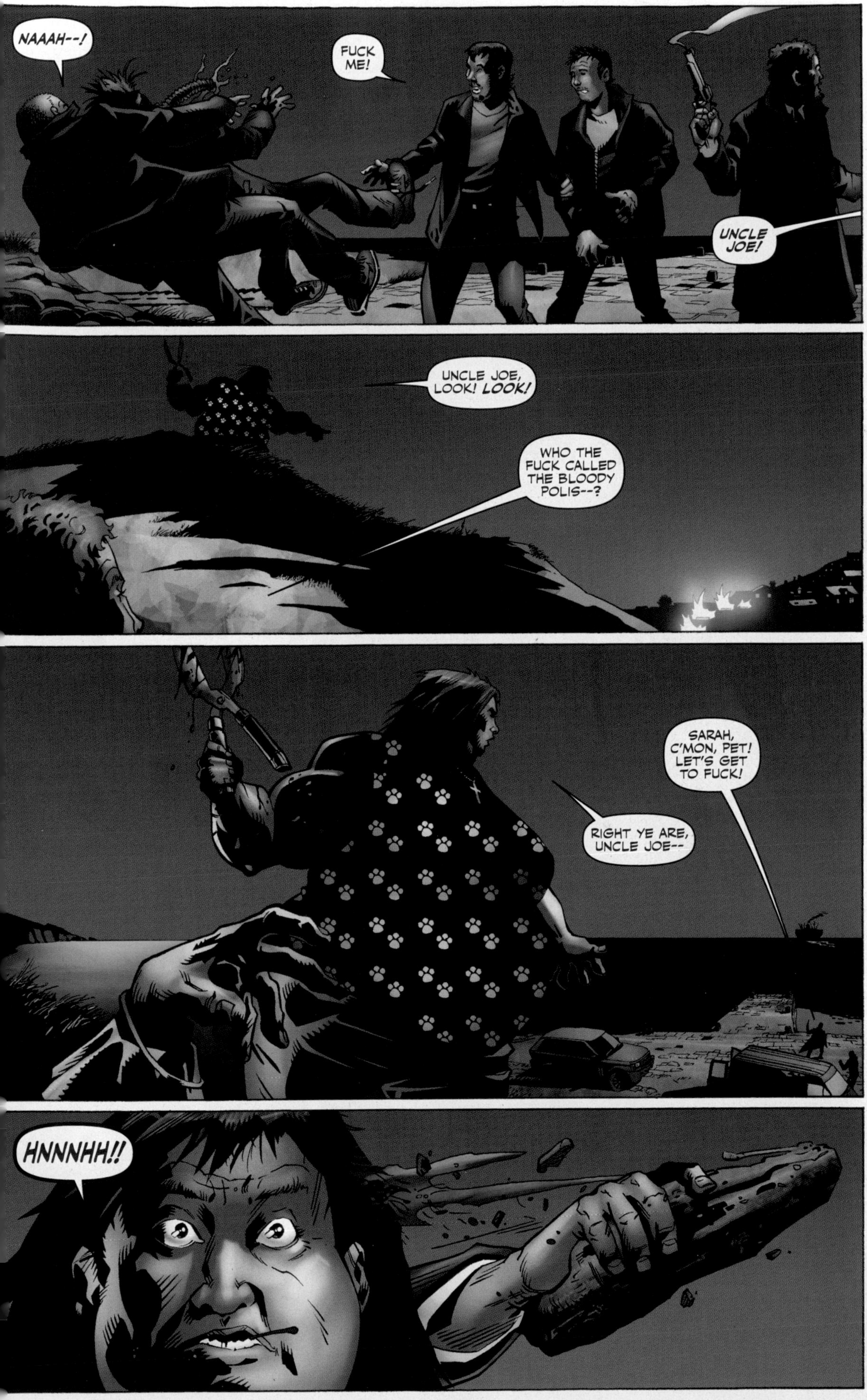
NAAAH--!
FUCK ME!
UNCLE JOE!
UNCLE JOE, LOOK! LOOK!
WHO THE FUCK CALLED THE BLOODY POLIS--?
SARAH, C'MON, PET! LET'S GET TO FUCK!
RIGHT YE ARE, UNCLE JOE--
HNNNHH!!

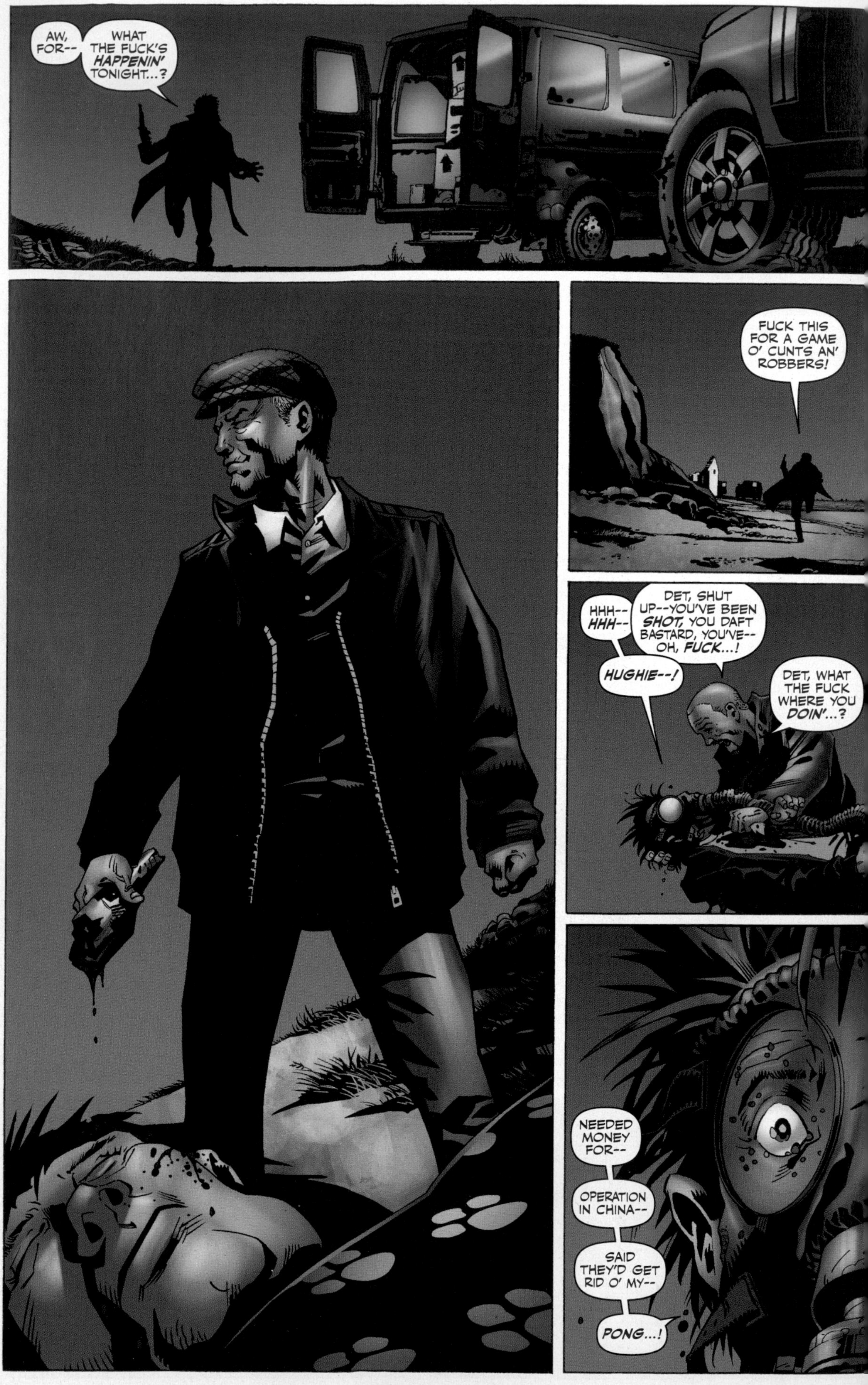
AW, FOR--
WHAT THE FUCK'S HAPPENIN' TONIGHT...?
FUCK THIS FOR A GAME O' CUNTS AN' ROBBERS!
HHH-- HHH--
DET, SHUT UP--YOU'VE BEEN SHOT, YOU DAFT BASTARD, YOU'VE-- OH, FUCK...!
HUGHIE--!
DET, WHAT THE FUCK WHERE YOU DOIN'...?
NEEDED MONEY FOR--
OPERATION IN CHINA--
SAID THEY'D GET RID O' MY--
PONG...!

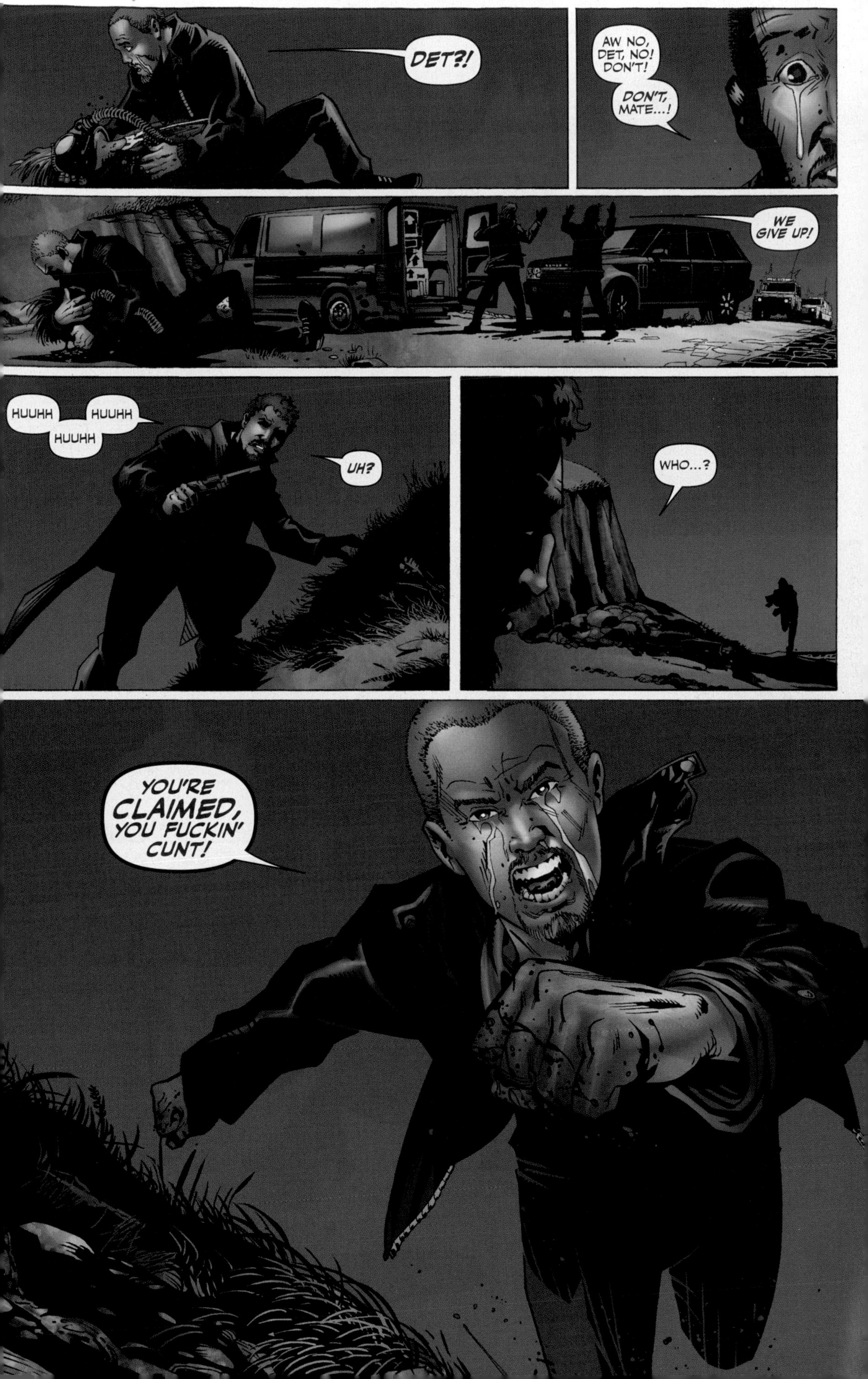
DET?!
AW NO, DET, NO! DON'T!
DON'T, MATE...!
WE GIVE UP!
HUUHH
HUUHH
HUUHH
UH?
WHO...?
YOU'RE CLAIMED, YOU FUCKIN' CUNT!

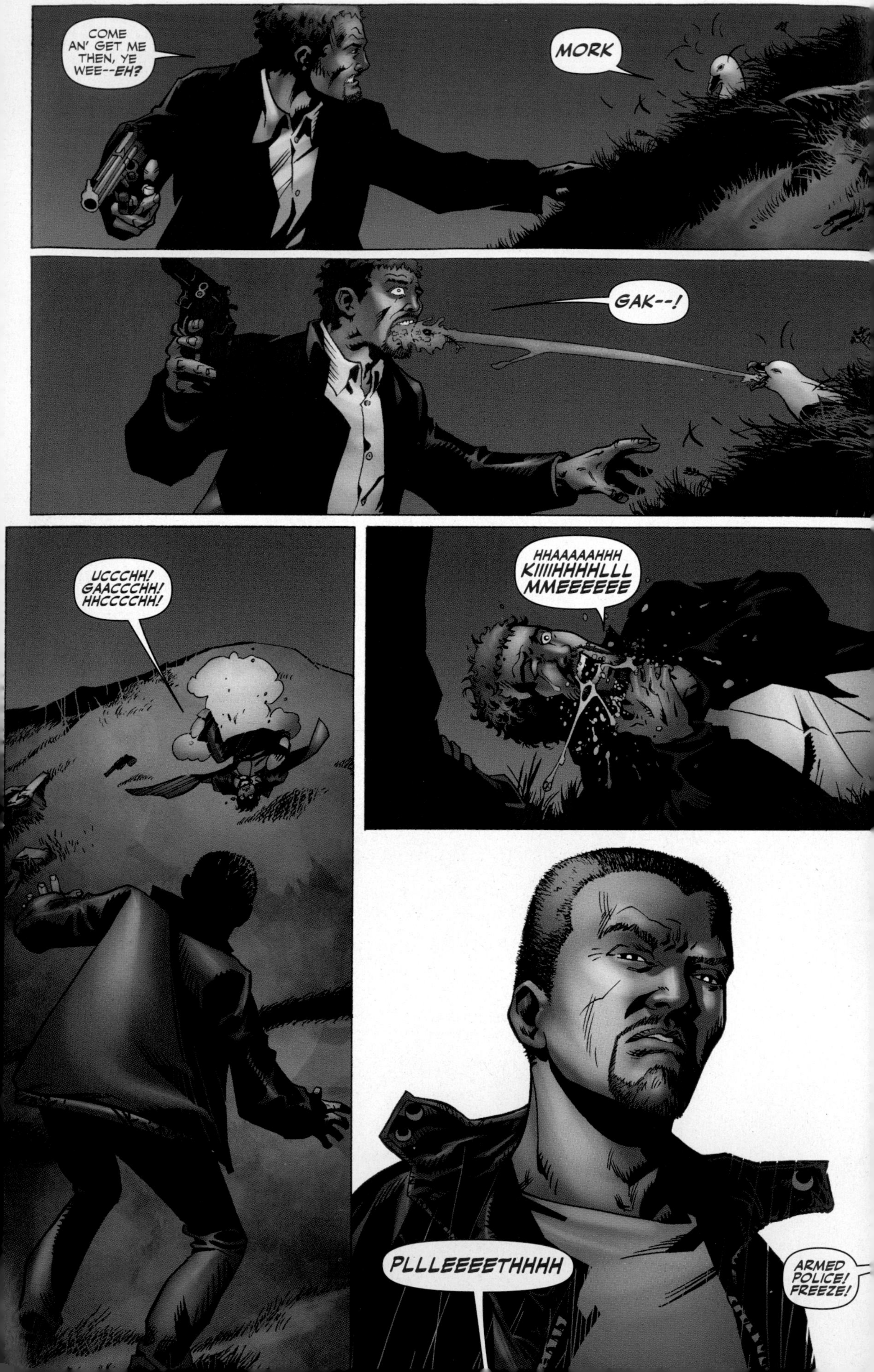
COME AN' GET ME THEN, YE WEE--EH?
MORK
GAK--!
UCCCHH! GAACCCHH! HHCCCCHH!
HHAAAAAAHHH KIIIIHHHLLL MMEEEEEE
PLLLEEEETHHHH
ARMED POLICE! FREEZE!

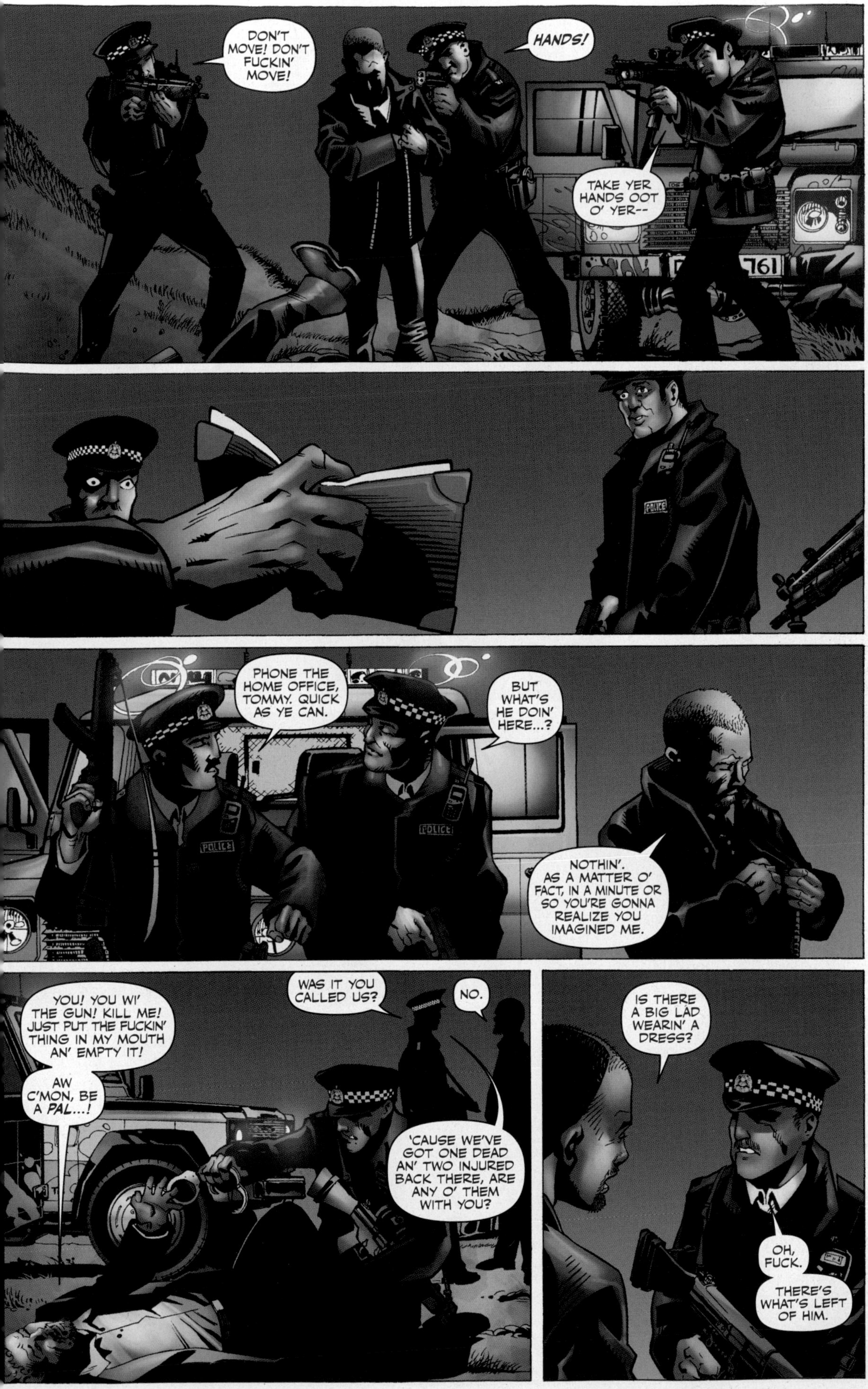
DON'T MOVE! DON'T FUCKIN' MOVE!
HANDS!
TAKE YER HANDS OOT O' YER--
PHONE THE HOME OFFICE, TOMMY. QUICK AS YE CAN.
BUT WHAT'S HE DOIN' HERE...?
NOTHIN'. AS A MATTER O' FACT, IN A MINUTE OR SO YOU'RE GONNA REALIZE YOU IMAGINED ME.
YOU! YOU WI' THE GUN! KILL ME! JUST PUT THE FUCKIN' THING IN MY MOUTH AN' EMPTY IT!
AW C'MON, BE A *PAL*...!
WAS IT YOU CALLED US?
NO.
'CAUSE WE'VE GOT ONE DEAD AN' TWO INJURED BACK THERE, ARE ANY O' THEM WITH YOU?
IS THERE A BIG LAD WEARIN' A DRESS?
OH, FUCK.
THERE'S WHAT'S LEFT OF HIM.

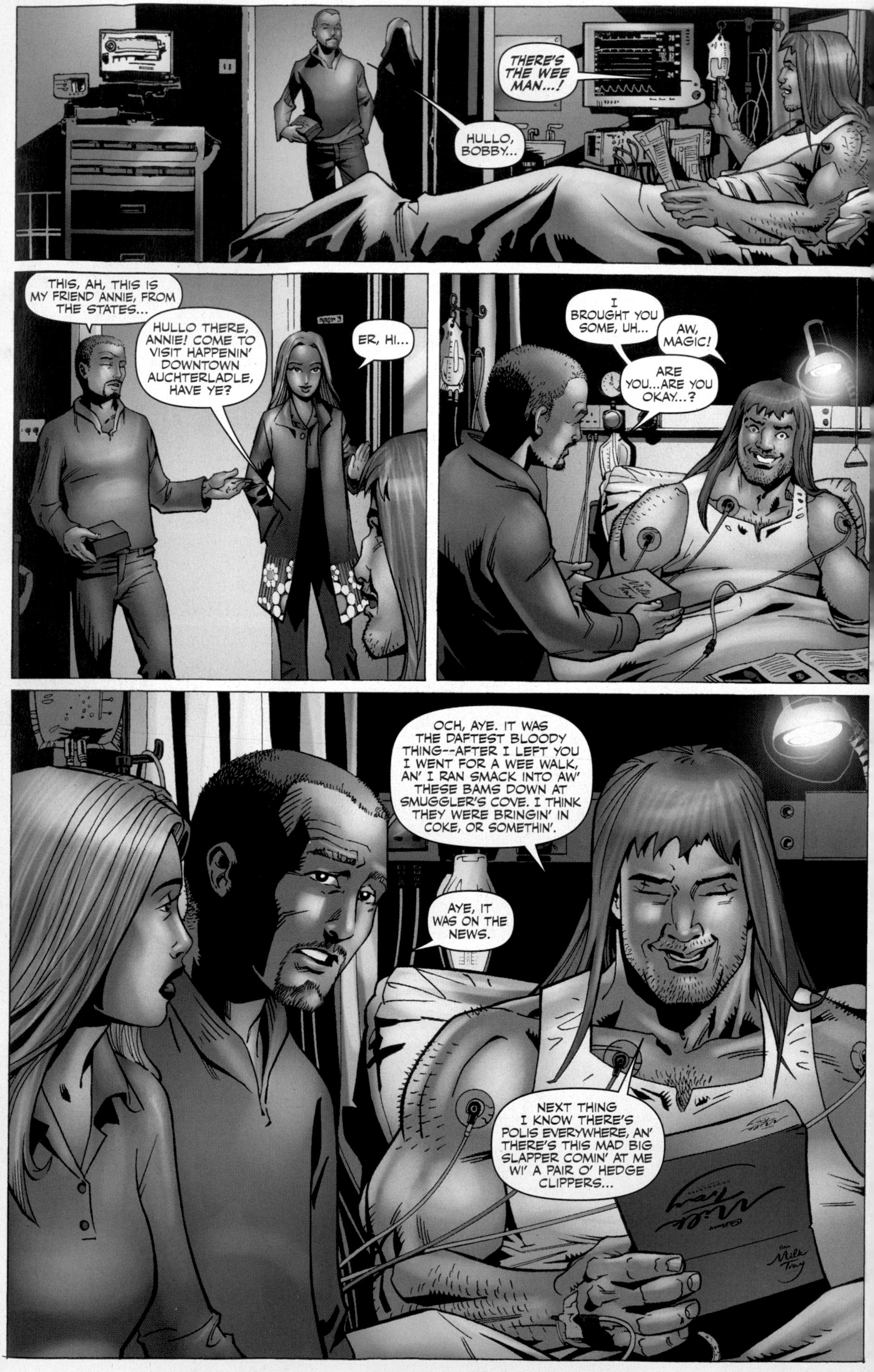
THERE'S THE WEE MAN...!
HULLO, BOBBY...
THIS, AH, THIS IS MY FRIEND ANNIE, FROM THE STATES...
HULLO THERE, ANNIE! COME TO VISIT HAPPENIN' DOWNTOWN AUCHTERLADLE, HAVE YE?
ER, HI...
I BROUGHT YOU SOME, UH...
AW, MAGIC!
ARE YOU...ARE YOU OKAY...?
OCH, AYE. IT WAS THE DAFTEST BLOODY THING--AFTER I LEFT YOU I WENT FOR A WEE WALK, AN' I RAN SMACK INTO AW' THESE BAMS DOWN AT SMUGGLER'S COVE. I THINK THEY WERE BRINGIN' IN COKE, OR SOMETHIN'.
AYE, IT WAS ON THE NEWS.
NEXT THING I KNOW THERE'S POLIS EVERYWHERE, AN' THERE'S THIS MAD BIG SLAPPER COMIN' AT ME WI' A PAIR O' HEDGE CLIPPERS...

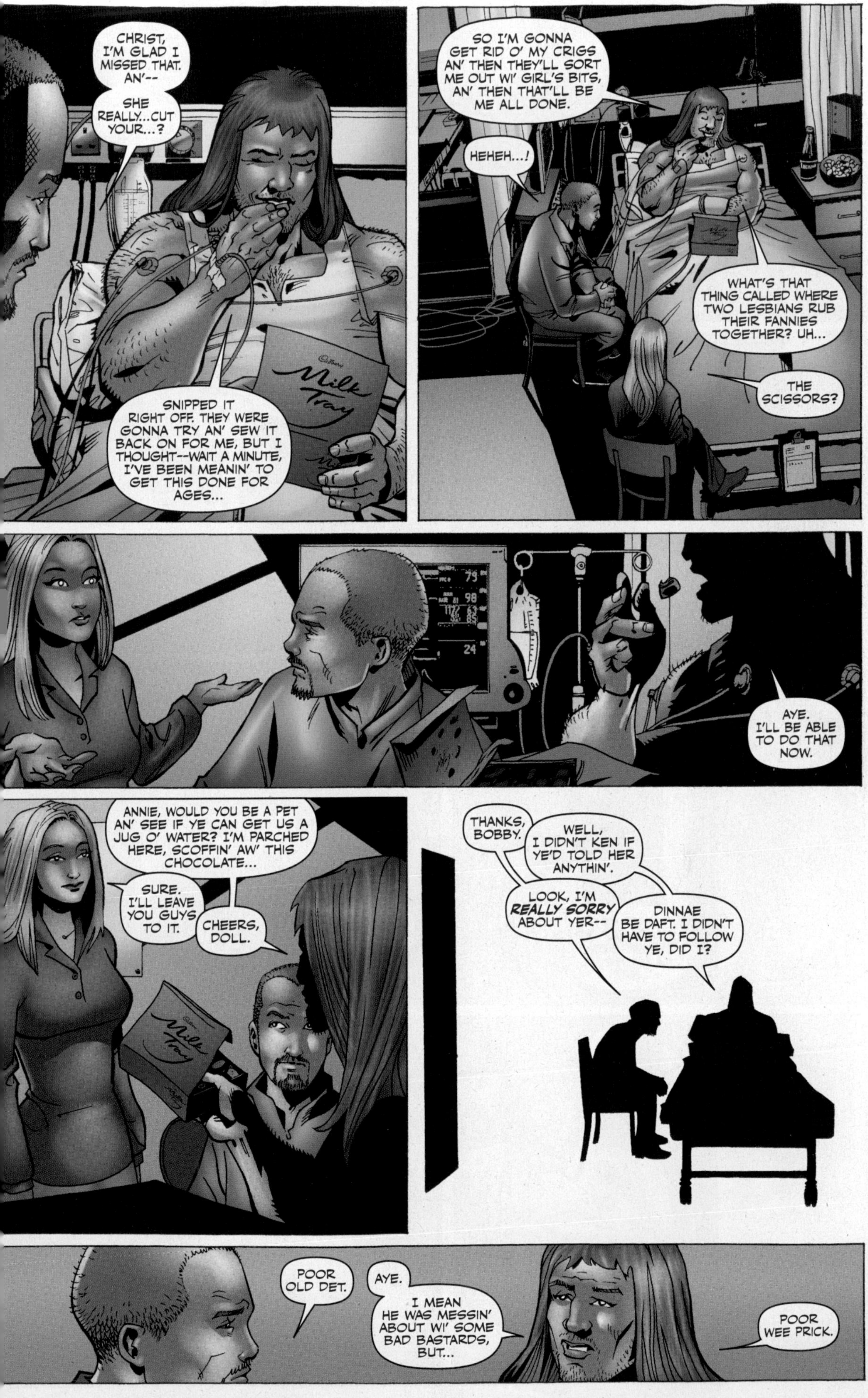
CHRIST, I'M GLAD I MISSED THAT. AN'--
SHE REALLY...CUT YOUR...?
SNIPPED IT RIGHT OFF. THEY WERE GONNA TRY AN' SEW IT BACK ON FOR ME, BUT I THOUGHT--WAIT A MINUTE, I'VE BEEN MEANIN' TO GET THIS DONE FOR AGES...
Milk Tray
SO I'M GONNA GET RID O' MY CRIGS AN' THEN THEY'LL SORT ME OUT WI' GIRL'S BITS, AN' THEN THAT'LL BE ME ALL DONE.
HEHEH...!
WHAT'S THAT THING CALLED WHERE TWO LESBIANS RUB THEIR FANNIES TOGETHER? UH...
THE SCISSORS?
AYE. I'LL BE ABLE TO DO THAT NOW.
ANNIE, WOULD YOU BE A PET AN' SEE IF YE CAN GET US A JUG O' WATER? I'M PARCHED HERE, SCOFFIN' AW' THIS CHOCOLATE...
SURE. I'LL LEAVE YOU GUYS TO IT.
CHEERS, DOLL.
Milk Tray
THANKS, BOBBY.
WELL, I DIDN'T KEN IF YE'D TOLD HER ANYTHIN'.
LOOK, I'M *REALLY SORRY* ABOUT YER--
DINNAE BE DAFT. I DIDN'T HAVE TO FOLLOW YE, DID I?
POOR OLD DET.
AYE.
I MEAN HE WAS MESSIN' ABOUT WI' SOME BAD BASTARDS, BUT...
POOR WEE PRICK.

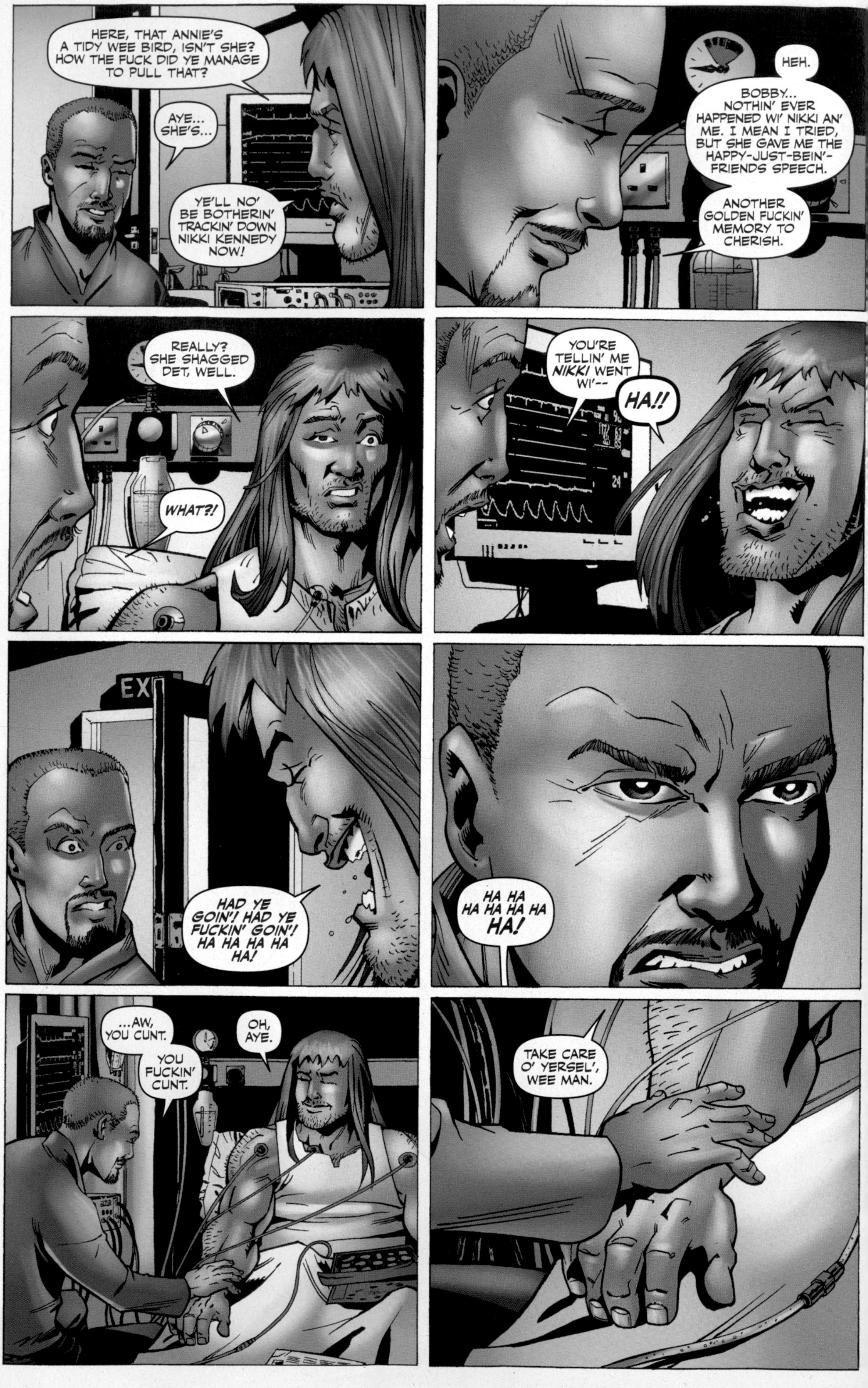
HERE, THAT ANNIE'S A TIDY WEE BIRD, ISN'T SHE? HOW THE FUCK DID YE MANAGE TO PULL THAT?
AYE... SHE'S...
YE'LL NO' BE BOTHERIN' TRACKIN' DOWN NIKKI KENNEDY NOW!
HEH.
BOBBY... NOTHIN' EVER HAPPENED WI' NIKKI AN' ME. I MEAN I TRIED, BUT SHE GAVE ME THE HAPPY-JUST-BEIN'-FRIENDS SPEECH.
ANOTHER GOLDEN FUCKIN' MEMORY TO CHERISH.
REALLY? SHE SHAGGED DET, WELL.
WHAT?!
YOU'RE TELLIN' ME NIKKI WENT WI'--
HA!!
EX
HAD YE GOIN'! HAD YE FUCKIN' GOIN'! HA HA HA HA HA!
HA HA HA HA HA HA HA!
...AW, YOU CUNT.
YOU FUCKIN' CUNT.
OH, AYE.
TAKE CARE O' YERSEL', WEE MAN.

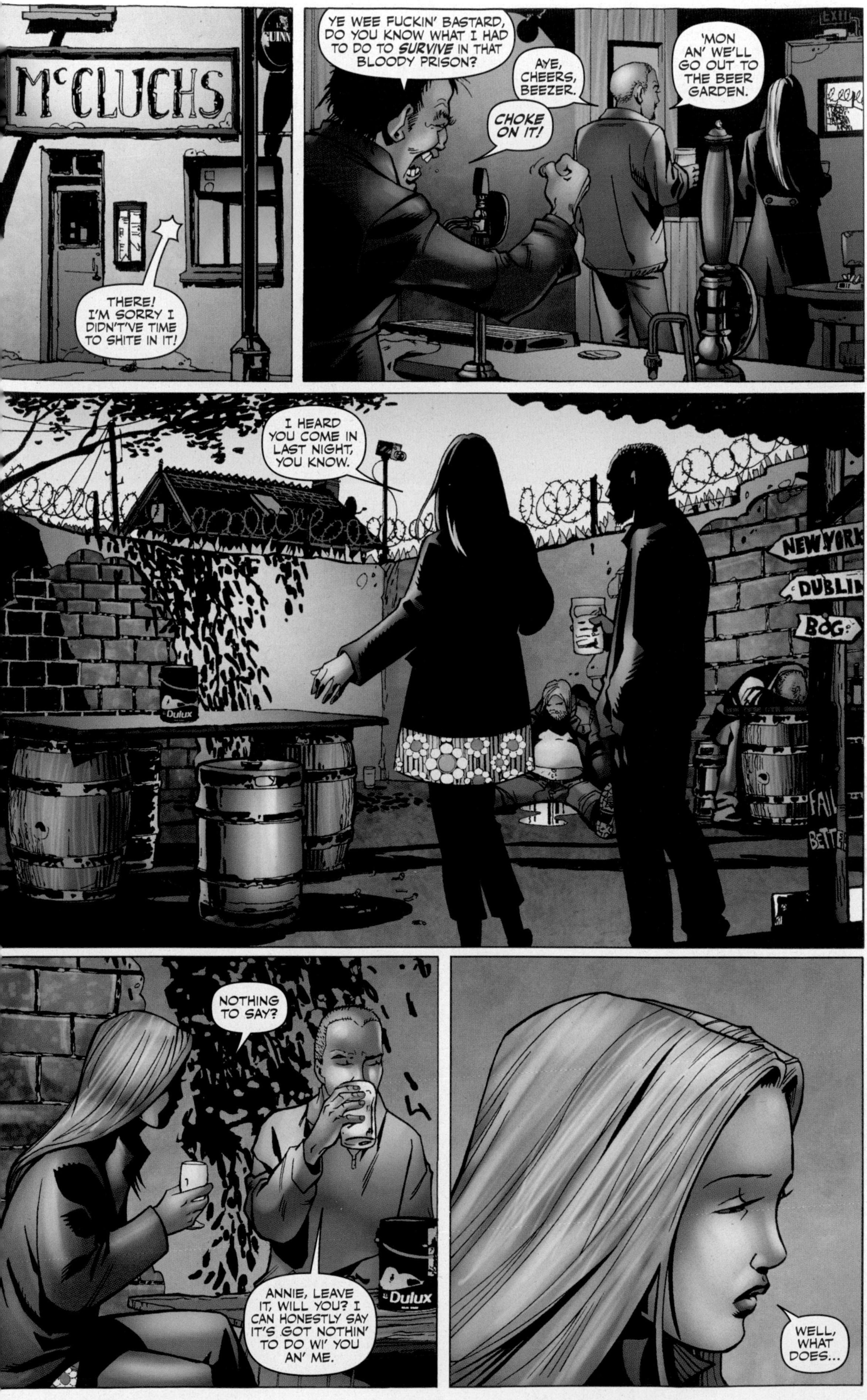
McCLUCHS
THERE! I'M SORRY I DIDN'T'VE TIME TO SHITE IN IT!
YE WEE FUCKIN' BASTARD, DO YOU KNOW WHAT I HAD TO DO TO *SURVIVE* IN THAT BLOODY PRISON?
AYE, CHEERS, BEEZER.
CHOKE ON IT!
'MON AN' WE'LL GO OUT TO THE BEER GARDEN.
I HEARD YOU COME IN LAST NIGHT, YOU KNOW.
NEW YORK
DUBLIN
BOG
Dulux
NOTHING TO SAY?
ANNIE, LEAVE IT, WILL YOU? I CAN HONESTLY SAY IT'S GOT NOTHIN' TO DO WI' YOU AN' ME.
Dulux
WELL, WHAT DOES...

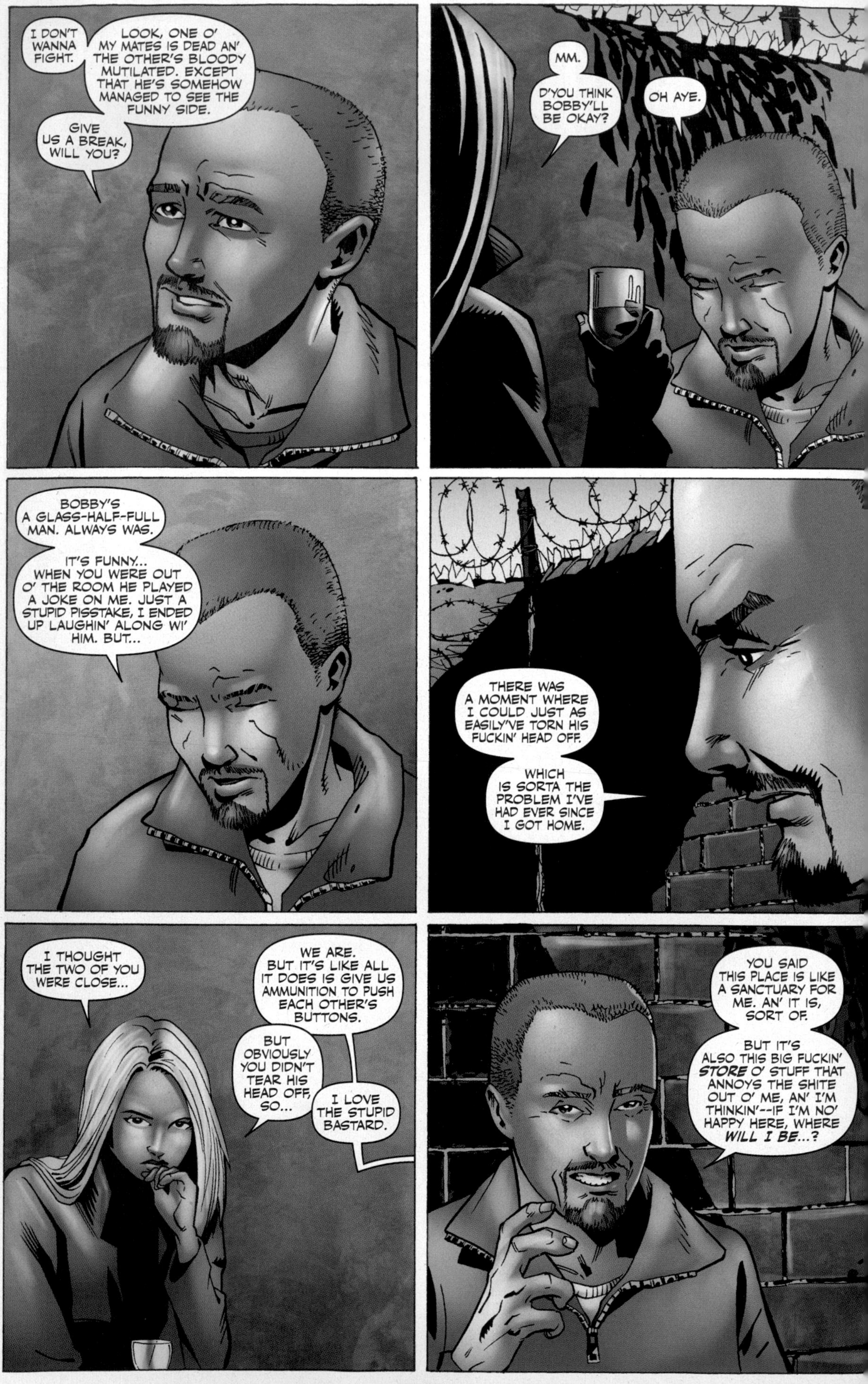
I DON'T WANNA FIGHT.
LOOK, ONE O' MY MATES IS DEAD AN' THE OTHER'S BLOODY MUTILATED. EXCEPT THAT HE'S SOMEHOW MANAGED TO SEE THE FUNNY SIDE.
GIVE US A BREAK, WILL YOU?
MM.
D'YOU THINK BOBBY'LL BE OKAY?
OH AYE.
BOBBY'S A GLASS-HALF-FULL MAN. ALWAYS WAS.
IT'S FUNNY... WHEN YOU WERE OUT O' THE ROOM HE PLAYED A JOKE ON ME. JUST A STUPID PISSTAKE, I ENDED UP LAUGHIN' ALONG WI' HIM. BUT...
THERE WAS A MOMENT WHERE I COULD JUST AS EASILY'VE TORN HIS FUCKIN' HEAD OFF.
WHICH IS SORTA THE PROBLEM I'VE HAD EVER SINCE I GOT HOME.
I THOUGHT THE TWO OF YOU WERE CLOSE...
WE ARE. BUT IT'S LIKE ALL IT DOES IS GIVE US AMMUNITION TO PUSH EACH OTHER'S BUTTONS.
BUT OBVIOUSLY YOU DIDN'T TEAR HIS HEAD OFF, SO...
I LOVE THE STUPID BASTARD.
YOU SAID THIS PLACE IS LIKE A SANCTUARY FOR ME. AN' IT IS, SORT OF.
BUT IT'S ALSO THIS BIG FUCKIN' *STORE* O' STUFF THAT ANNOYS THE SHITE OUT O' ME, AN' I'M THINKIN'--IF I'M NO' HAPPY HERE, WHERE *WILL I BE*...?

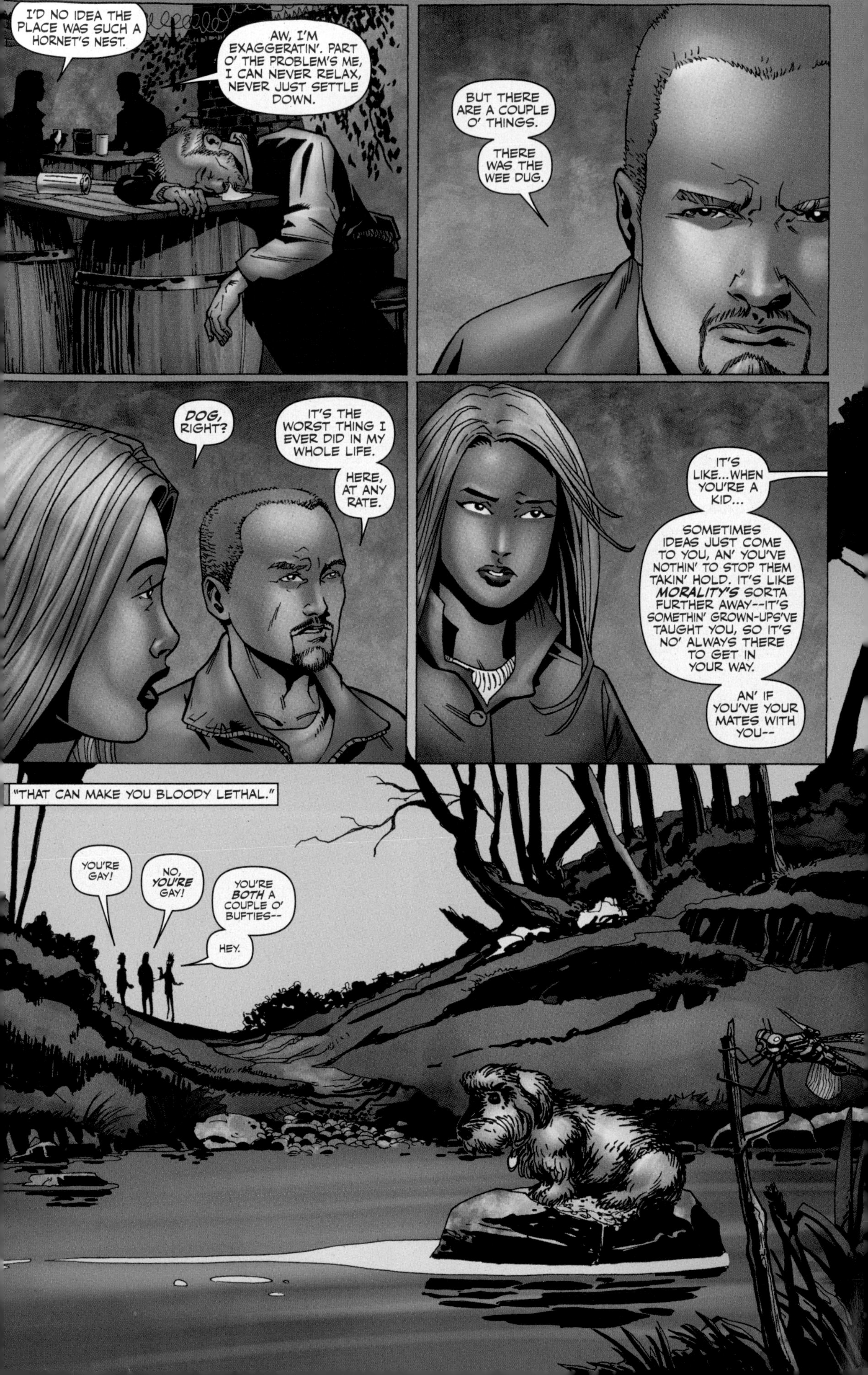
I'D NO IDEA THE PLACE WAS SUCH A HORNET'S NEST.
AW, I'M EXAGGERATIN'. PART O' THE PROBLEM'S ME, I CAN NEVER RELAX, NEVER JUST SETTLE DOWN.
BUT THERE ARE A COUPLE O' THINGS.
THERE WAS THE WEE DUG.
DOG, RIGHT?
IT'S THE WORST THING I EVER DID IN MY WHOLE LIFE.
HERE, AT ANY RATE.
IT'S LIKE...WHEN YOU'RE A KID...
SOMETIMES IDEAS JUST COME TO YOU, AN' YOU'VE NOTHIN' TO STOP THEM TAKIN' HOLD. IT'S LIKE MORALITY'S SORTA FURTHER AWAY--IT'S SOMETHIN' GROWN-UPS'VE TAUGHT YOU, SO IT'S NO' ALWAYS THERE TO GET IN YOUR WAY.
AN' IF YOU'VE YOUR MATES WITH YOU--
"THAT CAN MAKE YOU BLOODY LETHAL."
YOU'RE GAY!
NO, YOU'RE GAY!
YOU'RE BOTH A COUPLE O' BUFTIES--
HEY.

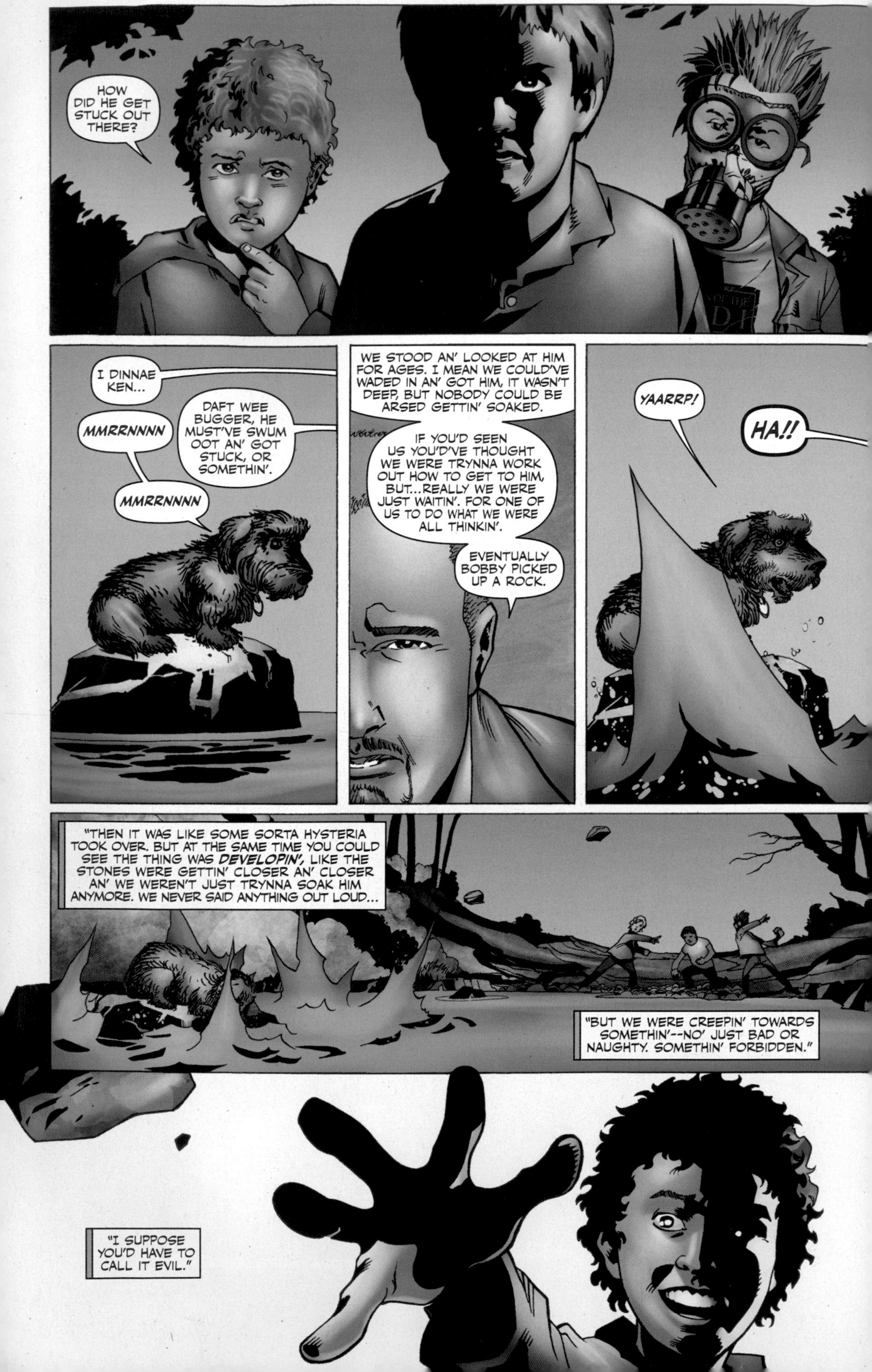
HOW DID HE GET STUCK OUT THERE?
I DINNAE KEN...
MMRRNNNN
DAFT WEE BUGGER, HE MUST'VE SWUM OOT AN' GOT STUCK, OR SOMETHIN'.
MMRRNNNN
WE STOOD AN' LOOKED AT HIM FOR AGES. I MEAN WE COULD'VE WADED IN AN' GOT HIM, IT WASN'T DEEP, BUT NOBODY COULD BE ARSED GETTIN' SOAKED.
IF YOU'D SEEN US YOU'D'VE THOUGHT WE WERE TRYNNA WORK OUT HOW TO GET TO HIM, BUT...REALLY WE WERE JUST WAITIN'. FOR ONE OF US TO DO WHAT WE WERE ALL THINKIN'.
EVENTUALLY BOBBY PICKED UP A ROCK.
YAARRP!
HA!!
"THEN IT WAS LIKE SOME SORTA HYSTERIA TOOK OVER. BUT AT THE SAME TIME YOU COULD SEE THE THING WAS DEVELOPIN', LIKE THE STONES WERE GETTIN' CLOSER AN' CLOSER AN' WE WEREN'T JUST TRYNNA SOAK HIM ANYMORE. WE NEVER SAID ANYTHING OUT LOUD...
"BUT WE WERE CREEPIN' TOWARDS SOMETHIN'--NO' JUST BAD OR NAUGHTY. SOMETHIN' FORBIDDEN."
"I SUPPOSE YOU'D HAVE TO CALL IT EVIL."

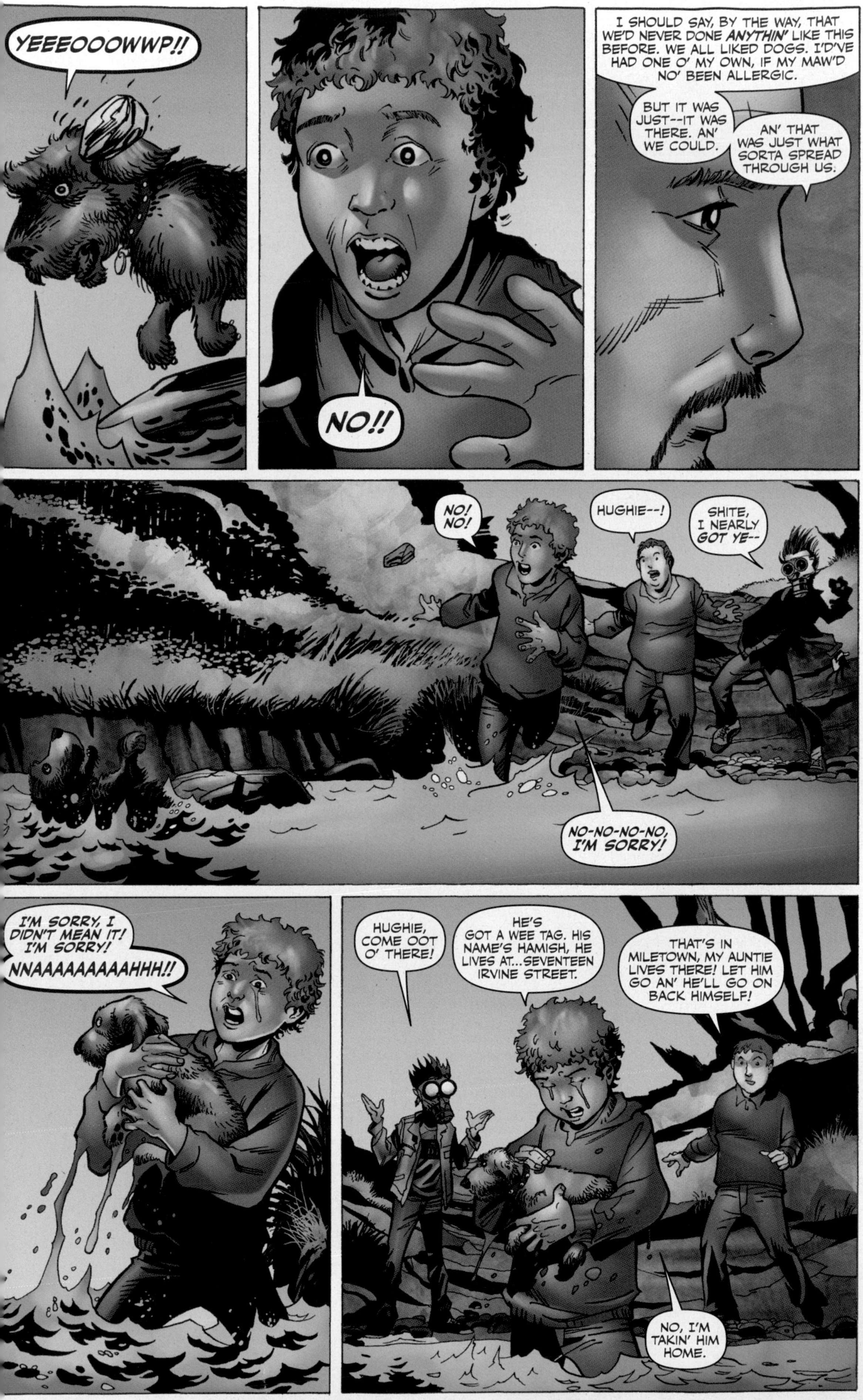
YEEEOOOWWP!!
NO!!
I SHOULD SAY, BY THE WAY, THAT WE'D NEVER DONE ANYTHIN' LIKE THIS BEFORE. WE ALL LIKED DOGS. I'D'VE HAD ONE O' MY OWN, IF MY MAW'D NO' BEEN ALLERGIC.
BUT IT WAS JUST--IT WAS THERE. AN' WE COULD.
AN' THAT WAS JUST WHAT SORTA SPREAD THROUGH US.
NO! NO!
HUGHIE--!
SHITE, I NEARLY GOT YE--
NO-NO-NO-NO, I'M SORRY!
I'M SORRY, I DIDN'T MEAN IT! I'M SORRY!
NNAAAAAAAAAAHHH!!
HUGHIE, COME OOT O' THERE!
HE'S GOT A WEE TAG. HIS NAME'S HAMISH, HE LIVES AT...SEVENTEEN IRVINE STREET.
THAT'S IN MILETOWN, MY AUNTIE LIVES THERE! LET HIM GO AN' HE'LL GO ON BACK HIMSELF!
NO, I'M TAKIN' HIM HOME.

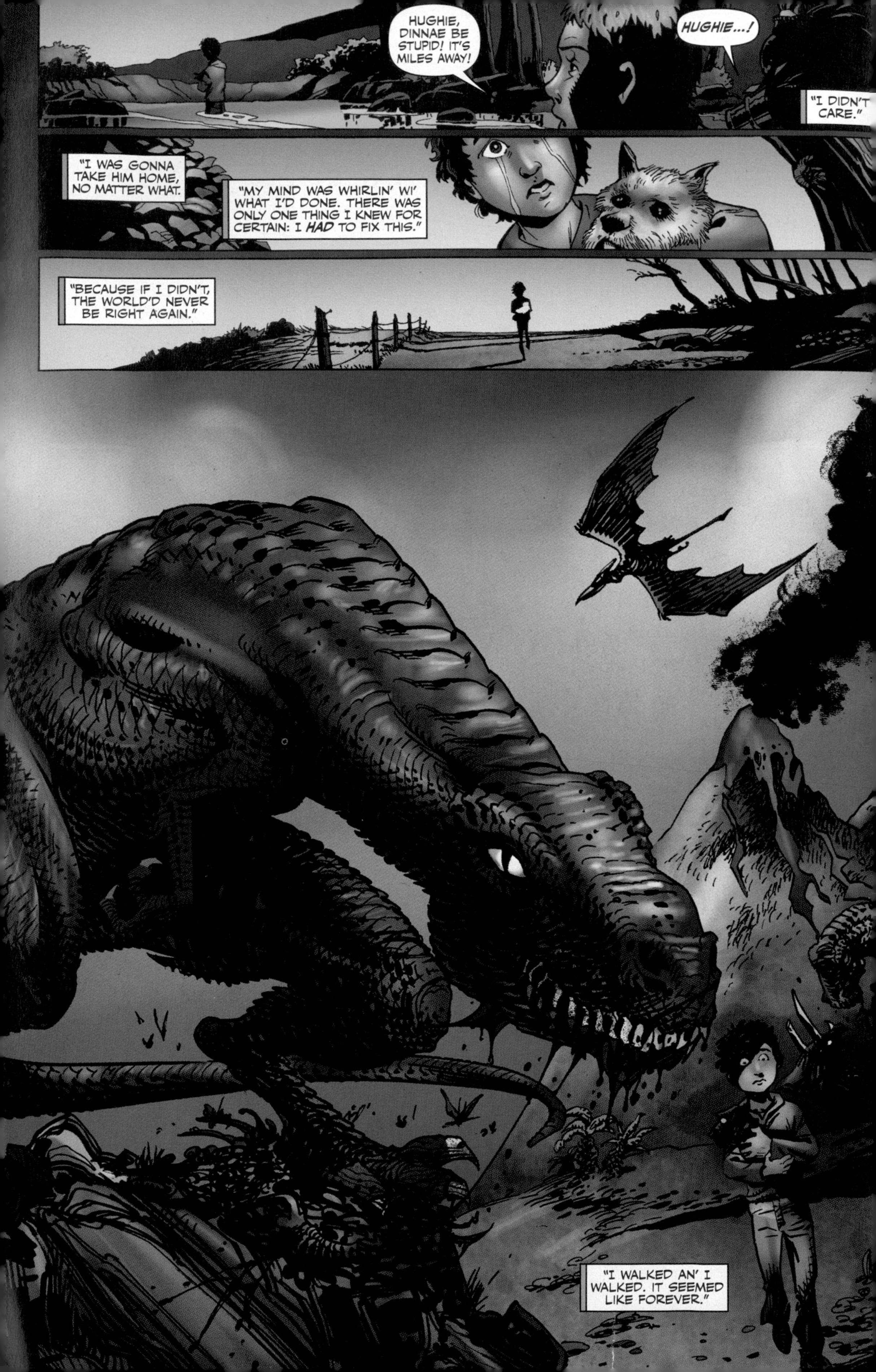

HUGHIE, DINNAE BE STUPID! IT'S MILES AWAY!
HUGHIE...!
"I DIDN'T CARE."
"I WAS GONNA TAKE HIM HOME, NO MATTER WHAT.
"MY MIND WAS WHIRLIN' WI' WHAT I'D DONE. THERE WAS ONLY ONE THING I KNEW FOR CERTAIN: I HAD TO FIX THIS."
"BECAUSE IF I DIDN'T, THE WORLD'D NEVER BE RIGHT AGAIN."
"I WALKED AN' I WALKED. IT SEEMED LIKE FOREVER."

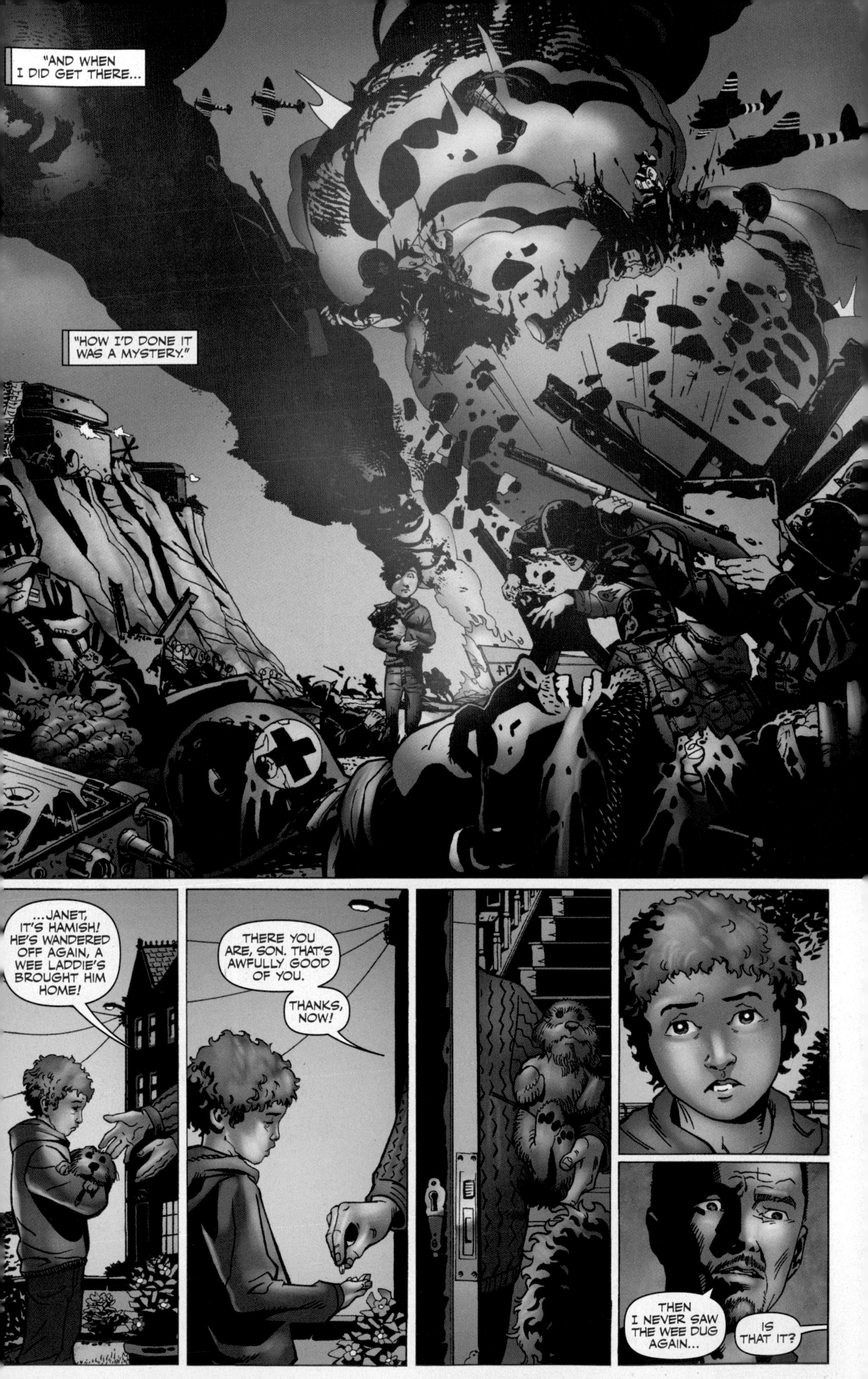
"AND WHEN I DID GET THERE...
"HOW I'D DONE IT WAS A MYSTERY."
...JANET, IT'S HAMISH! HE'S WANDERED OFF AGAIN, A WEE LADDIE'S BROUGHT HIM HOME!
THERE YOU ARE, SON. THAT'S AWFULLY GOOD OF YOU.
THANKS, NOW!
THEN I NEVER SAW THE WEE DUG AGAIN...
IS THAT IT?

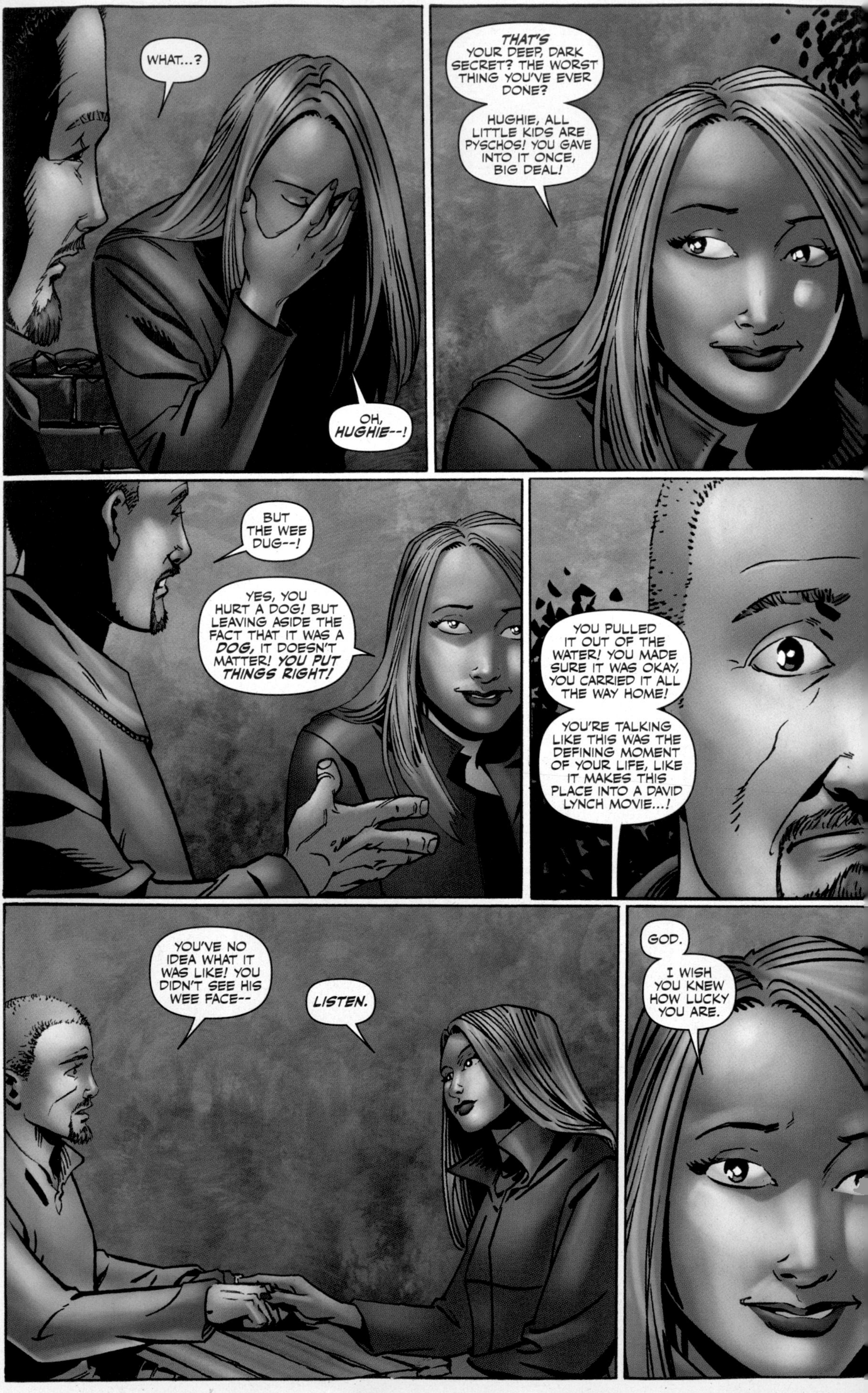
WHAT...?
OH, *HUGHIE*--!
THAT'S YOUR DEEP, DARK SECRET? THE WORST THING YOU'VE EVER DONE?
HUGHIE, ALL LITTLE KIDS ARE PYSCHOS! YOU GAVE INTO IT ONCE, BIG DEAL!
BUT THE WEE DUG--!
YES, YOU HURT A DOG! BUT LEAVING ASIDE THE FACT THAT IT WAS A *DOG*, IT DOESN'T MATTER! *YOU PUT THINGS RIGHT!*
YOU PULLED IT OUT OF THE WATER! YOU MADE SURE IT WAS OKAY, YOU CARRIED IT ALL THE WAY HOME!
YOU'RE TALKING LIKE THIS WAS THE DEFINING MOMENT OF YOUR LIFE, LIKE IT MAKES THIS PLACE INTO A DAVID LYNCH MOVIE...!
YOU'VE NO IDEA WHAT IT WAS LIKE! YOU DIDN'T SEE HIS WEE FACE--
LISTEN.
GOD.
I WISH YOU KNEW HOW LUCKY YOU ARE.

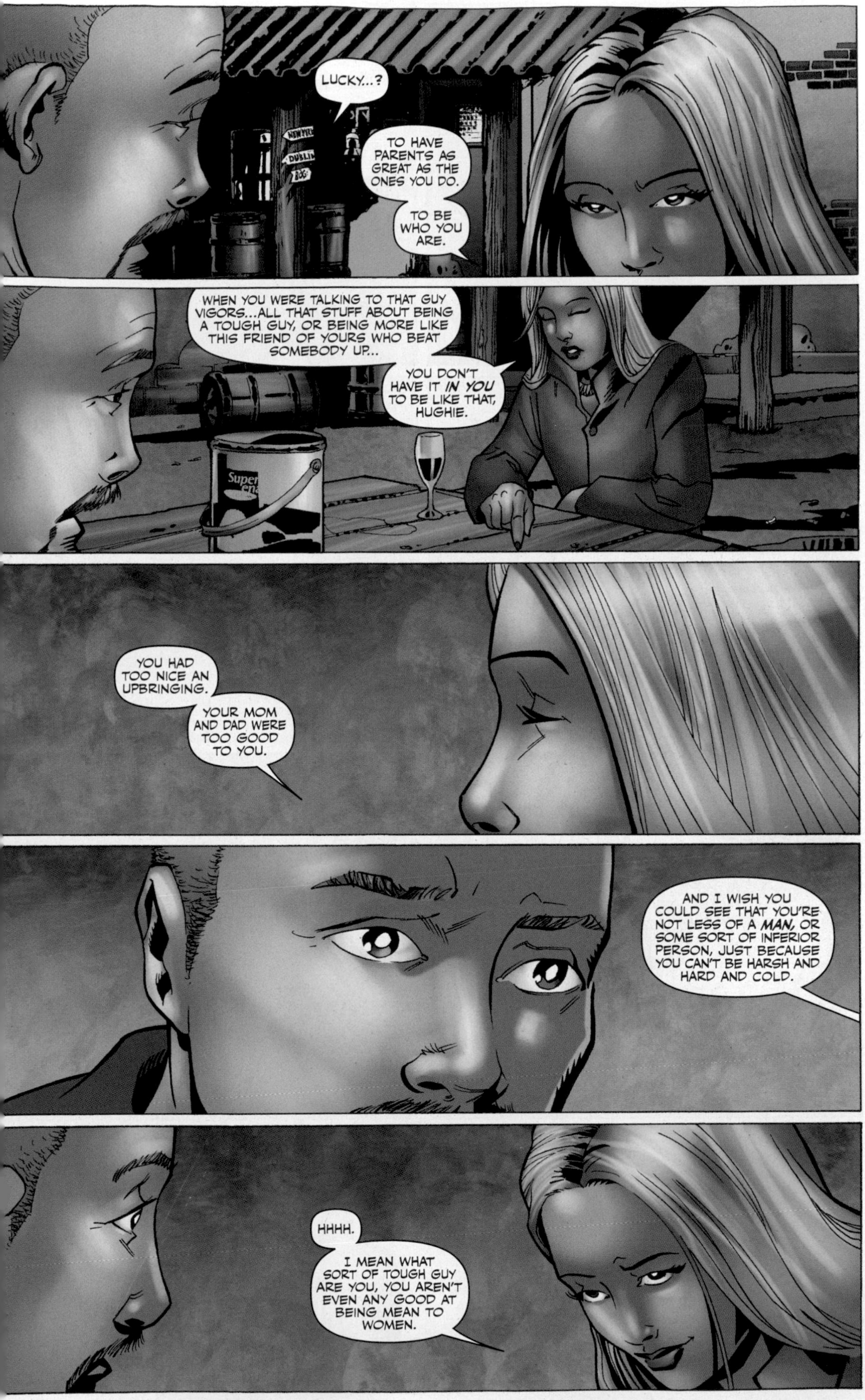
LUCKY...?
TO HAVE PARENTS AS GREAT AS THE ONES YOU DO.
TO BE WHO YOU ARE.
WHEN YOU WERE TALKING TO THAT GUY VIGORS...ALL THAT STUFF ABOUT BEING A TOUGH GUY, OR BEING MORE LIKE THIS FRIEND OF YOURS WHO BEAT SOMEBODY UP...
YOU DON'T HAVE IT *IN YOU* TO BE LIKE THAT, HUGHIE.
YOU HAD TOO NICE AN UPBRINGING.
YOUR MOM AND DAD WERE TOO GOOD TO YOU.
AND I WISH YOU COULD SEE THAT YOU'RE NOT LESS OF A *MAN,* OR SOME SORT OF INFERIOR PERSON, JUST BECAUSE YOU CAN'T BE HARSH AND HARD AND COLD.
HHHH.
I MEAN WHAT SORT OF TOUGH GUY ARE YOU, YOU AREN'T EVEN ANY GOOD AT BEING MEAN TO WOMEN.

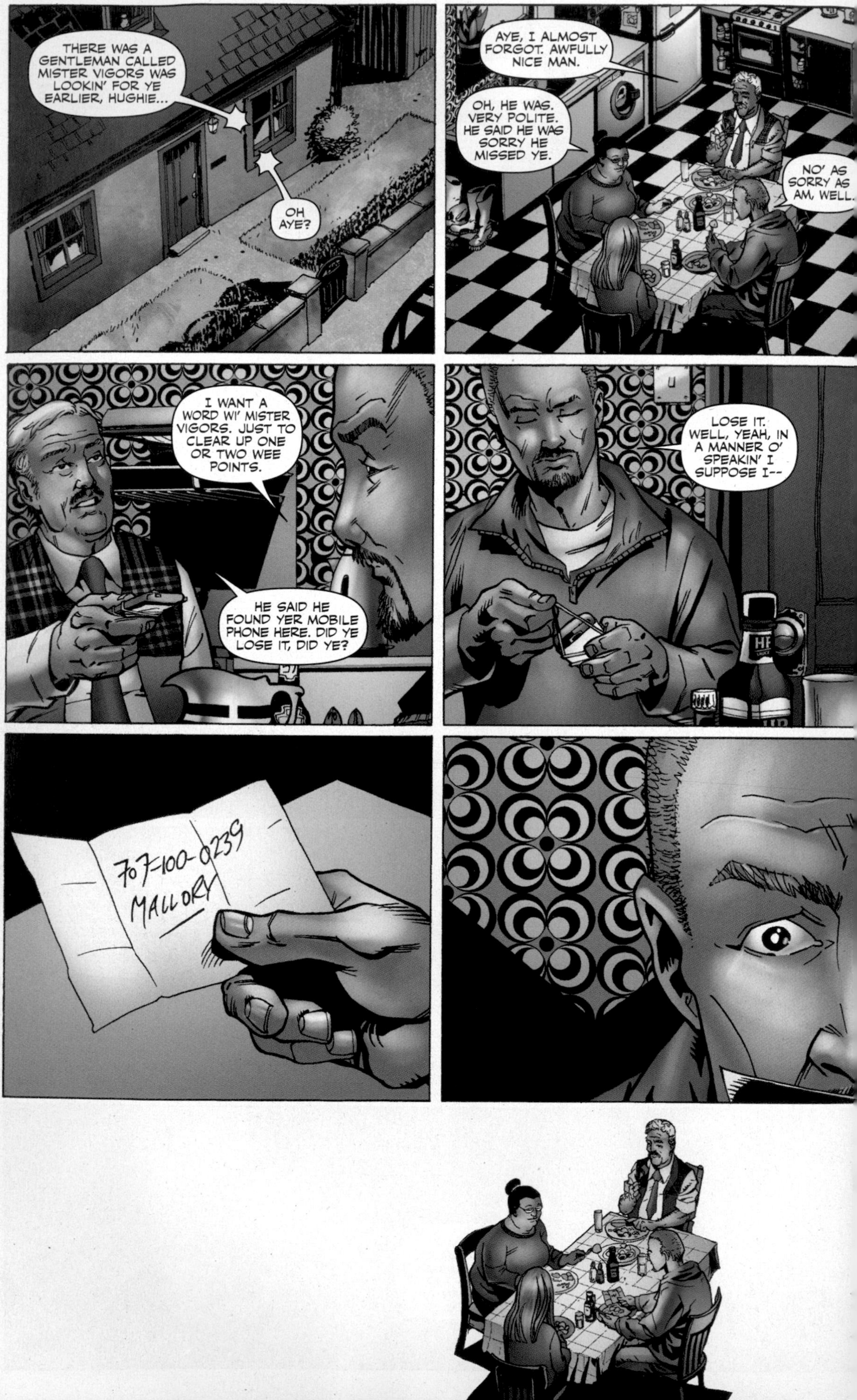
THERE WAS A GENTLEMAN CALLED MISTER VIGORS WAS LOOKIN' FOR YE EARLIER, HUGHIE...
OH AYE?
AYE, I ALMOST FORGOT. AWFULLY NICE MAN.
OH, HE WAS. VERY POLITE. HE SAID HE WAS SORRY HE MISSED YE.
NO' AS SORRY AS AM, WELL.
I WANT A WORD WI' MISTER VIGORS. JUST TO CLEAR UP ONE OR TWO WEE POINTS.
HE SAID HE FOUND YER MOBILE PHONE HERE. DID YE LOSE IT, DID YE?
LOSE IT. WELL, YEAH, IN A MANNER O' SPEAKIN' I SUPPOSE I--
707-100-0239
MALLORY

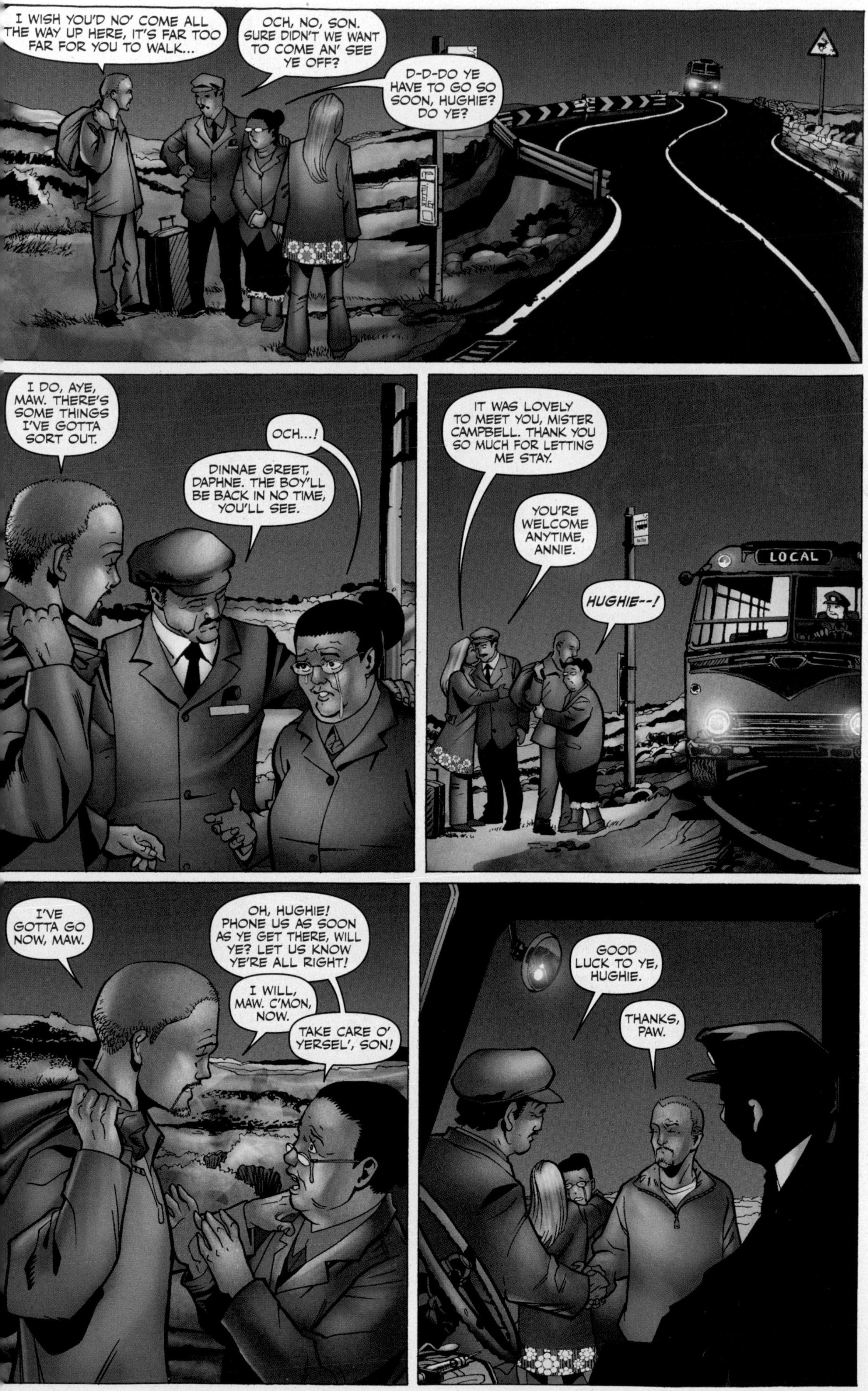
I WISH YOU'D NO' COME ALL THE WAY UP HERE, IT'S FAR TOO FAR FOR YOU TO WALK...
OCH, NO, SON. SURE DIDN'T WE WANT TO COME AN' SEE YE OFF?
D-D-DO YE HAVE TO GO SO SOON, HUGHIE? DO YE?
I DO, AYE, MAW. THERE'S SOME THINGS I'VE GOTTA SORT OUT.
OCH...!
DINNAE GREET, DAPHNE. THE BOY'LL BE BACK IN NO TIME, YOU'LL SEE.
IT WAS LOVELY TO MEET YOU, MISTER CAMPBELL. THANK YOU SO MUCH FOR LETTING ME STAY.
YOU'RE WELCOME ANYTIME, ANNIE.
HUGHIE--!
LOCAL
I'VE GOTTA GO NOW, MAW.
OH, HUGHIE! PHONE US AS SOON AS YE GET THERE, WILL YE? LET US KNOW YE'RE ALL RIGHT!
I WILL, MAW. C'MON, NOW.
TAKE CARE O' YERSEL', SON!
GOOD LUCK TO YE, HUGHIE.
THANKS, PAW.

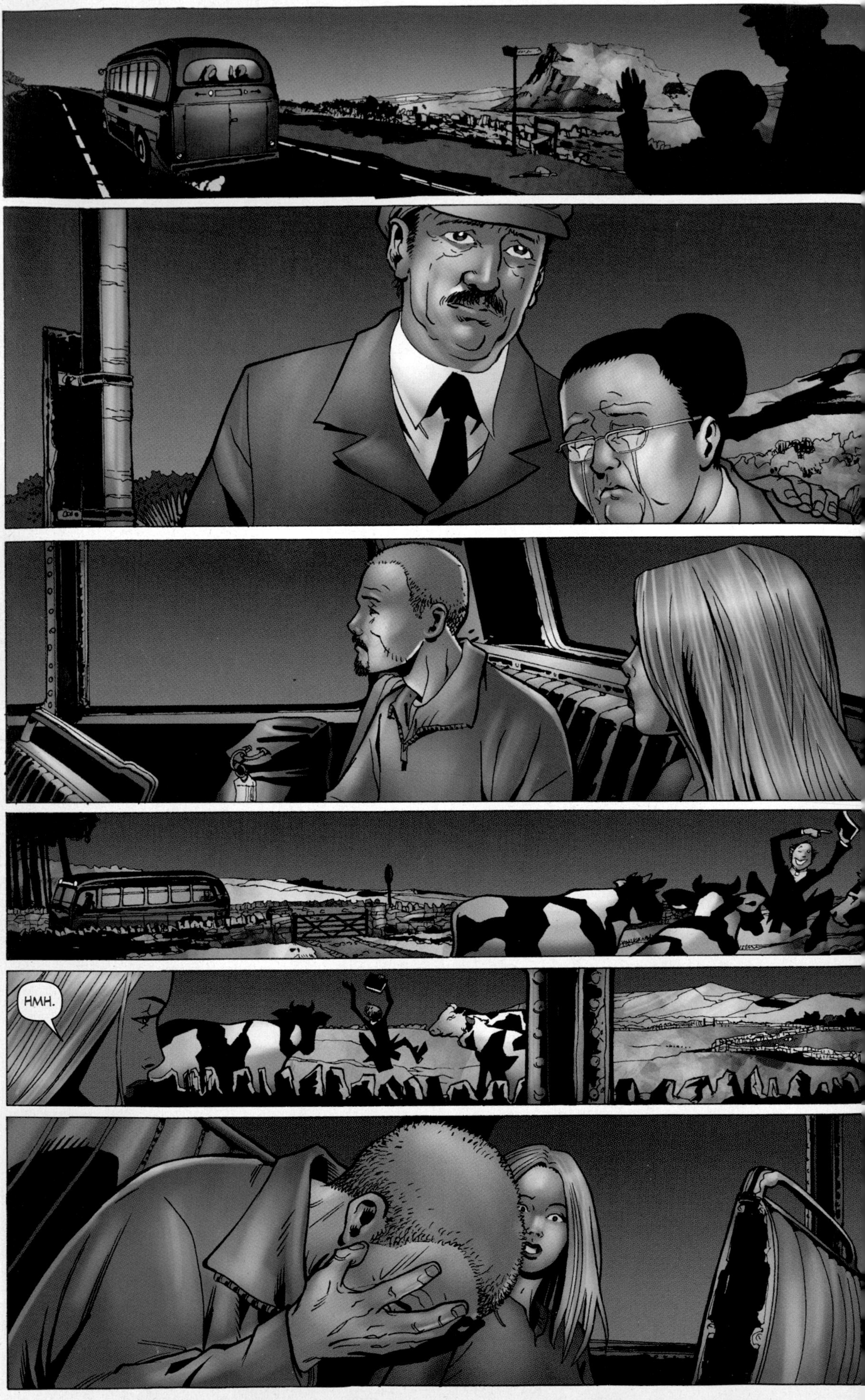
HMH.

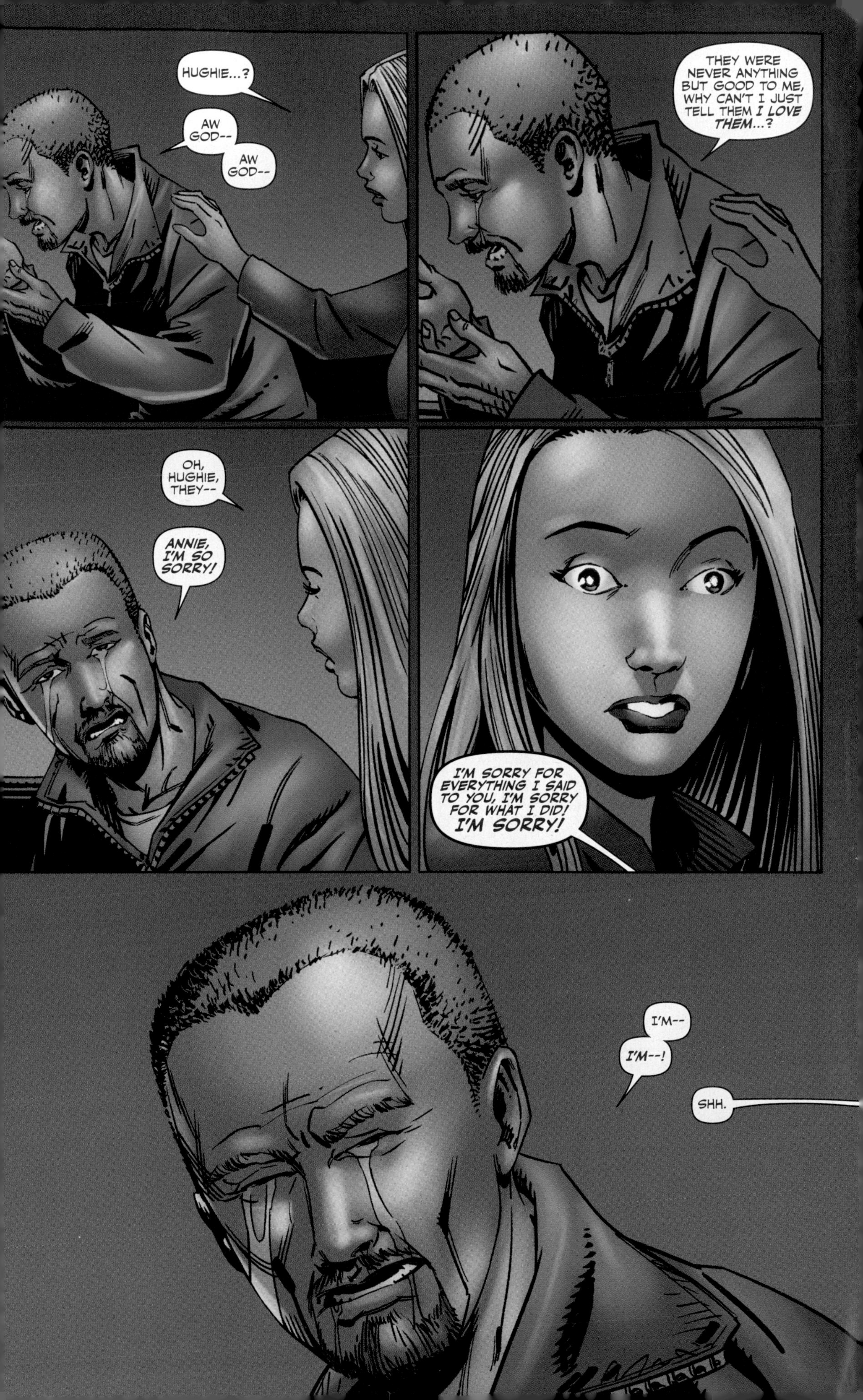
HUGHIE...?
AW GOD--
AW GOD--
THEY WERE NEVER ANYTHING BUT GOOD TO ME, WHY CAN'T I JUST TELL THEM *I LOVE THEM*...?
OH, HUGHIE, THEY--
ANNIE, I'M SO SORRY!
I'M SORRY FOR EVERYTHING I SAID TO YOU, I'M SORRY FOR WHAT I DID! **I'M SORRY!**
I'M--
I'M--!
SHH.

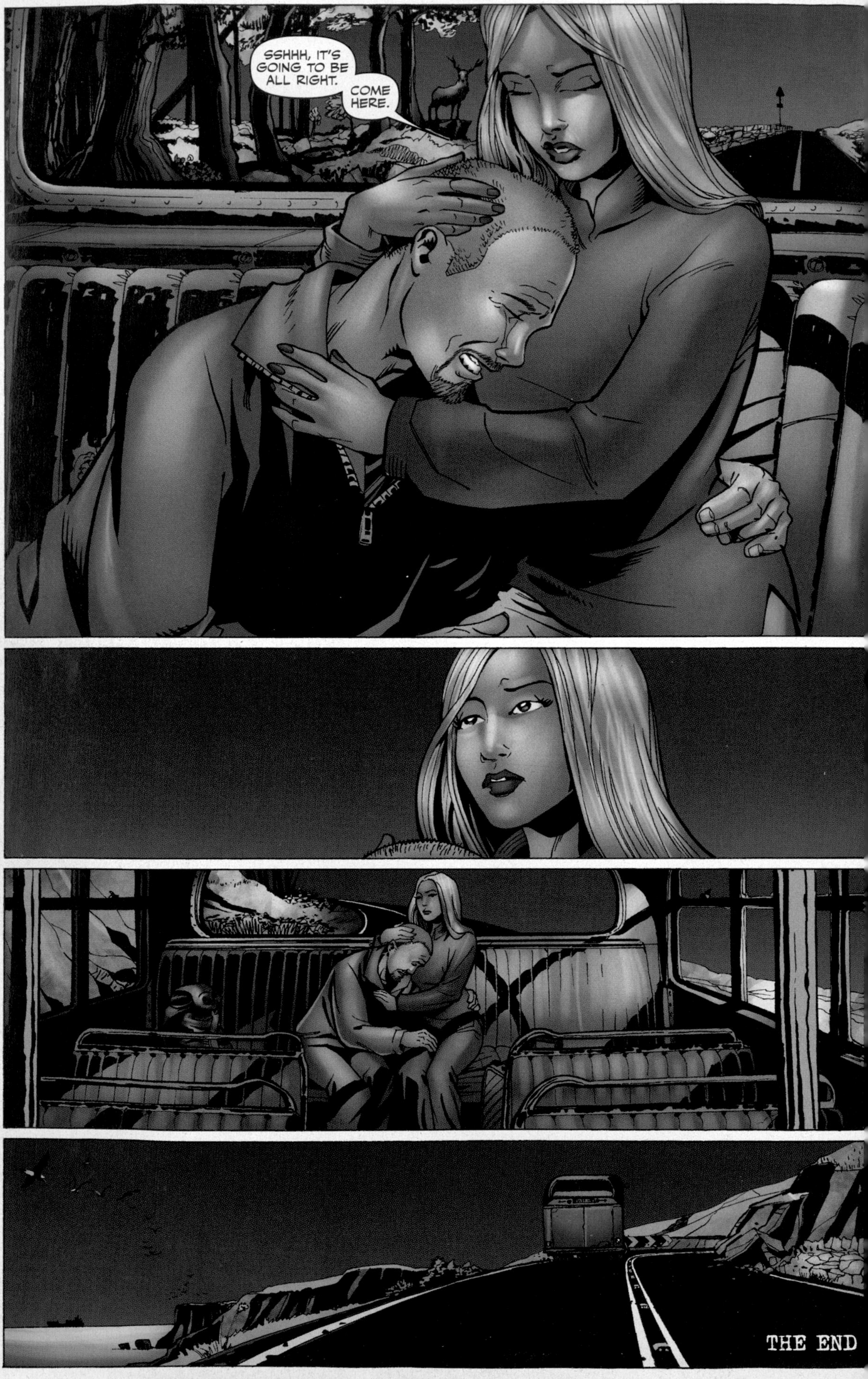
SSHHH, IT'S GOING TO BE ALL RIGHT.
COME HERE.
THE END

DON'T MISS THESE GREAT COLLECTIONS FROM *NEW YORK TIMES* BEST-SELLING AUTHOR

GARTH ENNIS & DYNAMITE

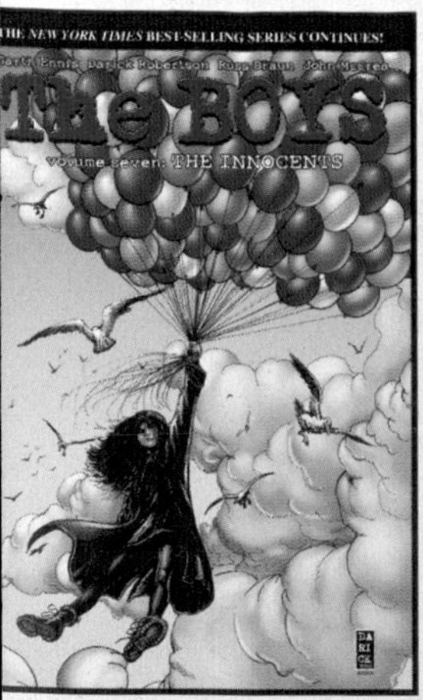
THE NEW YORK TIMES BEST-SELLING SERIES CONTINUES!
The BOYS
volume seven: THE INNOCENTS
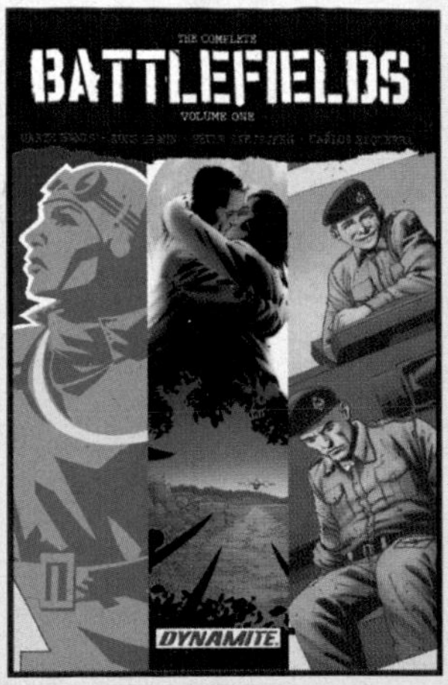
THE COMPLETE
BATTLEFIELDS
VOLUME ONE
DYNAMITE
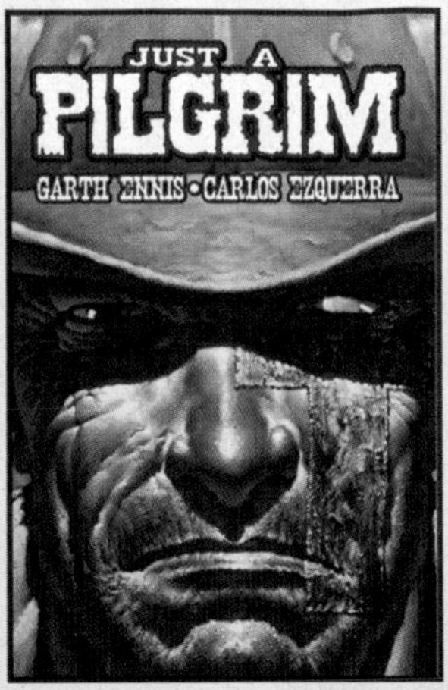
JUST A
PILGRIM
GARTH ENNIS • CARLOS EZQUERRA
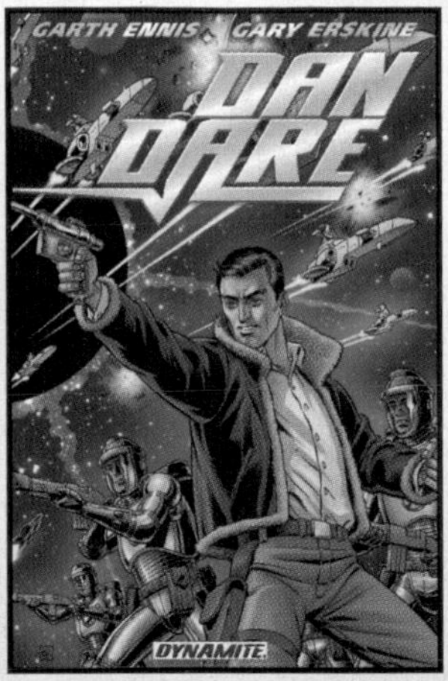
GARTH ENNIS GARY ERSKINE
DAN DARE
DYNAMITE

HARDCOVERS

THE BOYS DEFINITIVE EDITION VOL. 1 HARDCOVER..........(SOLD OUT!).............**1933305800**
- Collecting issues 1-14 of the hit series by Ennis and Robertson

THE BOYS DEFINITIVE EDITION VOL. 2 HARDCOVER.............**1606900730**
- Collecting issues 15-30 of the hit series by Ennis and Robertson

THE COMPLETE BATTLEFIELDS VOL. 1 HARDCOVER.............**160690079X**
- Collecting the first 3 Battlefields mini-series by Ennis, Braun, Snejbjerg and Ezquerra

THE COMPLETE BATTLEFIELDS VOL. 2 HARDCOVER.............**1606902229**
- Collecting the final 3 Battlefields mini-series by Ennis, Braun, Holden and Ezquerra

THE COMPLETE JUST A PILGRIM HARDCOVER.............**160690003X**
- Both mini-series by Ennis and Ezquerra collected together for the first time

DAN DARE OMNIBUS HARDCOVER.............**1606900277**
- Collecting issues 1-7 by Ennis and Erskine

TRADE PAPERBACKS

THE BOYS VOL. 1: THE NAME OF THE GAME.............**1933305738**
- Collects issues 1-6 by Ennis & Robertson

THE BOYS VOL. 2: GET SOME.............**1933305681**
- Collects issues 7-14 by Ennis, Robertson and Snejbjerg

THE BOYS VOL. 3: GOOD FOR THE SOUL.............**1933305924**
- Collects issues 15-22 by Ennis & Robertson

THE BOYS VOL. 4: WE GOTTA GO NOW.............**1606900358**
- Collects issues 23-30 by Ennis, Robertson and Higgins

THE BOYS VOL. 5: HEROGASM.............**160690082X**
- Collects issues 1-6 of the hit mini-series by Ennis and McCrea

THE BOYS VOL. 6: THE SELF-PRESERVATION SOCIETY.............**1606901257**
- Collects issues 31-38 by Ennis, Robertson and Ezquerra

THE BOYS VOL. 7: THE INNOCENTS.............**1606901508**
- Collects issues 39-47 by Ennis, Robertson, Braun & McCrea

THE BOYS VOL. 8: HIGHLAND LADDIE.............**1606902075**
- Collects issues 1-6 by Ennis & McCrea

BATTLEFIELDS VOL. 1: THE NIGHT WITCHES.............**1606900285**
- Collects issues 1-3 by Ennis and Braun

BATTLEFIELDS VOL. 2: DEAR BILLY.............**1606900579**
- Collects issues 1-3 by Ennis and Snejbjerg

BATTLEFIELDS VOL. 3: THE TANKIES.............**1606900757**
- Collects issues 1-3 by Ennis and Ezquerra

BATTLEFIELDS VOL. 4: HAPPY VALLEY.............**1606901281**
- Collects issues 1-3 by Ennis and Holden

BATTLEFIELDS VOL. 5: THE FIREFLY AND HIS MAJESTY.............**1606901451**
- Collects issues 4-6 by Ennis and Ezquerra

BATTLEFIELDS VOL. 6: MOTHERLAND.............**1606902210**
- Collects issues 7-9 by Ennis and Braun

THE COMPLETE JUST A PILGRIM.............**1606900072**
- Both mini-series by Ennis and Ezquerra collected together for the first time

DAN DARE OMNIBUS.............**1606900404**
- Collecting issues 1-7 by Ennis and Erskine

DYNAMITE ENTERTAINMENT **WWW.DYNAMITEENTERTAINMENT.COM** Newsletters • Contests • Downloads • Forums • More

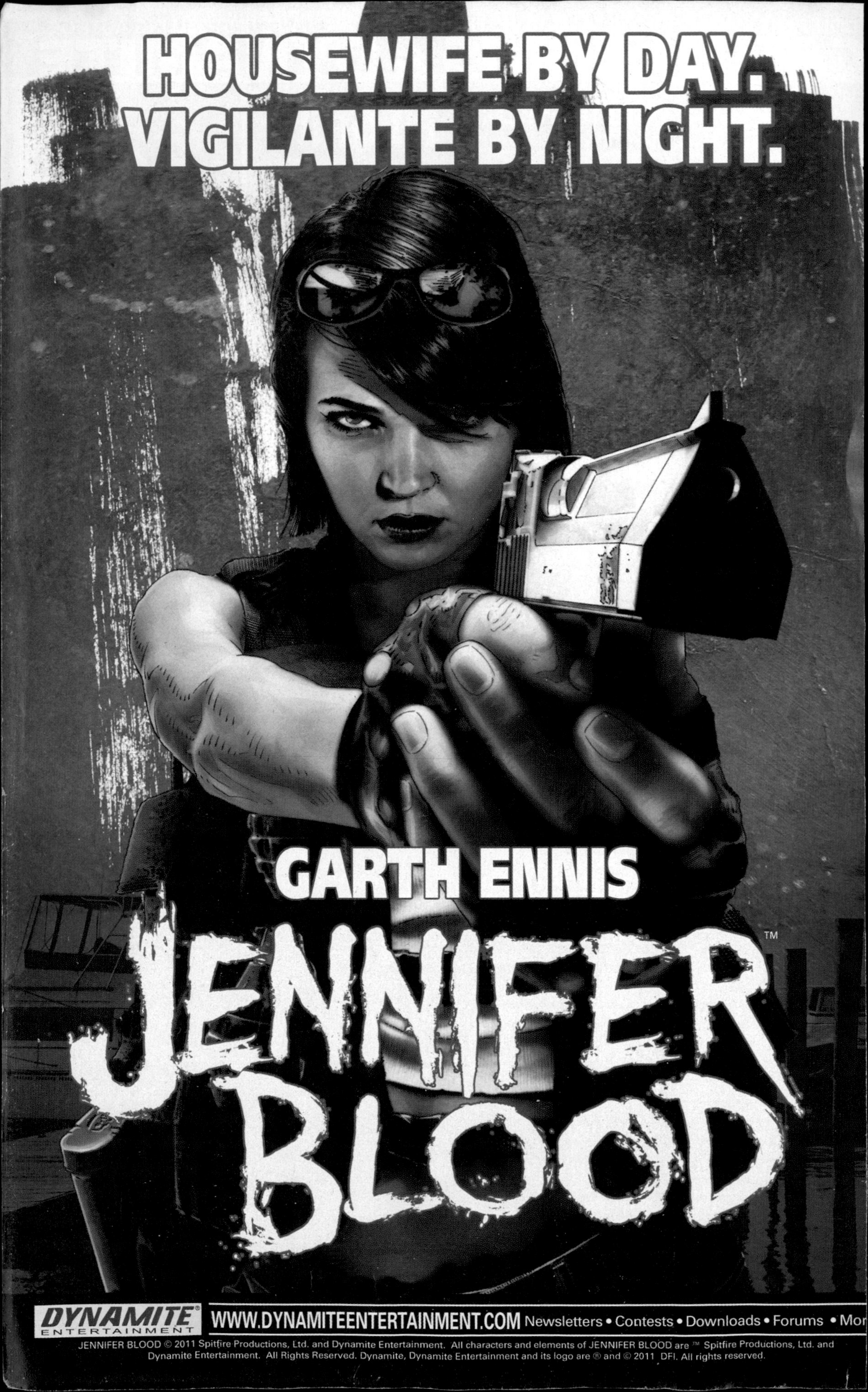
HOUSEWIFE BY DAY.
VIGILANTE BY NIGHT.
GARTH ENNIS
JENNIFER BLOOD™